Another Earth, Another Sky

HBJ HARCOURT BRACE JOVANOVICH, PUBLISHERS
New York   Chicago   San Francisco   Atlanta   Dallas   *and*   London

Another Earth, Another Sky

ODYSSEY An HBJ Literature Program

Sam Leaton Sebesta

Consultants

Elaine M. Aoki   Myra Cohn Livingston

Willard E. Bill   Daphne P. Muse

Sylvia Engdahl   Margaret D. Simpson

Carolyn Horovitz   Barre Toelken

Copyright © 1982 by Harcourt Brace Jovanovich, Inc.

All rights reserved. No part of this publication may be reproduced or transmitted in any form or by any means, electronic or mechanical, including photocopy, recording, or any information storage and retrieval system, without permission in writing from the publisher.

Printed in the United States of America

ISBN 0–15–333359–6

Acknowledgments

For permission to reprint copyrighted material, grateful acknowledgment is made to the following sources:

Hugh Agee and Greystone Publishers Inc.: "The Man Who Saved the Yankees" by Hugh Agee. Copyright 1977. First appeared in *Sandlapper, The Magazine of South Carolina,* March 1977, volume 10, number 3.

Arkham House Publishers, Inc., Sauk City, Wisconsin: "The Calamander Chest" from *Weird Tales* by Joseph Payne Brennan. Copyright 1953.

Atheneum Publishers: Adapted from *A Proud Taste for Scarlet and Miniver* (titled "Eleanor of Aquitaine") by E. L. Konigsburg. Copyright © 1973 by E. L. Konigsburg. Excerpt (titled "Rescue at the Dragon Stones"), quotations, and map of Pern (by Laura Lydecker) adapted from *Dragonsong* by Anne McCaffrey. Copyright © 1976 by Anne McCaffrey. "Thumbprint" from *It Doesn't Always Have to Rhyme* by Eve Merriam. Copyright © 1964 by Eve Merriam. "Victory" and excerpt from "Victory" in *Selected Poems of Robert Watson.* Copyright © 1963, 1964, 1965, 1966, 1974 by Robert Watson.

Curtis Brown, Ltd.: "Something Bright" by Zenna Henderson. Copyright © 1959 by Galaxy Publishing Company. "Creature of the Snows" by William Sambrot. Copyright © 1960 by William Sambrot. "The Bracelet" and excerpts from "The Bracelet" by Yoshiko Uchida. Copyright © 1976 by Yoshiko Uchida.

Leo E. Cardenas: "The Other Pioneers" by Roberto Felix Salazar from *LULAC News,* July 1939.

Chilton Book Company, Radnor, PA: From *Hey, Dummy* (titled "The Dummy") by Kin Platt. Copyright © 1971 by Kin Platt.

Constable Publishers: From *The Book of Songs: VIII,* a poem translated from the Chinese by Helen Waddell in *Lyrics from the Chinese.*

Darien House, Inc.: "Who's On First?" by Bud Abbott and Lou Costello from *Who's on First?,* edited by Richard J. Anobile. Copyright © 1972 by Darien House, Inc.

Delacorte Press/Seymour Lawrence: "It's Raining in Love" from *The Pill Versus the Springhill Mine Disaster* by Richard Brautigan. Copyright © 1968 by Richard Brautigan.

Norma Millay Ellis: Two lines from "Renascence" and six lines from "God's World" (which appear in *Up a Road Slowly* by Irene Hunt), copyright 1917, 1945 by Edna St. Vincent Millay, and "The Ballad of the Harp-Weaver," copyright 1923, 1951 by Edna St. Vincent Millay and Norma Millay Ellis, all reprinted from *Collected Poems* by Edna St. Vincent Millay, Harper & Row, Publishers, Inc.

Norma Farber: "The Hatch" from *The Hatch: Poems, Poets of Today II* by Norma Farber, Charles Scribner's Sons. Copyright © 1955 by Norma Farber.

Farrar, Straus & Giroux, Inc.: "Galante Garden: II" from *The Selected Writings of Juan Ramón Jiménez* translated by H. R. Hays. Copyright © 1957 by Juan Ramón Jiménez.

Follett Publishing Company, a division of Follett Corporation: From *Up a Road Slowly* (titled "Aggie") by Irene Hunt. Copyright © 1966 by Irene Hunt.

Grove Press, Inc.: "On the Mountain: Question and Answer" by Li Po from *Anthology of Chinese Literature* compiled and edited by Cyril Birch. Copyright © 1965 by Grove Press, Inc.

Harcourt Brace Jovanovich, Inc.: "Lazy Peter and His Three-Cornered Hat" from *The Three Wishes: A Collection of Puerto Rican Folk Tales* by Ricardo E. Alegría. "maggie and milly and molly and may," copyright © 1956 by E. E. Cummings. Reprinted from his volume *Complete Poems 1913–1962.* "To Look at Any Thing" from *The Living Seed* by John Moffitt. Copyright © 1961 by John Moffitt. Illustrations, and text, slightly abridged and adapted (titled "A Fox and a Rose"), from *The Little Prince* by Antoine de Saint-Exupéry. Copyright 1943, 1971 by Harcourt Brace Jovanovich, Inc. Slightly adapted version of "Big Chris" from *The Human Comedy* by William Saroyan. Copyright 1943, 1971 by William Saroyan. "Women," copyright © 1970 by Alice Walker. Reprinted from her volume *Revolutionary Petunias and Other Poems.*

Harper & Row, Publishers, Inc.: Adapted excerpt (titled "The Battle of the Rosebud") and quotations from *Only Earth and Sky Last Forever* by Nathaniel Benchley. Copyright © 1972 by Nathaniel Benchley. "The Presence" from *The Nightmare Factory* by Maxine Kumin. Copyright © 1969 by Maxine Kumin.

Holt, Rinehart and Winston, Publishers: "The Bedquilt" from *Hillsboro People* by Dorothy Canfield Fisher. Copyright 1915 by Holt, Rinehart and Winston. Copyright 1943 by Dorothy Canfield Fisher.

Houghton Mifflin Company: "A Song of Greatness" from *The Children Sing in the Far West* by Mary Austin. Copyright renewed 1956 by Kenneth M. Chapman and Mary C. Wheelwright. Selection (titled "The Loosing of the Shadow") and quotations from *A Wizard of Earthsea* by Ursula K. Le Guin. Copyright 1968 by Ursula K. Le Guin. From *Carlota* (titled "The Secret of Blue Beach") by Scott O'Dell. Copyright © 1977 by Scott O'Dell.

Houghton Mifflin/Clarion Books, New York: "Johanna" from *Shape Shifters: Fantasy and Science Fiction Tales About Humans Who Can Change Their Shapes* by Jane Yolen. Copyright © 1978 by Jane Yolen.

International Creative Management c/o Monica McCall, and Laurence Pollinger Limited: "The News in English" from *Danger Is the Password: Stories of Wartime Spies* by Graham Greene. Copyright 1944 by Graham Greene.

Francisco Jiménez: "I Am Not I" (translated by Robert Bly) and "Yo No Soy Yo" by Juan Ramón Jiménez.

Alfred A. Knopf, Inc.: From "The Man with the Blue Guitar" in *The Palm at the End of the Mind* by Wallace Stevens. Copyright 1936 by Wallace Stevens; renewed 1964 by Holly Stevens.

Maxine Kumin: "The Microscope" by Maxine Kumin. Copyright © 1963 by The Atlantic Monthly Company. Excerpt from "The Presence" in *The Nightmare Factory* by Maxine Kumin. Copyright © 1969 by Maxine Kumin.

Little, Brown and Company: Slightly adapted from "Lucas and Jake" in *I Thought You Were a Unicorn and Other Stories* by Paul Darcy Boles. Copyright © 1963 by Paul Darcy Boles.

Liveright Publishing Corporation: "Those Winter Sundays" from *Angle of Ascent, New and Selected Poems* by Robert Hayden. Copyright © 1975, 1972, 1970, 1966 by Robert Hayden.

Lothrop, Lee & Shepard Company, a division of William Morrow & Company: "Night Game" from *The Sidewalk Racer and Other Poems of Sports and Motion* by Lillian Morrison. Copyright © 1967 by Lillian Morrison.

Maclen Music, Inc.: Lyrics to "I'm Only Sleeping" by John Lennon and Paul McCartney. Copyright © 1966 by Northern Songs Ltd.

Macmillan Publishing Company, Inc.: "I Shall Not Care" from *Collected Poems* by Sara Teasdale. Copyright 1915 by Macmillan Publishing Co., Inc.; renewed 1943 by Mamie T. Wheless.

Macmillan Publishing Company, Inc., and Faber and Faber Limited: From *Bagthorpes Unlimited* (titled "The Great Bagthorpe Daisy Chain") by Helen Cresswell. Copyright © 1978 by Helen Cresswell.

McIntosh and Otis, Inc.: From *The Incredible Deborah* (titled "Private Deborah") by Cora Cheney. Copyright © 1967 by Cora Cheney. "The Affair at 7, Rue de M——" by John Steinbeck. Copyright © 1955 by John Steinbeck. Originally appeared in *Harper's Bazaar.*

William Morrow & Company: "Nahuatl: A Song of Nezahualcoyotl" from *The Magic World: American Indian Songs and Poems Selected and Edited by William Brandon.* Copyright © 1971 by William Brandon. "Winter Poem" from *My House* by Nikki Giovanni. Copyright © 1972 by Nikki Giovanni. From "I brought to the New World the gift of devotion" in *North Star Shining* by Hildegarde Hoyt Swift. Copyright 1947, 1974 by Hildegarde Hoyt Swift and Lynd Ward.

The New American Library, Inc.: "I Hear America Singing" from *Leaves of Grass* by Walt Whitman.

Pantheon Books, a division of Random House, Inc.: From *Working: People Talk About What They Do All Day and How They Feel About What They Do* by Studs Terkel. Copyright © 1972, 1974 by Studs Terkel.

Paragon Book Reprint Corporation: The Chinese and English texts of "The Ching-ting Mountain" from *The Works of Li Po, The Chinese Poet* by Shigeyoshi Obata.

Penguin Books Ltd.: "The Door" from *Selected Poems* by Miroslav Holub, translated by Ian Milner and George Theiner, *Penguin Modern European Poets,* 1967. Copyright © 1967 by Miroslav Holub.

G. P. Putnam's Sons: From "Fresh Air Will Kill You" in *Have I Ever Lied to You?* by Art Buchwald. Copyright © 1966, 1967, 1968 by Art Buchwald.

Random House, Inc.: "On Aging" from *And Still I Rise* by Maya Angelou. Copyright © 1978 by Maya Angelou. From *Alfred Hitchcock's Ghostly Gallery.* Copyright © 1962 by Random House, Inc.

Ishmael Reed: "beware: do not read this poem" from *Conjure: Selected Poems, 1963–1970* by Ishmael Reed, The University of Massachusetts Press. Copyright © 1972 by Ishmael Reed.

Reed & Cannon Company: "Side 31" from *Tropicalization* by Victor Hernandez Cruz. Copyright © 1967 by Victor Hernandez Cruz.

Paul R. Reynolds, Inc., 12 East 41st Street, New York, N.Y. 10017: "The Purple Moccasin" by MacKinlay Kantor. Copyright 1937 by The Curtis Publishing Company.

Russell & Volkening, Inc. as agent for the author: "A Wagon Load of Bricks" from *Harriet Tubman: Conductor on the Underground Railroad* by Ann Petry. Copyright © 1955 by Ann Petry.

St. Martin's Press, Inc., New York, and Harold Ober Associates: From *All Creatures Great and Small* (titled "Putting Things Right") by James Herriot. Copyright © 1972 by James Herriot.

Scott, Foresman and Company: "Happy Birthday" by Toni Cade Bambara in *What's Happening* by Marvin L. Greene. Copyright © 1969 by Scott, Foresman and Company.

Samuel Seiffer: "The Television" by Geoffrey Godbey. First appeared in *Congress/2.*

The Sterling Lord Agency, Inc.: "The King's Wishes" by Robert Sheckley. Copyright 1953 by Robert Sheckley.

Tomorrow Entertainment, Inc.: From the Tomorrow Entertainment, Inc. production of *I Know Why the Caged Bird Sings,* a teleplay written by Leonora Thuna and Maya Angelou, based on the book by Maya Angelou.

Universal Press Syndicate: From *Any Grooming Hints for Your Fans, Rollie?* (titled "The Typical Student") by G. B. Trudeau. Copyright © 1977 by G. B. Trudeau. All rights reserved.

University of Notre Dame Press: From *Barrio Boy* (titled "Lincoln School") by Ernesto Galarza. Copyright © 1971 by University of Notre Dame Press, Notre Dame, IN 46556.

Viking Penguin Inc.: From *The Last Unicorn* (titled "The Quest of the Unicorn") by Peter S. Beagle. Copyright © 1968 by Peter S. Beagle. All rights reserved.

Walker and Company, Inc.: "Preoccupation" from *Ants Will Not Eat Your Fingers: A Collection of Traditional African Poetry* by Leonard Doob. Copyright © 1966 by Leonard Doob.

The Washington Post Company: "I Hate Mornings" by Richard Cohen in *The Washington Post,* May 29, 1977. Copyright © 1977 by The Washington Post Company.

Art Acknowledgments

Allen Atkinson: 485; Chuck Bowden: 25, 74, 128, 136, 175, 198, 279, 305, 315, 324, 359, 412, 458, 481 (adapted from photographs from the following sources: 25, courtesy Brown Brothers; 74, courtesy Macmillan Publishing Co.; 128, courtesy Follett Publishing Co.; 136, © Nikky Finney, Random House, Inc.; 175, courtesy Culver Pictures; 198, courtesy Wide World Photos; 279, courtesy Wide World Photos; 305, HBJ photo by Rick Der; 315, courtesy Wide World Photos; 324, George Fry, Addison-Wesley Publishing Co., Inc.; 359, courtesy Culver Pictures; 412, courtesy Viking Press; 458, Wes Guderian, Harper and Row Publishers, Inc.; 481, Jack McManus, Houghton Mifflin Company); Kinuko Craft: 364; Kitty Diamantis: 363; Sharon Harker: top of pages 50–51, 52–53, 54–55, 158–159, 160, 230–231, 232–233, 336–337, 338–339, 340, 362–363, 364–365, 484–485, 486–487, 488; Lyle Miller: 159; Don Petersen: 51, 53, 54–55, 336–337, 338–339; Sharron O'Neil: 232, 365, 487, 488; Sue Rother: 97, 161, 237, 341, 401, 489; Pat Traub: 160; David Wiesner: 486.

Cover: Richard Brown.

Unit Openers: Jon Goodell.

Photo Acknowledgments

HBJ PHOTO by Marcy Maloy: 138–139.

RESEARCH CREDITS: © Ron Dahlquist, After-Image: 149; NASA: 230–231, 233; Thomas Hart Benton, *Internal Improvements* (detail), courtesy Indiana University at Bloomington: 240; Lian K'ai, *Li Po Chanting a Poem* (detail), courtesy the collection of the Tokyo National Museum: 357; Courtesy Cluny Museum, Paris, France: 484.

5

Contents

4 We, the People *239*

6 Another Where, Another When *403*

1 On the Funny Side

Big Chris

A chapter from the novel *The Human Comedy* by William Saroyan

Illustrated by V. Douglas Snow

The story of a different kind of American war hero, William Saroyan's first novel presents a light-hearted view of life in a California farm town during World War II. The "hero" is fourteen-year-old Homer Macauley, the fastest telegram messenger in the San Joaquin Valley. Since his father died and his older brother Marcus joined the Army, Homer is work-ing hard to help his mother hold the family together. Often he helps by looking after his four-year-old brother, Ulysses. Today, though, speedy Homer is running the hurdles for Ithaca High, leaving Ulysses to wander around town on his own. With so much going on in town, Ulysses is finding out that he doesn't need anyone to look after him: he can get into trouble all by himself.

WHEN HOMER MACAULEY swung onto his bicycle after the track meet to get to work as soon as possible, a man named Big Chris walked into Covington's Sporting Goods Store on Tu-lare Street. He was a huge man, tall, lean and hard, with a great blond beard. He had just come down from the hills around Piedra to see about some new grub and shells and traps. Mr. Covington, the founder and proprietor of the store, began immediately to demonstrate to Big Chris the workings of a rather involved new trap that had just been invented by a man out in Friant. The trap was enormous and complicated. It was made of steel, lemonwood, springs and ropes. Its principle seemed to be to take the animal, swing it up and around, and hold it off its feet until the trapper arrived.

"This is brand new," Mr. Covington said, "invented by a man named Safferty out in Friant. He's applied for a patent and so far he's made only two of them, one a model, which he sent to the patent office, and this one, which he sent to me, to sell. The trap is for any kind of animal that walks. Mr. Safferty calls it 'THE LIFT-THEM-OFF-THEIR-FEET, SWING-THEM-AROUND AND-HOLD-THEM SAFFERTY ALL-ANIMAL-TRAP.' He's asking twenty dollars for it. Of course the trap hasn't been tested, but as you can see for yourself, it is strong and could very likely lift, swing and hold a full grown bear with no difficulty at all.''

Big Chris listened to the proprietor of the sporting goods store as a child listens, and behind him Ulysses Macauley listened with the same fascination, ducking in between the two men for a better view of the trap. Mr. Covington was under the impression that Ulysses belonged to Big Chris and Big Chris was under the impression that Ulysses belonged to Mr. Covington, so that between the two of them they had no reason to account for the small boy's presence. As for Ulysses himself, he was under the impression that he belonged wherever there was something interesting to see.

"The remarkable thing about this trap," Mr. Covington said, "is that it will not *hurt* the animal, leaving the fur whole and undamaged. The trap is guaranteed by Mr. Safferty himself for a period of eleven years. This includes all parts — the pliancy of the wood, the endurance of the springs, the steel, the ropes, and all the other parts. Mr. Safferty, although not a trapper himself, believes this is the most effective and humane trap in the world. A man close to seventy, he lives quietly in Friant, reading books and inventing things. He has invented, all told, thirty-seven separate and distinct items of practical usefulness." Mr. Covington stopped his work with the trap. "Now," he said, "I believe the trap is set."

Ulysses, crowding in to watch, moved too far: the trap closed on him gently but swiftly, lifted him off his feet, turned him around and held him three feet off the floor, straight out, horizontally, clamped in. No sound came from the boy, even though he was a little bewildered. Big Chris, however, did not take the event so lightly.

"Careful there!" he said to Covington. "I don't want your son to be hurt."

"My son?" Covington said. "I thought he was *your* son. I never saw the boy before in my life. He came in with you."

"He did?" Big Chris said. "I didn't notice. Well, now, hurry! Get him out of the trap — get him out!"

"Yes, sir," Covington said. "Now let me see."

Big Chris was worried and confused. "What's your name, boy?" he said.

"Ulysses," the boy in the trap said.

"My name is Big Chris. Now you just hold tight there, Ulysses, and the man here will get you right out and set you free." Big Chris turned to Mr. Covington. "Well, come on now," he said, "get the boy back on his feet."

Mr. Covington, however, was just as confused as Big Chris. "I'm not sure I remember how Mr. Safferty explained *that* part of the trap. He didn't *demonstrate* the trap, you see, because — well — we didn't have anything to demonstrate it *on*. Mr. Safferty only *explained* it. I believe *this* is supposed to move out — no, it seems to be immovable."

Now, Big Chris and Mr. Covington went to work on the trap together, Big Chris holding Ulysses so that if the trap opened suddenly Ulysses wouldn't fall on his face, and the other man fooling around with the various parts of the trap to see if anything would give way.

"Well, hurry now," Big Chris said. "Let's not keep the boy in the air all day. You're not hurt, are you, Ulysses?"

"No, sir," Ulysses said.

"Well, you just hold tight. We'll get you out of this." He looked sharply at the boy and then said, "What made you crowd in there?"

"Watching," Ulysses said.

"Yes, it *is* a fascinating sort of contraption, isn't it? Now the man here will get you right out and I won't let you fall. How old are you?"

"Four," Ulysses said.

"Four," Big Chris said. "Well, I'm fifty years older than you. Now the man here will get you right out, won't you?" And Big Chris looked sharply at Mr. Covington. "What's *your* name?" he said.

"Walter Covington. I own this store."

"Well, that's fine. Now, Walter, get the boy out. Move that piece of wood there. I'm holding him. Don't you worry, Ulysses. What's your *father's* name?"

"Matthew," Ulysses said.

"Well, he's a lucky man to have a boy like you. A fellow with his eyes open. I'd give the world to have a boy like you, but I never met the right woman. I met a girl in Oklahoma thirty years ago but she went off with another fellow. Have you got it there, Walter?"

"Not yet," Mr. Covington said. "But I'll get it. I believe *this* is supposed to — no. Mr. Safferty *explained* how to get the animal out of the trap, but it seems I just can't get the hang of it. Maybe the principle changes when it's a small boy instead of an animal."

Two men, a woman with a small girl, and two boys of nine or ten came into the store to watch.

"What's the matter?" one of the boys said.

"We've got a boy caught in a trap here," Mr. Covington said. "A boy named Ulysses."

"How'd he get in?" one of the men said. "Shall I call a doctor?"

"No, he isn't hurt," Big Chris said. "The boy's all right. He's just off his feet, that's all."

"Maybe you ought to call the police," the woman said.

"No, lady," Big Chris said. "He's just caught in the trap. The man here — Walter — he'll get the boy out."

"Well," the lady said, "it's a shame the way little boys are made to suffer by all sorts of ridiculous mechanical devices."

"The boy's all right, lady," Big Chris said. "He *isn't* suffering."

"Well," the lady said, "if he were *my* boy, I'd have the police on you in two minutes." She went away in a huff, dragging her little daughter along.

"I want to see, I want to see!" the little girl cried. "Everybody gets to see but *me!*" The woman shook the little girl and dragged her out of the store.

"Now, don't you worry, Ulysses," Big Chris said. "We'll get you out of this in no time at all."

Mr. Covington, however, gave up. "Maybe I'd better telephone Mr. Safferty," he said. "*I* can't get the boy out."

"Got to stay here?" Ulysses said.

"No, you don't, boy," Big Chris said. "No, by gosh, you don't."

A boy with a dozen afternoon papers under his arm came into the store, crowded into the scene, looked at Ulysses, looked at the people, looked at Ulysses again, and then spoke.

"Hello, Ulysses," he said. "What you doing?"

"Hello, Auggie," Ulysses said. "Caught."

"What for?"

"Got caught."

The newsboy tried to help Big Chris, but only got in the way. He looked around, panic-stricken and paralyzed, but after a moment of confusion bolted for the street. He ran straight to the telegraph office. Homer wasn't there, so he ran into the street again, running one way and then the other,

bumping into people and shouting the day's headline all at the same time.

A woman who had been bumped said to herself, "Crazy! — from trying to sell papers!"

Auggie ran a full block, got out into the middle of the street to look around in four directions for Homer. As luck would have it, Homer appeared around a corner on his bicycle. Auggie ran toward Homer, shouting at him with all his might.

"Homer! You've got to come right away!"

Homer got off his bicycle. "What's the matter, Auggie?"

"Something's happened!" Auggie shouted, even though Homer was right beside him. "You've got to come with me!" He took Homer by the arm.

"But what's the matter?"

"Over at Covington's. Hurry — you've got to come!"

"Ah," Homer said, "you want to show me some new fishing tackle or a rifle or something in the window. I can't go around looking at things any more, Auggie. I'm working now. I've got to go to work."

Homer got back on his wheel and began to ride away, but Auggie took hold of the bike seat and trotted beside him, pushing the bike toward Covington's. "Homer, you've got to come with me! He's caught — he can't get out!"

"What are you talking about?"

Now, they were across the street from Covington's. There was a small crowd in front of the store, and Homer began to be a little frightened. Auggie pointed at the people. The two boys pushed through the crowd into the store, to the trap. There in the trap was Homer's brother Ulysses, and around the trap were Big Chris, Mr. Covington, and a number of strange men and women and boys.

"Ulysses!" Homer shouted.

"Hello, Homer," Ulysses said.

Homer spoke to Mr. Covington. "What's my brother doing in *that* thing?" he said.

"He got caught," Mr. Covington said.

"What are all these people doing here? Go home," he said to the people. "Can't a small boy get caught in a trap without the whole world hanging around?"

"Yes," Mr. Covington said, "I'll have to ask you people to go, who are not customers." Mr. Covington studied the people. "Mr. Wallace," he said, "you can stay. You trade here, and you, Mr. Sickert. George. Mr. Spindle. Shorty."

"*I* trade here," a man said. "I bought fish hooks here not more than a week ago."

"Yes," Mr. Covington said, "fish hooks. The rest of you will have to go." Only two people moved away a little.

"Don't worry, Ulysses," Homer said. "Everything's going to be all right now. It's a good thing Auggie found me. Auggie, run over to the telegraph office and tell Mr. Spangler my brother Ulysses is caught in a trap at Covington's and I'm trying to get him out. I'm late already but tell him I'll be over as soon as I get Ulysses out of the trap. Hurry now."

Auggie turned and ran. He bumped into a policeman who was coming into the store and almost knocked the man down.

"What's all the commotion about?" the policeman said.

"We've got a small boy caught in a trap here," Mr. Covington said. "Can't get him out."

"Let me look into this," the policeman said. He looked at Ulysses, and then at the people.

"All right now," he said, "get along with you, all of you. These things happen every day. You've got better things to do than stand around and watch a small boy in a trap." The policeman moved the people out of the store and locked the front door. He went to Mr. Covington and Big Chris. "Now, let's get this boy out of this thing and send him home."

"Yes," Mr. Covington said, "and the sooner the better. You've got my shop closed at four-thirty in the afternoon."

"Well, how does this thing work?" Homer said.

"It's a new trap," Mr. Covington said — "just invented by Mr. Wilfred Safferty of Friant. He's asking twenty dollars for it and a patent's been applied for."

"Well, get my brother out of it," Homer said, "or get someone who *can*. Get Mr. Safferty."

"I've already tried to telephone Mr. Safferty, but the telephone is out of order," Mr. Covington said.

"Out of order?" Homer shouted. He was very angry about

the whole thing. "What do I care if the phone's out of order? Get the man down here and get my brother out of the trap."

"Yes, I think you'd better do that," the policeman said to Mr. Covington.

"Officer," Mr. Covington said, "I'm trying to run a legitimate business. I'm a law-abiding citizen and I pay my taxes, out of which, I might say, you obtain your salary. I have already tried to reach Mr. Safferty by telephone. The telephone appears to be out of order. I cannot leave my shop in the middle of the day to go looking for him."

Homer looked at Mr. Covington straight in the eye and placed a wagging finger under his nose. "You go get the inventor of this torture machine," he said, "and get my brother out of it. That's all."

"It's not a torture machine," Mr. Covington said. "It's the most improved animal trap on the market. It holds the animal aloft without damage to fur or body. No squeezing, cutting or crushing. It operates on the principle of dislocating the animal from its base and thereby rendering it powerless. Besides, Mr. Safferty may not be at home."

"Ah," Homer said, "what are you talking about?"

Now the policeman decided to study the trap. "Maybe," he suggested, "we'd better *saw* the boy out."

"Saw steel?" Mr. Covington said. "How?"

"Ulysses," Homer said, "do you want anything? Are you all right?"

Big Chris, working hard over the trap, looked from one brother to the other, deeply moved by the calm of the boy in the trap and the furious devotion of his brother.

"Ulysses," Homer said, "can I get you anything?"

"Papa," Ulysses said.

"Ah," Homer said, "can I get you anything besides Papa?"

"Marcus," the boy in the trap said.

"Marcus is in the Army," Homer said. "Do you want an ice cream cone or anything like that?"

"No," Ulysses said, "just Marcus."

"Well, Marcus is in the Army," Homer said. He turned to Covington. "Get my brother out of this thing and hurry up about it, too!"

"Wait a minute," Big Chris said. "Hold your brother there, boy! Don't let him fall!" Big Chris was very busy with the trap now.

"You're *breaking* the trap!" Mr. Covington said. "It's the only one of its kind in the world. You mustn't break it! I'll go get Mr. Safferty. You're wrecking a great invention. Mr. Safferty's an old man. He may never be able to make another trap like this. The boy's all right. He's unhurt. I'll go get Mr. Safferty. I'll only be an hour or two."

"An hour or two!" Homer shouted. He looked at Mr. Covington with the most terrible contempt in the world, and then all around at the store. "I'll break this whole store," he said. He looked back at Big Chris. "Go ahead, mister. Break the trap — break it!"

Big Chris tugged at the trap with every muscle in his fingers, arms, shoulders and back, and little by little the trap began to give way to the force of his strength.

Ulysses twisted around to watch the man. At last Big Chris destroyed the trap.

Ulysses was free.

Holding him so that he would not fall on his face, Homer set his little brother on his feet. The crowd in front of the store cheered, but not effectively, as they were unorganized and had no leader. Ulysses tried out his legs. As everything seemed to be all right now, Homer put his arms around his brother. Ulysses looked at Big Chris. The big man was almost exhausted.

"Somebody's got to pay for that trap," Mr. Covington said. "It's ruined. Somebody's got to pay for it."

Without a word, Big Chris brought some currency out of his pocket, counted out twenty dollars and tossed it onto the counter. He took Ulysses by the head and rubbed the boy's hair, as a father sometimes does. Then he turned and walked out of the store.

Homer talked to his brother. "Are you all right? How do you get into these terrible things?" Homer looked at the ruined trap and then kicked it.

"Careful there, boy," the policeman said. "That's some kind of a new invention. There's no telling what it's liable to do."

Mr. Covington went out into the street to speak to the people. "The store is open for business again. Covington's opens at eight every morning, closes at seven every night, except Saturdays when we are open till ten. Closed all day Sunday. Everything in the sporting line. Fishing tackle, guns, ammunition, and athletic goods. We're open for business, ladies and gentlemen. Come right in."

The people slowly walked away.

Homer turned to the policeman before leaving the store. "Who was that man that got my brother out of the trap?"

"Never saw the man before in my life," the policeman said.

"Big Chris," Ulysses said to Homer.

"Is that his name — Big Chris?"

"Yes. Big Chris."

Now, Auggie ran into the store. He looked at Ulysses. "Did you get out, Ulysses? How did you get out, Ulysses?"

"Big Chris," Ulysses said.

"How did he get out, Homer?" Auggie said. "What happened? What happened to the trap? Where's the big man with the beard? What happened while I was gone?"

"Everything's all right, Auggie," Homer said.

About **WILLIAM SAROYAN**

William Saroyan came from a large, closely knit Armenian family, who made storytelling a part of daily life. During his childhood, he heard countless tales from his aunts, uncles, and grandparents. Saroyan started writing down many of those stories when he was only thirteen, and by the time he left school two years later, he knew that he would be a writer.

William Saroyan trained himself to listen, watch, and remember. When he sat down to write, he just let the writer part of his personality take over. He called this part of his personality "the presence." "I do not know a great deal about what the words come to," he once wrote, "but the presence says, now, don't get funny, just sit down and say something; it'll be all right. Say it wrong, it'll be all right anyway. Half the time I do say it wrong, but somehow or other, just as the presence says, it's right anyhow. . . . It's the presence, doing everything for me."

Of course Saroyan's "presence" did not do all the work. He put a great deal of time and effort into his writing. For years he wrote regularly, often producing a short story in a day. During a six-year period, he wrote over five hundred short stories as well as numerous novels and plays, many of which remain unpublished. It does not seem possible that one person could have had so many stories to tell, but Saroyan kept writing up until his death in 1981.

Understanding the Story

1. How did Ulysses get out of the trap?

2. What is unusual about Mr. Safferty's invention?

3. The author shows you the kind of person the shopkeeper is by letting you hear what he says. For example, when Big Chris starts to break the trap, Mr. Covington says, "You mustn't break it! . . . I'll go get Mr. Safferty. I'll only be an hour or two." Find one other statement that reveals Covington's character.

4. Do you think it was fair for Mr. Covington to charge twenty dollars for the ruined trap? Explain your reasons.

5. Homer is very protective of his little brother, Ulysses. Perhaps you have a brother or sister about whom you feel the same way. Explain how you might react if someone close to you was in danger.

Understanding Literature

Clues to the meaning of a story may come from the names that the author has chosen for his or her characters. Think about the names in "Big Chris." Ulysses, the name of the child who thought "he belonged wherever there was something interesting to see," is the Latin name for Odysseus, the legendary Greek hero who had many perilous adventures as he tried to find his way home after the Trojan War. Why do you think Saroyan chose the name Ulysses for the child in this story?

Authors often choose names that will give some hint of a character's personality. In this story, Ulysses' brother, Homer, has the same name as the Greek poet who is said to have written the *Iliad* and the *Odyssey* many centuries ago. Both long poems are about the gods, goddesses, and heroes of ancient Greece.

Homer's and Ulysses' last name is Macauley. It was also the family name of Thomas Macauley, a nineteenth-century writer and historian who was noted for his honesty, perseverance, and willingness to work hard. Big Chris is big in heart as well as in name, while the first part of Mr. Covington's name sounds a bit like *covet,* which means to want something (like money) badly.

Do you know what your name means? Perhaps you were named for a famous person in literature or history. If *your* name were the name of a character in a story, what qualities would it suggest?

Writing About the Story

"Invent" and draw an item or machine that could be used for some practical (or funny) purpose. Label the parts. Write the kind of description that would help you sell your invention. Explain how it works and how much it costs.

Preoccupation

A Mbundu (African) poem
Translated by Merlin Ennis

Chaff[1] is in my eye,
A crocodile has me by the leg,
A goat is in the garden,
A porcupine is cooking in the pot,
Meal is drying on the pounding rock,
The King has summoned me to court,
And I must go to the funeral of my mother-in-law:
In short, I am busy.

Illustration by Willi Baum

_____

1. **chaff**: grain husks, usually separated out during threshing.

Who's On First?

A comedy sketch by Bud Abbott and Lou Costello
Illustrated by Tim Boxell

Here is a classic comedy sketch of a failure to communicate,
first performed in 1946 on radio by Abbott (Dexter)
and Costello (Sebastian).

Sebastian: Peanuts!

Dexter: Peanuts!

Sebastian: Popcorn!

Dexter: Popcorn!

Sebastian: Crackerjack!

Dexter: Crackerjack!

Sebastian: Get your packages of Crackerjack here!

Dexter: — Crackerjack — will you keep quiet? Sebastian! Sebastian, please! Don't interrupt my act!

Sebastian: Ladies and gentlemen and also the children — will you excuse me for a minute, please? Thank you.

Dexter: What do you want to do?

Sebastian: Look, Mr. Broadhurst —

Dexter: What are you doing?

Sebastian: I love baseball!

Dexter: Well, we all love baseball.

Sebastian: When we get to St. Louis, will you tell me the guys' names on the team so when I go to see them in that St. Louis ball park I'll be able to know those fellows?

Dexter: Then you'll go and peddle your popcorn and don't interrupt the act anymore?

Sebastian: Yes, sir.

Dexter: All right. But you know, strange as it may seem, they give ballplayers nowadays very peculiar names.

Sebastian: Funny names?

Dexter: Nicknames. Nicknames.

Sebastian: Not — not as funny as my name — Sebastian Dinwiddie.

Dexter: Oh, yes, yes, yes!

Sebastian: Funnier than that?

Dexter: Oh, absolutely. Yes. Now, on the St. Louis team we have Who's on first, What's on second, I Don't Know is on third —

Sebastian: That's what I want to find out. I want you to tell me the names of the fellows on the St. Louis team.

Dexter: I'm telling you. Who's on first, What's on second, I Don't Know is on third —

Sebastian: You know the fellows' names?

Dexter: Yes.

Sebastian: Well, then, who's playin' first?

Dexter: Yes!

Sebastian: I mean the fellow's name on first base.

Dexter: Who.

Sebastian: The fellow playin' first base for St. Louis.

Dexter: Who.

Sebastian: The guy on first base.

Dexter: Who is on first.

Sebastian: Well, what are you askin' me for?

Dexter: I'm not asking you — I'm telling you. *Who is on first.*

Sebastian: I'm asking you — who's on first?

Dexter: That's the man's name!

Sebastian: That's whose name?

Dexter: Yes.

Sebastian: Well, go ahead and tell me!

Dexter: Who.

Sebastian: The guy on first.

Dexter: Who.

Sebastian: The first baseman.

Dexter: Who is on first.

Sebastian: Have you got a first baseman on first?

Dexter: Certainly.

Sebastian: Then who's playing first?

Dexter: Absolutely.

Sebastian: When you pay off the first baseman every month, who gets the money?

Dexter: Every dollar of it. And why not, the man's entitled to it.

Sebastian: Who is?

Dexter: Yes.

Sebastian: So who gets it?

Dexter: Why shouldn't he? Sometimes his wife comes down and collects it.

Sebastian: Whose wife?

Dexter: Yes. After all, the man earns it.

Sebastian: Who does?

Dexter: Absolutely.

Sebastian: Well, all I'm trying to find out is what's the guy's name on first base.

Dexter: Oh, no, no. What is on second base.

Sebastian: I'm not asking you who's on second.

Dexter: Who's on first.

Sebastian: That's what I'm trying to find out.

Dexter: Well, don't change the players around.

Sebastian: I'm not changing nobody.

Dexter: Now, take it easy.

Sebastian: What's the guy's name on first base?

Dexter: What's the guy's name on second base.

Sebastian: I'm not askin' ya who's on second.

Dexter: Who's on first.

Sebastian: I don't know.

Dexter: He's on third. We're not talking about him.

Sebastian: How could I get on third base?

Dexter: You mentioned his name.

Sebastian: If I mentioned the third baseman's name, who did I say is playing third?

Dexter: No. Who's playing first.

Sebastian: Stay offa first, will ya?

Dexter: Well, what do you want me to do?

Sebastian: Now what's the guy's name on first base?

Dexter: What's on second.

Sebastian: I'm not asking ya who's on second.

Dexter: Who's on first.

Sebastian: I don't know.

Dexter: He's on third.

Sebastian: There I go back on third again.

Dexter: Well, I can't change their names.

Sebastian: Say, will you please stay on third base, Mr. Broadhurst.

Dexter: Please. Now, what is it you want to know?

Sebastian: What is the fellow's name on third base?

Dexter: What is the fellow's name on second base.

Sebastian: I'm not askin' ya who's on second.

Dexter: Who's on first.

Sebastian: I don't know.

Dexter and Sebastian: *Third base!*

Sebastian: You got a pitcher on the team?

Dexter: Wouldn't this be a fine team without a pitcher?

Sebastian: I don't know. Tell me the pitcher's name.

Dexter: Tomorrow.

Sebastian: You don't want to tell me today?

Dexter: I'm telling you, man.

Sebastian: Then go ahead.

Dexter: Tomorrow.

Sebastian: What time?

Dexter: What time what?

Sebastian: What time tomorrow are you gonna tell me who's pitching?

Dexter: Now listen, Who is not pitching. Who is on —

Sebastian: I'll break your arm if you say who's on first.

Dexter: Then why come up here and ask?

Sebastian: I want to know what's the pitcher's name.

Dexter: What's on second.

Sebastian: I don't know.

Sebastian and Dexter: *Third base!*

Sebastian: Gotta catcher?

Dexter: Yes.

Sebastian: I'm a good catcher, too, you know.

Dexter: I know that.

Sebastian: I would like to play for the St. Louis team.

Dexter: Well, I might arrange that.

Sebastian: I would like to catch. Now, I'm being a good catcher, Tomorrow's pitching on the team, and I'm catching.

Dexter: Yes.

Sebastian: Tomorrow throws the ball and the guy up bunts the ball.

Dexter: Yes.

Sebastian: Now, when he bunts the ball — me being a good catcher — I want to throw the guy out at first base, so I pick up the ball and throw it to who?

Dexter: Now that's the first thing you've said right.

Sebastian: I DON'T EVEN KNOW WHAT I'M TALKING ABOUT.

Dexter: Well, that's all you have to do.

Sebastian: Is to throw it to first base.

Dexter: Yes.

Sebastian: Now who's got it?

Dexter: Naturally.

Sebastian: Who has it?

Dexter: Naturally.

Sebastian: Naturally.

Dexter: Naturally.

Sebastian: O.K.

Dexter: Now you've got it.

Sebastian: I pick up the ball and I throw it to Naturally.

Dexter: No you don't, you throw the ball to first base.

Sebastian: Then who gets it?

Dexter: Naturally.

Sebastian: O.K.

Dexter: All right.

Sebastian: I throw the ball to Naturally.

Dexter: You don't. You throw it to Who.

Sebastian: Naturally.

Dexter: Well, naturally. Say it that way.

Sebastian: That's what I said.

Dexter: You did not.

Sebastian: I said I'd throw the ball to Naturally.

Dexter: You don't. You throw it to Who.

Sebastian: Naturally.

Dexter: Yes.

Sebastian: So I throw the ball to first base and Naturally gets it.

Dexter: No. You throw the ball to first base ——

Sebastian: Then who gets it?

Dexter: Naturally.

Sebastian: That's what I'm saying.

Dexter: You're not saying that.

Sebastian: Excuse me, folks.

Dexter: Now, don't get excited. Now, don't get excited.

Sebastian: I throw the ball to first base.

Dexter: Then Who gets it.

Sebastian: He better get it.

Dexter: That's it. All right now, don't get excited. Take it easy.

Sebastian: Now I throw the ball to first base, whoever it is grabs the ball, so the guy runs to second.

Dexter: Uh-huh.

Sebastian: Who picks up the ball and throws it to What. What throws it to I Don't Know. I Don't Know throws it back to Tomorrow — a triple play.

Dexter: Yeah. It could be.

Sebastian: And I don't care.

Dexter: What was that?

Sebastian: I said, *I don't care.*

Dexter: Oh, that's our shortstop!

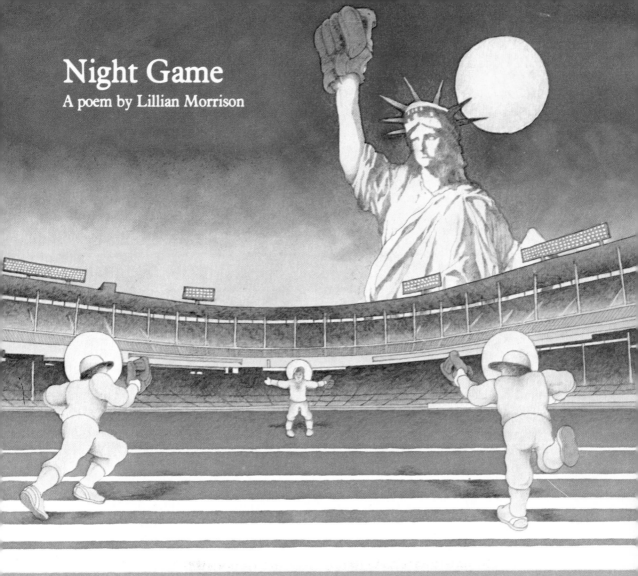

Night Game

A poem by Lillian Morrison

At first I thought it was the moon
gliding down with one
shining arm outstretched
carrying something dark.
Then I realized
it was the Statue of Liberty
arcing slowly through the sky
with a baseball glove on her
uplifted hand. She was saying,
"Umpire, you blind burglar,
You can't throw me out of the game."

Illustration by Brian Cody

The Man Who Saved the Yankees

A short story by Hugh Agee

Illustrated by George Ulrich

*The following correspondence was recently uncovered by
Jiggs Weston, sports editor of the Gravely, S.C.* Independent.[1]
*Knowing the widespread interest in baseball among our
readers, we wish to share the unusual story revealed herein.
We think you will agree with Mr. Weston's somewhat astonished comment to us that only in America are such things
possible.*

From Cyrus Bean to Casey Stengel:[2]

Route 1
Gravely, South Carolina

Mr. Casey Stengel, Manager
The New York Yankees Baseball Club
New York, N.Y.

Dear Mr. Stengel:

I was at Miss Nettie Stone's house this afternoon to hear
the game between the Yankees and the Red Sox on the radio
and Mr. Stengel, it was awful! I'm seventy-four years old and
a Yankee fan for most of those years, but for the life of me I
can't remember a time when the Yankees have done so
poorly and with players like Mantle, Berra, and Ford, too!

Mister Stengel, you don't know what it does to the American way of life to see the Yankees down like they are now. It
wouldn't surprise me to see the Stock Market take a big dip
any day now. I'd even bet the sale of hot dogs is off at the
Ball Park.

There's no getting around it: the manager of the World

---

1. *Independent:* the local newspaper of an imaginary town in South Carolina.
2. **Casey Stengel**: manager of the New York Yankees, 1949–1960.

Champion New York Yankees has an obligation to the American people. Take my grandson, for instance. He's only eleven, but he plays Little League ball. Since the Yankee slump, his hitting has fallen off something awful. Can't you see his future in baseball is threatened?

Don't think I'm just another loudmouth criticizing you unjustly. I'm not one to do that. Judge a man fair, my Pa always told me. All I want is to see the Yankees back on top where they belong.

It's like I was telling the fellows down at Jim Sykes' Service Station. Jim has a television set where folks watch the games on weekends. I said if the Yankees could start playing like they did in the old days, they'd be ten games out front now instead of ten behind. You get those Yankees going good again and see if the whole country don't get better overnight.

Respectfully,
Cyrus Bean

Telegram from Casey Stengel to Cyrus Bean:
APPRECIATE CONCERN. CAN'T DECIDE IF NEED YOU OR GRANDSON MORE. MAYBE YOU SHOULD COME AND SHOW HOW TO PLAY LIKE IN OLD DAYS.

CASEY STENGEL

Letter from Cyrus Bean to Casey Stengel:
Dear Mr. Stengel:

The mail carrier brought your telegram this morning. The boys at Jim Sykes' Service Station swear it's a fake but they get too many tricks played on them to know the real thing when they see it. Besides, I know what a serious man you are.

My grandson's laid up with the measles, but I'll be glad to come and see what I can do. I'm catching the next train for New York, although Nettie Stone don't think much of the whole business. Miss Nettie was my late wife's best friend.

Respectfully,
Cyrus Bean

P.S.   I won't expect any pay, but you can give me my train fare back to Gravely if the club can afford it.

Letter from Jimmy Bean to Cyrus Bean:
Dear Grandpa Cyrus:

The whole team has the measles now. Miss Nettie is letting me use her radio while I'm sick. She acts halfway mad at you for going off like you did. You just think about getting those Yankees back on the right track and make them play like you told us Little Leaguers to play.

Love,
Jimmy

Letter from Cyrus Bean to Jim Sykes:
Dear Jim:

Seems like I got to New York ahead of my answer to Mr. Stengel's telegram. He was very surprised, but since the Yankees lost this afternoon, he acted like he didn't half mind. The front office people were even more surprised that Mr. Stengel would ask me to help out without first checking with them. When I asked them what they had to lose, they calmed down enough to talk and realized I knew baseball. Finally, they agreed I could take over for two weeks.

Mr. Stengel said he'd rest at home and watch the games on television. I told him what a good set you had. Also told him how you boys thought his telegram was a joke. He said he halfway thought it was, too. A real keen wit, that Mr. Stengel. Just like you read about in the papers.

Sincerely,
Cyrus Bean

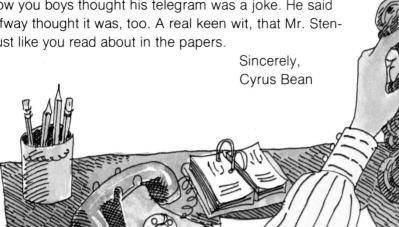

37

Letter from Fred Bates to Ethel Bates:
Mrs. Fred Bates
Gravely, South Carolina

Dear Ethel:

We finished our sales meeting a little early and the old man thought we ought to have a little recreation, so a bunch of us went out to see the Yankees play Detroit. Honey, imagine my surprise when I saw *Mr. Cyrus* turning in his lineup to the umpire. I told everyone how he ruled the roost around Jim Sykes' Service Station and how I was sure this had to be his first time out of the state.

But there he was, and Detroit pitching Lary,[3] which is usually a sure victory. What happened was the craziest thing I've seen in a long time. After they got Detroit out in the first inning, it all started. Bauer bunted and was thrown out. Kubek bunted safely and stole second. Mantle then bunted safely while Kubek took third. Berra bunted and Kubek scored while they were throwing out Berra. Then Skowron bunted out to end the inning. That's the way it was all night. Cyrus had every batter bunting through the first five innings until the whole Detroit infield was playing almost on top of home plate. Then for the rest of the game Mr. Cyrus ran Detroit half to death with bunts and little Texas league singles.[4] Before it was over he had the Tigers so unnerved they made half a dozen errors. At first the crowd didn't like it because they've been used to a lot of home run hitting, but after the Yankees got ahead they were about to tear the stadium apart with excitement.

I tried to go down to the locker room after the game, but the reporters were so thick I couldn't get in to speak to Mr. Cyrus. Kiss the children for me, and if you can, go over to Jim Sykes' place for the game Saturday.

Love,
Fred

---

3. **Detroit pitching Lary:** Frank Lary was pitching for the Detroit Tigers.
4. **Texas league singles:** softly hit balls landing just beyond the reach of the infielders and far in front of the outfielders.

Letter from Jim Sykes to Cyrus Bean:
Dear Cyrus:

   We all watched the game this afternoon, and we think you should have won by more than six runs. Now if I were you I'd swing Mantle around a little more in center when Kaline bats. The Yankees may bunt themselves into a pennant if they keep this up. Your five game winning streak has the whole county talking.

   The station was packed for the game and business was better than it's been in years.

Sincerely,
Jim Sykes

P.S.   *You forgot to wave.* Everybody was disappointed. In fact, Ben Landry almost waved his arm off trying to get your attention.

Letter from Cyrus Bean to Jimmy Bean:
Dear Jimmy:

I'm glad to get through that Chicago series. It sure was rough. I was afraid we might drop one or two of those games, but the boys came through. It's Cleveland tomorrow. A sweep will run our string to twelve games and give us second place, with the Baltimore series following to give us a shot at first before Mr. Stengel takes over again.

Sonny, I wish you could meet the team. I've told them how you hope to be a Yankee someday. Also told Mickey Mantle how you studied his bunting tips in *The Progressive Farmer.* He said I could teach you more about bunting than anybody he knew, himself included. He's a real modest fellow. Hope you can watch a television game soon.

Love,
Grandpa Cyrus

Telegram from seven American League[5] managers to the American League president:
ANYTHING IN THE RULE BOOK COVERING CYRUS BEAN? URGENT. IMMEDIATE REPLY REQUESTED.

Telegram from the American League president to seven American League managers:
SORRY. NOTHING THAT WILL HELP YOU. GOOD LUCK.

Letter from Nettie Stone to Cyrus Bean:
Dear Mr. Bean:

Since you are obviously too busy to write to me, I guess it's up to me to do the writing. I was going to make one of those applesauce cakes you like so well and send it to you, but I figured you were too busy even for that. I baked one anyway and served it to John David Dawson when he

---

5. **American League:** Professional baseball is divided into two major leagues, the National and the American.

escorted me home from prayer meeting. He's a mighty nice man with one of the nicest farms in the county. I know he gets lonesome since Miss Ella died, so I invited him back for Sunday dinner.

Hope you don't get sick eating all that highly seasoned food in those fancy restaurants.

Yours truly,
Nettie Stone

Telegram from Cyrus Bean to Nettie Stone:

IF YOU THINK YOU ARE MAKING ME JEALOUS BY PLAYING UP TO JOHN DAVID DAWSON YOU ARE WRONG AND I DON'T EAT HIGHLY SEASONED FOOD EITHER.

Letter from Jim Sykes to Cyrus Bean:
Dear Cyrus:

Congratulations on that Cleveland series. Never thought I'd see Colavito bunt four times in a row. Looks like they're fighting fire with fire. The Baltimore game Sunday will be your last, I hear, and it'll likely be for first place. Folks are already claiming seats at the station. You've got to remember to wave this time. Some are getting notions you're feeling high and mighty these days, but I know that ain't so.

I've got the drink box filled to the brim, and I'll have two wash tubs full of ice and drinks in the back room just in case. Sure hope the game isn't rained out.

Yours truly,
Jim Sykes

P.S.   I believe I'd pitch Turley Sunday since he once played for Baltimore and will know the hitters better.

Letter from Cyrus Bean to Casey Stengel:
Dear Mr. Stengel:

It sure is good to be back home again. Except for eating a little too much applesauce cake on the train, I had a pleasant trip. Mainly, I'm writing to thank you for giving me the opportunity to be with the Yankees, and to make a confession about Sunday's game with Baltimore. I could have lost that game and first place if it hadn't been for Jim Sykes and the people here in Gravely. I told you about Jim Sykes once before.

Anyway, when things got rough for us in the ninth with bases loaded and one man out, I knew it was time to change pitchers. If you remember, I had a lefthander and a righthander warming up with a lefthanded power coming to bat. Well, as I walked to the mound I knew I was going to call the lefthander, but remembering all those folks watching the game in Jim Sykes' Service Station and what Jim wrote me about some folks thinking me uppity because I didn't wave, I just turned loose with a big wave, and me being righthanded, the righthander started in from the bullpen. The Baltimore manager must have thought I was crazy, I suppose, so he sat his righthanded pinchhitters down and let those lefthanders swing away. Well, our man made a shambles of percentages and struck out their fellows to give us first place.

What I'm asking is that you not mention this to anyone, since I don't want Jimmy to think his grandpa didn't know what he was doing. I will tell him later when he's a little older and can understand that I'm human like everybody else. Good luck in the World Series.

Respectfully,
Cyrus Bean

Telegram from Cyrus Bean to fifteen major league teams:
APPRECIATE ALL OFFERS. SORRY I CAN'T ACCEPT ANY OF THEM. WHEN PEOPLE LIKE JIM SYKES, WHO NEVER PLAYED A DAY OF BASEBALL, STARTS TELLING ME HOW TO MANAGE A TEAM, IT'S HIGH TIME I GAVE IT ALL UP FOR GOOD.

Telegram from Casey Stengel to Cyrus Bean:
TEAM VOTED YOU SHARE WORLD SERIES MONEY PLUS TICKETS TO GAMES. GRANDSON GUARANTEED TRYOUT WITH YANKEES WHEN OF AGE.

CASEY STENGEL

Letter from Cyrus Bean to Casey Stengel:
Dear Mr. Stengel:
I accept the share and the tickets gratefully. Miss Nettie Stone has agreed to join Jimmy, his mother, and me for the trip. The boy's as happy as I've ever seen him.
Interest in baseball has increased so sharply around Gravely that Jim Sykes has bought a second television set and is renting a tent from the funeral parlor to pitch next to the station for the overflow crowd. Didn't I tell you the whole country would get better overnight if the Yankees started winning again?
Luck to you and the boys.

Respectfully,
Cyrus Bean

Understanding the Story

1. Why did Cyrus Bean say that it was important for the Yankees to start winning again?

2. What was Cyrus Bean's strategy for winning the Detroit game?

3. Why do you think the American League managers wanted to know if there was anything in the rule book covering Cyrus Bean?

4. The hero of a funny story is often an underdog, someone with average or less-than-average ability who manages to become amazingly successful against all odds. Why do you think people like to read this kind of story?

5. Some people think of age groups in terms of *stereotypes*. For example, they may think that all teenagers are alike or that all elderly people are alike. (In printing, a stereotype is a piece of metal that is used to make copies; each copy is exactly the same as the others.) How is Cyrus Bean like or different from any elderly person that you know?

Understanding Literature

Much of the humor in "The Man Who Saved the Yankees" comes from your being able to read the letters of several people, so that you can see a situation from several different points of view. These letters are written in an informal style and contain *slang* and *jargon*. Although slang, which tends to be colorful and exaggerated, begins as a new way of stating an idea, it becomes dated quickly. In "The Man Who Saved the Yankees," were there any slang expressions that sounded old-fashioned? If so, which ones?

Jargon is the language of people who have developed special words and phrases to talk about a job, hobby, or interest that they share. Often jargon is made up of the technical terms used in a business or in a sport, such as baseball.

Decide if each of the following sentences contains an example of slang, jargon, or both.

a. I told everyone how he ruled the roost around Jim Syke's Service Station.

b. Then for the rest of the game Mr. Cyrus ran Detroit half to death with bunts and little Texas league singles.

c. The Yankees may bunt themselves into a pennant if they keep this up.

Writing About the Story

Imagine that you have been granted an interview with the athletic star you most admire. In a paragraph, explain why you admire this person and list the three questions you would most like to ask him or her.

The Microscope

A poem by Maxine Kumin

Anton Leeuwenhoek[1] was Dutch.
He sold pincushions, cloth, and such.
The waiting townsfolk fumed and fussed
As Anton's dry goods gathered dust.

He worked, instead of tending store,
At grinding special lenses for
A microscope. Some of the things
He looked at were:
                        mosquitoes' wings,
the hairs of sheep, the legs of lice,
the skin of people, dogs, and mice;
ox eyes, spiders' spinning gear,
fishes' scales, a little smear
of his own blood,
                  and best of all,
the unknown, busy, very small
bugs that swim and bump and hop
inside a simple water drop.

Impossible! Most Dutchmen said.
This Anton's crazy in the head.
We ought to ship him off to Spain.
He says he's seen a housefly's brain.
He says the water that we drink
Is full of bugs. He's mad, we think!

They called him *domkop*,[2] which means dope.
That's how we got the microscope.

---

1. **Anton Leeuwenhoek** (LAY·vuhn·HOOK).
2. *domkop* (DUM·KAWF) Dutch word for a stupid person (literally, *stupid-head*).

I Hate Mornings

An article by Richard Cohen

Illustrated by Don Madden

IT IS FRIDAY MORNING in the city of Washington as I am writing this, and it is, I suppose, a beautiful morning. The sky is blue, the Celsius[1] is climbing to a number that means nothing to me, the air is so clean, and the birds, I swear, are singing. I have been up for several hours already and I have accomplished quite a bit and now there is something I very much want to do. I want to go back to bed.

I am pretending to be a morning person. I have been pretending now for some time, getting up early, running my two point six miles, eating a real breakfast like in the movies, showering, dressing, reading the papers — pretending, in short, to be awake. I am

not. Under no circumstances am I awake before 11 a.m. at the earliest. I am, in fact, asleep as this is being written.

The fact of the matter is that I cannot handle mornings. I never have, probably never will and resent the notion that I am expected to. I am not a morning person. It is not my fault. It is a handicap, like having freckles when you're young and want to look tough. I am expected to function when others function, to come out of the house with a smile on my face, kicking my heels like in the commercials, to greet the blasted morning with a smile and to function, function, function. It is useless. It is unfair. People like me need to organize. We need to sit in at some government building — in the afternoon, if that's all right.

___
1. **Celsius** (SEL·see·uhs): the metric temperature reading.

People who can function in the morning, which is to say most people, simply don't understand the problem. To them, late sleepers lack character. Weak people sleep late. Strong people are up with the sun. My father thought that way. He is your typical non-understanding morning person who thinks it is a sin to stay in bed when the sun is in the sky. He would come into my room when I was a kid, look down at me and order me out of bed. I would ask why and he would say — with absolute conviction — because it was time to get up.

I was just a kid, but already I was learning that I was different from most other people. Friends would come to my window in the morning and yell for me to come out and play. Snore. The smells of breakfast would come up the stairs to my room. Snore. Food beckoned. Baseball beckoned. Snore. Snore. I learned that I had to watch myself in the morning. I was likely to do anything, I could fall back to sleep while getting dressed and I did it once while leaning over to tie a shoe. I learned that I had this ability to believe I was dreaming anything that threatened to wake me up. Once, for instance, I dreamed my father had been locked out of the house and was calling me. I dreamed that because my father had been locked out of the house and was calling me.

By then I knew I was different. I became a reader of minibiographies — those "people-in-the-news" things you see in newspapers. I kept looking for the successful man or woman who got up late — the one who would say something like, "Never got out of bed until noon. That's how I made a million." But that was never the case. Instead, I read about people who had done a day's work by eight in the morning — who had risen with the dawn and gone straight to work. By the time I was just starting to come out of my nightly coma, they had already made a fortune.

Over the years I learned to cope, to treat myself as a crazy person who was likely to do anything in the morning. I learned the hard way. I bought and then threw out several alarm clocks, until I realized that it was me who was turning them off in the morning. The conclusion was inescapable. There was no one else in the room. I started to plan my wardrobe at night, knowing that I just could not handle major decisions like what shirt to wear in the morning. I could stand before the closet, looking at my clothes, having a virtual breakdown over this important decision. I would pace and then sit down and then pace some more. Finally, I would sit down on the bed to think things over. Then I would fall asleep.

Well, I know the psychiatrists out there are going to have their theories about all this — how maybe I'm afraid to face life or some such thing. I assure you that is not the case. I love life.

It's mornings I hate.

I'm Only Sleeping

A song by John Lennon and Paul McCartney

When I wake up early in the morning,
Lift my head, I'm still yawning.
When I'm in the middle of a dream,
Stay in bed, float up stream (float up stream),
Please don't wake me, no, don't shake me,
Leave me where I am, I'm only sleeping.
Everybody seems to think I'm lazy.
I don't mind, I think they're crazy
Running everywhere at such a speed,
Till they find there's no need (there's no need),
Please don't spoil my day, I'm miles away,
And after all, I'm only sleeping.
Keeping an eye on the world going by my window,
Taking my time, lying there and staring at the ceiling,
Waiting for a sleepy feeling.
Please don't spoil my day, I'm miles away,
And after all, I'm only sleeping.
Keeping an eye on the world going by my window,
Taking my time.
When I wake up early in the morning,
Lift my head, I'm still yawning.
When I'm in the middle of a dream,
Staying in bed, float up stream (float up stream),
Please don't wake me, no, don't shake me,
Leave me where I am, I'm only sleeping.

Illustration by Christa Kieffer

Learn About

An essay is a short piece of writing that presents the author's ideas and feelings about one subject. It is said to be *exposition,* because it *exposes,* or puts forth, these thoughts. An essay may contain narration or description, but it is primarily a statement of personal opinion.

Essayists aim to catch the interest of readers and provoke thought or action. To do this, they may focus on the highlights of a topic rather than try to cover it completely. Some essays deal with social and political issues and are serious in tone and purpose. Editorials and many newspaper columns fall into this category. Yet quite a few essays make readers smile as well as think.

An essay should focus on one main idea. Different paragraphs should develop the main idea with details in the form of examples, reasons, and factual information. The first paragraph of an essay should introduce the author's subject. It should also give some idea of his or her purpose in writing about that subject. By the end of the first paragraph the reader should know whether the author means to be serious or funny. The concluding words of the first paragraph may include a "hook"—something that catches your interest and makes you want to continue reading.

Read through the first paragraph of "Teenagers and Ghosts," an essay by Alfred Hitchcock. Think about what the writer accomplishes in the first paragraph.

> Good evening, and welcome to Alfred Hitchcock's Ghostly Gallery. This is your perennial host speaking. It seems to me that I am continually introducing things. Through my motion pictures, I introduce new stars; in television, I introduce the commercials, and now — here I am again. In this instance, I presume, you would call me a ghost host.

Here Alfred Hitchcock immediately catches the reader's attention by introducing his essay as if he were speaking to a radio or television audience. His last sentence names his subject—ghosts—and with the play on words, "ghost host," he indicates that this is a humorous essay.

The paragraphs that follow the first one explain what Hitchcock is introducing — a collection of ghost stories for teenagers — and why he is introducing them.

. . . and now I should say a word about the type of story you will find lurking between these covers. After all, I don't want you to begin to read under false pretenses. This is not *David Copperfield,* or *Rebecca of Sunnybrook Farm.* These are ghost stories and are designed both to frighten and instruct. You see, my aim is to teach you about ghosts and I feel you will be a very sympathetic audience. Let me explain.

The two most misunderstood groups of our society are teenagers and ghosts. When an adult hears a screech (of tires?) sounding through the night air, who gets the blame? When hub caps mysteriously disappear, whose fault is it? I am sure you are already feeling more sympathetic toward our ectoplasmic[1] friends.

---

1. ectoplasmic (EK•toh•PLAZ•mik): here, ghostly (literally, outside the body).

Now read the following brief essay by journalist Art Buchwald. Check to see if the first paragraph makes clear the subject, purpose, and tone of the essay. As you read, notice whether Buchwald sticks to one central idea.

Fresh Air Will Kill You

Smog, which was once the big attraction of Los Angeles, can now be found all over the country from Butte, Montana, to New York City, and people are getting so used to polluted air that it's very difficult for them to breathe anything else.

I was lecturing recently, and one of my stops was Flagstaff, Arizona, which is about 7,000 miles above sea level.

As soon as I got out of the plane, I smelled something peculiar.

"What's that smell?" I asked the man who met me at the plane.

"I don't smell anything," he replied.

"There's a definite odor that I'm not familiar with," I said.

"Oh, you must be talking about the fresh air. A lot of people come out here who have never smelled fresh air before."

"What's it supposed to do?" I asked suspiciously.

"Nothing. You just breathe it like any other kind of air. It's supposed to be good for your lungs."

"I've heard that story before," I said. "How come if it's air, my eyes aren't watering?"

"Your eyes don't water with fresh air. That's the advantage of it. Saves you a lot in paper tissues."

I looked around and everything appeared crystal clear. It was a strange sensation and made me feel very uncomfortable.

My host, sensing this, tried to be reassuring. "Please don't worry about it. Tests have proved that you can breathe fresh air day and night without its doing any harm to the body."

"You're just saying that because you don't want me to leave," I said. "Nobody who has lived in a major city can stand fresh air for a very long time. He has no tolerance for it."

"Well, if the fresh air bothers you, why don't you put a handkerchief over your nose and breathe through your mouth?"

"Okay, I'll try it. If I'd known I was coming to a place that had nothing but fresh air, I would have brought a surgical mask."

We drove in silence. About fifteen minutes later he asked, "How do you feel now?"

"Okay, I guess, but I sure miss sneezing." . . .

The fresh air was making me feel dizzy. "Isn't there a diesel bus around here that I could breathe into for a couple of hours?"

"Not at this time of day. I might be able to find a truck for you."

We found a truck driver, and slipped him a five-dollar bill, and he let me put my head near his exhaust pipe for a half-hour. I was immediately revived and able to give my speech.

Nobody was as happy to leave Flagstaff as I was. My next stop was Los Angeles, and when I got off the plane, I took one big deep breath of the smog-filled air, my eyes started to water, I began to sneeze, and I felt like a new man again.

You may still have the idea that an essay is a very formal, very difficult form of prose. Many people hold this misconception. Actually, the essay may be the simplest type of creative writing. If you come up with one good idea and then explore and expand it logically, you can write an entertaining essay. Of course there is one hurdle you must clear in order to do this. This common obstacle might be referred to as Writer's Paradox: the only time you don't have something really clever to say is when you are attempting to write something really clever. The other half of this law is that whenever you think of a great subject for a story or an essay, you have no pencil, no paper, and no time.

How can you overcome Writer's Paradox? One way is to write down your ideas as they occur and save the jottings for the day you finally sit down to write. If you do this, you will have the luxury of choosing among several interesting possibilities, instead of having to settle for whatever you can think of in a few moments. Of course, this useful suggestion is not very helpful if today is the day you want to write your essay. But there are some other proven ways to generate ideas. You may find one of these helpful as you prepare to write a humorous essay.

1. *Complain about something that people seldom complain about.* There is a popular saying that "nobody loves a grouch." This is not necessarily true, at least as it applies to essayists. Many humorous essays are half-serious gripes about some innocent practice or idea. For

example, Eric Nicol wrote an essay called "Pets in the Press." In it he tells how he hates news stories about remarkable animals.

2. *Make something unimportant into something important.* Robert Benchley wrote an essay, "Call for Mr. Kenworthy," on the practice of paging people in hotels. An everyday occurrence like this can become interesting when a writer singles it out for more attention than it deserves. The same holds true for objects.

3. *Make something seem like its opposite.* In "Fresh Air Will Kill You," Art Buchwald makes polluted air sound pleasant and fresh air sound awful. Many writers use this kind of flip-flop as a way to humorously examine a subject.

4. *Present a difficult problem and offer a ridiculous solution.* Many humorous essays about political or social issues follow this formula. Both the writer and the reader recognize the silliness of the proposed solution. But while the writer tries to prove that the ridiculous answer is a good one, he or she is able to point out weaknesses in answers that other people have seriously proposed. This sort of essay normally ends by suggesting a sensible answer to the problem.

Now look back at the suggestions one through four. For each of the four suggestions, write down at least one idea for a humorous essay. You may want to jot down a few examples and details to support each of these main ideas. Be prepared to share your ideas.

THE GREAT BAGTHORPE DAISY CHAIN

From the novel *Bagthorpes Unlimited* by Helen Cresswell

Illustrated by Lane Yerkes

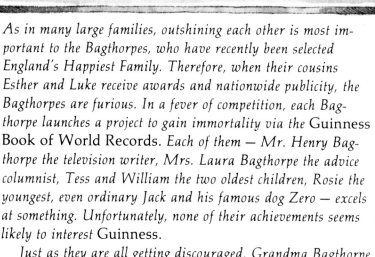

As in many large families, outshining each other is most important to the Bagthorpes, who have recently been selected England's Happiest Family. Therefore, when their cousins Esther and Luke receive awards and nationwide publicity, the Bagthorpes are furious. In a fever of competition, each Bagthorpe launches a project to gain immortality via the Guinness Book of World Records. Each of them — Mr. Henry Bagthorpe the television writer, Mrs. Laura Bagthorpe the advice columnist, Tess and William the two oldest children, Rosie the youngest, even ordinary Jack and his famous dog Zero — excels at something. Unfortunately, none of their achievements seems likely to interest Guinness.

Just as they are all getting discouraged, Grandma Bagthorpe renews the competition by forming an "Unholy Alliance" with another Bagthorpe cousin, four-year-old Daisy, daughter of Aunt Celia and Uncle Parker. In the past, Daisy's claim to fame has been her extraordinary ability to create disasters, but under Grandma's guidance Daisy has turned her attentions to the Bagthorpe quest for fame.

As we join the Happiest Family in England, Mr. Bagthorpe has just arranged to be interviewed at home by England's most prestigious newspaper. On the eve of this important interview, which he hopes will assure his fame as a serious writer, he returns home with Mrs. Bagthorpe and Jack to find Grandma and Daisy on the front lawn amidst an elaborate arrangement of floodlights. Sensing potential disaster, Mr. Bagthorpe storms up to the Unholy Alliance.

"Mother," Mr. Bagthorpe began, "what in the name of all that is wonderful — is — going — on?"

"There is no need to space your words out at me like that, Henry," Grandma told him. "I am not interfering with your life. Pray do not interfere with mine."

"Grandma Bag and me's going to make the longest daisy chain in the whole world, Uncle Bag," Daisy then piped up. "We'll be in the Beginners' Book of Records."

Jack at once saw the light.

"You — are — what?"

"I think you heard, Henry," said Grandma. "And you are still spacing out your words."

"Will you help, Uncle Bag?" asked Daisy.

This optimistic request met with a sound more like an animal growl than a human rejoinder, and Mr. Bagthorpe turned on his heel and lurched back toward the house, holding his head with his hands.

"Oh, dear," said Mrs. Bagthorpe. "Mother, is this true?"

"Perfectly true, Laura," replied Grandma, "and I am astonished that there should be all this ridiculous fuss. I should have thought that making a daisy chain was the most harmless occupation in the world. I should have thought that even Henry could not have taken exception to it. One really begins to wonder if one can ever do anything right."

"We had better go and have a cup of tea," said Mrs. Bagthorpe weakly at length. "Whatever have floodlights to do with daisy chains?"

This point was clarified over tea in the kitchen, when Grandma outlined her scheme to an interested audience which did not include Mr. Bagthorpe. Grandma was a schemer of the first order. If she had a project in hand, she executed it with the ruthless efficiency of a military genius. The present case was no exception.

The reason for the floodlights, she explained, was that darkness might fall the following day before the daisy chain was long enough. She had telephoned the vicar[1] and asked for the loan of the floodlights that had been used for the *son et lumière*[2] performance in the vicarage garden by the Ladies' Fellowship. In this, Grandma had played the part of Queen Elizabeth I and had, according to Mr. Bagthorpe, been playing it ever since.

"If necessary, Daisy and I will work through till dawn breaks the following day," Grandma informed them all.

No one had reason to doubt this.

"It would be a pity, however," she continued, "for an elderly lady and a delicate child to have to sit out all night in a heavy dew."

---

1. vicar (VIK•uhr): a local minister whose residence (usually at the church) is known as the **vicarage**.
2. *son et lumière* (SAWN ay loo•MYAYR): French for *sound and light.*

"It would be madness, Mother," agreed Mrs. Bagthorpe instantly, visualizing Aunt Celia's reaction to this proposal. "I think you must forget all about it."

"Also," continued Grandma, ignoring her, "there has been an unfortunate development during the afternoon. We wish, as I have told you, to establish a record for the longest daisy chain in the world. I believed this to be an entirely original enterprise. However, I find that I am mistaken. One of Daisy's friends has told us that a record for this already exists."

"And there aren't enough of us," Daisy chipped in. "We've got enough daisies, we've got bags and

bags of daisies, but we haven't got enough of us."

The Bagthorpes waited for this obscure utterance to be clarified.

"What Daisy is saying," Grandma told them obligingly, "is that we shall have to enlist your help. Fetch me that book, Daisy."

Daisy trotted out and soon reappeared carrying the *Guinness Book of Records*, which was beginning to look very thumbed round the edges, having been gone through many times with a fine-toothed comb by Bagthorpes bent on immortality.

"I will read the appropriate entry," Grandma told them. Accordingly she read: " 'The longest daisy chain on record is one of 3,234 ft.,

985 m., made of 18,000 daisies by the members of the Deanery Players,[3] Harrogate, North Yorkshire, England, in 8½ hours on 12th July 1975.'"

"Crikey!"[4] Rosie exclaimed. "Three thousand and *how* many feet?"

"I don't think you'll manage it, Grandma," Jack told her.

"Precisely," she nodded. "The chain, you will note, was not made single-handedly by an elderly lady and a delicate child. It was made by some people called the Deanery Players. I do not know who these people are, or how many of them there were, but I should imagine they were in rude health, and numbered more than two."

"There's only two of us, you see," Daisy elaborated helpfully.

"Daisy and I could, of course, make the attempt to establish a record for the longest chain made by a four-year-old child and her grandmother," Grandma said.

"But if we *all* helped," cried Rosie, "we'd all be in! Instead of those Player people, it would say, 'the Bagthorpes.' It might even give all our names separately. That'd show that Esther."

"That is exactly the point," Grandma nodded. "I am willing to

share with you all my chance of immortality."

There was a pause while people thought about this offer. There seemed, particularly to Tess and William, something intrinsically frivolous and undeserving of serious acclaim about the making of a daisy chain, however long. It was not at all what they had had in mind. On the other hand, Esther and Luke were unlikely, whatever their current successes, to achieve the kind of kudos[5] that goes with being an entry in the *Guinness Book of Records*.

"I'll help," Rosie said.

"And me," Jack said.

"It will mean, of course, my sacrificing my own immortality," Tess said ponderingly, "but naturally, family honor must come first. Very well, Grandma, I shall give you my assistance."

"Thank you, Tess," said Grandma, and looked inquiringly at William. He was well aware that sixteen-year-old males do not normally make daisy chains, but unwilling to miss out on the immortality stakes.

"All right," he said at length. "But I'm not doing any of the picking."

"There will be no need," Grandma told him. "The picking has already been done. I should imagine that we already have at least eighteen thousand daisies. But there are further supplies in at least two fields

3. **Players**: here, a name for a group of actors.
4. **crikey** (CRY·kee): an English slang word expressing surprise or astonishment.
5. **kudos** (KOO·dohz, KYOO·dohz): praise; glory.

that Daisy and I know of, and if we require them, we shall send for them."

"They've got lots of little girls picking for them," Jack told him. "I saw them this morning. They had bags full."

"I wonder how many of those Deanery people there were," William said. "Three thousand whatever it was feet sounds an awful lot. Can we beat them, do you think?"

"Of course we can," Grandma returned calmly. "We can beat anybody."

"I will certainly lend a hand during the odd moment," Mrs. Bagthorpe volunteered, not wishing to appear discouraging of any efforts on the part of her offspring to extend themselves. (Though she did not consider that daisy-chain-making constituted an Extra String to anybody's Bow.)[6]

"You will not be allowed to," Grandma told her.

Mrs. Bagthorpe looked startled by this outright rejection of her services.

"You are not a Blood Bagthorpe, Laura," Grandma explained. "You are related only by marriage, and not strictly one of the family. We do not wish to risk being disqualified on a technical point."

"Oh!" Mrs. Bagthorpe was quite

nonplused. She could see that Grandma's ruling would qualify Aunt Celia and Mr. Bagthorpe, but hoped that Grandma would have the wisdom not to invite the latter. Grandma went on to say that she had explained the matter to Grandpa, and he would be happy to help.

"Just a minute," William said. "If Mother's not a true Bagthorpe, nor are you. *You* only married one."

Grandma drew herself up exceedingly at this heresy.

"I am at the head of the line," she stated. "You are all descended from me. I hope you are not going to deny that?"

No one did, though they all thought her logic shaky.

---

6. **Extra String to anybody's Bow:** an accomplishment worthy of praise and attention. (A string added to a violin bow makes it sound louder.)

"I shall telephone Celia," she went on, "and enlist her aid. She is, of course, hopeless at most things, but daisy chains might turn out to be one of her strengths."

Aunt Celia was, indeed, ecstatic about the venture, and said what poetry Daisy had in her soul to think of something like this, appearing not to hear Grandma's frequently repeated assertions that it was *she* who had had the idea. Aunt Celia also saw the project as symbolic.

"I shall write a poem about it," she promised.

Once the Bagthorpes had thrown in their lot with Grandma, they became wholly involved in it. Jack, who had thought the little girls he had seen in the meadow had looked rather silly and unreliable, volunteered to go down and check on their bags of daisies.

"Tell them to lay them on sheets of plastic," Grandma instructed, "and water them frequently with a fine mist."

Rosie offered to take Daisy on a further picking expedition, because she was afraid they might run out of daisies. William said that he would set his alarm clock for 2 A.M., and go down and check on their own daisies and water them further if necessary. He then went out to ensure that the floodlights were working. Tess had pointed out that the Deanery Players had made their chain in only eight and a half hours and had had no need of floodlights. William told her that a mathematical equation would be involved, and spelled it out to her.

"It is a question of persons per number of daisies per hour," he said.

Grandma said that she did not care if there had been a hundred Deanery Players. The Bagthorpes would beat all comers, she proclaimed, and this, in fact, was by now the general feeling.

The only member of the household not now obsessively involved in the Great Bagthorpe Daisy Chain was Mr. Bagthorpe himself. He accused Grandma of plotting the whole thing in order to ruin his reputation.

"I shall telephone *The Sunday Times* and tell them not to come interview me," he said.

He did not, of course, do this. He could not feel sufficiently confident that they would then arrange an alternative date.

"I may well sit up all night," he stated. "I shall not be able to close my eyes. Any chance of my ever being taken seriously as a writer has now gone, knocked from my grasp by my own family."

"If you do," William said, "it would save me setting the alarm. Could you go out from time to time and see if the daisies need watering, do you think?"

Next day the Bagthorpes were up

at dawn, raring to go. They had a hasty and noisy breakfast — with the exception of Mr. Bagthorpe, who was still fast asleep. William collected all the waterproofs[7] in the house, because there had been a very heavy dew, and everyone except Grandma and Grandpa would be sitting on the ground.

With enormous anticipation they then set out into the unaccustomed stillness of early morning. The birds were whistling, and a milky haze hung in the distance.

---

7. **waterproofs:** raincoats.

"It feels like going on holiday," Jack said. "Come on, Zero, old chap. You're going to guard."

"My fingers feel all shaky," Rosie confided in them all. "I'm so excited, I don't know if I'll be able to use them properly."

"Then you must pull yourself together," Grandma told her. "Daisies are a precious commodity. We do not want any unnecessary wastage."

The daisies were pulled out and spread in the middle of the lawn. There seemed acres of them, lying thickly in the kind of quantities nobody had ever seen them before.

Their appearance produced a temporary, awed silence.

"We are embarking on a task of Herculean proportions," Tess remarked at last. "Personally, I would rather tackle the Augean stables."[8]

"We want none of that kind of defeatist talk!" Grandma snapped. "Where is your spirit?"

They all arranged themselves round, and Grandma picked up a handful of daisies and placed them in her lap.

"I shall now thread the first two daisies," she announced, making this moment into a kind of grand opening ceremony. "Daisy will then thread the next. The rest of you can start in whatever order you like."

They watched as she carefully nipped the stem of one daisy and passed through the slit the stem of another. She then looked triumphantly about her, as if expecting a round of applause. None was forthcoming.

"It is fortunate that none of us bite our nails," Grandma observed — and it was, of course. (Jack had used to, but had given it up after Zero became famous.)

After that, they all began. They worked fast, and in almost total silence, because they were as yet overcome by the enormity of what they were attempting.

They had been working for well over an hour, and getting to the point where they were having to spread farther apart to avoid tangling their chains, when Mrs. Fosdyke, the housekeeper, arrived. She came up the drive at a brisk hedgehog[9] trot and they heard her footsteps though they could not see her.

"Here, Mrs. Fosdyke!" called Mrs. Bagthorpe. (She was not being allowed to thread, but Grandma had said she could keep everybody else supplied with daisies.) She realized afterward that she should have got up, joined Mrs. Fosdyke and explained slowly and carefully what was taking place, to break her in gently.

As it was, next moment Mrs. Fosdyke's head poked through a shrub, disembodied like the Cheshire Cat's,[10] but unlike that cat, not smiling. Her expression was one of horror and downright disbelief. She blinked her eyes rapidly, evidently not trusting them.

"Oh, my good gracious!" she exclaimed at last. "Now what?"

"We are making the longest daisy chain in the world, Mrs. Fosdyke!" Grandma called gaily. She had by now worked into a kind of rhythm

---

8. **task of Herculean proportions:** a huge job. In Greek myth, the hero Hercules performed twelve extraordinary tasks in order to gain immortality; one of these labors was the cleaning of the huge **Augean stables,** where King Augeas (aw•JEE•uhs) kept 3000 oxen.

9. **hedgehog:** a porcupine.
10. **disembodied like the Cheshire Cat's:** from *Alice's Adventures in Wonderland*, by Lewis Carroll.

with her daisies, and her hands were moving with a regular action as though she were crocheting, or knitting. She gave the impression that now she had started, she was never going to stop.

"I don't believe it!" Mrs. Fosdyke said flatly. She pushed right past the shrub and stood there clutching her black plastic carrier, staring about her. "I don't believe it!" she repeated, as if by so doing she could make the whole scene disappear.

It seemed to Mrs. Fosdyke, who had been the witness of innumerable Bagthorpian holocausts, that the peaceful, innocent tableau[11] that

now lay before her was the most unnerving sight of her career with them. It was still not yet eight o'clock, and they sat steadily and patiently threading as if they might have been there all night — or even from time immemorial.

Later, at The Fiddler's Arms with her friends, she struggled to find the right words to describe how she had felt.

"You don't expect a turn like that, eight o'clock in the morning," she told her interested audience. "It ain't in nature. Young and old alike, sitting like statchers,[12] putting daisies

---

11. **tableau** (tab·LOH): scene.

12. **statchers:** Mrs. Fosdyke's pronunciation of the word *statues.*

together as if they was Snow White. If I was ten years older I should have dropped dead at my own feet."

At the time, she simply stood rooted to the spot, trying to order her thoughts.

"We have breakfasted already," Grandma told her, "but I am sure we would all appreciate a cup of tea, when you have a moment."

"Cup of tea," Mrs. Fosdyke repeated mechanically. "Cup of tea."

She disappeared among the foliage away toward the sanity of her kitchen, the kettle and the teapot. Jack was excused for several minutes, to go and help her carry the trays of tea. He found her tracking about the kitchen and talking to herself.

"I've come to help carry," he told her, in a fairly loud voice, to be sure of getting through to her. She stopped and stared at him.

"They're sitting out there making daisy chains," she told him, as if hoping to be contradicted. "I saw them. I saw them with me own eyes."

"That's right," he agreed. "I know it seems a bit funny, but — "

"Ought I to telephone somebody?" she wondered aloud.

At this point Mr. Bagthorpe entered.

"Where are they?" he demanded.

"On the front lawn," Jack told him.

"Making daisy chains?"

"Yes. Well, we did tell you we were."

Mrs. Fosdyke was astonished to see Mr. Bagthorpe. She had assumed that he, as the maddest of the lot, had been among the chain-makers — that he was, in fact, their organizer. If all the Bagthorpes had gone mad *except* him, then the plot, so far as she was concerned, was thickening.

"*The Sunday Times* will approach my house, and will find my entire family, including my own mother, up to their ears in daisies," said Mr.

Bagthorpe, summing up the situation for himself. "Nothing like this can ever have happened to a serious writer before. Would Shakespeare have survived, I wonder, or Tolstoy, or Milton,[13] if any of their families were on record as having been discovered like this? Could we now take *Othello* seriously, or *Paradise Lost*, if this were so?"

"I suppose you couldn't pretend

we *weren't* your family," Jack suggested helpfully.

Mr. Bagthorpe turned on him a weary gaze.

"So the situation improves," he said. "I have a bunch of complete strangers in my garden looping miles of daisy chains around, and I pass it off. I say, 'Sorry the family isn't here to meet you — just ignore that bunch of lunatics on the front lawn. It happens every day in the daisy season.'"

"I suppose not," Jack admitted.

A loud rush of gravel was heard in the ensuing silence.

"That," said Mr. Bagthorpe, "is all I need."

Uncle Parker had arrived to bring his wife to the daisy-chaining. He was himself debarred from taking part because of Grandma's ruling about blood.

"No reason why *you* shouldn't lend a hand, though, Henry," he told Mr. Bagthorpe, appropriating two of Mrs. Fosdyke's cups of tea for himself and Aunt Celia. "What a scoop for the Color Supplement[14] this will be."

"If it were not for your accursed daughter Daisy," Mr. Bagthorpe told him, "none of this would have happened."

"That is the truth!" cried Aunt Celia surprisingly. "And we are proud to own it! Such poetry, such

---

13. **Shakespeare . . . or Tolstoy, or Milton:** William Shakespeare, English playwright, author of the tragedy *Othello*; Leo Tolstoy, Russian writer; John Milton, English poet, famous for the poem *Paradise Lost*.

14. **Color Supplement:** newspaper section.

symbolism — and only four years of age!"

There was a moment's silence while everyone else present thought his or her own thoughts about Daisy.

"Better get out there and see how they're doing," Uncle Parker said. "And get Celia started. Sure you won't come, Henry?"

Aunt Celia, with cooing and exclamations of bliss, took her place among the daisy-threaders. Jack and Mrs. Fosdyke darted among them passing cups of tea.

"Delicious!" remarked Grandma, pausing to take a sip. "I always think tea tastes so much better when one is making daisy chains."

The morning wore on and the chains lengthened by the minute. By lunchtime the Bagthorpe lawn looked like a miniature maze with a lot of people lost in it. William, feeling this to be a marginally more manly role, had appointed himself overseer and measurer. Being Bagthorpes, they had been unable to resist setting up a race within a race, and were vying with one another to produce the longest individual chain. At present it looked as if Tess would win this, or Grandma. Aunt Celia was very nimble with her fingers, but lost much time going into reveries, during which she would sit with her hands folded in her lap, dreamily gazing about her and presumably drinking in all the poetry and symbolism.

It was stew for lunch, as luck would have it, and Grandma did not say anything about this tasting so much better being eaten in conjunction with daisy chains.

"I should have thought cucumber sandwiches would have been more apt," she told Mrs. Fosdyke, "followed by raspberries and cream."

"There's bakewell tart[15] and custard to follow," Mrs. Fosdyke told her.

It was unfortunate that a photographer from the *Aysham Gazette*[16] arrived during the forking up of mouthfuls of stew between daisy-threading, because the resulting picture was anything but poetic and symbolic. The photographer came and went without Mr. Bagthorpe's knowledge, and had been invited, of course, by Grandma. Mr. Bagthorpe was exaggerating only a little when he said, as he often did, that Grandma had become drunk with the heady wine of publicity.

By two o'clock, the Bagthorpes had been working for six and a half hours, and tension was running high. William had told them that their individual quota of daisies to be threaded was to be in the region of four and a half thousand each, if the existing record was to be broken.

"Though if we beat it by only one

---

15. **bakewell tart**: a dessert that originated in Bakewell, Derbyshire, England.
16. *Aysham Gazette:* the Bagthorpes' local newspaper.

daisy," he added, "it will still constitute an authentic record."

If the time record was to be broken too, the Great Bagthorpe Daisy Chain was due to be completed by 3:22 P.M. William, dizzied by his task of looping and numbering daisies by the yard, and by the complexity of the calculations to be made, panicked, and rang for three of his friends to come and assist. William himself counted Grandma's chain and made it three thousand seven hundred and one. He calculated rapidly, and realized that if this was accurate, and roughly matched by the rest, the record was as good as in the bag. This announcement caused so much excitement and jubilation that William began to wonder if he had perhaps made an error, and started a recount.

At just before half past two, Jack said, "I think it's going to rain again."

Grandma looked up.

"Alfred!" she called loudly to Grandpa. "Alfred."

He carried on picking at his daisies with his short, blunt fingers.

"Go and fetch all the umbrellas in the house," she ordered Jack. "Fetch the two large garden umbrellas from the shed."

He did so. As he returned with them the first heavy drops of rain were splashing down.

"The rain will help to keep the daisies fresh," Grandma observed.

She was enthroned under one of the striped sun umbrellas with Grandpa, as her consort, occupying a marginal position on the other side of the handle. The other Bagthorpes fended for themselves as best they could, retiring under trees, and wedging umbrellas above themselves in the boughs.

"Isn't it *lovely!*" squealed Daisy, crouched under her umbrella like a gnome under a deadly toadstool. "Rain, rain, bootiful rain, bootiful pea-green rain. . . ."

William's three friends arrived, and once they had recovered from the shock of what they saw, set about checking William's reckonings. Conversation among the daisy-chainers themselves was now banned.

"No one must speak," William told them, "including you, Grandma. If we are distracted, and lose count, we are lost."

What the men from *The Sunday Times* found, then, when they arrived at around three, was what looked at first sight like a heavy local fall of snow being sat in by a large number of people. And what they heard, when they stepped out of the car and gingerly approached, was the low murmur of people counting.

"Seven ninety-six, seven ninety-seven, seven ninety-eight. . . ."

Running beneath this, like a counterpoint, was a soft refrain,

"Rain, rain, bootiful rain, bootiful pea-green rain. . . ."

The *Sunday Times* men stood baffled, taking in this bizarre scene. They had heard rumors about Mr. Bagthorpe's unpredictability. Some people had even used the word "unbalanced." Was this, they wondered, an elaborate tableau staged for their benefit? Was its perpetrator,[17] perhaps, concealed nearby, watching to see its effect? They shook their heads in unison. Both these men had been all over the world, and were not easily impressed by anything, but they were impressed by this.

"What," muttered one to the other under his breath, "in the name of heaven is going on, do you think?"

The photographer took another long look.

"They're making daisy chains, I think," he pronounced.

At this point Mr. Bagthorpe, carefully dressed with careless negligence, emerged. He at once started in on an apology for his family, making strenuous denials of any involvement with their present activities. His voice got louder and louder until he was finally yelling.

"Be quiet!" called Grandma from under her canopy. "We shall lose count."

The photographer was already making adjustments to his camera.

"Switch on the floodlights!" came Grandma's voice. "This poor light is trying to my eyes."

The photographer became almost hysterical when the powerful floodlights suddenly bathed his subjects under their umbrellas.

"Floodlights!" he gibbered. "It's too good to be true. I've even got them *lit!*"

Then he was in among them, crouching and leaping, his shutter clicking nonstop. Gerald Pike started to try and interview the daisy-chainers, but was severely rebuked by Grandma, who was not so impressed by *The Sunday Times* as her son was.

"This morbid prying into personal lives must stop," she told him. "When we have made the longest daisy chain in the world, then I will interview you."

Mr. Bagthorpe, gritting his teeth, started to stroll among the workers, hoping that Gerald Pike would remember his original intention of interviewing *him.*

"Oh, go 'way, Uncle Bag!" Daisy squealed as he tripped over her thread and snapped it.

Gerald Pike did then turn his attention to Mr. Bagthorpe.

"Which chain is yours?" he inquired.

---

17. **perpetrator:** one who performs a crime or prank.

"I don't have a chain," Mr. Bagthorpe told him. "I am a serious creative ——"

"But I understood this was a family effort. The Great Bagthorpe Daisy Chain. Perhaps you feel it is beneath you?" (Gerald Pike was sufficiently seasoned a journalist to recognize that the story as it stood was good, but with Mr. Bagthorpe also deeply involved, would be better.)

"Perhaps you feel it is beneath you?" he repeated, seeing that Mr. Bagthorpe was trying to restrain himself.

"Perhaps I do!" shouted Mr. Bagthorpe, rising to this. "Perhaps I think the whole mutton-headed,[18] half-baked. . . ."[19]

He stopped. Gerald Pike was making notes. Mr. Bagthorpe looked wildly about him. It was like a nightmare. His whole family was sitting in the rain under umbrellas and lit eerily by floodlights, patiently threading daisies. He was evidently now expected to join them. His wife appeared at his elbow.

"Look, Henry dear," she said, "this is how you do it. . . ."

At this point a distraction occurred in the shape of Tess accusing Grandma of appropriating several yards of her daisies. The two had been running almost neck and neck for the individual title, and now, all of a sudden, Grandma was unassailably in the lead.

"You took some of my chain while I was fixing my umbrella!" Tess cried.

"Tess, dear," said Grandma piously, "the day I am reduced to cheating will be the day I retire from all forms of competitive activity."

This shameless denial left everybody speechless. Grandma always cheated, at everything, and the Bagthorpes knew it. If on this occasion she had *not* cheated, then this would in itself constitute a record. Matters were taking a dangerous turn, with Tess threatening to snap off the end of Grandma's chain in retaliation, when William, who had been in consultation with his aides, shouted, "That's it! We've done it!"

A concerted cheer set up from the Bagthorpes. They stood up and let the rain pour down on them, and cheered themselves hoarse. They all began boasting at once.

"We're in the *Guinness Book of Records!*" shouted Rosie.

"Hurray, hurray, aren't we clever!" squealed Daisy.

"William, kindly go and ask Mrs. Fosdyke to fetch out the champagne I laid in the refrigerator last night," Grandma told him.

"But, Mother," protested Mrs. Bagthorpe, "surely now that we have achieved our objective — and I *do* congratulate you, everybody, I think it quite wonderful — surely now we

---

18. **mutton-headed:** stupid (as a mutton, or sheep).
19. **half-baked:** crazy; not well thought-out.

can retire, and drink the champagne where it is dry?"

Grandma drew herself up.

"Achieved our objective?" she repeated. "Laura, after all these years, you evidently do not understand me."

"But surely," faltered Mrs. Bagthorpe, "you have now established a world record?"

"What we have done," Grandma corrected her, "has been child's play. We have merely toppled the record of those trumpery[20] Deanery people. Daisy and I are not satisfied with such half measures. The real work will now begin."

"The Great Bagthorpe Daisy Chain," exclaimed Jack, seeing what she was getting at. She was going to set up a Daisy Chain that nobody would ever beat.

"We've got millions of daisies left," cried Rosie.

"And there will be further supplies growing all summer," said Mr. Bagthorpe gloomily to himself.

William and Mrs. Fosdyke advanced slowly through the pouring rain, bearing trays of glasses.

"The champagne, Henry!" Grandma ordered.

---

20. **trumpery**: worthless; no-good.

Mr. Bagthorpe set to work with his thumbs.

"We shall work far into the night," Grandma told everyone. "And this time you, Henry, will assist us."

Mr. Bagthorpe was beaten, and knew it. He took his own glass of champagne and went and sat on a waterproof, the rain dripping off his eyebrows.

"The toast, Henry," said Grandma relentlessly.

Mr. Bagthorpe struggled back to his feet. He raised his glass.

"The Great Bagthorpe Daisy Chain!" he croaked.

"And its instigators,[21] of course," added Grandma, draining her own glass.

She had had, as usual, the last word.

---

21. **instigators:** those who began something; here, Grandma and Daisy.

About HELEN CRESSWELL

"I began writing at the age of six or seven, in fact I don't ever remember *not* writing," Helen Cresswell remarks. Though she has, she says, "a passion for words," becoming a professional writer took years of hard work. Cresswell experimented with countless writing techniques during her teens and early twenties, a period she considers essential to the development of her skill.

Helen Cresswell's first book was published when she was twenty-six. Since then she has written more than fifty books as well as stories and plays for television. Much of her work is as popular in this country as it is in her native England.

Helen Cresswell's writing frequently tends toward fantasy, humor, and contradiction. She loves the whimsical and the unlikely. "The qualities I most admire are courage and gaiety," she says. All her characters possess liberal amounts of both.

She drew on childhood memories for her popular series *The Bagthorpe Saga.* A most unusual family, the Bagthorpes seem to stumble into absurd situations all the time. Who else could burn down the dining room while trying to light the candles on a birthday cake?

■ Understanding the Story

1. Why did Mr. Bagthorpe refuse to join the rest of the family in making the daisy chain?

2. Why did Grandma say that Mrs. Bagthorpe could not help set a new daisy-chain record? What is funny about the reason she gives for excluding her daughter-in-law?

3. One of Grandma Bagthorpe's good qualities is that she is very clever. She gets her whole family to work with her on the daisy chain. Explain one other good quality and one bad quality that Grandma has.

4. Most stories contain at least one *conflict,* or struggle between opposing forces, that is important to the plot of the story. The conflict may be *external*—for instance, an actual physical fight, a struggle with natural elements, or a battle of wills between people. In other cases, the conflict may be *internal*—a conflict within a character. What is the most important conflict in this story? Who or what wins?

5. What do you think would be some advantages and disadvantages of living in a large family?

■ Understanding Literature

Authors who write funny stories use a variety of methods to create humor. Sometimes a writer will use *exaggera-* *tion,* making something seem larger, greater, much worse, or much better than ordinary. There is nothing funny about making a daisy chain, but most people would laugh at Grandma Bagthorpe's project to achieve immortality.

Another way to create humor in a story is to include characters, behavior, and situations that surprise the reader because they are so *unexpected.* Although she describes herself as a frail "elderly lady," Grandma is an unexpectedly strong, forceful character who rules her family with an iron will.

A third way of creating humor is by *playing with words,* using unusual words, making up puns and nonsense words, or having a character use words incorrectly. For example, Daisy tells the family, "We'll be in the Beginner's Book of Records."

■ Writing About the Story

What record would you like to set for the *Guinness Book of World Records?* After you choose a record to set, write up an imaginary entry for yourself. Be sure to include the title of the record (for example, "The Biggest Banana Split" or "The Fastest Window Cleaner"), your name, the city, state, and country where you live, and the activity you completed.

The King's Wishes

A short story by Robert Sheckley

Illustrated by Mordecai Gerstein

AFTER SQUATTING behind a glassware display for almost two hours, Bob Granger felt his legs begin to cramp. He moved to ease them, and his number-ten iron[1] slipped off his lap, clattering on the floor.

"Shh," Janice whispered, her mashie[2] gripped tightly.

"I don't think he's going to come," Bob said.

"Be quiet, honey," Janice whispered again, peering into the darkness of their store.

There was no sign of the burglar yet. He had come every night in the past week, mysteriously removing generators, refrigerators and air conditioners. Mysteriously — for he tampered with no locks, jimmied no windows, left no footprints. Yet somehow, he was able to sneak in, time after time, and slink out with a good part of their stock.

"I don't think this was such a good idea," Bob whispered. "After all, a man capable of carrying several hundred pounds of generator on his back — "

"We'll handle him," Janice said, with the certainty that had made her a master sergeant in the WAC Motor Corps.[3] "Besides, we have to stop him — he's postponing our wedding day."

Bob nodded in the darkness. He and Janice had built and stocked the Country Department Store with their army savings. They were planning on getting married, as soon as the profits enabled them to. But when someone stole refrigerators and air conditioners — —

"I think I hear something," Janice said, shifting her grip on the mashie.

There was a faint noise somewhere in the store. They waited. Then they

---

1. **number-ten iron**: Irons are a series of golf clubs.
2. **mashie**: a golf club; specifically, a number-five iron.

3. **WAC Motor Corps**: the section of the Women's Army Corps responsible for servicing vehicles.

heard the sound of feet, padding over the linoleum.

"When he gets to the middle of the floor," Janice whispered, "switch on the lights."

Finally they were able to make out a blackness against the lesser blackness of the store. Bob switched on the lights, shouting, "Hold it there!"

"Oh, no!" Janice gasped, almost dropping her mashie. Bob turned and gulped.

Standing in front of them was a being at least ten feet tall. He had budding horns on his forehead, and tiny wings on his back. He was dressed in a pair of dungarees and a white sweat shirt with EBLIS TECH written across it in scarlet letters. Scuffed white buckskins were on his tremendous feet, and he had a blond crewcut.

"Rats," he said, looking at Bob and Janice. "Knew I should have taken Invisibility in college." He wrapped his arms around his stomach and puffed out his cheeks. Instantly his legs disappeared. Puffing out his cheeks still more, he was able to make his stomach vanish. But that was as far as it went.

"Can't do it," he said, releasing his stored-up air. His stomach and legs came back into visibility. "Haven't got the knack."

"What do you want?" Janice asked, drawing herself to her full slender five foot three.

"Want? Let me see. Oh, yes. The fan." He walked across the room and picked up a large floor fan.

"Just a minute," Bob shouted. He walked up to the giant, his golf club poised. Janice followed close behind him. "Where do you think you're going with that?"

"To King Alerian," the giant said. "He wished for it."

"Oh, he did, did he?" Janice said. "Better put it down." She poised the mashie over her shoulder.

"But I *can't*," the young giant said, his tiny wings twitching nervously. "It's been wished for."

"You asked for it," Janice said. Although small, she was in fine condition from the WACs, where she had spent her time repairing jeep engines. Now, blond hair flying, she swung her club.

"Ouch!" she said. The mashie bounced off the being's head, almost knocking Janice over with the recoil. At the same time, Bob swung his club at the giant's ribs.

It passed *through* the giant, ricocheting against the floor.

"Force is useless against a ferra," the young giant said apologetically.

"A what?" Bob asked.

"A ferra. We're first cousins of the jinn,[4] and related by marriage to the devas."[5] He started to walk back to the center of the room, the fan gripped in one broad hand. "Now if you'll excuse me — "

"A demon?" Janice stood open-mouthed. Her parents had allowed no talk of ghosts or demons in the house, and Janice had grown up a hard-headed realist. She was skilled at repairing anything mechanical; that was her part of the partnership. But anything more fanciful she left to Bob.

Bob, having been raised on a liberal feeding of Oz[6] and Burroughs,[7] was more credulous. "You mean you're out of the *Arabian Nights*?"[8] he asked.

"Oh, no," the ferra said. "The jinn of Arabia are my cousins, as I said. All demons are related, but I am a ferra, of the ferras."

"Would you mind telling me," Bob asked, "what you are doing with my generator, my air conditioner, and my refrigerator?"

"I'd be glad to," the ferra said, putting down the fan. He felt around the air, found what he wanted, and sat down on nothingness. Then he crossed his legs and tightened the laces of one buckskin.

"I graduated from Eblis Tech just about three weeks ago," he began.

---

4. **jinn:** spirits (either good or evil) that appear in human or animal form.

5. **devas:** in Hindu myth, good spirits.
6. **Oz:** fantasy adventures by L. Frank Baum about the Kingdom of Oz.
7. **Burroughs:** Edgar Rice Burroughs, modern American author of fantasy novels.
8. *Arabian Nights: The Arabian Nights' Entertainments* (also known as *The Thousand and One Nights),* a collection of Eastern folk tales from the tenth century.

"And of course, I applied for civil service. I come from a long line of government men. Well, the lists were crowded, as they always are, so I —"

"Civil service?" Bob asked.

"Oh, yes. They're all civil-service jobs — even the jinni in Aladdin's lamp[9] was a government man. You have to pass the tests, you know."

"Go on," Bob said.

"Well — promise this won't go any farther — I got my job through pull." He blushed orange. "My father is a ferra in the Underworld Council, so he used his influence. I was appointed over four thousand higher-ranking ferras, to the position of ferra of the King's Cup. That's quite an honor, you know."

There was a short silence. Then the ferra went on.

"I must confess I wasn't ready," he said sadly. "The ferra of the cup has to be skilled in all branches of demonology.[10] I had just graduated from college — with only passing grades. But of course, I thought I could handle anything."

The ferra paused, and rearranged his body more comfortably on the air.

"But I don't want to bother you with my troubles," he said, getting off the air and standing on the floor. "If you'll excuse me —" He picked up the fan.

"Just a minute," Janice said. "Has this king commanded you to get our fan?"

"In a way," the ferra said, turning orange again.

"Well, look," Janice said. "Is this king rich?" She had decided, for the moment, to treat this superstitious entity as a real person.

"He's a very wealthy monarch."

"Then why can't he buy this stuff?" Janice wanted to know. "Why does he have to steal it?"

"Well," the ferra mumbled, "there's no place where he can buy it."

"Why can't he import the goods? Any company would be glad to arrange it."

---

9. **Aladdin's lamp:** in the *Arabian Nights*, Aladdin rubs the magic lamp, and a jinni appears.

10. **demonology:** the study of demons.

"This is all very embarrassing," the ferra said, rubbing one buckskin against another. "I wish I could make myself invisible."

"Out with it," Bob said.

"If you must know," the ferra said sullenly, "King Alerian lives in what you would call two thousand B.C."

"Then how ——"

"Oh, just a minute," the young ferra said crossly. "I'll explain everything." He rubbed his perspiring hands on his sweat shirt.

"As I told you, I got the job of ferra of the King's Cup. Naturally, I expected the king would ask for jewels or beautiful women, either of which I could have supplied easily. We learn that in first-term conjuration.[11] But the king had all the jewels he wanted, and more wives than he knew what to do with. So what does he do but say, 'Ferra, my palace is hot in the summer. Do that which will make my palace cool.'

"I knew right then I was in over my head. It takes an advanced ferra to handle climate. I guess I spent too much time on the track team. I was stuck.

"I hurried to the master encyclopedia and looked up "Climate." The spells were just too much for me. And of course, I couldn't ask for help. That would have been an admission of incompetence. But I read that there was artificial climate control in the twentieth century. So I walked here, along the narrow trail to the future, and took one of your air conditioners. When the king wanted me to stop his food from spoiling, I came back for a refrigerator. Then it was ——"

"You hooked them all to the generator?" Janice asked, interested in such details.

"Yes. I may not be much with spells, but I'm pretty handy mechanically."

It made sense, Bob thought. After all, who could keep a palace cool in 2,000 B.C.? Not all the money in the world could buy the gust of icy air from an air conditioner, or the food-saving qualities of a refrigerator. But what still bothered Bob was, what kind of a demon was he? He didn't look Assyrian. Certainly not Egyptian . . .

"No, I don't get it," Janice said. "In the *past*? You mean time travel?"

"Sure. I majored in time travel," the ferra said, with a proud, boyish grin.

Aztec perhaps, Bob thought, although that seemed unlikely . . .

"Well," Janice said, "why don't you go somewhere else? Why not steal from one of the big department stores?"

"This is the only place the trail to the future leads," the ferra said.

He picked up the fan. "I'm sorry to be doing this, but if I don't make good here, I'll never get another appointment. It'll be limbo for me."[12]

He disappeared.

---

11. conjuration: the act of casting a magical spell.

12. limbo: here, oblivion — a "place" for out-of-date or useless persons or things.

Half an hour later, Bob and Janice were in a corner booth of an all-night diner, drinking black coffee and talking in low tones.

"I don't believe a word of it," Janice was saying, all her skepticism back in force. "Demons! Ferras!"

"You have to believe it," Bob said wearily. "You saw it."

"I don't have to believe everything I see," Janice said staunchly. Then she thought of the missing articles, the vanishing profits and the increasingly distant marriage. "All right," she said. "Oh, honey, what'll we do?"

"You have to fight magic with magic," Bob said confidently. "He'll be back tomorrow night. We'll be ready for him."

"I'm in favor of that," Janice said. "I know where we can borrow a Winchester ——"

Bob shook his head. "Bullets will just bounce off him, or pass through. Good, strong magic, that's what we need. A dose of his own medicine."

"What kind of magic?" Janice asked.

"To play safe," Bob said, "we'd better use all kinds. I wish I knew where he's from. To be really effective, magic ——"

"You want more coffee?" the counterman said, appearing suddenly in front of them.

Bob looked up guiltily. Janice blushed.

"Let's go," she said to Bob. "If any-one hears us, we'll be laughed out of town."

They met at the store that evening. Bob had spent the day at the library, gathering his materials. They consisted of twenty-five sheets covered on both sides with Bob's scrawling script.

"I still wish we had that Winchester," Janice said, picking up a tire iron from the hardware section.

At eleven forty-five, the ferra appeared.

"Hi," he said. "Where do you keep your electric heaters? The king wants something for winter. He's tired of open hearths. Too drafty."

"Begone," Bob said, "in the name of the cross!" He held up a cross.

"Sorry," the ferra said pleasantly. "The ferras aren't connected with Christianity."

"Begone in the name of Namtar and Idpa!" Bob went on, since Mesopotamia was first on his notes. "In the name of Utuq, dweller of the desert, in the name of Telal and Alal ——"

"Oh, here they are," the ferra said. "Why do I get myself into these jams? This is the electric model, isn't it? Looks a little shoddy."

"I invoke Rata, the boatbuilder," Bob intoned, switching to Polynesia "And Hina, the tapa maker."

"Shoddy nothing," Janice said, her business instincts getting the better of her. "That stove is guaranteed for a year. Unconditionally."

"I call on the Heavenly Wolf," Bob
went on, moving into China when
Polynesia had no effect. "The Wolf
who guards the gates of Shang Ti. I invoke the thunder god, Lei Kung ——"

"Let's see, I have an infrared
broiler," the ferra said. "And I need a
bathtub. Have you got a bathtub?"

"I call Bael, Buer, Forcas, Marcho-
cias, Astaroth ——"

"These are bathtubs, aren't they?"
the ferra asked Janice, who nodded involuntarily. "I think I'll take the largest.
The king is a good-sized man."

" —— Behemoth, Theutus, Asmo-
deus and Incubus!" Bob finished. The
ferra looked at him with respect.

Angrily Bob invoked Ormazd,

Persian king of light, and then the
Ammonitic[13] Beelphegor, and Dagon
of the ancient Philistines.

"That's all I can carry, I suppose,"
the ferra said.

Bob invoked Damballa. He called
upon the gods of Arabia. He tried
Thessalian magic, and spells from
Asia Minor. He nudged Aztec gods
and stirred Mayan spirits. He tried
Africa, Madagascar, India, Ireland,
Malaya, Scandinavia and Japan.

"That's impressive," the ferra said,
"but it'll really do no good." He lifted
the bathtub, broiler and heater.

---

13. **Ammonitic:** from Ammon, an ancient kingdom
east of the Jordan River.

"Why not?" Bob gasped, out of breath.

"You see, ferras are affected only by their own indigenous[14] spells. Just as jinn are responsible only to magic laws of Arabia. Also, you don't know my true name, and I assure you, you can't do much of a job of exorcising anything if you don't know its true name."

"What country are you from?" Bob asked, wiping perspiration from his forehead.

"Sorry," the ferra said. "But if you knew that, you might find the right spell to use against me. And I'm in enough trouble as it is."

"Now look," Janice said. "If the king is so rich, why can't he pay?"

"The king never pays for anything he can get free," the ferra said. "That's why he's so rich."

Bob and Janice glared at him, their marriage fading off into the future.

"See you tomorrow night," the ferra said.

He waved a friendly hand, and vanished.

———✦———

"Well, now," Janice said, after the ferra had left. "What now? Any more bright ideas?"

"All out of them," Bob said, sitting down heavily on a sofa.

"Any more magic?" Janice asked, with a faint touch of irony.

"That won't work," Bob said. "I couldn't find ferra or King Alerian listed in any encyclopedia. He's probably from some place we'd never hear of. A little native state in India, perhaps."

"Just our luck," Janice said, abandoning irony. "What are we going to do? I suppose he'll want a vacuum cleaner next, and then a phonograph." She closed her eyes and concentrated.

"He really is trying to make good," Bob said.

"I think I have an idea," Janice said, opening her eyes.

"What's that?"

"First of all, it's our business that's important, and our marriage. Right?"

"Right," Bob said.

"All right. I don't know much about spells," Janice said, rolling up her sleeves, "but I do know machines. Let's get to work."

The next night the ferra visited them at a quarter to eleven. He wore the same white sweater, but he had exchanged his buckskins for tan loafers.

"The king is in a special rush for this," he said. "His newest wife has been pestering the life out of him. It seems that her clothes last for only one washing. Her slaves beat them with rocks."

"Sure," Bob said.

"Help yourself," Janice said.

"That's awfully decent of you," the ferra said gratefully. "I really appreciate it." He picked up a washing machine. "She's waiting now."

He vanished.

---

14. **indigenous** (in·DIJ·uh·nuhs): native, from their own land.

84

Bob and Janice sat down on a couch and waited. In half an hour the ferra appeared again.

"What did you do?" he asked.

"Why, what's the matter?" Janice asked sweetly.

"The washer! When the queen started it, it threw out a great cloud of evil-smelling smoke. Then it made some strange noises and stopped."

"In our language," Janice said, "we would say it was gimmicked."

"Gimmicked?"

"Rigged. Fixed. Strung. And so's everything else in this place."

"But you can't do that!" the ferra said. "It's not playing the game."

"You're so smart," Janice said venomously. "Go ahead and fix it."

"I was boasting," the ferra said in a small voice. "I was much better at sports."

Janice smiled and yawned.

"Well, gee," the ferra said, his little wings twitching nervously.

"Sorry," Bob said.

"This puts me in an awful spot," the ferra said. "I'll be demoted. I'll be thrown out of civil service."

"We can't let ourselves go bankrupt, can we?" Janice asked.

Bob thought for a moment. "Look," he said. "Why *don't* you tell the king you've met a strong countermagic?

Tell him he has to pay a tariff to the demons of the underworld if he wants his stuff.''

"He won't like it," the ferra said doubtfully.

"Try it anyhow," Bob suggested.

"I'll try," the ferra said, and vanished.

"How much do you think we can charge?" Janice asked.

"Oh, give him standard rates. After all, we've built this store on fair practices. We wouldn't want to discriminate. I still wish I knew where he was from, though."

"He's so rich," Janice said dreamily. "It seems a shame not to —— "

"Wait a minute!" Bob shouted. "We can't do it! How can there be refrigerators in two thousand B.C.? Or air conditioners?"

"What do you mean?"

"It would change the whole course of history!" Bob said. "Some smart guy is going to look at those things and figure out how they work. Then the whole course of history will be changed!"

"So what?" Janice asked practically.

"So what? So research will be carried out along different lines. The present will be changed."

"You mean it's impossible?"

"Yes!"

"That's just what I've been saying all along," Janice said triumphantly.

"Oh, stop that," Bob said. "I wish I could figure this out. No matter what country the ferra is from, it's bound to

have an effect on the future. We can't have a paradox."

"Why not?" Janice asked, but at that moment the ferra appeared.

"The king has agreed," the ferra said. "Will this pay for what I've taken?" He held out a small sack.

Spilling out the sack, Bob found that it contained about two dozen large rubies, emeralds and diamonds.

"We can't take it," Bob said. "We can't do business with you."

"Don't be superstitious!" Janice shouted, seeing their marriage begin to evaporate again.

"Why not?" the ferra asked.

"We can't introduce modern things into the past," Bob said. "It'll change the present. This world may vanish or something."

"Oh, don't worry about that," the ferra said. "I guarantee nothing will happen."

"But why? I mean, if you introduced a washer in ancient Rome —— "

"Unfortunately," the ferra said, "King Alerian's kingdom has no future."

"Would you explain that?"

"Sure." The ferra sat down on the air. "In three years King Alerian and his country will be completely and irrevocably destroyed by forces of nature. Not a person will be saved. Not even a piece of pottery."

"Fine," Janice said, holding a ruby to the light. "We'd better unload while he's still in business."

"I guess that takes care of that,"

Bob said. Their business was saved, and their marriage was in the immediate future. "How about you?" he asked the ferra.

"Well, I've done rather well on this job," the ferra said. "I think I'll apply for a foreign transfer. I hear there are some wonderful opportunities in Arabian sorcery."

He ran a hand complacently over his blond crewcut. "I'll be seeing you," he said, and started to disappear.

"Just a minute," Bob said. "Would you mind telling me what country you're from? And what country King Alerian is from?"

"Oh, sure," the ferra said, only his head still visible, "I thought you knew. Ferras are the demons of Atlantis."[15]

And he disappeared.

---

15. **Atlantis:** a legendary island whose advanced civilization disappeared when an earthquake sank the island into the Atlantic Ocean.

■ Understanding the Story

1. Janice wanted to fight the ferra with physical force. How did Bob hope to fight him? What does the choice of weapons tell about each person?

2. The ferra guarantees that the future will not be changed as a result of his work. What event will prevent the change that Bob fears?

3. Although the ferra claims to be a demon, he is funny rather than scary because his appearance, behavior, and speech combine the real world of the twentieth century A.D. with an ancient, supernatural world. For example, he wears jeans and a sweatshirt, but he also has tiny wings and budding horns. Find two other examples of how the author combines real and supernatural worlds in this story.

4. Bob has no power over the ferra because he does not know the ferra's "true name." Make up a true name for the ferra. Try to think of a name that will suggest magical power or have some other special and important meaning.

5. Suppose you had your own personal ferra who could walk a "narrow trail to the future" and bring back objects that would satisfy three of your wishes. What would you wish for and why?

■ Understanding Literature

Satire is writing that makes fun of a kind of person, behavior, or situation that the author considers foolish or evil. Satire can be bitterly critical, attacking something that is seriously wrong. By calling attention to a real problem in society, such as air pollution or crime, the satirist hopes to bring about a change. Satire can also be gentle and witty, with the author poking fun at something that he or she thinks is ridiculous but not terribly harmful or wrong.

The satire in "The King's Wishes" is light-hearted and humorous. Robert Sheckley satirizes, for example, the clothes that a college athlete might have worn in the 1950s. In addition to college athletes, some of the other targets for Sheckley's satire are business people and civil servants.

■ Writing About the Story

Suppose you are the royal record-keeper of King Alerian's court in Atlantis, and you see the strange contraptions the king's ferra brought back from the future. Choose one machine and explain how you would describe it to your friends. What might you guess about the culture it came from? Write a one-page description of this machine. Remember you are living almost two thousand years in the past.

Side 31

A poem by Victor Hernandez Cruz

In Coney Island they have a sign hanging
Outside one of those spooky house rides
That reads: Come inside and see the
Invisible man

Illustration by Richard Brown

Lazy Peter and His Three-Cornered Hat

A Puerto Rican folk tale adapted by Ricardo E. Alegría

Illustrated by Lisa French

HIS IS THE STORY of Lazy Peter, a shameless rascal of a fellow who went from village to village making mischief.

One day Lazy Peter learned that a fair was being held in a certain village. He knew that a large crowd of country people would be there selling horses, cows, and other farm animals and that a large amount of money would change hands. Peter, as usual, needed money, but it was not his custom to work for it. So he set out for the village, wearing a red three-cornered hat.

The first thing he did was to stop at a stand and leave a big bag of money with the owner, asking him to keep it safely until he returned for

it. Peter told the man that when he returned for the bag of money, one corner of his hat would be turned down, and that was how the owner of the stand would know him. The man promised to do this, and Peter thanked him. Then he went to the drugstore in the village and gave the druggist another bag of money, asking him to keep it until he returned with one corner of his hat turned up. The druggist agreed, and Peter left. He went to the church and asked the priest to keep another bag of money and to return it to him only when he came back with one corner of his hat twisted to the side. The priest said fine, that he would do this.

Having disposed of three bags of

money, Peter went to the edge of the village where the farmers were buying and selling horses and cattle. He stood and watched for a while until he decided that one of the farmers must be very rich indeed, for he had sold all of his horses and cows. Moreover, the man seemed to be a miser who was never satisfied but wanted always more and more money. This was Peter's man! He stopped beside him. It was raining; and instead of keeping his hat on to protect his head, he took it off and wrapped it carefully in his cape, as though it were very valuable. It puzzled the farmer to see Peter stand there with the rain falling on his head and his hat wrapped in his cape.

After a while he asked, "Why do you take better care of your hat than of your head?"

Peter saw that the farmer had swallowed the bait, and smiling to himself, he said that the hat was the most valuable thing in all the world and that was why he took care to protect it from the rain. The farmer's curiosity increased at this reply, and he asked Peter what was so valuable about a red three-cornered hat. Peter told him that the hat worked for him; thanks to it, he never had to work for a living because, whenever he put the hat on with one of the corners turned over, people just handed him any money he asked for.

The farmer was amazed and very interested in what Peter said. As money-getting was his greatest ambition, he told Peter that he couldn't believe a word of it until he saw the hat work with his own eyes. Peter assured him that he could do this, for he, Peter, was hungry, and the hat was about to start working since he had no money with which to buy food.

With this, Peter took out his three-cornered hat, turned one corner down, put it on his head, and told the farmer to come along and watch the hat work. Peter took the farmer to the stand. The minute the owner looked up, he handed over the bag of money Peter had left with him. The farmer stood with his mouth open in astonishment. He didn't know what to make of it. But of one thing he was sure — he had to have that hat!

Peter smiled and asked if he was satisfied, and the farmer said yes, he was. Then he asked Peter if he would sell the hat. This was just what Lazy Peter wanted, but he said no, that he was not interested in selling the hat because, with it, he never had to work and he always had money. The farmer said he thought that was unsound reasoning because thieves could easily steal a hat, and wouldn't it be safer to invest in a farm with cattle? So they talked, and Peter pretended to be impressed with the farmer's arguments. Finally

he said yes, that he saw the point, and if the farmer would make him a good offer, he would sell the hat. The farmer, who had made up his mind to have the hat at any price, offered a thousand pesos. Peter laughed aloud and said he could make as much as that by just putting his hat on two or three times.

As they continued haggling over the price, the farmer grew more and more determined to have that hat until, finally, he offered all he had realized[1] from the sale of his horses and cows — ten thousand pesos in gold. Peter still pretended not to be interested, but he chuckled to him-

self, thinking of the trick he was about to play on the farmer. All right, he said, it was a deal. Then the farmer grew cautious and told Peter that, before he handed over the ten thousand pesos, he would like to see the hat work again. Peter said that was fair enough. He put on the hat with one of the corners turned up and went with the farmer to the drugstore. The moment the druggist saw the turned-up corner, he handed over the money Peter had left with him. At this the farmer was convinced and very eager to set the hat to work for himself. He took out a bag containing ten thousand pesos in gold and was about to hand it to Peter when he had a change of heart

_____

1. **realized:** collected; made as income or profit.

and thought better of it. He asked Peter please to excuse him, but he had to see the hat work just once more before he could part with his gold. Peter said that that was fair enough, but now he would have to ask the farmer to give him the fine horse he was riding as well as the ten thousand pesos in gold. The farmer's interest in the hat revived, and he said it was a bargain!

Lazy Peter put on his hat again, doubled over one of the corners, and told the farmer that, since he still seemed to have doubts, this time he could watch the hat work in the church. The farmer was delighted with this, his doubts were stilled, and he fairly beamed thinking of all the money he was going to make once that hat was his.

They entered the church. The priest was hearing confession, but when he saw Peter with his hat, he said, "Wait here, my son," and he went to the sacristy[2] and returned with the bag of money Peter had left with him. Peter thanked the priest, then knelt and asked for a blessing before he left. The farmer had seen everything and was fully convinced of the hat's magic powers. As soon as they left the church, he gave Peter the ten thousand pesos in gold and told him to take the horse, also. Peter tied the bag of pesos to the

saddle, gave the hat to the farmer, begging him to take good care of it, spurred his horse, and galloped out of town.

As soon as he was alone, the farmer burst out laughing at the thought of the trick he had played on Lazy Peter. A hat such as this was priceless! He couldn't wait to try it. He put it on with one corner turned up and entered the butcher shop. The butcher looked at the hat, which was very handsome indeed, but said nothing. The farmer turned around, then walked up and down until the butcher asked him what he wanted. The farmer said he was waiting for the bag of money. The butcher laughed aloud and asked if he was crazy. The farmer thought that there must be something wrong with the way he had folded the hat. He took it off and doubled another corner down. But this had no effect on the butcher. So he decided to try it out some other place. He went to the Mayor of the town.

The Mayor, to be sure, looked at the hat but did nothing. The farmer grew desperate and decided to go to the druggist who had given Peter a bag of money. He entered and stood with the hat on. The druggist looked at him but did nothing.

The farmer became very nervous. He began to suspect that there was something very wrong. He shouted at the druggist, "Stop looking at me and hand over the bag of money!"

---

2. **sacristy** (SAK·rih·stee): a room (or small building) in a church for storing religious objects.

The druggist said he owed him nothing, and what bag of money was he talking about, anyway? As the farmer continued to shout about a bag of money and a magic hat, the druggist called the police. When they arrived, he told them that the farmer had gone out of his mind and kept demanding a bag of money. The police questioned the farmer, and he told them about the magic hat he had bought from Lazy Peter. When he heard the story, the druggist explained that Peter had left a bag of money, asking that it be returned when he appeared with a corner of his hat turned up. The owner of the stand and the priest told the same story. And I am telling you the farmer was so angry that he tore the hat to shreds and walked home.

Understanding the Story

1. Why did Peter go to the village fair?

2. How did Peter decide which farmer he would try to trick?

3. With how many people did Peter leave bags of money? After he had bought the hat from Peter, from how many people did the farmer try to get money?

4. "Lazy Peter and His Three-Cornered Hat" is a *folk tale,* a story that people told and passed down to their children for hundreds of years. Folk tales often contain a *moral,* or a lesson, that is important to the people who made up the story. What do you think is the moral of this folk tale?

5. In one or two words, how would you describe Peter? What two qualities in the farmer's character make him exactly the opposite of Peter?

Understanding Literature

The folk tales of the different peoples of the world have similar plots, characters, and morals, perhaps because all people share similar needs, hopes, and feelings. Usually the *plot,* what happens in the story, is the most important element in a folk tale because it teaches the moral. Most folk tales have relatively simple plots. The plot of "Lazy Peter and His Three-Cornered Hat" can be summarized easily:

Lazy Peter, a trickster, uses his wit and a hat to trick a greedy miser. At the end of the tale, we have learned a lesson, but we don't know much about Peter or the farmer.

Because plot and moral are most important, there is usually little time spent developing characters in folk tales. Folk tale characters are often *flat characters;* that is, they stand for a particular type of person and have only one or two personality traits. (Characters who have fully developed personalities are called *round characters.*) We find out immediately that Peter is a trickster, a type of character appearing in many folk tales. The farmer is greedy and easily deceived.

As in most folk tales, the person-to-person conflict in this story is simple and direct—a battle of wits in which the powerful person is hopelessly outclassed by the clever underdog. The uncomplicated conflict and plot make the moral apparent: Even a lazy rascal can trick a powerful person who is blinded by greed.

Writing About the Story

In many folk tales and fairy tales, the main character finds a magical device that produces gold, jewels, or money. For example, there is a story about a goose that lays golden eggs. Make up a similar device that could make you rich. Write a paragraph explaining what the device could do and what you would do with your wealth.

BOOKSHELF

The Mouse That Roared by Leonard Wibberley. Bantam Books, 1971. The tiny, impoverished duchy of Grand Fenwick invents a madcap solution to their financial woes.

Ordinary Jack; Absolute Zero; Bagthorpes Unlimited by Helen Cresswell. Macmillan, 1977; 1978; 1978. This comic series presents the daffy doings of the talented and eccentric Bagthorpe clan.

No He's Not a Monkey, He's An Ape and He's My Son by Hester Mundis. Crown Publishers, 1976. This true tale about a chimp raised in a New York City apartment will have you hysterical with laughter.

The Dog Who Wouldn't Be by Farley Mowat. Little, Brown, 1957. The hilarious adventures of a dog who much preferred to act like a human being.

The Star Diaries by Stanislaw Lem. Seabury Press, 1976. These stories will take you careening through time and deep space with a wacky spaceman and his interstellar Model T.

The Great Desert Race by Betty Baker. Macmillan, 1980. Trudy and Alberta team up to drive in a desert auto race, and their wild adventures begin.

The Devil's Dictionary by Ambrose Bierce. Stemmer House, 1978. A diabolical little dictionary filled with irreverent humor and all the spite you would expect of its author.

What Now, Charlie Brown? Selected Cartoons from the Unsinkable Charlie Brown, Vol. I by Charles M. Schulz. Fawcett Books, 1978. Good old Charlie Brown is back in this volume of unforgettably funny cartoons.

The Grass Is Always Greener Over the Septic Tank by Erma Bombeck. McGraw-Hill, 1976. Share the author's zany world of suburbia — where crabgrass grows instead of trees, and where anything hilarious can happen.

2 Spectrum

The Dummy

From the novel *Hey, Dummy* by Kin Platt

Illustrated by Dennis Scofield

The big, slow-moving boy picked up the football and looked at it as if he'd never seen a football in his life.

"Hey, Dummy," Neil yelled. "Throw the ball back." From then on, Neil's eighth-grade friends had a target for their jokes, and the Dummy had a name.

Neil isn't intentionally cruel. When he realizes that the big boy, whose real name is Alan Harper, is retarded, Neil regrets having made fun of him. But his wisecrack catches on, and Neil soon has to suffer the consequences of his cleverness.

E VERY WEEK we're given a topic to write about, and read aloud in English class. None of us are great writers or have anything important to say, but our teacher Mr. Alvarado doesn't mind. He says the main idea is to get our brains accustomed to observing and thinking, and then telling about it.

The subject this week was about people we had met and found interesting. I couldn't think of anybody else so I wrote about the Dummy.

My turn came to stand up and read. The first time I mentioned the name Dummy a few guys snickered. As I went on more and more of the class started laughing until finally everybody was roaring, stamping feet, laughing so hard and so loud I could hardly hear my own words.

All I'd done was write about how we met and so on. I didn't think it was so funny, but the waves of laughter bouncing off the walls got to me and before I finished reading I was grinning like everybody else. Some kids sat doubled over, holding their sides, and girls were wiping tears off their eyes from laughing. There was a lot of clapping. Everybody's face seemed split into a wide smile.

I felt the room quieting down and glanced at Mr. Alvarado leaning in front of his desk. He wasn't smiling. His arms were crossed over his chest. His face was grim, set in hard lines, his black eyes glittering. He waited patiently until the laughter died down, and the coughing spasms[1] and foot stamping subsided.

"Is that all, Comstock?" he asked softly. "Are you finished?"

---

1. **spasms:** sudden bursts of muscle contractions.

I had a terrible sinking feeling in my stomach. Something was wrong. I looked down at the pages in my notebook.

"Yes, sir. That's it."

"Be seated," he said curtly.

I flopped down fast, feeling suddenly very warm. He looked at me without expression, then surveyed the rest of the class, his eyes flicking from one seat to another. Normally, he's a very good-natured man. I could recognize the change right away.

"Congratulations, Comstock," he said. His eyes lifted to the others. "You are all to be congratulated — for your total lack of humanity and understanding."

There were nervous coughs from behind me. I felt hot, my ears burning, and I sank back in my seat, keeping my eyes on Mr. Alvarado. There wasn't any place to go and hide.

Mr. Alvarado's eyes touched me again, then flicked away to stare bleakly at the others. I could feel the contempt in his voice now, a low growling note.

"I was never before aware that there was the slightest thing funny about being retarded," he said. "Maybe I've been missing something." His eyes returned to me. "Is your subject brain-damaged?"

I shrugged. My voice sounded weak. "I don't know."

He nodded curtly. "You don't know," he said. He rubbed the dark stubble of his chin. "It doesn't make

too much difference, really. One such state is as helpless as the other. If you'll laugh at one, you'll find the other equally amusing.''

I cleared my throat. ''I didn't mean it to be funny. I only wrote about it. I mean, like that's the way it was.''

His glance was gloomy, his voice sharp and unforgiving.

''Did you ever stop to wonder how some politicians and demagogues[2] manage to hold and influence their audiences?''

I shook my head dumbly. It wasn't anything I'd ever done any thinking about.

''They use the same tactics,'' he continued. ''They hold up to ridicule what neither they nor their audience can understand. I'd hoped we could do better here.''

''Yes, sir,'' I mumbled.

I felt everybody's eyes on my back, and knew they'd never forgive me for sucking them all into this.

Mr. Alvarado's hard eyes levelled at me again.

''You did your assignment but I can't let it pass. You got your laughs cheap at the expense of an unfortunate and innocent victim.''

Feet shuffled behind me and there were nervous uncomfortable coughs. Nobody was prepared for this side of Mr. Alvarado.

''All of you were equally at fault,'' he

said, ''for letting yourselves be taken in. A certain amount of courage is needed to resist mass opinion. But we're supposed to have made some progress since the last lynching. Being mentally retarded means being crippled, in a sense. I'm willing to listen if anybody cares to explain what's funny about being a cripple. Anybody?''

He waited but nobody volunteered. The room got very quiet. Mr. Alvarado nodded.

''All right, Comstock. It was a mistake and we all have to live or fall with our thoughts. If you want a mark you'll have to try again. Perhaps next time you'll be able to come up with something better suited to your assignment. Our topic was contact with another person. By contact, I mean understanding. . . . Any questions?'' He waited again. Then he turned away. ''Class dismissed.''

I pushed myself out of my chair, picked up my books, and got out of there fast.

On my way home from school, I heard yelling and cheering around the corner, like a big game was in progress.

When I got there I could see why everybody sounded so happy. They were playing the game where you drive somebody crazy. I'm not sure this game has a name, but everybody knows what it is. It could be called Grab-your-hat, for example.

Here's how it works. Somebody

2. **demagogues:** those who gain power by appealing to the people's fears and prejudices.

grabs something of yours. If that happens to be your hat, then that's it. The idea of the game is for you to try to get your hat back from whoever has it. He passes it over your head, or to the person nearest him, or anybody available who can catch it out of your reach. You run back and forth, trying to guess which way it's going, jumping, trying to get it before somebody else does. If you accomplish that, then you've won and it's somebody else's turn to chase back and forth and be frustrated. I suppose the first big bully who grabbed a smaller kid's hat started the whole dumb game.

There were a lot of kids spread out in a big circle. When I saw who was in the middle, chasing back and forth, I could understand why they were all having such a good time.

They had the Dummy's hat, a funny kind of floppy red baseball cap with a long bill. The kid who had it held it up. The Dummy charged. Somebody stuck his foot out and tripped him. He fell, and everybody laughed. When he got up and went after his hat again, the kid who had it waited till the Dummy was almost on top of him before passing it off to the fellow next to him.

"Aaaah!" the Dummy said.

That's the way it went, over and over again, until I got sick watching. The Dummy was too slow and clumsy, he didn't have the right reflexes, he couldn't move right when he had to. It was pathetic. He would make a rush for his cap, eyes and mouth wide open,

his hands outstretched, making that awful "aaaah" sound. They'd trip him, let him get up, fool him, trip him again, allow him to get close, almost touch the cap, and then — off it would go to somebody else.

He was sucking wind, his chest heaving, tears of frustration streaking his face. He didn't get angry. Maybe he didn't know how.

I couldn't stand it any longer. The next time the hat was flipped I was able to reach up and grab it. Everybody cheered. They thought they had another soldier. "That's all," I said. "He's had enough. Give somebody else a chance to go crazy."

I walked out of the circle and they began to yell and yammer, crowding up close, their faces mean and angry, asking me what the idea was. I had to push a few of them away.

"Can't you tell he's a sick kid?" I said. "Come on — you've had your fun."

I beckoned to the Dummy. "It's okay. I got it," I said and showed him the hat.

He smiled through the tears. "Aaaah!" he said. His arms went up, hands outstretched.

"Yeah. Sure. We got it. Come on."

He walked toward me, his eyes fixed on his red cap like it was a magnet. Somebody booted him from behind and then shoved him forward, knocking him off-balance right into me. I managed to keep us both from falling.

I put his cap back on his head and

looked directly at the kid who had knocked him forward. He glared at me for a second, then backed up. I was mad enough to hit him, and I guess I showed it. He stepped out of the way as I came through. So did a few others. I walked right up to them like I never intended to stop, pulling the Dummy along behind me by one arm. His hand felt hot and heavy. There were a lot of dumb remarks as we passed through but we kept going and I didn't look back. When we were clear, I turned to the Dummy.

"Come on. I'll take you home. Where do you live?"

A slight frown passed over his face. He thought about it a while. One arm suddenly shot up.

"My . . . my . . . " he said.

"Okay," I said. "Lead the way."

It wasn't very far but it took a long time to get there. Almost everything that caught the Dummy's eye interested him and he would stop to look it over. He was like a bee buzzing from flower to flower sipping the nectar.

The first thing that interested him was a fire hydrant. He looked it over from all sides, squatting to peer at it, walking all around it, touching it.

"Nice," he said. "Nice . . . thing."

I never thought before about a fire hydrant being nice.

"Yeah," I said. "It's okay."

He touched it again. "I . . . I . . . " he said.

"It's iron, I guess."

That wasn't what he meant. He touched his cap. "My . . . my . . . "

I got it.

"That's right," I said. "They're both the same color. Red."

He beamed. He took his cap off and looked at it lovingly.

"My," he said. "My red."

"It's a hat," I said hastily. "Or maybe you call it a cap. A red hat or a red cap."

"Aaaah," he said. He put it back on his head and touched it proudly. "My . . . red . . . huh . . . huh . . . hat."

I nodded. My face felt red, too.

"Yeah," I said.

He turned to look back to the direction we'd come from. He touched his hat again.

"You . . . you," he said.

"It's okay," I said.

We were having a real conversation.

He liked a telephone pole next. Just an ordinary telephone pole, the wood splintered or gouged out where some kids had cut their initials. He put his hand on the pole.

"Woo," he said. "Woo. Woo."

He leaned against the wood, hugging the pole. He looked up, smiled and pointed. A blue jay was sitting on a wire at the top.

"Brrr," the Dummy said, waving his arms.

I nodded.

He surprised me then by whistling. It was a beautiful trilling whistle, sharp and clear. A bird call.

"Hey, that's pretty good," I said.

The little bird high on the wire cocked its head. It bent down and

trilled its own reply. The Dummy smiled.

"Brrr," he said.

I tapped his arm. "We were going home, remember? Let's go."

We were moving again but it didn't last long. After a few more steps he was peering down at a stain on the sidewalk. Rain and weather had done something to the cement, and people walking on it, and passing traffic. I noticed it was very much like a painting. Cloudlike effects separated by tiny pebbles and some streaks of tar stains. The more I looked at it, the more interesting it became. I walked around the square indentations framing the picture, looking at it from all angles. I never noticed before how interesting a dirty street sidewalk could be.

Suddenly I realized the Dummy had moved on. Now he was staring down at a chip in the cement curb. I looked at that, too, but it didn't seem to me to be anything more than just a chipped curb. The Dummy passed on to examine a wall next to a vacant lot. It had bits of paper poster stuck on it, green stains, a lot of holes and scars on the bricks. It looked like a dirty old wall but, after my first annoyed glance, I saw it had the same effect on me the sidewalk had. This was like a modern painting, too, the stains and blotches and scraps of faded paper somehow making a very interesting design.

I could tell by now that, at the rate we were going, it would take about a week to walk the Dummy home. He

liked to look at fences, garbage cans, thrown scraps, pieces of paper the wind had blown along the street, old cans, bottles, a lot of crummy things. After a while, I felt I was looking at the world through a microscope.

"Nice," he would say every once in a while. "Things."

I never dreamed I'd be agreeing with him. But by the time I got the Dummy home, I had discovered there was a whole new world inside the world I took for granted. Something had been added to the original by time or accident, making everything more interesting than before. Sometimes, if you looked closely enough, you saw it was even beautiful.

I sort of wondered who was the real Dummy, after all.

■ Understanding the Story

1. Why did Mr. Alvarado refuse to accept Neil Comstock's paper?

2. The *narrator* is the person who tells the story. In "The Dummy," the narrator is Neil Comstock. What kind of person is Neil at the beginning of the story?

3. By the end of the story, how has Neil changed? What has caused the change?

4. "The Dummy" ends with the sentence, "I sort of wondered who was the real Dummy, after all." Explain what Neil means by this statement. Have you ever felt this way?

5. With both *verbal irony* and *sarcasm,* a person says or writes the opposite of what he or she means. Sarcasm, however, refers to remarks that are intended to hurt or criticize someone. Often sarcasm is used in hopes of affecting someone's behavior. When Mr. Alvarado says, "You are all to be congratulated for your total lack of humanity and understanding," he is being sarcastic. Write another sarcastic statement that Mr. Alvarado might have said to the class.

■ Understanding Literature

The author of a well-written story creates fictional people that you are interested in and care about. You may remember the characters in a story long after you forget its plot. As you know, a character who has the qualities of a real person is called a *round character.* A lifelike character has bad qualities as well as good ones. Like a real person, he or she makes mistakes and may sometimes be jealous, impatient, or cruel. At the beginning of "The Dummy," for example, Neil Comstock is indifferent to the problems of Alan Harper, the handicapped boy.

In some stories, an important event will change the major character. Because people do not change suddenly in real life, the author must carefully prepare you for the change in the major character. Although the change may seem sudden, you should be able to see reasons for the change, or you will feel that the author has tricked you.

Neil changes when he looks closely at the world through the eyes of the boy everyone calls "The Dummy." What prepares you for the change in Neil?

■ Writing About the Story

Mr. Alvarado gave Neil Comstock another chance to write a composition about making contact with another person. Pretend that you are Neil and write the first paragraph of the paper he might have written after walking the Dummy home. Remember that this composition will be read aloud to Mr. Alvarado's eighth-grade class.

Yo No Soy Yo/I Am Not I

A poem by Juan Ramón Jiménez

Translated by Robert Bly

Yo no soy yo.
           Soy este
que va a mi lado sin yo verlo;
que, a veces, voy a ver,
y que, a veces, olvido.
El que calla, sereno, cuando hablo,
el que perdona, dulce, cuando odio,
el que pasea por donde no estoy,
el que quedará en pie cuando yo muera.

I am not I.
        I am this one
walking beside me whom I do not see;
whom at times I manage to visit,
and whom at other times I forget;
who remains calm and silent while I talk
and forgives, gently, when I hate,
who walks where I am not,
who will remain standing when I die.

Illustration by Arvis Stewart

Aggie

A chapter from the novel *Up a Road Slowly*
by Irene Hunt
Illustrated by Bert Dodson

*When their mother died, Julie and her brother Chris went to live
on their aunt's farm. Aunt Cordelia was also "Miss Cordelia,"
the teacher in the one-room local school, and she had very definite
ideas about how the strong-willed Julie should behave at home and
at school.*

    *Aggie Kilpin was another of Miss Cordelia's students. Under-
nourished and retarded, Aggie was the youngest child of "a
shiftless, vicious father and a mother who had been beaten down
by the cruelties of her life." Julie and her friends did their best to
avoid Aggie until Miss Cordelia forced them to let Aggie join
their circle at lunch. Julie countered by mockingly crowning Aggie
"the queen of the lunch hour" and placing her in the center of their
circle — a safe distance from all her "subjects."*

MY TWELFTH YEAR, we supposed, would be my last
one with Aunt Cordelia, since I would be enter-
ing high school the next year and be going into
town to live with Father; therefore Aunt Cordelia agreed
that I might have a birthday party that spring and the talk
among the girls at school centered for a period of several
weeks upon the social event of the season. Word of it got
to Aggie Kilpin, who still sat in the center of a wide circle
of peasants during the noon hour; Aggie gleefully told me
that yes, kid, she would be coming to my party too. I
didn't think she would.

Alicia Allison sent me a box of tiny pink notes and matching envelopes on which I could write, "Miss Julie Trelling requests the pleasure," and so on. I spent a happy and satisfying hour in preparing these notes and addressing each tiny envelope. Aunt Cordelia had said, "Boys and girls, or just girls?" when I had suggested the party, and I had decided in favor of just girls, including some of the girls from town. Since she hadn't demurred at[1] the exclusion of boys, I rather hoped that she would not notice one other omission. She did, of course. Ruffling through the little pile of envelopes, she said quietly, "Julia, you have forgotten to include Agnes."

"Oh, Aunt Cordelia, I can't. I simply can't have Aggie. She would spoil the whole party. You know that."

"She knows about your party, Julia, and it has been something she's looked forward to for weeks. You can't do this to another child; it would be too cruel."

"I can't invite her. I simply can't have the town girls thinking that she is my friend. I'm sorry for Aggie, awfully sorry, but let's face it, Aunt Cordelia: Aggie smells."

Aunt Cordelia sighed. "Julia, that child has been in my classroom since she was five; that means she's been there almost ten years, and she has stood at my desk, learning nothing, but giving off a more unbearable stench each year. I know Agnes very well; I know that she's smelly as you say, but I also know that if you stab her, she feels pain. I can't encourage cruelty on your part."

I shook my head. "I'd rather not have a party if I have to ask her," I said shortly.

"That's up to you, Julia; think it over," Aunt Cordelia answered.

I made my decision. The little pink envelopes went into the wastebasket, and I had to tell all the girls at school that there would be no party. There was general indignation directed toward Aunt Cordelia, indignation coming from my closest friends, from some of their mothers, even from Aggie, who muttered that Miss

---

1. **demurred** (dih·MURD, dih·MYURD) **at:** objected to.

Cordelia was mean to Julie, never once suspecting that she herself was the cause of all our broken plans.

Aunt Cordelia maintained her usual calm. No one of us was fool enough to believe that she would change her mind though the whole school should rise in mutiny. Her only nod to our disappointment was a casual remark that, although the party had been cancelled, there would be birthday cake for everyone, a remark that delighted the boys, who had not been especially pained at the disappointment of the girls in the first place.

Father never interfered with Aunt Cordelia's disciplinary measures, but I think that he felt a little sorry for me at this time. He came out and took me for a long drive the night before my birthday, and he brought me a silver pen and a quire[2] of good white paper in a leather box, material for the stories I wanted to write. Father's friend Alicia sent me a gift too, a beautifully bound volume of Edna St. Vincent Millay's[3] poems. In a little note Alicia said, "There is something about you, Julie, that reminds me of Millay's early poems; read them now and save the darker ones for later years." She had placed her note in the book so that it opened to the lines:

> God, I can push the grass apart
> And lay my finger on Thy heart!

And turning a few pages, I found lines that mirrored an ache and longing I had so often felt when the beauty around my woods cathedral was too intense, when the need to grasp and keep loveliness left me with a sense of desolate frustration.

> Thy winds, thy wide grey skies!
> Thy mists, that roll and rise!
> Thy woods, this autumn day, that ache and sag

---

2. **quire:** one-twentieth of a ream of paper; 24 or 25 sheets.
3. **Edna St. Vincent Millay** (1892–1950): an American poet. The first lines quoted here are from her poem "Renascence."

And all but cry with colour! That gaunt crag
To crush! To lift the lean of that black bluff!
World, World, I cannot get thee close enough![4]

When I was through, my eyes were wet and I loved not only Millay but Alicia and my sister Laura and Aunt Cordelia — almost everyone in the world except poor little Aggie Kilpin.

Compassion was not yet aroused within me, and the better nature that loved poetry and beauty was completely overshadowed the day of my twelfth birthday. Aunt Cordelia drove her car to school that morning because she was taking the two huge angel-food cakes that she had baked and iced the night before. I was invited to cut the cakes at noon and after sliding each piece on a napkin, to place my birthday offering on each pupil's desk. It was a poor substitute for a party, and most of the girls felt as downcast and low spirited that noon as I did.

But not Aggie. She grinned in delight when I placed the cake before her, and she clambered out of her seat when she saw the rest of us preparing to go outside.

"I won't be queen today, kid," she garbled eagerly. "I'm goin' to set by you 'cause it's your birthday. I'm goin' to be your best friend."

And then I did it, a thing one does not forget. I turned on an innocent human being in fury, and I threw Aggie's love for me back into her simple, uncomprehending face.

"Don't you dare follow me, Aggie; don't you dare come near me," I told her, and I didn't care in the least what measures of discipline Aunt Cordelia might think up for me. I flashed a hostile look toward her as I strode past her desk, and I noticed that she looked quite tired and a little drawn. She said nothing to me, but she held out her hand to Aggie.

"Would you like to go with the little children and me, Agnes? We're going out to the woods and get a bunch of wild flowers for Julia's birthday."

---

4. The lines are from ''God's World'' by Edna St. Vincent Millay.

Aggie seemed to be afraid of me after that. She would grin timidly at me and nod her head as if encouraging me to be kind. Sometimes in shame, I returned her smile, but it was always a weak thing, and Aggie was never reassured. I did not read Edna St. Vincent Millay's poems during those last few weeks of school; belatedly, I had a miserable feeling that the gentle young poet would not have liked me.

It was a hot, dry summer that year, and in early August, when the heat seemed almost unbearable, we heard that Agnes Kilpin was very ill with a fever resulting from the infection of a cut foot for which she had received no medical attention. Aunt Cordelia immediately drove up to the Kilpins', taking ice and cool fruit drinks with her. That evening she told me something of the condition in which she had found Aggie and of the futility of trying to help her.

"I wanted to bathe the poor child and put clean sheets on her bed, but Mrs. Kilpin wouldn't allow me to touch her — said she wasn't going to have her girl catch pneumonia by having a bath." Aunt Cordelia closed her eyes briefly in exasperation. "Afraid of pneumonia, but not of filth and the agony of heat and fever. I wanted to tie that woman up outside the room and see to it that Agnes was cared for properly — for just once in her life."

A few days later on a hot Sunday when tempers were shorter than usual, Aunt Cordelia and I had one of our not infrequent clashes. She had given my room a quick inspection after church that morning, and had found its condition unsatisfactory.

"You will put your books and clothing in their proper places, Julia, and you will dust the room, including — especially including — the windowsills, which I find absolutely white with dust. And understand this, Julia: no lady has a right to that title unless she is not only clean of body and clothing, but is equally clean in her surroundings. Never let it be said that you have grown up in my home and have been so remiss[5] as to throw your discarded underclothing under the bed — which is exactly where I found yours just now."

Her wrath was formidable;[6] mine was rather intense too, for I felt that I might have been instructed to clean my room with considerably less sermonizing. Our clash was brief and bitter, and Aunt Cordelia was the victor. I spent the next hour converting the energy of rage into a zest for cleaning which resulted in an immaculate state that would have satisfied any top-sergeant.

Aunt Cordelia inspected my work and nodded approvingly. "I should think now that after a shower and a brief apology for your impertinence you might feel very much better, Julia."

"I am very sorry that I was impertinent, Aunt Cordelia," I managed to say, and then fled for the bathroom

---

5. **remiss:** careless; negligent.
6. **Her wrath was formidable:** Her anger was frighteningly great.

and a shower. I wished as I stood under the cooling, cleansing flood of water that I were as fortunate as Uncle Haskell, Aunt Cordelia's brother, living apart in the old carriage house, working on a magnum opus[7] and communicating with Aunt Cordelia only infrequently.

That was the afternoon that Carlotta Berry called, asking me to go driving with her. To receive an invitation to go driving with Lottie that summer was a coveted honor. Being an only child of unusually indulgent[8] parents, Lottie had a great deal more in the way of clothes and expensive toys than most of us, and for her birthday that year she had received a gift that was the envy of all her classmates. The gift was a pony, a snowy, dainty-hoofed little creature, a wonderful gift in itself, but this one was harnessed to a wicker and patent leather cart. Carlotta had power in the possession of that pony cart: those who pleased her might share it, but there were no rides for those who did not.

I supposed no favors would be granted me that afternoon, but Aunt Cordelia was a much fairer person than I sometimes believed her to be.

"I see no reason why you shouldn't go," she said pleasantly. "You have fulfilled your duties and are entitled to some recreation."

"I can go!" I told Lottie joyfully, and when she arrived, cool and pretty in blue and white organdy, Aunt Cordelia looked at me thoughtfully and suggested that I might wear the dress from Laura's wardrobe which she had altered to fit me, a fine white linen embroidered with tiny wreaths of rosy flowers and tied with a gay sash. It was plain that Aunt Cordelia wanted me to look no less well-dressed than the darling of the Berry household.

Our gladiolas were in full bloom that week and while I dressed, Aunt Cordelia cut a great armful of the bright flowers and then sat in the porch swing waiting for Carlotta and me to come downstairs.

---

7. **magnum opus:** a Latin phrase meaning "great work"; an important book.
8. **indulgent:** extremely generous; pampering; lenient.

"Since you're going to be driving all around the neighborhood, I think it would be nice of you girls to take this bouquet to Agnes. You won't mind doing that, will you?" she asked.

Aunt Cordelia was too much the voice of authority for either Carlotta or me to resist her suggestion. We didn't want to think of Aggie, much less to visit her, but a sense of decency prodded by the determination which we knew was back of my aunt's quiet suggestion, led us to accept the errand.

"Isn't it just like her?" Carlotta sputtered when we were out of hearing. "She spoils your party on account of Aggie, and now, she spoils our afternoon by making us stop at the dirty Kilpins'. Sometimes I can't *stand* Miss Cordelia; I mean it — I just can't *stand* her."

I had been annoyed too, but at that speech I turned loyal niece and remarked that if Lottie didn't like my aunt, she might well have invited someone other than a relative of Aunt Cordelia's to go riding with her, and Lottie replied that since the pony and cart were hers, she might rescind[9] her invitation.

I wanted the ride enough to tolerate Carlotta's airs. Both of us were conscious that we made a pretty picture on the country road, our gay dresses and the bright flowers filling the little cart with color, Lottie's blonde hair and my black shining as brightly as the pony's silver coat. Uncle Haskell took off his hat and made us a sweeping bow when we met him driving home from town, and a mile or so farther on, Danny Trevort and Jimmy Ferris chased us on their bicycles, scorning our elegance although we were pretty sure that they secretly envied us.

"O, ki-tinka, ka-tonka," they shrilled in pained mockery. Then, riding close to the cart and holding on to the sides, they gave us the benefit of their supreme contempt. "Slurp, slurp," they added as if the sight of us was a little more than either of them could bear.

Their behavior bothered me a little. Danny was still as close to me as in the days when he and my brother Chris and I rode and swam and skated together. Danny was often at Aunt Cordelia's, and I was just as often at his home where gentle Mrs. Trevort always made me welcome. Now, in the presence of Carlotta and Jimmy, he was scornful of me, and I found myself acting as haughtily toward him as if we were foes of long standing.

There is something wrong with this world, I thought. And then, a few minutes later, I found a world in which there was a greater wrong than I had ever known.

Carlotta refused to go inside when we reached the Kilpin house.

"I don't have to mind Miss Cordelia while it's summer vacation, Julie," she said, and I had to respect her point of view. "I guess you'll just have to take the flowers in yourself — since you can't help being her niece." She glanced back down the road, obviously hoping the boys would soon appear again.

---

9. **rescind** (rih•SIND): withdraw; take back.

I climbed out of the elegant cart and crossed the road in some trepidation.[10] I had heard stories of the Kilpins. The cluttered dooryard and the sagging front steps added to the ominous look of the place; I rather hoped that no one would hear my light knock on the half-open screen door.

But Mrs. Kilpin had seen my approach, and she came to the door as soon as I knocked. She was a withered, bent woman with a narrow strip of forehead wrinkling above close-set, sullen eyes. She motioned me to come in, but she didn't speak; when I offered her the flowers and told her they were for Aggie, she nodded toward a table where I laid them, pretty sure that they wouldn't be touched until they were thrown away.

Aggie was lying on a bed in the corner of the room. It was a filthy bed, sheetless and sagging in the middle, and Aggie rolled restlessly upon it, her mouth parched with fever and her eyes glazed and unseeing. The heat, the stench, and the closeness of death made the place so unbearable that I wanted nothing so much as to break away and run from it. Somehow, however, I managed to walk closer to the bed and speak to the girl who lay there.

I really think that I half expected to see Aggie grin again, to hear her call me "Kid" and declare that we were friends. But Aggie was another person that day; she was a part of the dignity of a solemn drama, no longer the phony "queen" seated in the center of a mocking circle of her subjects. Aggie was as indifferent to my presence as if I'd been one of the houseflies crawling along the edge of a spoon that lay on the table beside a bottle of medicine.

I was awed and unsure of what I should do. "Is she going to get well?" I finally whispered to the shadowy woman who stood beside me.

"No, she ain't a-goin' to git well. She's a-goin' to die," the woman said without emotion.

"I'm sorry," I said, and Mrs. Kilpin answered in the same dead voice.

---

10. **trepidation:** trembling fright.

"No, you ain't. You ain't sorry. Nobody's sorry that my girl's a-goin' to die. Not even her pa's sorry. Nobody."

I couldn't answer that. "I guess I must go, Mrs. Kilpin," I said miserably. "I guess I'll have to go."

"Yes, you go," she said, and I saw her eyes studying me from head to foot. "Them clothes is too fine for this place. You go 'long."

I turned toward the bed with agony in my throat. If I could have kept Aggie from dying by ignoring the stench and the ugliness, it would have been such an easy thing to do; it would have been a privilege to put my cheek next to hers and to tell her that yes, I was her friend. But Aggie would not look at me, and her mother's look held only sullen hatred for me.

"I know that sometimes I've been mean to Aggie. I'm sorry, Mrs. Kilpin; I wish that you'd believe me. I'm really sorry."

"I said that you'd best be gittin' on," Mrs. Kilpin said, without looking at me. She pointed toward the door.

When I was out of the house, I ran to the cart where Carlotta was waiting. "Hurry, Julie," she said, her doll-like face pink with anticipation. "We're going to go north at the corner. The boys just went that way, and I almost know they're hiding to surprise us. We won't even speak to them," she added, the instincts of the born coquette[11] asserting themselves more strongly by the minute.

"Take me home, Lottie," I said desperately, as I climbed into the seat beside her. "Please. Just take me home — then you can do whatever you like."

"Don't be silly, Julie. For goodness sake, was it *that* bad? I didn't know you liked Aggie so much."

"Will you take me home?" I asked her once again, my voice sharp because of the tumult inside me.

"No, I won't. Your old aunt had to spoil things by making us come up here. My mother didn't say that I had to come and see Aggie, but I just brought you up here because I supposed that Miss Cordelia would have a fit if I didn't. Now, I'm going to go wherever I please, and I just don't please to take you home."

It wasn't the first time we had quarreled. Lottie and I were at swords' points as often as we were bound together in friendship. And beside the fact that our friendship was not very deep, the day was ghastly hot and beyond the discomfort of heat I was sickened by the glimpse I'd had of "something terribly wrong in this world." I jumped from the seat into the dusty road.

"Go right ahead," I told her. "I'll walk."

"Very well, Miss Trelling," Carlotta said loftily, and off she drove, her pony and cart, her blonde curls and organdy dress as beautiful as a picture.

There were two miles before me, and I was already tired. The thick yellow dust felt hot through my thin slippers, and the half-burned weeds stung when they swished about my bare ankles. It would have been a long

---

11. **coquette** (koh·KET): a flirt.

and wretched walk if Danny hadn't rescued me, but he did, and there wasn't a trace of the taunts he had yelled at Carlotta and me hardly a half hour earlier.

"What's the matter, Julie?" he asked as he stopped his bicycle at my side. "What did Lottie do to you?"

"Nothing. She just won't take me home." I looked at Danny bleakly. "I think Aggie is going to die, Danny, and her mother almost hates me. I can't ride around the country in a pony cart after I've seen Aggie and her mother."

Danny looked down at the ground. Somehow the subject of death embarrassed us both. I wondered about it later.

I rode for the remainder of the two miles home on the handlebars of Danny's bicycle. We didn't talk much, and Aunt Cordelia didn't say much either when I told her briefly what had happened. Some grease from the spokes of a wheel had soiled my white dress, but she didn't scold; she made cold lemonade for Danny and me and the three of us sat together on the wide porch, all of us grave and thoughtful.

Mrs. Kilpin had been right; we heard of Aggie's death the next morning, and Aunt Cordelia again drove up to the bare, wretched home where she and Mrs. Trevort and Mrs. Peters got Aggie ready for a decent burial.

The three women looked pale and tired when they came back from the Kilpins that night. Aunt Cordelia and I sat together in the high-ceilinged library where a cross-current of air made the room cool and pleasant.

"She's clean, at last, poor little creature." Aunt Cordelia shuddered involuntarily when she spoke. "I washed her hair. It was a task the like of which I hope never to have to do again. But do you know, Julia, the child had pretty hair. When it was clean I was able to press two big waves in it above her forehead, and when it dried it was a deep brown color with bright lights in it."

Aggie's hair clean. Not only clean, but pretty. It seemed impossible, but I knew that it was true or Aunt Cordelia would not have said so. I wished that Aggie

could have known. It seemed such a terrible waste — ugliness all one's life, and something pretty discovered only after one was dead.

I had never attended a funeral; Aunt Cordelia had always excused me from going with her for one reason or another. But four of us, Elsie Devers, Margaret Moore, Carlotta and I, were pressed into attending Aggie's funeral. We carried big armfuls of flowers and followed Aggie's casket to the altar of the little country church.

When I looked at Aggie lying in her coffin that afternoon, I was filled with wonder as I saw that she was gently, almost gracefully pretty in death. She was clean, so beautifully clean in the soft ivory-colored dress that my aunt and other neighbors had bought for her, a dress that would have sent Aggie into ecstasies if she could have had it while she lived. I noticed that her hair was, indeed, bright with copper lights in it, lights that sparkled when the afternoon sunlight, channeled in through the church windows, touched Aggie's head and face. It had

been the filth and the stench and the silly grimaces,[12] the garbled speech and the stupid responses that had made Aggie revolting. And now she was pretty.

But it was a prettiness touched with a cold aloofness that reproached and tormented me. I knew with a terrible certainty that I might beg her forgiveness until I was exhausted, that I might kneel before her as we had done in mockery when we first made her queen of the lunch hour, and that she would remain as coldly indifferent to me as I had once been to her.

There was a poem of Sara Teasdale's[13] which I had heard Aunt Cordelia read many times. It hadn't meant much to me until that afternoon when, I found to my surprise, that I was able to recall every word of it. I whispered the lines to myself:

> "When I am dead and over me bright April
> Shakes out her rain-drenched hair,
> Tho' you should lean above me broken-hearted,
> I shall not care.
>
> I shall have peace, as leafy trees are peaceful
> When rain bends down the bough,
> And I shall be more silent and cold-hearted
> Than you are now."

When we walked home after the funeral, Carlotta said, "You were saying poetry to yourself in the church, Julie. I think that's very bad manners, with poor Aggie lying there dead — and all that."

At twilight that evening I wandered out to the carriage house, where Uncle Haskell sat on his porch enjoying the light breeze that stirred the leaves of our surrounding wooded acres. He laughed lightly as I seated myself on the steps at his feet.

---

12. **grimaces** (GRIM•uhs•uhz): facial expressions.
13. **Sara Teasdale** (1884–1933): an American poet. The lines that follow are from her poem "I Shall Not Care."

"Your face, my treasure, has a funereal aspect this evening. Are you responding to our popular stereotype — the proper mourner who must tense his muscles for the correct number of days before he can cheerfully thank Heaven that it was the other fellow and not he, who had succumbed?"[14]

I didn't answer immediately. Sometimes Uncle Haskell seemed like a bad-mannered child, someone who deserved to be ignored.

"Do you know what it means to feel guilty, Uncle Haskell?" I asked after a minute.

"No. I thank whatever gods may be that no such emotion has ever disrupted my equanimity."[15] He toyed for a while with the pipe which he always carried but never smoked. "Now, why should you feel guilty, my little Julie? You know very well that if this Kilpin girl could approach you again, as moronic and distasteful as she was a month ago, that you'd feel the same revulsion for her. You couldn't help it."

He was right, of course. I thought how awkward it would be to have to say, "Oh, Aggie, you were so nice when you were dead, and now here you are — the same old mess again." That wouldn't do, naturally; one couldn't say *that*, even to Aggie.

Uncle Haskell was speaking again. "Hadn't you rather thank Heaven that she has escaped what life had to offer her? Come, Julie, death may be the great equalizer; let's not give in to the hypocrisy that it is the great glorifier."

We sat in silence after that, and I listened to the sounds of night around us. Uncle Haskell's words beat in upon me as I sat there; I knew that he expressed something that was true, but I knew as well that he was missing something. In Aggie's life and death there was something more than a distasteful little unfortunate's few barren years and her fever-driven death. But what it was I could not put into words; it was strange that I should have sought out a

---

14. **succumbed** (suh·KUMBD): here, died.
15. **equanimity** (EE·kwuh·NIM·ih·tee, EK·wuh·NIM·ih·tee): calmness; composure.

cynic[16] such as Uncle Haskell with the hope of finding an answer.

Finally I rose, the need for action of some sort strong within me. "I think I'll saddle Peter the Great and ride for a while," I said.

Then, for some reason, I suddenly felt very sorry for Uncle Haskell. Obeying an impulse which I did not understand, I mounted the five steps up to the porch, and standing beside his chair, I bent and kissed him on his forehead. It was the first time in my life that I had ever done anything of the kind.

He didn't move. He muttered, "Don't ride too far," and that was all. I ran out to the barn, saddled the big old horse who was much gentler than his namesake, and rode away through the woods, pondering for the first time over the mysteries of life and death.

Uncle Haskell's light was on when I returned, and I could see that he was working at his typewriter. That was unusual. His writings never seemed to reach his typewriter; one supposed, innocently at first and then in mocking derision, that his magnum opus was being done in longhand.

I slept rather late the next morning and when I opened my eyes, I saw the folded white paper which had been slipped underneath my door. I jumped out of bed to pick it up and then propped myself comfortably against the pillows in order to enjoy whatever it was that I was about to read.

The letter read as follows:

Dear Julie:

What you were seeking tonight was a good, gray uncle, full of wisdom, and you came to an uncle who is neither good nor gray nor very wise.

I am annoyed with you, my sweet. I do not like stepping out of character even for a little niece who

---

16. **cynic** (SIN·ik): a person who believes that people are basically selfish and who doubts the sincerity of generous acts or feelings.

kisses me good-night, and by that token, makes a
vapid[17] old fool of me. But I'll be for a few minutes
your good, gray uncle, full of wisdom. I'll say to my
sad-faced little Julie: Guilt feelings will do nothing for
either you or the Kilpin child. But your compassion as
you grow into womanhood may well become immortality for the girl you call "Aggie."

Uncle Haskell

I read his letter several times and then secreted it in
the little leather box where I hid other treasures.

---

17. **vapid:** dull; tiresome; spiritless.

About IRENE HUNT

Irene Hunt's father died when she was only seven
years old. She went to live with her grandparents,
and because they lived on an isolated farm, Hunt
made no close friends. "My early childhood years
were happy," she says, "but after my father died I
was a very lonely child."

Fortunately her grandfather was a born storyteller,
and Irene Hunt soon developed her own talent. "I
spent much time making up stories of my own as a
child . . . and I often told stories to other children."

When Irene Hunt grew up, she became a teacher.
Throughout her teaching career, Hunt always remembered that she had learned a great deal about American history from
her grandfather's stories. She wanted her students to realize that history is more than just a collection of names and dates. Her first book,
Across Five Aprils, is based on her grandfather's stories about the
Civil War.

Now retired from teaching, Irene Hunt lives in Florida. She loves to
garden, and she enjoys reading, cooking, golfing, and playing the
organ. She likes to have young people visit often because, she says,
"I do miss the classroom at times."

■ Understanding the Story

1. The most important conflict in this story happens inside a person. What is the conflict?

2. A story is made up of a sequence of events called *incidents* that reveal character traits and develop the plot. What does the incident of Julie's birthday party reveal about her personality?

3. What did Uncle Haskell mean when he wrote to Julie, ". . . your compassion as you grow into womanhood may well become immortality for the girl you call 'Aggie' "?

4. If Aggie had lived, do you think Julie would have been any nicer to her?

5. Do Julie's remorse and her apology to Mrs. Kilpin make up for her previous cruelty? Explain. Do you feel more sympathy for Julie or for Aggie? Explain.

■ Understanding Literature

Notice how author Irene Hunt uses the following methods of characterization to develop the characters in her story "Aggie":

a. *By giving a physical description.* On arriving at Julie's house, Carlotta is described as looking "cool and pretty in blue and white organdy."

b. *By revealing the character's actions and speech.* When Aunt Cordelia tells Julie that she must invite Aggie, Julie says, "I'd rather not have a party if I have to ask her."

c. *By revealing the character's thoughts and feelings.* Since Julie is telling the story, we are often told what she is thinking. For example, Julie says that she and Carlotta "were conscious that we made a pretty picture on the country road."

d. *By revealing what others think of the character.* Carlotta says of Aunt Cordelia, "She spoils your party on account of Aggie. . . . Sometimes I can't *stand* Miss Cordelia."

e. *By commenting directly on the characters.* Julie comments directly on herself when she says, "And then I did it, a thing one does not forget. I turned on an innocent human being in fury, and I threw Aggie's love for me back into her simple, uncomprehending face."

By using all of these methods of characterization, author Irene Hunt reveals her characters' personality traits and thus makes those characters seem real.

■ Writing About the Story

Think of two people you know who are a strong contrast to one another in personality and character. List some character traits of each. Then describe the people by contrasting them. After you have your ideas on paper, organize and write a paragraph contrasting these two people for your classmates. Use fictional names.

Happy Birthday

A short story by Toni Cade Bambara

Illustrated by Nancy Schill

OLLIE SPENT the whole morning waiting. First she tried shaking Granddaddy Larkins, who just wouldn't wake up. She thought he was just playing, but he was out. His teeth weren't even in the glass and there was a bottle on the bedstand. He'd be asleep for days. Then she waited on the cellar steps for Chalky, the building superintendent, to get through hauling garbage and come talk. But he was too busy. And then Ollie sat on the stairs waiting for Wilma. But it was Saturday and Wilma'd be holed up somewhere stuffing herself with potato chips and crunching down on jaw breakers, too greedy to cool it and eat 'em slow. Wilma'd come by tomorrow, though, and lie her behind off. "I went to Bear Mountain yesterday on a big boat with my brother Chestnut and his wife," she'd say, "and that's why I didn't come by for you cause we left so early in the morning that my mother even had to get me up when it was still dark out and we had a great time and I shot bows and arrows when we got there, and do you like my new dress?" Wilma always had some jive tale and always in one breath.

Ollie tried to figure out why she was even friends with Wilma. Wilma was going to grow up to be a lady and marry a doctor and live in New York, Wilma's mother said. But Ollie, poor orphan, was going to grow up and marry a drinking man if she didn't get killed first, Wilma's mother said. Ollie never

told Granddaddy Larkins what Wilma's mother was all the
time saying. She just hated her in private.

Ollie spent the early afternoon sitting on the rail in front of
The Chicken Shack Restaurant, watching the cooks sling the
wire baskets of chicken in and out of the frying fat. They were
too sweaty and tired to tell her to move from in front. "Ruin-
ing the business," the owner used to fuss. Later she stood
between the laundry and shoe store, watching some men
pitch pennies against the building. She waited for a while,
squeezing a rubber ball in her hand. If I can just get the wall
for a minute, she thought, maybe somebody'll come along

and we'll have us a good game of handball. But the men went right on pitching while other ones were waiting their turn. They'd be there for hours, so Ollie left.

She knocked on Mrs. Robinson's door to see if she wanted her dog walked. It was cool in the hallway at least. No one was home, not even the loud-mouth dog that usually slammed itself against the door like he was big and bad instead of being just a sorry little mutt. Then Ollie took the stairs two at a time, swinging up past the fourth floor to the roof. There was rice all over. Ronnie must have already fed his pigeons. The door to the roof was unlocked, and that meant that the big boys were on the roof. She planted her behind against the door and pushed. She kicked at a cluster of rice. Some grains bounced onto the soft tar of the roof and sank. When Ollie moved onto the roof, the blinding sun made her squint. And there they were, the big boys, jammed between the skylight and the chimney like dummies in a window, just doing nothing and looking half-asleep.

Peter Proper, as always, was dressed to the teeth. "I naturally stays clean," he was always saying. Today he said nothing, just sitting. Marbles, a kid from the projects, had an open book on his knees. James was there, too, staring at a fingernail. And Ferman, the nut from crosstown, and Frenchie, the athlete. A flurry of cinders floated down from the chimney and settled into their hair like gray snow.

"Why don't you just sit in the incinerator? You can get even dirtier that way," Ollie yelled. No one moved or said anything. She expected Frenchie to at least say, "Here comes Miss Freshmouth," or for Peter to send her to the store for eighteen cents' worth of American cheese. It was always eighteen cents' worth, and he always handed her a quarter and a nickel. Big Time. "Don't none of you want nothing from the store today?" She squinted with her hands on her hips, waiting for the store dummies to start acting like Marbles, Peter, James, and so forth.

Ferman straightened out a leg against the skylight. "Ollie, when are you going to learn how to play with dolls?"

"Ya want anything from the store, Ferman Fruitcake? I'm too big for dolls." Ollie hitched up her jeans.

Ferman started to say something, but his audience was nearly asleep. Frenchie's head was nodding. James was staring into space. The pages of the open book on Marble's knees were turning backward, three at a time, by themselves. Peter Proper was sitting very straight, back against the chimney with his eyes closed to the sun.

Ollie turned, looking over the edge of the roof. There was no one down in the park today. There was hardly anyone on the block. She propped a sticky foot against the roof railing and scraped off the tar. Everything below was gray as if the chimney had snowed on the whole block.

Chalky, the superintendent, was rolling a mattress onto a cart. Maybe he'd play cards with her. Just last Friday he had, but sometimes he wouldn't even remember her and would run and hide thinking she was King Kong come down just to hit him in the head or something. Ollie looked past the swings to the track. Empty. Frenchie should be out there trotting, she thought, looking back at him. He was dipping his head.

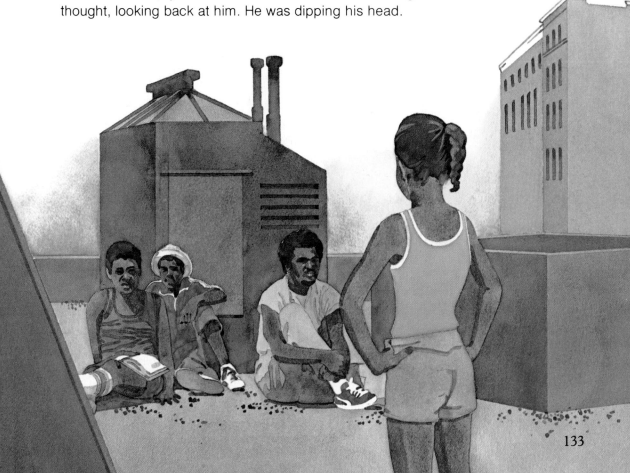

Sometimes she'd trot beside Frenchie, taking big jumps to keep up. He'd smile at her but never teased her about them silly little jumps. He'd tell her for the hundredth time how he was going to enter the Olympics and walk off with a cup full of money.

"Go away, little girl!" Ferman had just yelled at her as if he had forgotten her name or didn't know her any more. He's as crazy as Chalky, thought Ollie, slamming the big roof door behind her and running down the stairs to the street. They must be brothers.

It was now four o'clock by the bank clock. Ollie remembered the bar-b-que place that had burned down. But she'd already rummaged through the ruins and found nothing. No use messing up her sneakers any further. She turned around to look the block over. Empty. Everyone was either at camp or at work or was sleeping like the boys on the roof or dead or just plain gone off. She perched on top of the fire hydrant with one foot, balancing with her arms. She could almost see into the high windows of Mount Zion A.M.E.[1] Church. "This time I'm going to fly off and kill myself," she yelled, flapping her arms. A lady with bundles turned the corner and gave Ollie a look, crossed against the traffic, looking over her shoulder and shaking her head at what the kids of today had come to. Reverend Hall came out of the church basement, mopping his head with a big handkerchief.

"You go play somewhere else," he said, frowning into the sun.

"Where?" Ollie asked.

"Well, go to the park and play."

"With who?" she demanded. "I've got nobody to play with."

Reverend Hall just stood there trying to control his temper. He was always chasing the kids. That's why he's got no choir, Granddaddy Larkins was always saying. He always chases kids and dogs and pigeons and drunks.

"Little girl, you can't act up here in front of the church. Have you no ——"

---

1. **A.M.E.**: African Methodist Episcopal.

"How come you always calling me little girl, but you sure know my name when I'm walking with my grandfather?" Ollie said.

"Tell'm all about his sanctified self," said Miss Hazel, laughing out her window. But when the Reverend looked up to scowl, she ducked back in. He marched back into the church, shooing the pigeons off the steps.

"Wish me happy birthday," Ollie whispered to the pigeons. They hurried off toward the curb. "Better wish me happy birthday," she yelled, "or somebody around here is gonna get wasted."[2]

Miss Hazel leaned out the window again. "What's with you, Ollie? You sick or something?"

"You should never have a birthday in the summertime," Ollie yelled, "cause nobody's around to wish you happy birth-day or give you a party."

---

2. **get wasted**: get killed.

"Well, don't cry, sugar. When you get as old as me, you'll be glad to forget all about ——"

"I'm not crying." Ollie stamped her foot, but the tears kept coming and before she could stop herself she was howling, right there in the middle of the street and not even caring who saw her. And she howled so loudly that even Miss Hazel's great-grandmother had to come to the window to see who was dying and with so much noise and on such a lovely day.

"What's the matter with the Larkins child?" asked the old woman.

"Beats me." Miss Hazel shook her head and watched Ollie for a minute. "I don't understand kids sometimes," she sighed, and closed the window so she could hear the television good.

About TONI CADE BAMBARA

In northwest Africa there lives a group of people who are known for their fine, delicate woodcarvings. They are called *Bambara*. It is a name writer Toni Cade took for her own after finding it on a notebook in her great-grandmother's trunk.

The name seems to fit her; for like the wood-carvers whose name she shares, Toni Cade Bambara is very careful and precise in her work. For example, instead of settling for what she *thinks* a young person might say, she will talk with a group of young people to be sure that she expresses their true feelings in her writing.

Toni Cade Bambara describes herself as "the mother of Karma, the sister of Walter Cade the painter, and a writer since childhood who nevertheless wanted to be a doctor, lawyer, artist, musician, and everything else." Although she may not have fulfilled all those plans, she has many accomplishments to her credit. Among them are several books, short stories, and many poems and articles. She has studied dance, film, and mime. She has also been working on a series of books about children who have lived through difficult times in American history.

■ Understanding the Story

1. Who does Ollie live with? What else do you find out about her?

2. Why does Ollie cry at the end of the story?

3. Almost everything in "Happy Birthday" is told from the point of view of one character. Who is that character?

4. What do you think might have made the day happy for Ollie? Tell why you think so.

5. If it were your birthday and you could do anything you wanted, what would you do?

■ Understanding Literature

No matter how often you see an object, a well-written story or poem can make you see it as you never have before. Stories and especially poems also make you understand and experience ideas and feelings in a new way.

Writers take you by surprise when their words affect your senses. Vivid words and phrases create *images*. Images give you an immediate and intense experience of the writer's subject. They help you imagine not only how something looks, but also how it smells, tastes, sounds, and feels. The use of language to create images is called *imagery*.

Many of the images in "Happy Birthday" are visual: they help you to see what Ollie sees. For example, Ollie remarks that the chimney cinders had settled onto the boys' hair "like dry snow." This kind of *sense imagery* is often created through the use of *figurative language.* In figurative language, words are used in unusual rather than in exact or literal ways. When Ollie says "Everything below was gray as if the chimney had snowed on the whole block," she is using a *simile* in order to create an image of the hot, quiet street. A simile is a kind of figurative language that compares two things by using *like* or *as.* Find one other simile that has been used to create an image in "Happy Birthday."

■ Writing About the Story

Pick a place in your neighborhood. Look very carefully at what you see there. Pay special attention to colors, any smells or sounds, and other details. Write down what you see, hear, feel, taste, and smell. Then try to create four images, each appealing to a different sense, to describe something in that place. Try to create images that will make your classmates sense what you have sensed.

It's Raining in Love

A poem by Richard Brautigan

I don't know what it is,
but I distrust myself
when I start to like a girl
   a lot.

It makes me nervous.
I don't say the right things
or perhaps I start
   to examine,
          evaluate,
                compute
   what I am saying.

If I say, "Do you think it's going to rain?"
and she says, "I don't know,"
I start thinking: Does she really like me?

In other words
I get a little creepy.

A friend of mine once said,
"It's twenty times better to be friends
   with someone
than it is to be in love with them."

I think he's right and besides,
it's raining somewhere, programming flowers
and keeping snails happy.
   That's all taken care of.

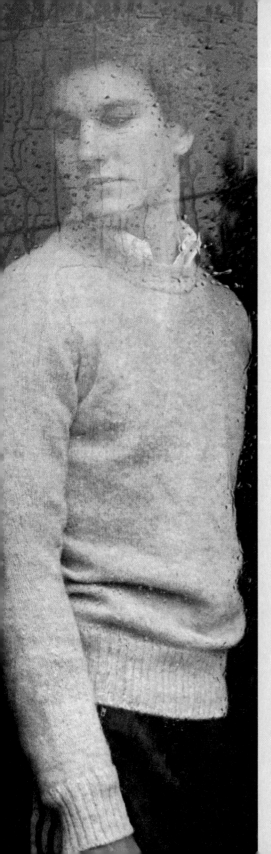

BUT
if a girl likes me a lot
and starts getting real nervous
and suddenly begins asking me funny questions
and looks sad if I give the wrong answers
and she says things like,
"Do you think it's going to rain?"
and I say, "It beats me,"
and she says, "Oh,"
and looks a little sad
at the clear blue California sky,
I think: Thank God, it's you, baby, this time
    instead of me.

139

Putting Things Right

A chapter from *All Creatures Great and Small* by James Herriot
Illustrated by Lyle Miller

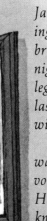

James Herriot, a young English veterinarian, has been daydreaming about Helen Alderson ever since he met her. Her animals keep bringing them together, but getting to know Helen has been a nightmare for Jim. He did well enough setting her calf's broken leg, but on their first date Jim was too nervous to talk. And the last time he ran into Helen, at a village dance, he was covered with mud!

Now, fellow vet Tristan announces that Helen Alderson is waiting in the office to see "Mr. Herriot." Jim is once again nervous and embarrassed — until he sees old Dan, the sheep dog Helen has brought in for treatment. With a dog, at least, Jim knows just where he stands.

"Could Mr. Herriot see my dog, please?"

Familiar enough words coming from the waiting room but it was the voice that brought me to a slithering halt just beyond the door.

It couldn't be, no of course it couldn't, but it sounded just like Helen. I tiptoed back and applied my eye without hesitation to the crack in the door. Tristan was standing there looking down at somebody just beyond my range of vision. All I could see was a hand resting on the head of a patient sheep dog.

I was still peering out when Tristan shot out of the room and collided with me. Stifling an oath, he grabbed my arm and hauled me along the passage into the dispensary.[1] He shut the door and spoke in a hoarse whisper.

"It's her! The Alderson woman! And she wants to see you! Not Siegfried, not me, but you, Mr. Herriot himself!"

He looked at me wide-eyed for a few moments; then, as I stood hesitating, he opened the door and tried to propel me into the passage.

"What are you waiting for?" he hissed.

"Well, it's a bit embarrassing,

---

1. dispensary (dis·PEN·suh·ree): a storeroom for medicines.

isn't it? I mean after the last time she saw me."

Tristan struck his forehead with his hand. "Good heavens! You worry about details, don't you? She's asked to see you — what more do you want? Go on, get in there!"

I was shuffling off irresolutely when he raised a hand. "Just a minute. Stay right there." He trotted off and returned in a few seconds holding out a white lab coat.

"Just back from the laundry," he said as he began to work my arms into the starched sleeves. "You'll look marvelous in this, Jim — the immaculate young surgeon."

I stood unresisting as he buttoned me into the garment but struck away his hand when he started to straighten my tie. As I left him he gave me a final encouraging wave before heading for the back stairs.

I didn't give myself any more time to think but marched straight into the waiting room. Helen looked up and smiled. And it was just the same smile. Nothing behind it. Just the same friendly, steady-eyed smile as when I first met her.

We faced each other in silence for some moments, then when I didn't say anything, she looked down at the dog.

"It's Dan in trouble this time," she said. "He's our sheep dog but we're so fond of him that he's more like one of the family."

The dog wagged his tail furiously at the sound of his name but yelped as he came towards me. I bent down and patted his head. "I see he's holding up a hind leg."

"Yes, he jumped over a wall this morning and he's been like that ever since. I think it's something quite bad — he can't put any weight on the leg."

"Right, bring him through to the other room and I'll have a look at him. But take him on in front of me, will you, and I'll be able to watch how he walks."

I held the door open and she went through ahead of me with the dog. I watched as Old Dan walked down the passage.

It was a dislocated hip. It had to be with that shortening of the limb and the way he carried it underneath his body with the paw just brushing the ground.

My feelings were mixed. This was a major injury but on the other hand the chances were I could put it right quickly and look good in the process. Because I had found, in my brief experience, that one of the most spectacular procedures in practice was the reduction of a dislocated hip. Maybe I had been lucky, but with the few I had seen I had been able to convert an alarmingly lame animal into a completely sound one as though by magic.

In the operating room I hoisted Dan on to the table. He stood without moving as I examined the hip. There was no doubt about it at all — the head of the femur[2] was displaced upwards and backwards, plainly palpable[3] under my thumb.

The dog looked round only once — when I made a gentle attempt to flex the limb — but turned away immediately and stared resolutely ahead. His mouth hung open a little as he panted nervously, but like a lot of the placid animals which arrived on our surgery table, he seemed to have resigned himself to his fate. I had the strong impression that I could have started to cut his head off and he wouldn't have made much fuss.

"Nice, good-natured dog," I said. "And a bonny[4] one, too."

Helen patted the handsome head with the broad blaze of white down the face; the tail waved slowly from side to side.

"Yes," she said. "He's just as much a family pet as a working dog. I do hope he hasn't hurt himself too badly."

"Well, he has a dislocated hip. It's a nasty thing but with a bit of luck I ought to be able to put it back."

----

2. **femur** (FEE•muhr): the thigh bone.
3. **palpable**: able to be touched and felt.
4. **bonny**: from the Scottish word for pretty; used in England to mean healthy and lively.

"What happens if it won't go back?"

"He'd have to form a false joint up there. He'd be very lame for several weeks and probably always have a slightly short leg."

"Oh dear, I wouldn't like that," Helen said. "Do you think he'll be all right?"

I looked at the docile animal still gazing steadfastly to his front. "I think he's got a good chance, mainly because you haven't hung about for days before bringing him in. The sooner these things are tackled the better."

"Oh good. When will you be able to start on him?"

"Right now." I went over to the door. "I'll just give Tristan a shout. This is a two man job."

"Couldn't I help?" Helen said. "I'd very much like to if you wouldn't mind."

I looked at her doubtfully. "Well I don't know. You mightn't like playing tug of war with Dan in the middle. He'll be anesthetized[5] of course but there's usually a lot of pulling."

Helen laughed. "Oh, I'm quite strong. And not a bit squeamish. I'm used to animals, you know, and I like working with them."

"Right," I said. "Slip on this spare coat and we'll begin."

The dog didn't flinch as I pushed the needle into his vein and as the anesthetic flowed in, his head began to slump against Helen's arm and his supporting paw to slide along the smooth top of the table. Soon he was stretched unconscious on his side.

I held the needle in the vein as I looked down at the sleeping animal. "I might have to give him a bit more. They have to be pretty deep to overcome the muscular resistance."

Another cc.[6] and Dan was as limp as any rag doll. I took hold of the affected leg and spoke across the table. "I want you to link your hands underneath his thigh and try to hold him there when I pull. O.K.? Here we go, then."

It takes a surprising amount of force to pull the head of a displaced femur over the rim of the acetabulum.[7] I kept up a steady traction with my right hand, pressing on the head of the femur at the same time with my left. Helen did her part efficiently, leaning back against the pull, her lips pushed forward in a little pout of concentration.

I suppose there must be a foolproof way of doing this job — a method which works the very first time — but I have never been able to find it. Success has always come to me only after a fairly long period of

---

5. **anesthetized** (uh·NES·thuh·TYZD): made not to feel pain through the use of an anesthetic.

6. **cc.**: abbreviation of cubic centimeter(s), the unit of measure commonly used in medicine.

7. **acetabulum** (AS·uh·TAB·yuh·luhm): the hip socket.

trial and error and it was the same today. I tried all sorts of angles, rotations and twists on the flaccid[8] limb, trying not to think of how it would look if this just happened to be the one I couldn't put back. I was wondering what Helen, still hanging on determinedly to her end, must be thinking of this wrestling match when I heard the muffled click. It was a sweet and welcome sound.

I flexed the hip joint once or twice. No resistance at all now. The femoral head was once more riding smoothly in its socket.

"Well that's it," I said. "Hope it stays put — we'll have to keep our fingers crossed. The odd one does pop out again but I've got a feeling this is going to be all right."

Helen ran her hand over the silky ears and neck of the sleeping dog. "Poor old Dan. He wouldn't have jumped over that wall this morning if he'd known what was in store for him. How long will it be before he comes round?"

"Oh, he'll be out for the rest of the day. When he starts to wake up tonight I want you to be around to steady him in case he falls and puts the thing out again. Perhaps you'd give me a ring. I'd like to know how things are."

I gathered Dan up in my arms and was carrying him along the passage, staggering under his weight,

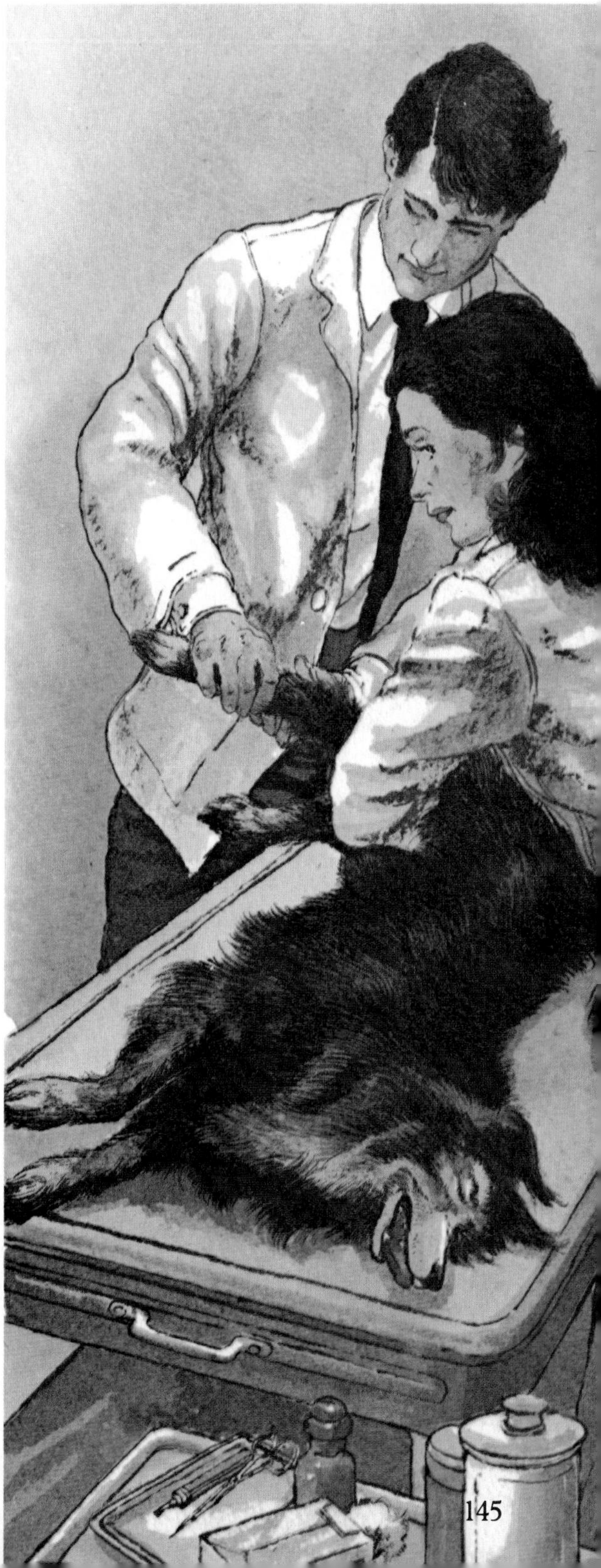

---

8. flaccid (FLAK·sid, FLA·sid): limp.

145

when I met Mrs. Hall.[9] She was carrying a tray with two cups.

"I was just having a drink of tea, Mr. Herriot," she said. "I thought you and the young lady might fancy a cup."

I looked at her narrowly. This was unusual. Was it possible she had joined Tristan in playing Cupid? But the broad, dark-skinned face was as unemotional as ever. It told me nothing.

"Well, thanks very much, Mrs. Hall. I'll just put this dog outside first." I went out and settled Dan on the back seat of Helen's car; with

9. **Mrs. Hall**: the housekeeper for the three veterinarians Tristan, Siegfried, and James.

only his eyes and nose sticking out from under a blanket he looked at peace with the world.

Helen was already sitting with a cup in her lap and I thought of the other time I had drunk tea in this room with a girl. This was a lot different. This time the conversation didn't lag. Maybe it was because I was on my own ground — perhaps I never felt fully at ease unless there was a sick animal involved somewhere, but at any rate I found myself prattling effortlessly just as I had done when we had first met.

Mrs. Hall's teapot was empty and the last of the biscuits gone before I finally saw Helen off and started on my round.

The same feeling of easy confidence was on me that night when I heard her voice on the phone.

"Dan is up and walking about," she said. "He's still a bit wobbly but he's perfectly sound on that leg."

"Oh great, he's got the first stage over. I think everything's going to be fine."

There was a pause at the other end of the line, then: "Thank you so much for what you've done. We were terribly worried about him, especially my young brother and sister. We're very grateful."

"Not at all, I'm delighted too. He's a grand dog." I hesitated for a moment — it had to be now. "Oh, you remember we were talking about Scotland today. Well, I was passing the Plaza this afternoon and I see they're showing a film about the Hebrides.[10] I thought maybe . . . I wondered if perhaps, er . . . you might like to come and see it with me."

Another pause and my heart did a quick thud-thud.

"All right." Helen said. "Yes, I'd like that. When? Friday night? Well, thank you — good-bye till then."

I replaced the receiver with a trembling hand. Why did I make such heavy weather of these things? But it didn't matter — I was back in business.

---

10. **Hebrides** (HEB·ruh·deez): a group of islands off the west coast of Scotland.

147

■ Understanding the Story

1. Why did Helen bring her sheep dog to Jim Herriot?

2. Like many other good titles, "Putting Things Right" has two meanings. What two things were put right?

3. How does Jim Herriot feel about animals? What actions in the story reveal this attitude?

4. The story ends with the sentence, "I was back in business." What do you think this sentence means?

5. Jim Herriot seems to enjoy his work as a veterinarian. If you could work at whatever job you wanted, what would you choose to do? Tell why you think you would like it. Mention any disadvantages, too.

■ Understanding Literature

Conversation between and among characters in a work of literature is called *dialogue*. Dialogue can bring a story to life for you. Rather than describing events directly, the writer uses the dialogue of characters to tell you what is happening.

Besides making a story more realistic and interesting, dialogue can reveal character traits and help move the story forward. For example, when Herriot says, "Nice, good-natured dog . . . and a bonny one, too," he is showing that he genuinely likes animals and appreciates their different personalities.

The following speech, in which Helen asks for the opportunity to assist Herriot, shows how dialogue works to move the plot along:

> "Couldn't I help?" Helen said. "I'd very much like to if you wouldn't mind."

Find in this story one other example of dialogue that furthers the plot.

Realistic dialogue sounds the way people speak naturally. Sentences are usually short and may be incomplete. Contractions and informal English are common, as in the following speech:

> "It's her! The Alderson woman! And she wants to see you! Not Siegfried, not me, but you, Mr. Herriot himself!"

Dialogue tags are phrases, such as "Helen said" or "I said," that tell you who is speaking. Notice in "Putting Things Right" that most conversation does not include dialogue tags. Find two places in the story where dialogue tags are not included. Can you explain why they are left out?

■ Writing About the Story

Suppose that you are writing a script for a TV show about an interesting encounter you have had. Write a page of dialogue that will let the audience know the speakers' personalities and characters. Feel free to use slang and incomplete sentences to make your dialogue as realistic as possible.

Victory

From the poem by Robert Watson

Moving furniture around my room
I can move stars, the streetlights and the dust
In rolls below our chairs. I can change weather
If I want.

. . . .

Putting on clothes I have not worn before
I sit on a shifted chair turning my body
To something new. I can be President
When I choose.

Opening the door to watch the snow
I walk frozen ground, past frozen trees,
Around the block, around. I can circle the universe
When I will.

Indoors I light a fire to warm the air,
I can move the chimney across the room,
Or doom the furniture in the hearth
If I please.

But you, like a frozen tree in frozen ground,
I'll walk around, I'll walk around the block,
I'll shift all the furniture in my room.
I'll move you yet.

Lucas and Jake

A short story by Paul Darcy Boles

Illustrated by Pat Traub

IT WAS THE TIME when he could relax a little, letting go in all the clean sun that showered down on this part of the zoo.

So Lucas, who would be sixty-five next Tuesday, July sixteenth, was sitting on a box beside Jake's cage down on one of the side paths where not many sightseers came. He was eating a winesap apple, a fine specimen of its kind. He took distinct pleasure in biting into it with teeth that were largely his own.

All morning he'd been thinking back to when he'd been a boy and, on a day like this, would have been footloose and free as a big bird. He'd always liked zoo work, even if it didn't give you much status with friends and fellow men. Yet a man needed somebody to look up to him. An admirer, maybe a relative. Lucas

didn't have one ring-tailed relative, admiring or not, on earth.

He finished his apple, flipped its core into a trash can and leaned back, hugging his knees and cutting an eye at Jake.

Jake lay quiet, cinnamon-colored body shadowed, just a few flecks of sunlight picking out bits of his mane, one splash of light in his left eye. The eye, large and golden, resembled some strange pirate coin. Jake possessed awful patience. He could watch an inconsequential bug on the cage floor hours on end, not even his tail twitching, its very tuft motionless.

Lucas sat up as two boys came around the lilac bush and moved toward Jake's cage. And Lucas's moustache bristled a bit. His eyes got the stern cool look of a TV

Westerner's — a town marshal, summing up transients.[1]

The older boy, about twelve, padded along on sneakers soundless as a brace[2] of leopards. The younger, eight or nine, with a thatch of sheepdoggish hair, was fiddling with a yo-yo. It reeled out smartly enough, but when he tried to flip it back it nearly banged his nose.

Both stopped at the cage and looked in at Jake. Lucas waited for their first smidge[3] of smart talk. But the bigger boy's voice sounded thoughtful, not smart talking at all. "Wonder how come they keep him here, Paddy? Not back with all the others?"

The smaller boy shrugged. He went on making his yo-yo climb up and roll down. "Maybe he *likes* it here."

That was as good an answer as Lucas had ever heard from a layman who couldn't know anything solid about lions. Most people thought they were lion experts.

The bigger boy's eyes widened toward Lucas. "Sir, how come he's here? Not messing around with the other lions up at the moat?"

Paddy let his yo-yo spin to a stop. He wanted to know too.

Lucas cleared his throat. But before he could say word one, information fountained out of the taller boy: "My name's Ridefield Tarrant. This is Patrick McGoll. Call him Paddy, sir. We came out on the bus. We each had two bits for Saturday. I didn't like the baboons, they make me nervous barking. But I sure like the lions and the tigers. Especially lions." He drew fresh breath. "We could have gone to the movies. But it felt like a better day for animals."

When he was sure Ridefield had finished, Lucas nodded. "You can't miss, with animals." He waited; the word coast still seemed clear. "You asked about this lion. His name's Jake. They keep Jake all by himself for" — Jake coughed — "for certain secret reasons."

Ridefield's face lighted all over. He owned very black hair and eyes that were bold. He was polite, but in a flash Lucas could tell nobody was ever going to break his inquiring spirit. The knowledge made Lucas happy about something in the universe no man ever really had a name for: glory, ecstasy; he wouldn't know.

With a glance at his own bronze knuckles, hard as oak roots soaking up sunlight, Lucas nodded again. "Going to tell you boys the secret. Because you look like you want to know. Listen real close."

Ridefield Tarrant was leaning toward Lucas like an arrow set on the bowstring, and the mouth of Paddy McGoll had come a trifle

---

1. **summing up transients:** checking out strangers who are passing through.
2. **brace:** a pair.
3. **smidge** (SMIJ): short for *smidgen*, a very small amount.

open like that of a young bird expecting food.

Lucas narrowed his eyes. "Ever hear of a Cape lion?"

Their heads shook.

"Well" — Lucas shook his head — "only the kings of the whole lion breed. That's all they are, gents. Never in your life see a Cape lion doing push-ups on a barrel in a circus. No, sir! Wouldn't catch him dead in such a place." Almost casually, Lucas added, "Jake's a Cape lion."

"Yike," murmured Ridefield.

Lucas folded his arms. "Yep. Took from his mother when he was a young brave. Fought all the way.

Killed . . . more'n you could count. Notice the bars of this here now cage." He pointed. "Put Jake in a cage with *lighter* bars, why, he'd be right out among you with a baseball bat. Put him up at the moat with the rest, he'd eat 'em like cornflakes. Cornflakes." Lucas touched his moustache reflectively. "He's my sole and particular charge. Jake's my special talent."

At this moment Jake twitched his left ear to discourage a bluebottle fly. Paddy McGoll stiffened like a little post with hair all over the top of it. Ridges and valleys leaped into the leather of Lucas's forehead. "Now, I hope I did right to tell you,

gents. Most people, you tell 'em about Jake, they'd write to editors about him, stir up trouble. I'd hate for the zoo to have to shoot him."

Ridefield said, "I won't say a thing! Neither will Paddy."

Paddy nodded. "I don't write so good, anyhow. In penmanship I use my fingers instead of my wrists. I wouldn't *tell* anybody."

"Good." Lucas stood. He felt his joints creak, but the looseness of the sun was warming him too. "Well, I got to be going. I won't be far off — but I hate to leave you here alone with him —"

Ridefield spoke rather swiftly. "We'll be going, we haven't seen the birds yet."

Lucas snorted. "Birds. They're all right, but a lion like Jake — now, he teaches you something. Well, c'mon."

The three started off. Lucas noted that Ridefield and Paddy were walking backward, taking one last look.

And it was just then that Paddy did the foolish thing. It happened because his yo-yo finger was too small for the string's loop. Suddenly, there went the whole yo-yo, string and all, sailing between the cage bars and coming to rest with a clack eight inches in front of Jake's nose.

"*Yike*," breathed Ridefield.

Lucas could feel all the radiance of the day pour itself into his veins as though he himself were about twelve again, or even nine, tough as

nails, but desperately searching for a key to the whole world and all the whirling planets. Low-voiced, he said, "Don't move an inch."

Ridefield's nostrils were white. Paddy stood as if whacked to the spot with spikes. Lucas walked back to Jake's cage.

He could hear the soda water fizz of Jake's breath through great nostrils. The gold coins of the eyes — sometimes pale green, at other times so full of sun they, too, were like suns — were tightly covered. Jake's chin lay on the backs of his paws.

Lucas put his right arm between the bars. The arm moved very slowly. Then his fingers were touching the yo-yo, his arm actually brushing Jake's whiskers. Lucas drew his arm out, stepped back to the boys, said, "Here y'ar," and put the yo-yo in Paddy's fingers.

Ridefield tried to speak, and couldn't. He stuck his right hand up to Lucas, and Lucas shook it. Then Paddy, dropping the yo-yo into a pocket, stuck his hand out, and he and Lucas shook. Then Ridefield and Paddy moved off. It was as if they held something so tremendous they might burst. Strength and wonder and greatness, all understood, all there . . .

They were out of sight around the lilac bush before Lucas smiled. It was the smile of a man who'd earned something: more than status. And after a moment Lucas strolled back

to Jake's cage. He thrust his arm in, took hold of the mane, which felt like rope fibers, and gave it a minor tug.

All at once Jake came awake, the eyes staring at Lucas with green-gold enigmatic quiet. Jake was no Cape lion. But he might have been. *All* animals of this kind were brave and glorious. If they got old and preferred to sleep, if they couldn't really be terrible any longer, or even roar much, that was their business. In some definite way Lucas felt he'd done something for Jake today; for the whole kingdom of lions.

He couldn't have put a finger on it. He tousled the dark mane, felt of the veinous surface behind the left ear — soft as a velvet mouse — and drew his arm back out of the cage. He turned away; there was plenty to do, and he didn't want to get chewed out for not doing it. He walked off.

Behind him, alone again to sleep out his years quietly, Jake kept his eyes open for a few more seconds. Then the eyelids trembled. The eyes shut. The body lay unmoving, powerful, in the huge green afternoon.

Understanding the Story

1. When the boys asked Lucas why Jake was in a cage away from the other lions, what reason did he give?

2. The real reason why Jake was in a cage by himself is implied but not stated directly in the story. What do you think was the real reason?

3. Why do you think Lucas did not tell the truth about the lion?

4. After Lucas gets the yo-yo from Jake's cage, what does he feel that he has achieved for himself and for Jake?

5. Think about the elderly people that you know. What kind of work do they do?

Understanding Literature

Often, in order to find the main point of a story, whether it is a short story such as "Lucas and Jake" or a contemporary novel, we must look for the *theme.*

If you were to tell someone what happened in this story, you would be describing the *plot.* But if you were to explain the main idea, the basic meaning, or the point of the story, you would be stating the theme.

While not every literary work has a theme, most authors *do* write stories with themes, which they want readers to recognize. Therefore, writers often include *key passages,* sections of a story that seem to speak directly to us. Key passages may sound like philosophical statements or words of wisdom. Often they state the lesson the characters in the story have learned, a lesson that the author wants us to learn, too.

In "Lucas and Jake," for example, author Paul Darcy Boles tells us:

> Jake was no Cape lion. But he might have been. *All* animals of this kind were brave and glorious. If they got old and preferred to sleep, if they couldn't really be terrible any longer, or even roar much, that was their business.

In this key passage, Boles is stating that even the fiercest creatures grow old but must still be allowed to keep their dignity. Can you think of any ways that Lucas and Jake might be alike?

Writing About the Story

Write a letter of inquiry to the director of a zoo, real or imaginary, and ask questions about zoo policies and about the animals. Here are some examples of questions you might ask:

a. Where does the zoo get its animals?

b. What is the oldest animal in this zoo?

c. Who cares for the animals when they are sick?

On Aging

A poem by Maya Angelou

When you see me sitting quietly,
Like a sack left on the shelf,
Don't think I need your chattering.
I'm listening to myself.
Hold! Stop! Don't pity me!
Hold! Stop your sympathy!
Understanding if you got it,
Otherwise I'll do without it!

When my bones are stiff and aching
And my feet won't climb the stair,
I will only ask one favor:
Don't bring me no rocking chair.

When you see me walking, stumbling,
Don't study and get it wrong.
'Cause tired don't mean lazy
And every goodbye ain't gone.
I'm the same person I was back then,
A little less hair, a little less chin,
A lot less lungs and much less wind.
But ain't I lucky I can still breathe in.

Learn About

"Good writing is true writing," according to novelist Ernest Hemingway. He went on to say that the quality of a story depends on the writer's knowledge of life. One kind of knowledge comes from personal experiences. A writer is most convincing when telling about the people, places, and events he or she knows best.

Many fine stories are retellings of incidents that writers have been unable to forget. Irene Hunt says that her novel *Up a Road Slowly* (the book from which "Aggie" was taken) grew out of a childhood experience that continued to haunt her. She says, "I was one of a thoughtless group of children who once rejected a retarded child."

Irene Hunt created a character named Julie to play the part she herself once played in the drama. She retells the incident from this character's point of view. What happens in "Aggie" is not identical to the real incident in Hunt's life. However, when Julie says to the retarded child's mother, "I know that sometimes I've been mean to Aggie. I'm sorry . . . I'm really sorry," there is little doubt that Irene Hunt is finally saying what she wishes she could have said long ago to the child whom she and her friends treated so cruelly.

"Aggie" is said to be *first-person narration*. It is told from a story character's point of view: *We did this; I thought this; She said to me. . . .* (*I* and *we* are first-person pronouns.) First-person point of view makes readers especially aware of the main character's feelings, since the readers see only what this one character sees, and know only what this character knows. Kin Platt also uses this type of narration in "The Dummy." This story tells about a young person, Neil Comstock, who changes his attitude toward a person with different capabilities.

In "Putting Things Right," James Herriot chooses first-person narration to re-create an emotionally charged personal experience. However, instead of inventing a character to narrate the story, Herriot makes himself the main character and narrator. He thus makes his story *autobiographical*. By telling the story from his own point of view, Herriot can share with readers what he saw and felt while he worked to reset a sheepdog's dislocated hip.

A writer can learn about life by doing careful research as well as by experiencing things. This type of research

is particularly necessary in writing stories about the past or about remote places. But learning only about such things as styles of dress and means of transportation does not mean that a writer will be able to make a distant time or place come alive on the pages of a book. The writer must use imagination to make the people in such a situation seem real and worth caring about.

In order to breathe life into a story, a writer often must imagine that he or she has *become* one of its characters. Scott O'Dell (the author of ''The Secret of Blue Beach,'' which appears in Unit Five of this book) tries to speak as a different person each time he narrates

a story. He wrote his award-winning novel *Island of the Blue Dolphins* from the point of view of Karana, a young girl left alone on an island for many years. This young girl's life is very different from O'Dell's own life. If O'Dell had not set aside his own feelings and ways of seeing things while he wrote the story, Karana's tale would not have seemed as real.

Personal experience can be told in ways other than first-person narration. ''Happy Birthday,'' by Toni Cade Bambara, is the story of Ollie, a girl who cannot find anyone to help her celebrate her birthday. The writer tells the story as if she were observing Ollie. This is *third-person narration: She did this; She thought this; He said this to her . . . . (She, he,* and *they* are third-person pronouns.)

It is impossible to guess what kind of incident led Toni Cade Bambara to write "Happy Birthday." Nevertheless, the rough-edged emotions and the sharply detailed surroundings give the reader the sense that some similar, saddening experience must have happened to the author.

"Lucas and Jake" is another story told through third-person narration. Again, the feelings of the characters are what give life to the story. Author Paul Darcy Boles seems to have put some part of himself into the lonely zookeeper, and perhaps into the two boys who talk with him. The third-person narration allows the author to communicate the thoughts and feelings of more than one character.

As you write stories and poems, you will draw on your experiences and feelings. Even the most imaginative piece of writing requires the use of memory. Allen Say, the author of the novel *The Ink-Keeper's Apprentice,* has said it well: "What we call imagination is rearrangement of memory. You cannot imagine without memory."

Choose one of the stories or poems in the unit. "Become" one of the characters and write either an autobiographical account or a journal entry about an incident in the story or poem. Be sure to use first-person narration. (A good choice would be Helen's account of her encounter with Jim Herriot at the veterinary office.)

BOOKSHELF

I, Juan de Pareja by Elizabeth Borton de Treviño. Farrar, Straus & Giroux, 1965. Juan de Pareja, a court painter's slave in seventeenth-century Spain, develops a unique friendship with his master.

The Language of Goldfish by Zibby Oneal. Viking Press, 1980. Carrie, thirteen, creates an imaginary world rather than face the pain of growing into adolescence.

To Be Young, Gifted and Black: A Portrait of Lorraine Hansberry In Her Own Words adapted by Robert Nemiroff. Samuel French, Inc., 1971. Lorraine Hansberry, who died at age thirty-four, left to the American theater, and to readers as well, a clear-eyed view of the human spirit.

When Thunders Spoke by Virginia Driving Hawk Sneve. Holiday House, 1974. Norman Two Bull respects his heritage but encounters family conflict when old customs collide with modern society.

Of Nightingales That Weep by Katherine Paterson. T. Y. Crowell, 1974. Takiko struggles to cope with a raging civil war and conflicting loyalties to the court, a warrior, and her severely deformed stepfather.

Roll of Thunder, Hear My Cry by Mildred D. Taylor. Dial Press, 1976. During the difficult Depression Era, Cassie and her family, like many other Black families, suffer the indignities of persecution and humiliation.

The Effect of Gamma Rays on Man-in-the-Moon Marigolds: A Drama in Two Acts by Paul Zindel. Harper & Row, 1971. Beatrice was an embittered mother with a crazed household to contend with, and no one baffled her more than her daughter Tillie — a keeper of rabbits and dreamer of dreams.

3 Only Darkness Ticking

The News In English

A short story by Graham Greene

Illustrated by Robert Steele

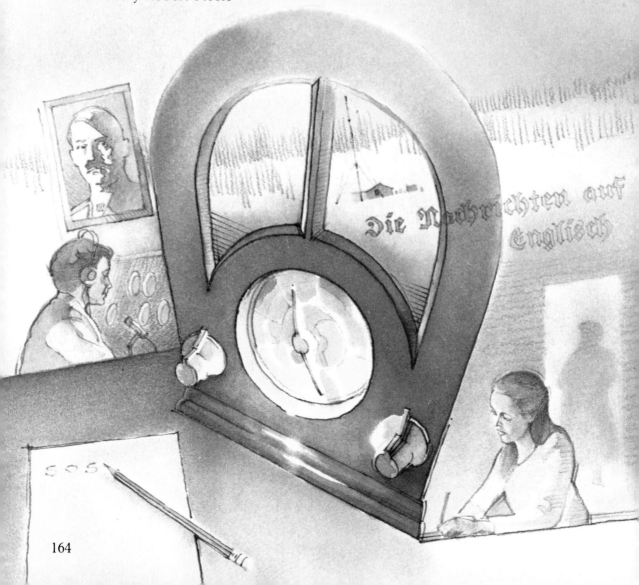

Graham Greene's World War II spy thriller is a study of a special kind of courage and trust shared by two people. It's difficult enough to risk your life, even when it's for those who trust and support you. But David and Mary Bishop meet an even greater test: he must face danger alone, with only Mary to aid and believe in him. Everyone else in England thinks David is a traitor. But the fact of the matter is ——

LORD HAW-HAW OF ZEESEN[1] was off the air.

All over England the new voice was noticed: precise and rather lifeless, it was the voice of a typical English don.[2]

In his first broadcast he referred to himself as a man young enough to sympathize with what he called "the resurgence of youth all over the new Germany," and that was the reason — combined with the pedantic[3] tone — he was at once nicknamed Dr. Funkhole.

It is the tragedy of such men that they are never alone in the world.

Old Mrs. Bishop was knitting by the fire at her house in Crowborough when young Mrs. Bishop tuned in to Zeesen. The sock was khaki; it was as if she had picked up at the point where she had dropped a stitch in 1918. The grim comfortable house stood in one of the long avenues, all spruce and laurel and a coating of snow, which are used to nothing but the footsteps of old retired people. Young Mrs. Bishop never forgot that moment; the wind beating up across Ashdown Forest against the blacked-out window, and her mother-in-law happily knitting, and the sense of everything waiting for this moment. Then the

---

1. **Zeesen** (TSAY·zuhn): a village in East Germany. Lord Haw-Haw was the name given William Joyce, an American-English Nazi who made nightly propaganda "news" broadcasts from Zeesen.
2. **don**: a senior professor at an English university.
3. **pedantic**: preachy; pretentious.

voice came into the room from Zee-sen in the middle of a sentence, and old Mrs. Bishop said firmly, "That's David."

Young Mary Bishop made a hopeless protest, "It can't be," but she knew.

"I know my son if you don't know your husband."

It seemed incredible that the man speaking couldn't hear them, that he should just go on, reiterating for the hundredth time the old lies, as if there were nobody anywhere in the world who knew him — a wife or a mother.

Old Mrs. Bishop had stopped knitting. She said, "Is that the man they've been writing about, Dr. Funkhole?"

"It must be."

"It's David."

The voice was extraordinarily convincing; he was going into exact engineering details — David Bishop had been a mathematics don at Oxford. Mary Bishop twisted the wireless off and sat down beside her mother-in-law.

"They'll want to know who it is," Mrs. Bishop said.

"We mustn't tell them," said Mary.

The old fingers had begun again on the khaki sock. She said, "It's our duty." Duty, it seemed to Mary Bishop, was a disease you caught with age: you ceased to feel the tug-tug of personal ties; you gave yourself up to the great tides of patriotism and hate. She said, "They must have made him do it. We don't know what threats. . . ."

"That's neither here nor there."

She gave in weakly to hopeless wishes. "If only he'd got away in time. I never wanted him to give that lecture course."

"He always was stubborn," said old Mrs. Bishop.

"He said there wouldn't be a war."

"Give me the telephone."

"But you see what it means," said Mary Bishop. "He may be tried for treason if we win."

"*When* we win," old Mrs. Bishop said.

The nickname was not altered, even after the interviews with the two Mrs. Bishops, even after the sub-acid derogatory little article about David Bishop's previous career. It was suggested now that he had known all along what was coming, that he had gone to Germany to evade military service, leaving his wife and his mother to be bombed. Mary Bishop fought, almost in vain, with the reporters for some recognition that he might have been forced — by threats or even physical violence. The most one paper would admit was that if threats had been used David Bishop had taken a very unheroic way out. We praise heroes as though they are rare, and yet we are always ready to blame another man

166

for lack of heroism. The name Dr. Funkhole stuck.

But the worst of it to Mary Bishop was old Mrs. Bishop's attitude. She turned a knife in the wound every evening at nine-fifteen. The radio set had to be tuned in to Zeesen, and there she sat listening to her son's voice and knitting socks for some unknown soldier on the Maginot Line.[4] To young Mrs. Bishop none of it made sense — least of all that flat, pedantic voice with its smooth, well-thought-out, elaborate lies. She was afraid to go out now into Crowborough; the whispers in the post office, the old faces watching her covertly in the library. Sometimes she thought almost with hatred, Why has David done this to me? Why?

Then suddenly she got her answer.

The voice for once broke new ground. It said, "Somewhere back in England my wife may be listening to me. I am a stranger to the rest of you, but she knows that I am not in the habit of lying."

A personal appeal was too much. Mary Bishop had faced her mother-in-law and the reporters; she couldn't face her husband. She began to cry, sitting close beside the radio set like a child beside its doll's house when something has been broken in it which nobody can re-

pair. She heard the voice of her husband speaking as if he were at her elbow from a country which was now as distant and as inaccessible as another planet.

"The fact of the matter is —"

The words came slowly out as if he were emphasizing a point in a lecture, and then he went on to what would concern a wife. The low price of food, the quantity of meat in the shops. He went into great detail, giving figures, picking out odd, irrelevant things — like mandarin oranges and toy zebras — perhaps to give an effect of richness and variety.

Suddenly Mary Bishop sat up with a jerk as if she had been asleep. She said, "Oh, God, where's that pencil?" and upset one of the too many ornaments looking for one. Then she began to write, but in no time at all the voice was saying, "Thank you for having listened to me so attentively," and Zeesen had died out on the air. She said, "Too late."

"What's too late?" said old Mrs. Bishop sharply. "Why did you want a pencil?"

"Just an idea," Mary Bishop said.

She was led next day up and down the cold, unheated corridors of a War Office in which half the rooms were empty, evacuated. Oddly enough, her relationship to David Bishop was of use to her now,

---

4. **Maginot** (MAZH•uh•noh) **Line:** a zone of fortifications set up by the French along their border with Germany in the years preceding World War II.

if only because it evoked some curiosity and a little pity. But she no longer wanted the pity, and at last she reached the right man.

He listened to her with great politeness. He was not in uniform. His rather good tweeds made him look as if he had just come up from the country for a day or two, to attend to the war. When she had finished he said, "It's rather a tall story, you know, Mrs. Bishop. Of course it's been a great shock to you — this — well — action of your husband's."

"I'm proud of it."

"Just because in the old days you had this — scheme, you really believe. . . ."

"If he was away from me and he telephoned 'The fact of the matter is,' it always meant, 'This is all lies, but take the initial letters which follow.' Oh, Colonel, if you only knew the number of unhappy week-ends I've saved him from — because, you see, he could always telephone to me, even in front of his host." She said with tears in her voice, "Then I'd send him a telegram."

"Yes. But still — you didn't get anything this time, did you?"

"I was too late. I hadn't a pencil. I only got this. I know it doesn't seem to make sense." She pushed the paper across. SOSPIC. "I know it might easily be coincidence — that it does seem to make a kind of word."

"An odd word."

"Mightn't it be a man's name?"

The officer in tweeds was looking at it, she suddenly realized, with real interest, as if it were a rare kind of pheasant. He said, "Excuse me a moment," and left her. She could hear him telephoning somebody from another room; the little ting of the bell, silence, and then a low voice she couldn't overhear. Then he returned, and she could tell at once from his face that all was well.

He sat down and fiddled with a fountain pen; he was obviously embarrassed. He started a sentence and stopped it. Then he brought out in an embarrassed gulp, "We'll all have to apologize to your husband."

168

"It meant something?"

He was obviously making his mind up about something difficult and out of the way; he was not in the habit of confiding in members of the public. But she had ceased to be a member of the public.

"My dear Mrs. Bishop," he said, "I've got to ask a great deal from you."

"Of course. Anything."

He seemed to reach a decision and stopped fiddling. "A neutral ship called the *Pic* was sunk this morning at four A.M., with a loss of two hundred lives. SOS *Pic*. If we'd had your husband's warning, we could have got destroyers to her in time. I've been speaking to the Admiralty."[5]

Mary Bishop said in a tone of fury, "The things they are writing about David. Is there one of them who'd have the courage. . . ."

"That's the worst part of it, Mrs. Bishop. They must go on writing. Nobody must know, except my department and yourself."

"His mother?"

"You mustn't even tell her."

"But can't you make them just leave him alone?"

"This afternoon I shall ask them to intensify their campaign — in order to discourage others. An article on the legal aspect of treason."

"And if I refuse to keep quiet?"

"Your husband's life won't be worth much, will it?"

"So he's just got to go on?"

"Yes. Just go on."

He went on for four weeks. Every night now she tuned in to Zeesen with a new horror — that he would be off the air. The code was a child's code. How could they fail to detect it? But they did fail. Men with complicated minds can be deceived by simplicity. And every night, too, she had to listen to her mother-in-law's indictment; every episode which she thought discreditable out of a child's past was brought out, the tiniest incident. Women in the last war had

---

5. **Admiralty:** the British naval office.

found a kind of pride in giving their sons; this, too, was a gift on the altar of a warped patriotism. But now young Mrs. Bishop didn't cry; she just held on — it was relief enough to hear his voice.

It wasn't often that he had information to give; the phrase "the fact of the matter is" was a rare one in his talks. Sometimes there were the numbers of the regiments passing through Berlin, or of men on leave — very small details, which might be of value to military intelligence, but to her seemed hardly worth the risk of a life. If this was all he could do, why, why hadn't he allowed them simply to intern[6] him?

_____

6. intern (in•TURN): to hold as a prisoner of war.

At last she could bear it no longer. She visited the War Office again. The man in tweeds was still there, but this time for some reason he was wearing a black tail coat and a black stock as if he had been to a funeral. He must have been to a funeral, and she thought with more fear than ever of her husband.

"He's a brave man, Mrs. Bishop," he said.

"You needn't tell me that," she cried bitterly.

"We shall see that he gets the highest possible decoration. . . ."

"Decoration!"

"What do you want, Mrs. Bishop? He's doing his duty."

"So are other men. But they come home on leave. Sometime. He can't go on forever. Soon they are bound to find out."

"What can we do?"

"You can get him out of there. Hasn't he done enough for you?"

He said gently, "It's beyond our power. How can we communicate with him?"

"Surely you have agents."

"Two lives would be lost. Can't you imagine how they watch him?"

Yes. She could imagine all that clearly. She had spent too many holidays in Germany — as the press had not failed to discover — not to know how men were watched, telephone lines tapped, table companions scrutinized.

He said, "If there was some way

we could get a message to him, it *might* be managed. We do owe him that."

Young Mrs. Bishop said quickly before he could change his mind, "Well, the code works both ways. The fact of the matter is! We have news broadcast in German. He might one day listen in."

"Yes. There's a chance."

She became privy to the plan because again they needed her help. They wanted to attract his notice first by some phrase peculiar to her. For years they had spoken German together on their annual holiday. That phrase was to be varied in every broadcast, and elaborately they worked out a series of messages which would convey to him the same instructions — to go to a certain station on the Cologne-Wesel line[7] and contact there a railway worker who had already helped five men and two women to escape from Germany.

Mary Bishop felt she knew the place well, the small country station which probably served only a few dozen houses and a big hotel where people went in the old days for cures. The opportunity was offered him, if he could only take it, by an elaborate account of a railway accident at that point — so many people killed — sabotage — arrests. It was

plugged in the news as relentlessly as the Germans repeated the news of false sinkings, and they answered indignantly back that there had been no accident.

It seemed more horrible than ever to Mary Bishop — those nightly broadcasts from Zeesen. The voice was in the room with her, and yet he couldn't know whether any message for which he risked his life reached home, and she couldn't know whether their messages to him just petered out unheard or unrecognized.

⚬⚬

Old Mrs. Bishop said, "Well, we can do without David tonight, I should hope." It was a new turn in her bitterness — now she would

---

7. **Cologne-Wesel** (ko·LOHN-VAY·zuhl) **line:** the main railway line along the Rhine River in Germany.

simply wipe him off the air. Mary Bishop protested. She said she must hear — then at least she would know that he was well.

"It serves him right if he's not well."

"I'm going to listen," Mary Bishop persisted.

"Then I'll go out of the room. I'm tired of his lies."

"You're his mother, aren't you?"

"That's not my fault. I didn't choose — like you did. I tell you I won't listen to it."

Mary Bishop turned the knob. "Then stop your ears," she cried in a sudden fury, and heard David's voice coming over.

"The lies," he was saying, "put over by the British capitalist press. There has not even been a railway accident, let alone any sabotage, at the place so persistently mentioned in the broadcasts from England. To-morrow I am leaving myself for the so-called scene of the accident, and I propose in my broadcast the day after tomorrow to give you an impartial observer's report, with records of the very railwaymen who are said to have been shot for sabotage. Tomorrow, therefore, I shall not be on the air. . . ."

"Oh, thank God, thank God," Mary Bishop said.

The old woman grumbled by the fire. "You haven't much to thank Him for."

"You don't know how much."

All next day she found herself praying, although she didn't much believe in prayer. She visualized that station "on the Rhine not far from Wesel" — and not far either from the Dutch frontier. There must be some method of getting across — with the help of that unknown worker — possibly in a refrigerating van. No idea was too fantastic to be true. Others had succeeded before him.

All through the day she tried to keep pace with him — he would have to leave early, and she imagined his cup of ersatz[8] coffee and the slow wartime train taking him south and west. She thought of his fear and of his excitement — he was coming home to her. Ah, when he landed safely, what a day that would be! The papers then would have to eat their words — no more Dr. Funkhole and no more of this place, side by side with his unloving mother.

At midday, she thought, he has arrived; he has his black disks with him to record the men's voices; he is probably watched, but he will find his chance — and now he is not alone. He has someone with him helping him. In one way or another he will miss his train home. The freight train will draw in; perhaps a signal will stop it outside the station. She saw it all so vividly, as the early winter dark came down, and she

---

8. **ersatz** (ER·sahts): artificial (from the German word for *substitute*).

blacked the windows out,[9] that she found herself thankful he possessed, as she knew, a white mackintosh.[10] He would be less visible waiting there in the snow.

Her imagination took wings, and by dinner time she felt sure that he was already on the way to the frontier. That night there was no broadcast from Dr. Funkhole, and she sang as she bathed, and old Mrs. Bishop beat furiously on her bedroom floor above.

In bed she could almost feel herself vibrating with the heavy movement of *his* train. She saw the landscape going by outside — there must be a crack in any van in which he lay hid, so that he could mark the distances. It was very much the landscape of Crowborough, spruces powdered with snow, the wide dreary waste they called a forest, dark avenues — she fell asleep.

⁕

When she woke she was still happy. Perhaps before night she would receive a cable from Holland, but if it didn't come she would not be anxious because so many things in wartime might delay it. It didn't come.

That night she made no attempt to turn on the radio, so old Mrs. Bishop changed her tactics again.

---

9. **she blacked the windows out:** During the war, people darkened their windows at night.
10. **mackintosh:** a raincoat.

"Well," she said, "aren't you going to listen to your husband?"

"He won't be broadcasting." Very soon now she could turn on his mother in triumph and say, "There, I knew it all the time, my husband's a hero."

"That was last night."

"He won't be broadcasting again."

"What do you mean? Turn it on and let me hear."

There was no harm in proving that she knew. She turned it on.

A voice was talking in German — something about an accident and English lies, she didn't bother to listen. She felt too happy. "There," she said, "I told you. It's not David."

And then David spoke.

He said, "You have been listening to the actual voices of the men your English broadcasters have told you were shot by the German police. Perhaps now you will be less inclined to believe the exaggerated stories you hear of life inside Germany today."

"There," old Mrs. Bishop said, "I told you."

And all the world, she thought, will go on telling me now, forever — Dr. Funkhole. He never got those messages. He's there for keeps. David's voice said with curious haste and harshness, "The fact of the matter is ——"

He spoke rapidly for about two minutes as if he were afraid they would fade him at any moment, and yet it sounded harmless enough, the old stories about plentiful food and how much you could buy for an English pound, figures. But some of the examples this time, she thought with dread, are surely so fantastic that even the German brain will realize something is wrong. How had he ever dared to show *this* copy to his chiefs?

She could hardly keep pace with her pencil, so rapidly did he speak. The words grouped themselves on her pad: "Five U's refueling *hodie* noon 53.23 by 10.5.[11] News reliable

---

11. **Five U's refueling *hodie* noon 53.23 by 10.5:** Five German submarines (U-boats) will be refueling at noon today, at latitude 53.23° north by longitude 10.5° east.

174

source Wesel so returned. Talk un-authorized. The end."

"This order. Many young wives I feel enjoy giving one" — he hesitated — "one's day's butter in every dozen — " the voice faded, gave out altogether. She saw on her pad: *To my wife, good-bie d. . . .*"

The end, good-by, the end — the words rang on like funeral bells. She began to cry, sitting as she had done before, close up against the radio set. Old Mrs. Bishop said with a kind of delight, "He ought never to have been born. I never wanted him. The coward!" Now Mary Bishop could stand no more of it.

"Oh," she cried to her mother-in-law across the little overheated, over-furnished Crowborough room, "if only he were a coward, if only he were. But he's a hero, a damned hero, a hero, a hero — " she cried hopelessly on, feeling the room reel round her, and dimly supposing behind all the pain and horror that one day she would have to feel, like other women, pride.

About GRAHAM GREENE

At some time in their lives most writers have had odd jobs of one sort or another. Graham Greene had one of the oddest. He sometimes disguised himself as a tramp and played the barrel organ, passing the hat to earn money.

Perhaps it was while wandering the city streets that Graham Greene acquired his curiosity about the facts and details of human experience. "I am journalistically minded," he comments. "I want to see the dead body, not just read about it."

It is characteristic of Graham Greene to mention a dead body in his remarks. Often it seems that he is fascinated by death and by the dark side of human nature. He feels that a fascination or a compulsion of some sort is necessary to the writer: "Every writer worth our consideration is a victim, a man given over to an obsession."

Some critics have said Graham Greene's obsession is with evil. But, as his writing shows, Greene also believes in divine mercy. Although his vision may be a dark one, it is true to his belief that "there are at least two duties the novelist owes—to tell the truth as he sees it and to accept no special privileges from the state."

■ Understanding the Story

1. The people who listened to David Bishop's propaganda broadcasts from Germany assumed that he was a traitor. What was the real reason he had agreed to broadcast for the Germans?

2. The plan for helping David escape from Germany didn't work. Why?

3. How did Mary Bishop and Mrs. Bishop differ in their attitudes toward duty, patriotism, and personal ties? Was David Bishop more like his wife or more like his mother in these matters? Explain.

4. Using the Bishops' code system, write a "secret message" of at least ten words. Be sure that your words make a sensible sentence.

5. American English and British English often use different words for the same object. In England you would take the *tube* to the *cinema* instead of taking the subway to the movies. Translate the following British terms into American English: bobby; pram; lift; chemist; petrol; braces.

■ Understanding Literature

When and where a story takes place is called the *setting.* An author can choose any time or place as a setting for a story, but that choice affects the plot, the characterizations, and the mood of the story.

Sometimes the writer immediately identifies the setting for us with a statement like "It was 1942 in England. World War II was raging, the Germans were bombing England nightly, and the sitting room of the small house in Sussex shook as Pam sat listening to the radio."

Authors don't always give us the setting so directly. Often, as in Graham Greene's short story "The News in English" we must figure out the setting as the story goes along. For example, a story may begin in the morning in a person's room. As the story unfolds, we may find out that the building is in New York City and that the story takes place at a particular time, perhaps the 1970s. Look back at page 165. What clues help you figure out the setting of this story? What is the immediate, specific setting? What is the larger, general setting?

■ Writing About the Story

What do you think might have happened to David Bishop after his last broadcast? Pretend that you are a reporter after the war ends. Write a news story in which you reveal the true facts about David Bishop's heroism. Begin your article with a lead sentence that tells who, what, when, where, why, and how. Look at a newspaper article if you need a model. You will also need to write a headline for your story.

The Door

A poem by Miroslav Holub
Translated from the Czech by
Ian Milner and George Theiner

Go and open the door.
   Maybe outside there's
   a tree, or a wood,
   a garden,
   or a magic city.

Go and open the door.
   Maybe a dog's rummaging.
   Maybe you'll see a face,
or an eye,
or the picture
         of a picture.

Go and open the door.
   If there's a fog
   it will clear.

Go and open the door.
   Even if there's only
   the darkness ticking,
   even if there's only
   the hollow wind,
   even if
        nothing
          is there,
go and open the door.

At least
there'll be
a draft.

Illustration by Jaclyne Scardova

The Calamander Chest

A short story by Joseph Payne Brennan

Illustrated by Lyle Miller

"From the Indies, sir!" said the secondhand dealer, pressing his palms together. "Genuine calamander wood — a rare good buy, sir!"

"Well — I'll take it," replied Ernest Maax somewhat hesitantly.

He had been strolling idly through the antique and secondhand shop when the chest caught his attention. It had a rich, exotic look which pleased him. In appearance the dark brown, black-striped wood resembled ebony. And the chest was quite capacious.[1] It was at least two feet wide and five feet long, with a depth of nearly three feet.

When Maax learned that the dealer was willing to dispose of it for only twelve dollars, he could not resist buying it.

What made him hesitate a little was the dealer's initial low price and quite obvious pleasure upon completing the transaction. Was that fine-grained wood only an inlay or did the chest contain some hidden defect?

When it was delivered to his room the next day, he could find nothing wrong with it. The calamander wood was solid and sound and the entire chest appeared to be in fine condition. The lid clicked smoothly into place when lowered, and the big iron key turned readily enough.

---

1. **capacious** (kuh·PAY·shuhs): roomy; large.

179

Feeling quite satisfied with himself, Maax carefully polished the dark wood and then slid the chest into an empty corner of his room. The next time he changed his lodgings, the chest would prove invaluable. Meanwhile it added just the right exotic touch to his rather drab chamber.

Several weeks passed, and although he still cast occasional admiring glances at his new possession, it gradually began to recede from his mind.

Then one evening his attention was returned to it in a very startling manner. He was sitting up, reading, late in the evening, when for some reason his eyes lifted from his book and he looked across the room toward the corner where he had placed the chest.

A long white finger protruded from under its lid.

He sat motionless, overwhelmed with sudden horror, his eyes riveted on this appalling object.

It just hung there unmoving, a long pale finger with a heavy knuckle bone and a black nail.

After his first shock, Maax felt a slow rage kindling within him. The finger had no right to be there; it was unreasonable—and idiotic. He resented it bitterly, much as he would have resented the sudden intrusion of an unsavory roomer from down the hall. His peaceful, comfortable evening was ruined by this outrageous manifestation.[2]

_____

2. **manifestation**: materialization; becoming visible or apparent.

With an oath, he hurled his book straight at the finger.

It disappeared. At least he could no longer see it. Tilting his reading light so that its beams shot across the room, he strode to the chest and flung open the lid.

There was nothing inside.

Dropping the lid, he picked up his book and returned to the chair. Perhaps, he reflected, he had been reading too much lately. His eyes, in protest, might be playing tricks on him.

For some time longer he pretended to read, but at frequent intervals he lifted his eyes and looked across the room toward the calamander chest. The finger did not reappear and eventually he went to bed.

A week passed and he began to forget about the finger. He stayed out more during the evening, and read less, and by the end of a week he was quite convinced that he had been the victim of nothing more than an odd hallucination brought on by simple eye strain.

At length, at the beginning of the second week, deciding that his eyes had had a good rest, he bought some current magazines and made up his mind to spend the evening in his room.

Some time after he took up the first magazine, he glanced over at the chest and saw that all was as it should be. Settling comfortably in his chair, he became absorbed in the magazine and did not put it aside for over an hour. As he finally laid it down and prepared to pick up another, his eyes strayed in the direction of the chest — and there was the finger.

It hung there as before, motionless, with its thick knuckle and repulsive black nail.

Crowding down an impulse to rush across the room, Maax slowly reached over to a small table which stood near his chair and felt for a heavy metal ash tray. As his hand closed on the tray, his eyes never left the finger.

Rising very slowly, he began to inch across the room. He was certain that the ash tray, if wielded with force, would effectively crush anything less substantial than itself which it descended on. It was made of solid metal, and it possessed a sharp edge.

When he was a scant yard away from the chest, the finger disappeared. When he lifted the lid, the chest, as he had expected, was empty.

Feeling considerably shaken, he returned to his chair and sat down. Although the finger did not reappear, he could not drive its hideous image out of his mind. Before going to bed, he reluctantly decided that he would get rid of the chest.

He was in sound health and his eyes had had a week's rest. Therefore, he

reasoned, whatever flaw in nature permitted the ugly manifestation rested not with him but with the chest itself.

Looking back, he recalled the secondhand dealer's eagerness to sell the chest at a ridiculously low price. The thing must already have had an evil reputation when the antique dealer acquired it. Knowing it, the unscrupulous[3] merchant had readily consented to part with it for a small sum.

Maax, a practical young man, admitted the possibility of a nonphysical explanation only with reluctance, but felt that he was not in a position to debate the matter. The preservation of stable nerves came first. All other considerations were secondary.

Accordingly, on the following day, before leaving for work, he arranged with his landlady to have the chest picked up and carted off to the city dump. He included specific directions that upon arrival it was to be burned.

When he arrived back at his room that evening, however, the first thing that met his gaze was the calamander chest. Furious, he hurried down the hall to his landlady's apartment and demanded an explanation. Why had his orders been ignored?

When she was able to get a word in, the patient woman explained that the chest actually had been picked up and carted off to the dump. Upon arrival, however, the man in charge of the dump had assured the men who

lugged in the chest that there must be some mistake. Nobody in his right mind, he asserted, would destroy such a beautiful and expensive article. The men must have picked up the wrong one; surely there must be another left behind, he said, which was the worthless one the owner wanted discarded.

The two men who had taken the chest to the dump, not feeling secure in their own minds about the matter, and not wishing to make a costly mistake, had returned the chest later in the day.

Completely nonplussed[4] by this information, Maax muttered an apology to the landlady and went back to his room, where he plopped into a chair and sat staring at the chest. He would, he finally decided, give it one more chance. If nothing further happened, he would keep it; otherwise he would take immediate and drastic measures to get rid of it once and for all.

Although he had planned to attend a concert that evening, it began to rain shortly after six o'clock and he resigned himself to an evening in his room.

Before starting to read, he locked the chest with the iron key and put the key in his pocket. It was absurd that he had not thought of doing so before. This would, he felt, be the decisive test.

While he read, he maintained a keen watch on the chest, but nothing happened until well after eleven, when he

---

3. **unscrupulous** (un·SKROOP·yoo·luhs): dishonest.

4. **nonplussed** (also nonplused): thoroughly puzzled.

put aside his book for the evening. As he closed the book and started to rise, he looked at the chest — and there was the finger.

In appearance it was unchanged. Instead of hanging slack and motionless, however, it now seemed to be imbued with faint life. It quivered slightly and it appeared to be making weak attempts to scratch the side of the chest with its long black nail.

When he finally summoned up sufficient courage, Maax took up the metal ash tray as before and crept across the room. This time he actually had the tray raised to strike before the finger vanished. It seemed to whisk back into the chest.

With a wildly thumping heart, Maax lifted the lid. Again the box was empty. But then he remembered the iron key in his pocket and a new thrill of horror coursed down his spine. The hideous digital apparition had unlocked the chest! Either that, or he was rapidly losing his sanity.

Completely unnerved, he locked the chest for a second time and then sat in a chair and watched it until two o'clock in the morning. At length, exhausted and deeply shaken, he sought his bed. Before putting out the light, he ascertained that the chest was still locked.

As soon as he fell asleep, he experienced a hideous nightmare. He dreamed that a persistent scratching sound woke him up, that he arose, lit a candle, and looked at the chest. The protruding finger showed just under the lid and this time it was galvanized[5] with an excess of life. It twisted and turned, drummed with its thick knuckle, scratched frantically with its flat black nail. At length, as if it suddenly became aware of his presence, it became perfectly still — and then very deliberately beckoned for him to approach. Flooded with horror, he nevertheless found himself unable to disobey. Setting down the candle, he slowly crossed the room like an automaton.[6] The monstrous beckoning finger drew him on like some infernal magnet which attracted human flesh instead of metal.

As he reached the chest, the finger darted inside and the lid immediately lifted. Overwhelmed with terror and yet utterly unable to stop himself, he stepped into the chest, sat down, drew his knees up to his chin and turned onto his side. A second later the lid slammed shut and he heard the iron key turn in the lock.

At this point in the nightmare he awoke with a ringing scream. He sat up in bed and felt the sweat of fear running down his face. In spite of the nightmare — or because of it — he dared not get up and switch on the light. Instead, he burrowed under the bedclothes and lay wide awake till morning.

After he had regained some measure of self-composure, he went out for

---

5. **galvanized**: jolted into action as if by an electric shock.
6. **automaton** (aw·TOM·uh·TON): a robot.

black coffee and then, instead of reporting to his job, rode across town to the modest home of a truck driver and mover whom he had hired at various times in the past. After some quite detailed and specific plans had been agreed upon, he paid the mover ten dollars and departed with a promise to pay him an equal amount when the job was done. After lunch, considerably relieved, he went to work.

He entered his room that evening with a confident air, but as soon as he looked around, his heart sank. Contrary to instructions, the mover had not picked up the chest. It remained in the corner, just where it had been.

This time Maax was more depressed than angry. He sought out a telephone and called up the mover. The man was profusely apologetic. His truck had broken down, he explained, just as he was starting out to pick up the chest. The repairs were nearly completed, however, and he would absolutely be out to carry off the chest the first thing in the morning.

Since there was nothing else he could do, Maax thanked him and hung up. Finding himself unusually reluctant to return to his room, he ate a leisurely dinner at a nearby restaurant and later attended a movie. After the movie he stopped and had a hot chocolate. It was nearly midnight before he got back to his room.

In spite of his nightmare of the previous evening, he found himself looking forward to bed. He had lost almost an entire night's sleep and he was beginning to feel the strain.

After assuring himself that the calamander chest was securely locked, he slipped the iron key under his pillow and got into bed. In spite of his uneasiness he soon fell asleep.

Some hours later he awoke suddenly and sat up. His heart was pounding. For a moment he was not aware of what had awakened him — then he heard it. A furious scratching, tapping, thumping sound came from one corner of the room.

Trembling violently, he got out of bed, crossed the room and pressed the button on his reading lamp. Nothing happened. Either the electricity was shut off, or the light bulb had burned out.

He pulled open a drawer of the lamp stand and frantically searched for a candle. By the time he found one and applied a match to its wick the scratching sound had redoubled in intensity. The entire room seemed filled with it.

Shuddering, he lifted the candle and started across the room toward the calamander chest. As the wavering light of the candle flickered into the far corner, he saw the finger.

It protruded far out of the chest and it was writhing with furious life. It thrummed[7] and twisted, dug at the chest with its horrible black nail, tapped and turned in an absolute frenzy of movement.

Suddenly, as he advanced, it became

_____

7. **thrummed:** drummed; tapped.

184

absolutely still. It hung down limp. Engulfed with terror, Maax was convinced that it had become aware of his approach and was now watching him.

When he was halfway across the room, the finger slowly lifted and deliberately beckoned to him. With a rush of renewed horror Maax remembered the ghastly events of his dream. Yet — as in the nightmare — he found himself utterly unable to disobey that diabolical[8] summons. He went on like a man in a trance.

_____

8. **diabolical** (DY•uh•BOL•uh•kuhl): evil; cruel.

Early the next morning the mover and his assistant were let into Maax's room by the landlady. Maax had apparently already left for work, but there was no need of his presence since he had already given the mover detailed instructions in regard to the disposal of the chest.

The chest, locked but without a key, stood in one corner of the room. The melted wax remains of a candle, burned to the end of its wick, lay nearby.

The landlady shook her head. "A good way to burn the house down," she complained. "I'll have to speak to

185

Mr. Maax. Not like him to be so careless."

The movers, burdened with the chest, paid no attention to her. The assistant growled as they started down the stairs. "Must be lined with lead. Never knew a chest so heavy before!"

"Heavy wood," his companion commented shortly, not wishing to waste his breath.

"Wonder why he's dumpin' such a good chest?" the assistant asked later as the truck approached an abandoned quarry near the edge of town.

The chief mover glanced at him slyly. "I guess I know," he said. "He bought it off Jason Kinkle. And Kinkle never told him the story on it. But he found out later, I figure — and that's why he's ditchin' it."

The assistant's interest picked up. "What's the story?" he asked.

They drove into the quarry grounds and got out of the truck.

"Kinkle bought it dirt cheap at an auction," the mover explained as they lifted out the chest. "Auction of old Henry Stubberton's furniture."

The assistant's eyes widened as they started up a steep slope with the chest. "You mean the Stubberton they found murdered in a . . . "

"*In a chest!*" the mover finished for him. "*This chest!*"

Neither spoke again until they set down the chest at the edge of a steep quarry shaft.

Glancing down at the deep water which filled the bottom of the shaft, the mover wiped the sweat from his face. "A pretty sight they say he was. All doubled up an turnin' black. Seems he wasn't dead when they shut him in, though. They say he must have tried to claw his way out! When they opened the chest, they found one of his fingers jammed up under the lid, near the lock! Tried to pick the lock with his fingernail, it looked like!"

The assistant shuddered. "Let's be rid of it, then. It's bad luck sure!"

The mover nodded. "Take hold and shove."

They strained together and in another second the calamander chest slipped over the edge of the quarry and hurtled toward the pool of black water far below. There was one terrific splash and then it sank from sight like a stone.

"That's good riddance and another tenner for me," the mover commented.

Oddly enough, however, he never collected the tenner, for after that day Mr. Ernest Maax dropped completely out of sight. He was never seen or heard of again. The disgruntled mover, never on the best of terms with the police, shrugged off the loss of the tenner and neglected to report the disposal of the chest. And since the landlady had never learned the mover's name, nor where he intended taking the chest, her sparse information was of no help in the search.

The police concluded that Maax had got into some scrape, changed his name, and effected a permanent change of locale.

Understanding the Story

1. When Ernest Maax bought the calamander chest, he was afraid that the low price might be due to a hidden defect. In a way, he was right. What was the chest's hidden defect?

2. What is the most important conflict in the story? What happens to Maax at the end of the story?

3. Edgar Allan Poe, one of the greatest writers of mystery stories, said that every event and detail in a short story should contribute to a single effect on the reader. What single effect does the author of "The Calamander Chest" try to achieve? Find the paragraph on page 183 that begins, "As soon as he fell asleep . . ." List five phrases in this paragraph that contribute to that single effect.

4. If you were Ernest Maax, what would you have done to escape from the chest?

Understanding Literature

"From the Indies, Sir! . . . Genuine calamander wood — a rare good buy, sir!" With these words, Joseph Payne Brennan gets both the reader and Ernest Maax interested in "The Calamander Chest," and he does not let either one off easily. The author of a short story or play plans every detail to catch and hold your interest. This careful arrangement of the setting, characters, and events around a basic conflict is called the *plot.*

Most stories and plays follow the same basic pattern. They begin by introducing the characters and the setting. They suggest at least one conflict that will catch your attention. Once the conflict is introduced, the events that follow, called *rising action,* help build your interest in what will happen.

As the action progresses, you become more and more involved until the story reaches the *climax,* or turning point. At this point, you learn how the main conflict will turn out. In "The Calamander Chest" the climax occurs on page 185, when Ernest Maax realizes he has fallen under the chest's mysterious spell, just as in his nightmare.

The events following the climax are called the *falling action,* or *resolution.* They answer your questions about the outcome and bring the story or play to an end. What do you find out from the resolution of "The Calamander Chest"?

Writing About the Story

Suppose you were producing a radio program that broadcasts horror shows. Think of a title and then write an introduction to be used each week in your broadcast. For example, one old radio show, "The Shadow," began each broadcast this way: "Who knows what evil lurks in the hearts of men? The Shadow knows."

Who knows what evil lurks in a pack of bubble gum? What if this "atrocious substance" we call gum were to come to life? What fiendish revenge would it seek on the giants who had crushed it between their jaws?

Steinbeck's tale is a **parody** (that is, a humorous imitation) of the great detective and horror stories of Edgar Allan Poe (1809–1849). The author's pretended reluctance to discuss the case is a Poe trademark, as is the stiff, formal style of the opening paragraphs. The stilted language Steinbeck imitates here may seem inappropriate for a tale about bubble gum, but once you get past the formal opening you'll find the gummy villain a formidable foe who can make you tremble with fear — and shake with laughter.

The Affair at 7, Rue de M–

A short story by John Steinbeck

Illustrated by Leslie Morrill

I HAD HOPED to withhold from public scrutiny those rather curious events which have given me some concern for the past month. I knew of course that there was talk in the neighborhood. I have even heard some of the distortions current in my district, stories, I hasten to add, in which there is no particle of truth. However, my desire for privacy was shattered yesterday by a visit of two members of the fourth estate[1] who assured me that the story, or rather *a* story, had escaped the boundaries of my *arrondissement.*[2]

In the light of impending publicity I think it only fair to issue the true details of those happenings which have come to be known as The Affair at 7, rue de M——, in order that nonsense may not be added to a set of circumstances which are not without their *bizarrerie.*[3] I shall set down the events as they happened without comment, thereby allowing the public to judge of the situation.

At the beginning of the summer I carried my family to Paris and took up residence in a pretty little house at 7, rue de M——, a building which in another period had been the mews[4] of the great house beside it. The whole property is now owned and part of it inhabited by a noble French family of such age and purity

---

1. **fourth estate:** the press; newspaper.
2. *arrondissement* (ah·RAWN·dees·MAHN): French word for *district;* the city of Paris, France, is divided into twenty such districts.

3. bizarrerie (bee·zahr·re·REE): French word for *strangeness, peculiarity.*
4. **mews:** stables built around a courtyard.

that its members still consider the Bourbons[5] unacceptable as claimants to the throne of France.

To this pretty little converted stable with three floors of rooms above a well-paved courtyard, I brought my immediate family, consisting of my wife, my three children, two small boys and a grown daughter, and of course myself. Our domestic arrangement — in addition to the concierge[6] who, as you might say, came with the house — consists of a French cook of great ability, a Spanish maid, and my own secretary, a girl of Swiss nationality whose high attainments and ambitions are only equaled by her moral altitude. This then was our little family group when the events I am about to chronicle were ushered in.

If one must have an agency in this matter, I can find no alternative to placing not the blame but rather the authorship, albeit innocent, on my younger son John who has only recently attained his eighth year, a lively child of singular beauty and buck teeth.

This young man has, during the last several years in America, become not so much an addict as an aficionado[7] of that curious American practice, the chewing of bubble gum, and one of the pleasanter aspects of the early summer in Paris lay in the fact that the Cadet[8] John had neglected to bring any of the atrocious substance with him from America. The child's speech became clear and unobstructed and the hypnotized look went out of his eyes.

Alas, this delightful situation was not long to continue. An old family friend traveling in Europe brought as a present to the children a more than adequate supply of this beastly gum, thinking to do them a kindness. Thereupon the old familiar situation reasserted itself. Speech fought its damp way past a huge wad of the gum and emerged with the sound of a faulty water trap. The jaws were in constant motion, giving the face at best a look of agony while the eyes took on a glaze like those of a pig with a recently severed jugular.[9] Since I do not believe in inhibiting[10] my children I resigned myself to a summer not quite so pleasant as I had at first hoped.

On occasion I do not follow my ordinary practice of laissez faire.[11] When I am composing the material for a book or play or essay, in a word, when the utmost of concentration is required, I am prone to establish tyrannical rules for my own comfort

---

5. **Bourbons:** the family that ruled in France from 1589 to 1792.
6. **concierge** (kon·see·AYRZH): a caretaker.
7. **aficionado** (uh·FISH·ee·uh·NAH·doh): an enthusiastic follower.

8. **Cadet** (kuh·DET): the youngest son in a family.
9. **severed jugular:** a slashed throat.
10. **inhibiting** (in·HIB·uh·ting): restricting.
11. **laissez faire** (LES·ay FAYR): from the French, *let be*; here, allowing children to act for themselves.

and effectiveness. One of these rules is that there shall be neither chewing nor bubbling while I am trying to concentrate. This rule is so thoroughly understood by the Cadet John that he accepts it as one of the laws of nature and does not either complain or attempt to evade the ruling. It is his pleasure and my solace for my son to come sometimes into my workroom, there to sit quietly beside me for a time. He knows he must be silent, and when he has remained so for as long a time as his character permits, he goes out quietly, leaving us both enriched by the wordless association.

Two weeks ago in the late afternoon, I sat at my desk composing a short essay for *Figaro Littéraire*,[12] an essay which later aroused some controversy when it was printed under the title "Sartre Resartus."[13] I had come to that passage concerning the proper clothing for the soul when, to my astonishment and chagrin, I heard the unmistakable soft plopping sound of a bursting balloon of bubble gum. I looked sternly at my offspring and saw him chewing away. His cheeks were colored with embarrassment and the muscles of his jaws stood rigidly out.

"You know the rule," I said coldly.

To my amazement tears came into his eyes and while his jaws continued to masticate[14] hugely, his blubbery voice forced its way past the huge lump of bubble gum in his mouth.

"I didn't do it," he cried.

"What do you mean, you didn't do it?" I demanded in a rage. "I distinctly heard and now I distinctly see."

"Oh sir!" he moaned, "I really didn't. I'm not chewing it, sir. It's chewing me."

---

12. *Figaro Littéraire* (FIG·ah·roh Lit·ay·RAYR): the weekly literary supplement to a Paris newspaper.
13. "Sartre Resartus" (SAHR·truh ri·SAHR·tuhs): The title of the narrator's article about French philosopher Jean-Paul Sartre is a pun on *Sartor Resartus* (The Barber Re-barbered), a famous philosophical satire by the nineteenth century writer Thomas Carlyle.

---

14. **masticate**: to chew.

For a moment I inspected him closely. He is an honest child, only under the greatest pressure of gain permitting himself an untruth. I had the horrible thought that the bubble gum had finally had its way and that my son's reason was tottering. If this were so, it were better to tread softly. Quickly I put out my hand. "Lay it here," I said kindly.

My child manfully tried to disengage the gum from his jaws. "It won't let me go," he sputtered.

"Open up," I said and then inserting my fingers in his mouth I seized hold of the large lump of gum and after a struggle in which my fingers slipped again and again, managed to drag it forth and to deposit the ugly blob on my desk on top of a pile of white manuscript paper.

For a moment it seemed to shudder there on the paper and then with an easy slowness it began to undulate, to swell and recede with the exact motion of being chewed while my son and I regarded it with popping eyes.

For a long time we watched it while I drove through my mind for some kind of explanation. Either I was dreaming or some principle as yet unknown had taken its seat in the pulsing bubble gum on the desk. I am not unintelligent. While I considered the indecent thing, a hundred little thoughts and glimmerings of understanding raced through my brain. At last I asked, "How long

has it been chewing you?"

"Since last night," he replied.

"And when did you first notice this, this propensity[15] on its part?"

He spoke with perfect candor, "I will ask you to believe me, sir," he said. "Last night before I went to sleep I put it under my pillow as is my invariable custom. In the night I was awakened to find that it was in my mouth. I again placed it under my pillow and this morning it was again in my mouth, lying very quietly. When, however, I became

---

15. **propensity:** a tendency (to do something).

thoroughly awakened, I was conscious of a slight motion and shortly afterward the situation dawned on me that I was no longer master of the gum. It had taken its head. I tried to remove it, sir, and could not. You yourself with all of your strength have seen how difficult it was to extract. I came to your workroom to await your first disengagement, wishing to acquaint you with my difficulty. Oh, Daddy, what do you think has happened?"

The cancerous thing held my complete attention.

"I must think," I said. "This is something a little out of the ordinary, and I do not believe it should be passed over without some investigation."

As I spoke a change came over the gum. It ceased to chew itself and seemed to rest for a while, and then with a flowing movement like those monocellular animals of the order *Paramecium*,[16] the gum slid across the desk straight in the direction of my son. For a moment I was stricken with astonishment and for an even longer time I failed to discern its intent.[17] It dropped to his knee, climbed horribly up his shirt front. Only then did I understand. It was trying to get back into his mouth. He looked down on it paralyzed with fright.

"Stop," I cried, for I realized that my third-born was in danger and at such times I am capable of a violence which verges on the murderous. I seized the monster from his chin and striding from my workroom, entered the salon, opened the window and hurled the thing into the busy traffic on the rue de M——.

I believe it is the duty of a parent to ward off those shocks which may cause dreams or trauma whenever possible. I went back to my study to find young John sitting where I had left him. He was staring into space.

---

16. monocellular animals of the order *Paramecium* (PAR·uh·MEE·see·uhm): one-celled protozoa.
17. **discern its intent:** understand its goal.

There was a troubled line between his brows.

"Son," I said, "you and I have seen something which, while we know it to have happened, we might find difficult to describe with any degree of success to others. I ask you to imagine the scene if we should tell this story to the other members of the family. I greatly fear we should be laughed out of the house."

"Yes, sir," he said passively.

"Therefore I am going to propose to you, my son, that we lock the episode deep in our memories and never mention it to a soul as long as we live." I waited for his assent and when it did not come, glanced up at his face to see it a ravaged field of terror. His eyes were starting out of his head. I turned in the direction of his gaze. Under the door there crept a paper-thin sheet which, once it had entered the room, grew to a gray blob and rested on the rug, pulsing and chewing. After a moment it moved again by pseudopodian progression[18] toward my son.

I fought down panic as I rushed at it. I grabbed it up and flung it on my desk, then seizing an African war club from among the trophies on the wall, a dreadful instrument studded with brass, I beat the gum until I was breathless and it a torn piece of plastic fabric. The moment I rested, it drew itself together and for a few moments chewed very rapidly as though it chuckled at my impotence, and then inexorably it moved toward my son, who by this time was crouched in a corner moaning with terror.

Now a coldness came over me. I picked up the filthy thing and wrapped it in my handkerchief, strode out of the house, walked three blocks to the Seine and flung the handkerchief into the slowly moving current.

I spent a good part of the afternoon soothing my son and trying to reassure him that his fears were over. But such was his nervousness that my wife insisted that I call a doctor. I did not at that time dare to tell her why I could not obey her wish.

I was awakened, indeed the whole house was awakened, in the night by a terrified muffled scream from the children's room. I took the stairs two at a time and burst into the room, flicking the light switch as I went. John sat up in bed squalling, while with his fingers he dug at his half-open mouth, a mouth which horrifyingly went right on chewing. As I looked a bubble emerged between his fingers and burst with a wet plopping sound.

What chance of keeping our secret now! All had to be explained, but with the plopping gum pinned to

18. **pseudopodian** (SOO·doh·POH·dee·uhn) **progression**: literally, *movement on a false foot* — the way in which one-celled animals move forward.

a breadboard with an ice pick the explanation was easier than it might have been. And I am proud of the help and comfort given me. There is no strength like that of the family. Our French cook solved the problem by refusing to believe it even when she saw it. It was not reasonable, she explained, and she was a reasonable member of a reasonable people.

For two weeks we were besieged by the monster. We burned it in the fireplace, causing it to splutter in blue flames and melt in a nasty mess among the ashes. Before morning it had crawled through the keyhole of the children's room, leaving a trail of wood ash on the door, and again we were awakened by screams from the Cadet.

In despair I drove far into the country and threw it from my automobile. It was back before morning. Apparently it had crept to the highway and placed itself in the Paris traffic until picked up by a truck tire. When we tore it from John's mouth it had still the nonskid marks of Michelin[19] imprinted in its side.

Fatigue and frustration will take their toll. In exhaustion, with my will to fight back sapped, and after we had tried every possible method to lose or destroy the bubble gum, I placed it at last under a bell jar which I ordinarily use to cover my microscope. I collapsed in a chair to gaze at it with weary defeated eyes. John slept in his little bed backed by my assurance that I would not let the Thing out of my sight.

I lighted a pipe and settled back to watch it. Inside the bell jar the gray tumorous lump moved restlessly about searching for some means of exit from its prison. Now and then it paused as though in thought and emitted a bubble in my direction. I could feel the hatred it had for me. In my weariness I found my mind slipping into an analysis which had so far escaped me.

The background I had been over hurriedly. It must be that from constant association with the lambent[20] life which is my son, the magic of life had been created in the bubble gum. And with life had come intelligence, not the manly open intelligence of the boy, but an evil calculating wiliness.

How could it be otherwise? Intelligence without the soul to balance it must of necessity be evil. The gum had not absorbed any part of John's soul.

Very well, said my mind, now we have a hypothesis[21] of its origin, let us consider its nature. What does it think? What does it want? What does it need? My mind leaped like a terrier. It needs and wants to get back to its host, my son. It wants to be chewed. It must be chewed to survive.

Inside the bell jar the gum inserted a thin wedge of itself under the heavy glass foot and constricted so that the whole jar lifted a fraction of an inch. I laughed as I drove it back. I laughed with almost insane triumph. I had the answer.

In the dining room I procured a clear plastic plate, one of a dozen my wife had bought for picnics in the country. Then turning the bell jar over and securing the monster in its bottom, I smeared the mouth of the jar with a heavy plastic cement guaranteed to be water-, alcohol- and acidproof. I forced the plate over the opening and pressed it down until the glue took hold and bound the plate to the glass, making an airtight container. And last I turned the jar upright again and adjusted the reading light so that I could observe every movement of my prisoner.

---

19. **Michelin**: a French manufacturer of tires.
20. **lambent**: softly bright or radiant.

---

21. **hypothesis** (hy·POTH·ih·sis): a theory.

Again it searched the circle for escape. Then it faced me and emitted a great number of bubbles very rapidly. I could hear the little bursting plops through the glass.

"I have you, my beauty," I cried. "I have you at last."

That was a week ago. I have not left the side of the bell jar since, and have only turned my head to accept a cup of coffee. When I go to the bathroom, my wife takes my place. I can now report the following hopeful news.

During the first day and night, the bubble gum tried every means to escape. Then for a day and a night it seemed to be agitated and nervous as though it had for the first time realized its predicament. The third day it went to work with its chewing motion, only the action was speeded up greatly, like the chewing of a baseball fan. On the fourth day it began to weaken and I observed with joy a kind of dryness on its once slick and shiny exterior.

I am now in the seventh day and I believe it is almost over. The gum is

lying in the center of the plate. At intervals it heaves and subsides. Its color has turned to a nasty yellow. Once today when my son entered the room, it leaped up excitedly, then seemed to realize its hopelessness and collapsed on the plate. It will die tonight I think and only then will I dig a deep hole in the garden, and I will deposit the sealed bell jar and cover it up and plant geraniums over it.

It is my hope that this account will set straight some of the silly tales that are being hawked in the neighborhood.

About JOHN STEINBECK

Rancher, cotton picker, road worker, deck hand, student, writer: John Steinbeck was all of these. He was born in Salinas, California, in 1902, and grew up on the rich farm lands there along the Pacific coast. He studied science at nearby Stanford University, and though he never finished his degree, it was there in the laboratory that he learned to pay close attention to whatever was in front of him and to write down clear, simple observations. He would use these skills all of his life.

As a young man, Steinbeck worked beside the farmers, fishermen, migrants, and ranchers of the Pacific coast. Out of his varied experiences came a deep respect for the ways his co-workers expressed their humanity. Later he wrote of what he had seen: courage, humor, poverty, endurance, cruelty, and compassion. Whether he wrote about California cannery workers or about Norwegian fishermen, his realistic insights have made his work popular in many countries and with many kinds of people. In 1962, Steinbeck was awarded the Nobel Prize for Literature; he was the seventh American-born author to earn that recognition.

John Steinbeck felt that writing was a very serious profession, an honor. He thought that the writer "is charged with exposing our many grievous faults and failures, with dredging up to the light our dark and dangerous dreams for the purpose of improvement . . . and is delegated to . . . celebrate man's proven capacity for greatness of heart and spirit—for gallantry in defeat—for courage, compassion, and love."

■ Understanding the Story

1. The narrator tries to kill the bubble gum by throwing it into traffic, fire, and water. How does he finally manage to outwit the gum?

2. What is the climax of the story?

3. Steinbeck often uses exaggeration to make you laugh. Find two examples of exaggeration in this story.

4. What television program or commercial would you most like to ridicule—that is, make fun of? Tell which program or commercial you most dislike, and why.

5. Make up a brand name for the bubble gum in the story, and write an advertising slogan to appear on the bubble gum package.

■ Understanding Literature

In "The Affair at 7, Rue de M——," John Steinbeck makes fun of Edgar Allan Poe's writing style and subject matter by imitating them. A humorous imitation of an author's style or of a type of literature is called a *parody*. Steinbeck's story is a parody of Poe's detective stories. Steinbeck mocks the following elements:

a. Poe's use of foreign settings. Like many of Poe's mystery stories, Steinbeck's "Affair" takes place in Paris, although the specific location (Rue de M——) is hidden to pretend a need for secrecy.

b. Poe's choice of subject matter: horror and the supernatural.

c. Poe's use of difficult words and words from other languages.

d. Poe's use of two adjectives or two verbs to increase the effect. For example, the narrator tried every possible method to *"lose or destroy* the bubble gum." He gazed at it with *"weary defeated* eyes."

The narrator figures out how to destroy the gum by using the process of *deductive reasoning.* This process begins with one statement; in this case: Life and intelligence had come into the gum because it had been so closely associated with the narrator's son — that is, it had been constantly chewed. Starting with this theory, the narrator then deduces that the gum must be chewed to survive.

Poe's use of deductive reasoning to solve crimes inspired the creation of the detective story and many legendary sleuths, from Sherlock Holmes to the film detectives of today.

■ Writing About the Story

Summarize the plot of a story that begins with someone or something digging up the bubble gum and breaking the glass bell jar. Tell who your main character will be. Next, describe the setting, and outline the important events leading up to the story's climax. Then explain the climax and its resolution.

From

An Old Cornish Litany

A traditional English verse

From Ghoulies and Ghosties,
And long-leggity Beasties,
And all Things that go bump in the Night,
Good Lord deliver us.

Illustration by Blanche Sims

The Television

A poem by Geoffrey Godbey

Unaccustomed
to movement
and real life
it crept
to the window
and
delicately
lifting the blind
with a long
aluminum
tentacle,
sat
looking out
at the night.

Illustration by Richard Brown

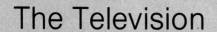

Johanna

A short story by Jane Yolen

Illustrated by Christa Kieffer

Deer appear in legends and myths from all over the world, often as enchanted animals that once were people. When the Greek hunter Acteon saw the goddess Artemis bathing, he was transformed into a stag and then killed by his own men. The mines of ancient Cornwall were thought to be haunted by buccas, the spirits of enslaved miners who had turned into deer. Deer were also common in Native American mythology, usually appearing as the hero's close friend or relative. In China, however, the Celestial Stag was a troublesome spirit who changed shape whenever it suited his mischievous purposes. Whatever the culture, the deer remains a source of mystery and magic.

THE FOREST WAS DARK and the snow-covered path was merely an impression left on Johanna's moccasined feet.

If she had not come this way countless daylit times, Johanna would never have known where to go. But Hartwood was familiar to her, even in the unfamiliar night. She had often picnicked in the cool, shady copses and grubbed around the tall oak trees. In a hard winter like this one, a family could subsist for days on acorn stew.

Still, this was the first night she had ever been out in the forest, though she had lived by it all her life. It was tradition — no, more than that — that members of the Chevril family did not venture into the midnight forest. "Never, never go to the woods at night," her mother said, and it was not a warning as much as a command. "Your father went though he was told not to. He never returned."

And Johanna had obeyed. Her father's disappearance was still in her memory, though she remembered nothing else of him. He was not the first of the Chevrils to go that way. There had been a great-uncle and two girl cousins who had likewise "never returned." At least, that was what Johanna had been told. Whether they had disappeared into the maw[1] of the city that lurked over several mountains to the west, or into the hungry jaws of a wolf or bear, was never made clear. But Johanna, being an obedient girl, always came into the house with the setting sun.

For sixteen years she had listened to that warning. But

---

1. **maw**: the mouth.

tonight, with her mother pale and sightless, breathing brokenly in the bed they shared, Johanna had no choice. The doctor, who lived on the other side of the wood, must be fetched. He lived in the cluster of houses that rimmed the far side of Hartwood, a cluster that was known as the "Village," though it was really much too small for such a name. The five houses of the Chevril family that clung together, now empty except for Johanna and her mother, were not called a village though they squatted on as much land.

Usually the doctor himself came through the forest to visit the Chevrils. Once a year he made the trip. Even when the grandparents and uncles and cousins had been alive, the village doctor came only once a year. He was gruff with them and called them "Strong as beasts," and went away never even offering a tonic. They needed none. They were healthy.

But the long, cruel winter had sapped Johanna's mother's strength. She lay for days silent, eyes cloudy and unfocused, barely taking in the acorn gruel that Johanna spooned for her. And at last Johanna had said: "I will fetch the doctor."

Her mother had grunted "no" each day, until this evening. When Johanna mentioned the doctor again, there had been no answering voice. Without her mother's no, Johanna made up her own mind. She *would* go.

If she did not get through the woods and back with the doctor before dawn, she felt it would be too late. Deep inside she knew she should have left before, even when her mother did not want her to go. And so she ran as quickly as she dared, following the small, twisting path through Hartwood by feel.

At first Johanna's guilt and the unfamiliar night were a burden, making her feel heavier than usual. But as she continued running, the crisp night air seemed to clear her head. She felt unnaturally alert, as if she had suddenly begun to discover new senses.

The wind moulded her short dark hair to her head. For the first time she felt graceful and light, almost beautiful.

Her feet beat a steady tattoo[2] on the snow as she ran, and she felt neither cold nor winded. Her steps lengthened as she went.

Suddenly a broken branch across the path tangled in her legs. She went down heavily on all fours, her breath caught in her throat. As she got to her feet, she searched the darkness ahead. Were there other branches waiting?

Even as she stared, the forest seemed to grow brighter. The light from the full moon must be finding its way into the heart of the woods. It was a comforting thought.

She ran faster now, confident of her steps. The trees seemed to rush by. There would be plenty of time.

She came at last to the place where the woods stopped, and cautiously she ranged along the last trees, careful not to be silhouetted against the sky. Then she halted.

She could hear nothing moving, could see nothing that threatened. When she was sure, she edged out onto the short meadow that ran in a downward curve to the back of the village.

Once more she stopped. This time she turned her head to the left and right. She could smell the musk of the farm animals on the wind, blowing faintly up to her. The moon beat down upon her head and, for a moment, seemed to ride on her broad, dark shoulder.

Slowly she paced down the hill toward the line of houses that stood like teeth in a jagged row. Light streamed out of the rear windows, making threatening little earthbound moons on the graying snow.

She hesitated.

A dog barked. Then a second began, only to end his call in a whine.

A voice cried out from the house furthest on the right, a woman's voice, soft and soothing. "Be quiet, Boy."

The dog was silenced.

She dared a few more slow steps toward the village, but her fear seemed to proceed her. As if catching its scent, the first dog barked lustily again.

---

2. **tattoo:** a drum beat.

"Boy! Down!" It was a man this time, shattering the
night with authority.

She recognized it at once. It was the doctor's voice. She
edged toward its sound. Shivering with relief and dread,
she came to the backyard of the house on the right and
waited. In her nervousness, she moved one foot restlessly,
pawing the snow down to the dead grass. She wondered
if her father, her great-uncle, her cousins had felt this fear
under the burning eye of the moon.

The doctor, short and too stout for his age, came out of
the back door, buttoning his breeches with one hand. In
the other he carried a gun. He peered out into the darkness.

"Who's there?"

She stepped forward into the yard, into the puddle of
light. She tried to speak her name, but she suddenly could
not recall it. She tried to tell why she had come, but nothing passed her closed throat. She shook her head to clear
the fear away.

The dog barked again, excited, furious.

"My heavens," the doctor said, "it's a deer."

She spun around and looked behind her, following his
line of sight. There was nothing there.

"That's enough meat to last the rest of this cruel winter,"
he said. He raised the gun, and fired.

206

◼ Understanding the Story

1. What command had Johanna received about the forest? What reason had her mother given for this command?

2. What happened to Johanna at the end of the story?

3. How does the setting contribute to the story? Could you change the setting without changing the way the story ends? If so, suggest a different setting.

4. Throughout the story, the author drops hints about what will happen at the end. For example, the doctor said that the Chevrils were ''strong as beasts.'' Find one other clue that prepares you for the ending.

5. If you could change into a wild or domestic animal, what animal would you choose? Explain why.

◼ Understanding Literature

Certain themes, plots, and types of characters occur over and over again in stories, no matter where or when they were written. The ability to recognize these universal elements in literature will add to your enjoyment and understanding of what you read.

''Johanna'' is a story about *metamorphosis*. The term *metamorphosis* means a change in form. Scientists use it to mean a marked change in the appearance of an animal during its life cycle. Some caterpillars, for instance, metamorphose, or change, into moths and butterflies.

In literature, metamorphosis refers to a magical change, especially of humans into animals or animals into humans. This theme, which is common to all cultures, seems to express the idea that humans, animals, and nature are closely related.

Though metamorphosis is a magical change, it usually does not occur suddenly. Before Johanna changes into a deer, author Jane Yolen prepares you for that change by giving animal qualities to Johanna and her family. For example, Johanna's mother ''grunted 'no' '' each day. When Johanna stumbles in the darkness, she goes down ''heavily on all fours.'' When she runs again, she runs so swiftly that ''the trees seemed to rush by.'' In order to understand the story, we have to realize what has happened to Johanna and why the doctor points the gun at her. These clues help us figure out the story's ending.

◼ Writing About the Story

Did Johanna get away? Was she killed? Write a paragraph that would follow the last sentence in the story. Tell what happened to Johanna.

The Ballad of the Harp-Weaver

A poem by Edna St. Vincent Millay

"Son," said my mother,
   When I was knee-high,
"You've need of clothes to cover you,
   And not a rag have I.

"There's nothing in the house
   To make a boy breeches,
Nor shears to cut a cloth with,
   Nor thread to take stitches.

"There's nothing in the house
   But a loaf-end of rye,
And a harp with a woman's head
   Nobody will buy,"
   And she began to cry.

That was in the early fall.
   When came the late fall,
"Son," she said, "the sight of you
   Makes your mother's blood crawl, —

"Little skinny shoulder-blades
   Sticking through your clothes!
And where you'll get a jacket from
   God above knows.

"It's lucky for me, lad,
   Your daddy's in the ground,
And can't see the way I let
   His son go around!"
   And she made a queer sound.

Illustrations by George Gershinowitz

That was in the late fall.
　　When the winter came,
I'd not a pair of breeches
　　Nor a shirt to my name.

I couldn't go to school,
　　Or out of doors to play.
And all the other little boys
　　Passed our way.

"Son," said my mother,
　　"Come, climb into my lap,
And I'll chafe[1] your little bones
　　While you take a nap."

And, oh, but we were silly
　　For half an hour or more,
Me with my long legs
　　Dragging on the floor,

A-rock-rock-rocking
　　To a mother-goose rhyme!
Oh, but we were happy
　　For half an hour's time!

But there was I, a great boy,
　　And what would folks say
To hear my mother singing me
　　To sleep all day,
　　In such a daft[2] way?

Men say the winter
　　Was bad that year;
Fuel was scarce,
　　And food was dear.

A wind with a wolf's head
　　Howled about our door,
And we burned up the chairs
　　And sat upon the floor.

---

1. **chafe:** to warm by rubbing.

2. **daft:** crazy.

All that was left us
  Was a chair we couldn't break,
And the harp with a woman's head
  Nobody would take,
  For song or pity's sake.

The night before Christmas
  I cried with the cold,
I cried myself to sleep
  Like a two-year-old.

And in the deep night
  I felt my mother rise,
And stare down upon me
  With love in her eyes.

I saw my mother sitting
  On the one good chair,
A light falling on her
  From I couldn't tell where,

Looking nineteen,
  And not a day older,
And the harp with a woman's head
  Leaned against her shoulder.

Her thin fingers, moving
  In the thin, tall strings,
Were weav-weav-weaving
  Wonderful things.

Many bright threads,
  From where I couldn't see,
Were running through the harp-strings
  Rapidly,

And gold threads whistling
  Through my mother's hand.
I saw the web grow,
  And the pattern expand.

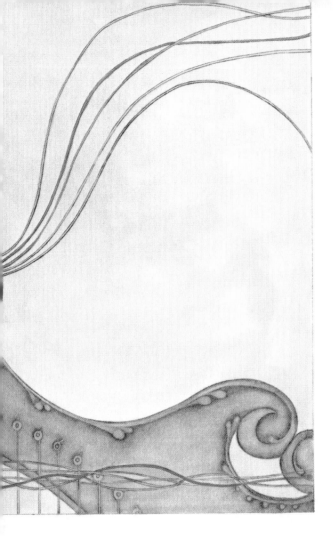

She wove a pair of breeches
    Quicker than that!
She wove a pair of boots
    And a little cocked hat.

She wove a pair of mittens,
    She wove a little blouse,
She wove all night
    In the still, cold house.

She sang as she worked,
    And the harp-strings spoke;
Her voice never faltered,
    And the thread never broke.
    And when I awoke, —

There sat my mother
    With the harp against her shoulder,
Looking nineteen,
    And not a day older,

A smile about her lips,
    And a light about her head,
And her hands in the harp-strings
    Frozen dead.

And piled up beside her
    And toppling to the skies,
Were the clothes of a king's son,
    Just my size.

She wove a child's jacket,
    And when it was done
She laid it on the floor
    And wove another one.

She wove a red cloak
    So regal[3] to see,
"She's made it for a king's son,"
    I said, "and not for me."
    But I knew it was for me.

---

3. **regal**: royal; "fit for a king."

Something Bright

A short story by Zenna Henderson

Illustrated by Nancy Schill

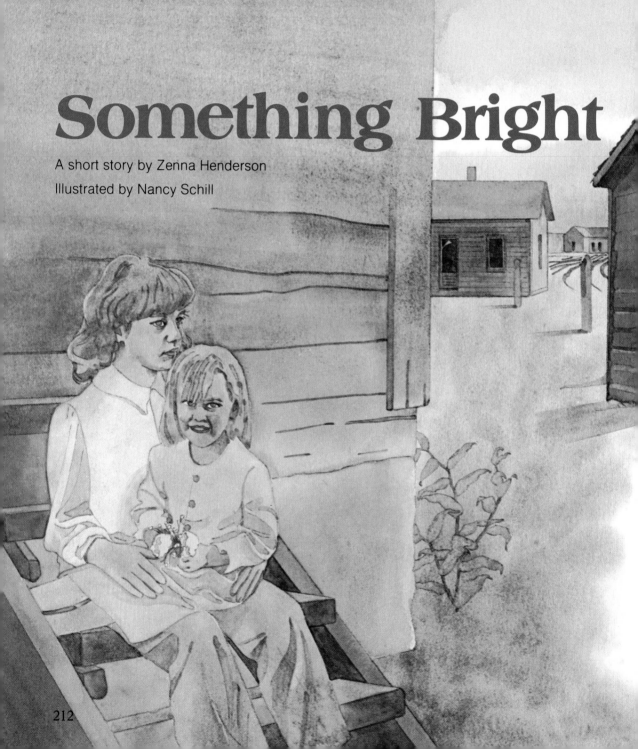

Most science fiction stories take place in the future or "long ago, in a galaxy far away." But in this strange tale, creatures from another dimension have traveled through time and space, arriving in America during the Great Depression of the 1930s when times were hard, and jobs and money scarce.

DO YOU REMEMBER the Depression? That black shadow across time? That hurting place in the consciousness of the world? Maybe not. Maybe it's like asking do you remember the Dark Ages.[1] Except what would I know about the price of eggs in the Dark Ages? I knew plenty about prices in the Depression.

If you had a quarter — *first find your quarter* — and five hungry kids, you could supper them on two cans of soup and a loaf of day-old bread, or two quarts of milk and a loaf of day-old bread. It was filling and — in an afterthought kind of way — nourishing. But if you were one of the hungry five, you eventually began to feel erosion set in, and your teeth ached for substance.

But to go back to eggs. Those were a precious commodity. You savored them slowly or gulped them eagerly — unmistakably as eggs — boiled or fried. That's one reason why I remember Mrs. Klevity. She had eggs for *breakfast!*

And *every day!* That's one reason why I remember Mrs. Klevity.

I didn't know about the eggs the time she came over to see Mom, who had just got home from a twelve-hour day, cleaning up after other people at thirty cents an hour. Mrs. Klevity lived in the same court as we did. Courtesy called it a court because we were all dependent on the same shower house and two toilets that occupied the shack square in the middle of the court.

All of us except the Big House, of course. It had a bathroom of its own and even a radio blaring "Nobody's Business" and "Should I Reveal" and had ceiling lights that didn't dangle nakedly at the end of a cord. But then it really wasn't a part of the court. Only its back door shared our area, and even that was different. It had *two* back doors in the same frame — a screen one and a wooden one!

Our own two-room place had a distinction, too. It had an upstairs. One room the size of our two. The Man

---

1. **Dark Ages:** the period A.D. 476–1000.

Upstairs lived up there. He was mostly only the sound of footsteps overhead and an occasional cookie for my sister Danna.

Anyway, Mrs. Klevity came over before Mom had time to put her shopping bag of work clothes down or even to unpleat the folds of fatigue that dragged her face down ten years or more of time to come. I didn't much like Mrs. Klevity. She made me uncomfortable. She was so solid and slow-moving and so nearly blind that she peered frighteningly wherever she went. She stood in the doorway as though she had been stacked there like bricks and a dress drawn hastily down over the stack and a face sketched on beneath a fuzz of hair. Us kids all gathered around to watch, except Danna who snuffled wearily into my neck. Day nursery or not, it was a long, hard day for a four-year-old.

"I wondered if one of your girls could sleep at my house this week." Her voice was as slow as her steps.

"At your house?" Mom massaged her hand where the shopping bag handles had crisscrossed it. "Come in. Sit down." We had two chairs and a bench and two apple boxes. The boxes scratched bare legs, but surely they couldn't scratch a stack of bricks.

"No, thanks." Maybe she couldn't bend! "My husband will be away several days and I don't like to be in the house alone at night."

"Of course," said Mom. "You must feel awfully alone."

The only aloneness she knew, what with five kids and two rooms, was the taut secretness of her inward thoughts as she mopped and swept and ironed in other houses. "Sure, one of the girls would be glad to keep you company." There was a darting squirm and LaNell was safely hidden behind the swaying of our clothes in the diagonally curtained corner of the other room, and Kathy knelt swiftly just beyond the dresser, out of sight.

"Anna is eleven." I had no place to hide, burdened as I was with Danna. "She's old enough. What time do you want her to come over?"

"Oh, bedtime will do." Mrs. Klevity peered out the door at the darkening sky. "Nine o'clock. Only it gets dark before then—"

"As soon as she has supper, she can come," said Mom, handling my hours as though they had no value to me. "Of course she has to go to school tomorrow."

"Only when it's dark," said Mrs. Klevity. "Day is all right. How much should I pay you?"

"Pay?" Mom gestured with one hand. "She has to sleep anyway. It doesn't matter to her where, once she's asleep. A favor for a friend."

I wanted to cry out: Whose favor for what friend? We hardly passed the time of day with Mrs. Klevity. I couldn't even remember Mr. Klevity except that he was straight and old and wrinkled. Uproot me and make me lie in a strange house, a strange dark, listening to

a strange breathing, feeling a strange warmth making itself part of me for all night long, seeping into me —

"Mom —" I said.

"I'll give her breakfast," said Mrs. Klevity. "And lunch money for each night she comes."

I resigned myself without a struggle. Lunch money each day — a whole dime! Mom couldn't afford to pass up such a gift.

"Thank you," I whispered as I went to get the can opener to open supper. For a night or two I could stand it.

—•◆•—

I felt all naked and unprotected as I stood in my flimsy crinkle cotton

pajamas, one bare foot atop the other, waiting for Mrs. Klevity to turn the bed down.

"We have to check the house first," she said thickly. "We can't go to bed until we check the house."

"Check the house?" I forgot my starchy stiff shyness enough to question. "What for?"

Mrs. Klevity peered at me in the dim light of the bedroom. They had *three* rooms for only the two of them! Even if there was no door to shut between the bedroom and the kitchen.

"I couldn't sleep," she said, "unless I looked first. I have to."

So we looked. Behind the closet

curtain, under the table — Mrs. Klevity even looked in the portable oven that sat near the two-burner stove in the kitchen.

When we came to the bed, I was moved to words again. "But we've been in here with the doors locked ever since I got here. What could possibly —"

"A prowler?" said Mrs. Klevity nervously, after a brief pause for thought. "A criminal?"

Mrs. Klevity pointed her face at me. I doubt if she could see me from that distance. "Doors make no difference," she said. "It might be when you least expect, so you have to expect all the time."

"I'll look," I said humbly. She was older than Mom. She was nearly blind.

"No," she said. "I have to. I couldn't be sure, else."

So I waited until she grunted and groaned to her knees, then bent stiffly to lift the limp spread. Her fingers hesitated briefly, then flicked the spread up. Her breath came out flat and finished. Almost disappointed, it seemed to me.

She turned the bed down and I crept across the gray, wrinkled sheets, and turning my back to the room, I huddled one ear on the flat pillow and lay tense and uncomfortable in the dark, as her weight shaped and reshaped the bed around me. There was a brief silence before I heard the soundless breathy shape of her words, "How long, how long?"

I wondered through my automatic *bless Mama and my brother and sisters* what it was that Mrs. Klevity was finding too long to bear.

After a restless waking, dozing sort of night that strange sleeping places held for me, I awoke to a thin chilly morning and the sound of Mrs. Klevity moving around. She had set the table for breakfast, a formality we never had time for at home. I would have preferred to run home to our usual breakfast of canned milk and Shredded Wheat, but instead I watched, fascinated, as Mrs. Klevity struggled with lighting the kerosene stove. She bent so close, peering at the burners with the match flaring in her hand that I

was sure the frowzy[2] brush of her hair would catch fire, but finally the burner caught instead and she turned her face toward me.

"One egg or two?" she asked.

"Eggs! Two!" Surprise wrung the exclamation from me. Her hand hesitated over the crumpled brown bag on the table. "No, no!" I corrected her thought hastily. "One. One is plenty," and sat on the edge of a chair watching as she broke an egg into the sizzling frying pan.

"Hard or soft?" she asked.

"Hard," I said casually, feeling very woman-of-the-worldish, dining out —

well, practically — and for breakfast, too! I watched Mrs. Klevity spoon the fat over the egg, her hair swinging stiffly forward when she peered. Once it even dabbled briefly in the fat, but she didn't notice, and as it swung back, it made a little shiny curve on her cheek.

"Aren't you afraid of the fire?" I asked as she turned away from the stove with the frying pan. "What if you caught on fire?"

"I did once." She slid the egg out onto my plate. "See?" She brushed her hair back on the left side and I could see the mottled[3] pucker of a large old scar. "It was before I got used to Here," she said, making Here more than the house, it seemed to me.

"That's awful," I said, hesitating with my fork.

"Go ahead and eat," she said. "Your egg will get cold." She turned back to the stove and I hesitated a minute more. Meals at a table you were supposed to ask a blessing, but — I ducked my head quickly and had a mouthful of egg before my soundless amen was finished.

After breakfast I hurried back to our house, my lunch-money dime clutched securely, my stomach not quite sure it liked fried eggs so early in the morning. Mom was ready to leave, her shopping bag in one hand, Danna swinging from the other, singing one of her baby songs. She *liked* the day nursery.

---

2. **frowzy**: dirty and untidy; messy.

3. **mottled**: spotted or blotched in coloring.

"I won't be back until late tonight," Mom said. "There's a quarter in the corner of the dresser drawer. You get supper for the kids and try to clean up this messy place. We don't have to be pigs just because we live in a place like this."

"Okay, Mom." I struggled with a snarl in my hair, the pulling making my eyes water. "Where you working today?" I spoke over the clatter in the other room where the kids were getting ready for school.

She sighed, weary before the day began. "I have three places today, but the last is Mrs. Paddington." Her face lightened. Mrs. Paddington sometimes paid a little extra or gave Mom discarded clothes or leftover food she didn't want. She was nice.

"You get along all right with Mrs. Klevity?" asked Mom as she checked her shopping bag for her work shoes.

"Yeah," I said. "But she's funny. She looks under the bed before she goes to bed."

Mom smiled. "I've heard of people like that."

"But, Mom, nothing coulda got in. She locked the door after I got there."

"People who look under beds don't always think straight," she said. "Besides, maybe she'd *like* to find something under there."

"But she's *got* a husband," I cried after her as she herded Danna across the court.

"There are other things to look for besides husbands," she called back.

I went back to put my shoes on and get my sweater. I looked at the bed. I got down on my stomach and peered under. *Other things to look for.* There was the familiar huddle of cardboard cartons we kept things in and the familiar dust fluffs and one green sock LaNell had lost last week, but nothing else.

I dusted my front off. I tied my lunch-money dime in the corner of a handkerchief, and putting my sweater on, left for school.

———————

I peered out into the windy wet semi-twilight. "Do I have to?"

"You said you would," said Mom. "Keep your promises. You should have gone before this. She's probably been waiting for you."

"I wanted to see what you brought from Mrs. Paddington's." LaNell and Kathy were playing in the corner with a lavender hug-me-tight[4] and a hat with green grapes on it. Deet was rolling an orange on the floor, softening it preliminary to poking a hole in it to suck the juice out.

"She cleaned a trunk out today," said Mom. "Mostly old things that belonged to her mother, but these two coats are nice and heavy. They'll be good covers tonight. It's going to be cold. Someday when I get time, I'll cut them up and make quilts." She sighed. Time was what she never had enough

——————

4. **hug-me-tight:** a type of woman's jacket that is warm and close-fitting.

of. "Better take a newspaper to hold over your head."

"Oh, Mom!" I huddled into my sweater. "It isn't raining now. I'd feel silly!"

"Well, then, scoot!" she said, her hand pressing my shoulder warmly, briefly.

I scooted, skimming quickly the flood of light from our doorway, and splishing through the shallow runoff stream that swept across the court. There was a sudden wild swirl of wind and a vindictive[5] splatter of heavy, cold raindrops that swept me, exhilarated, the rest of the way to Mrs. Klevity's house and under the shallow little roof that was just big enough to cover the back step. I knocked quickly, brushing

_____

5. **vindictive:** unforgiving; mean.

my disordered hair back from my eyes. The door swung open and I was in the shadowy, warm kitchen, almost in Mrs. Klevity's arms.

"Oh!" I backed up, laughing breathlessly. "The wind blew —"

"I was afraid you weren't coming." She turned away to the stove. "I fixed some hot cocoa."

I sat cuddling the warm cup in my hands, savoring the chocolate sip by sip. She had made it with milk instead of water, and it tasted rich and wonderful. But Mrs. Klevity was sharing my thoughts with the cocoa. In that brief moment when I had been so close to her, I had looked deep into her dim eyes and was feeling a vast astonishment. The dimness was only on top. Underneath — underneath —

I took another sip of cocoa. Her

eyes — almost I could have walked into them, it seemed like. Slip past the gray film, run down the shiny bright corridor, into the live young sparkle at the far end.

I looked deep into my cup of cocoa. Were all grownups like that? If you could get behind their eyes, were they different too? Behind Mom's eyes, was there a corridor leading back to youth and sparkle?

I finished the cocoa drowsily. It was still early, but the rain was drumming on the roof and it was the kind of night you curl up to if you're warm and fed. Sometimes you feel thin and cold on such nights, but I was feeling curl-uppy. So I groped under the bed for the paper bag that had my jamas in it. I couldn't find it.

"I swept today," said Mrs. Klevity, coming back from some far country of her thoughts. "I musta pushed it farther under the bed."

I got down on my hands and knees and peered under the bed. "Ooo!" I said. "What's shiny?"

Something snatched me away from the bed and flung me to one side. By the time I had gathered myself up off the floor and was rubbing a banged elbow, Mrs. Klevity's bulk was pressed against the bed, her head under it.

"Hey!" I cried indignantly, and then remembered I wasn't at home. I heard an odd whimpering sob and then Mrs. Klevity backed slowly away, still kneeling on the floor.

"Only the lock on the suitcase," she said. "Here's your jamas." She handed

me the bag and ponderously pulled herself upright again.

We went silently to bed after she had limped around and checked the house, even under the bed again. I heard that odd breathy whisper of a prayer and lay awake, trying to add up something shiny and the odd eyes and the whispering sob. Finally I shrugged in the dark and wondered what I'd pick for funny when I grew up. All grownups had some kind of funny.

The next night Mrs. Klevity couldn't get down on her knees to look under the bed. She'd hurt herself when she plumped down on the floor after yanking me away from the bed.

"You'll have to look for me tonight," she said slowly, nursing her knees. "Look good. Oh, Anna, look good!"

I looked as good as I could, not knowing what I was looking for.

"It should be under the bed," she said, her palms tight on her knees as she rocked back and forth. "But you can't be sure. It might miss completely."

"What might?" I asked, hunkering down by the bed.

She turned her face blindly toward me. "The way out," she said. "The way back again —"

"Back again?" I pressed my cheek to the floor again. "Well, I don't see anything. Only dark and suitcases."

"Nothing bright? Nothing? Nothing —" She tried to lay her face on her knees, but she was too unbendy to

manage it, so she put her hands over her face instead. Grownups aren't supposed to cry. She didn't quite, but her hands looked wet when she reached for the clock to wind it.

I lay in the dark, one strand of her hair tickling my hand where it lay on the pillow. Maybe she was crazy. I felt a thrill of terror fan out on my spine. I carefully moved my hand from under the lock of hair. How can you find a way *out* under a bed? I'd be glad when Mr. Klevity got home, eggs or no eggs, dime or no dime.

Somewhere in the darkness of the night, I was suddenly swimming to wakefulness, not knowing what was waking me but feeling that Mrs. Klevity was awake too.

"Anna." Her voice was small and light and silver. "Anna —"

"Hummm?" I murmured, my voice still drowsy.

"Anna, have you ever been away from home?" I turned toward her, trying in the dark to make sure it was Mrs. Klevity. She sounded so different.

"Yes," I said. "Once I visited Aunt Katie at Rocky Butte for a week."

"Anna . . ." I don't know whether she was even hearing my answers; her voice was almost a chant. ". . . Anna, have you ever been in prison?"

"No! Of course not!" I recoiled indignantly. "You have to be awfully bad to be in prison."

"Oh, no. Oh, no!" she sighed. "Not jail, Anna. Prison — prison. The weight of the flesh — bound about —"

"Oh," I said, smoothing my hands across my eyes. She was talking to a something deep in me that never got talked to, that hardly even had words. "Like when the wind blows the clouds across the moon and the grass whispers along the road and all the trees pull like balloons at their trunks and one star comes out and says 'Come' and the ground says 'Stay' and part of you tries to go and it hurts —" I could feel the slender roundness of ribs under my pressing hands. "And it hurts —"

"Oh Anna, Anna!" The soft, light voice broke. "You feel that way and you *belong* Here. You won't ever —"

The voice stopped and Mrs. Klevity rolled over. Her next words came thickly, as though a gray film were over them as over her eyes. "Are you awake, Anna? Go to sleep, child. Morning isn't yet."

I heard the heavy sigh of her breathing as she slept. And finally I slept too, trying to visualize what Mrs. Klevity would look like if she looked like the silvery voice in the dark.

I sat savoring my egg the next morning, letting thoughts slip in and out of my mind to the rhythm of my jaws. What a funny dream to have, to talk with a silver-voiced someone. To talk about the way blowing clouds and windy moonlight felt. But it wasn't a dream! I paused with my fork raised. At least not my dream. But how can you tell? If you're part of someone else's dream, can it still be real for you?

"Is something wrong with the egg?" Mrs. Klevity peered at me.

"No — no —" I said, hastily snatching the bite on my fork. "Mrs. Klevity —"

"Yes." Her voice was thick and heavy footed.

"Why did you ask me about being in prison?"

"Prison?" Mrs. Klevity blinked blindly. "Did I ask you about prison?"

"Someone did — I thought —" I faltered, shyness shutting down on me again.

"Dreams." Mrs. Klevity stacked her knife and fork on her plate. "Dreams."

——————

I wasn't quite sure I was to be at Klevity's the next evening. Mr. Klevity was supposed to get back sometime during the evening. But Mrs. Klevity welcomed me.

"Don't know when he'll get home," she said. "Maybe not until morning. If he comes early, you can go home to sleep and I'll give you your dime anyway."

"Oh, no," I said, Mom's teachings solidly behind me. "I couldn't take it if I didn't stay."

"A gift," said Mrs. Klevity.

We sat opposite one another until the silence stretched too thin for me to bear.

"In olden times," I said, snatching at the magic that drew stories from Mom, "when you were a little girl —"

"When I was a girl —" Mrs. Klevity rubbed her knees with reflective hands. "The other Where. The other When."

"In olden times," I persisted, "things were different then."

"Yes." I settled down comfortably, recognizing the reminiscent tone of voice. "You do crazy things when you are young." Mrs. Klevity leaned heavily on the table. "Things you have no business doing. You volunteer when you're young." I jerked as she lunged across the table and grabbed both my arms. "But I *am* young! Three years isn't an eternity. I *am* young!"

I twisted one arm free and pried at her steely fingers that clamped the other one.

"Oh." She let go. "I'm sorry. I didn't mean to hurt you."

She pushed back the tousled[6] brush of her hair.

"Look," she said, her voice almost silver again. "Under all this — this grossness, I'm still me. I thought I could adjust to anything, but I had no idea that they'd put me in such —" She tugged at her sagging dress. "Not the clothes!" she cried. "Clothes you can take off. But this —" Her fingers dug into her heavy shoulder and I could see the bulge of flesh between them.

"If I knew *anything* about the setup maybe I could locate it. Maybe I could call. Maybe —"

Her shoulders sagged and her eyelids dropped down over her dull eyes.

"It doesn't make any sense to you," she said, her voice heavy and thick again. "To you I'd be old even There.

6. **tousled** (TOW·suhld): tangled; mussed.

At the time it seemed like a perfect way to have an odd holiday and help out with research, too. But we got caught."

⊹⊱✾⊰⊹

She began to count her fingers, mumbling to herself. "Three years There, but Here that's — eight threes are —" She traced on the table with a blunt forefinger, her eyes close to the old, worn-out cloth.

223

"Mrs. Klevity." My voice scared me in the silence, but I was feeling the same sort of upsurge that catches you sometimes when you're playing-like and it gets so real. "Mrs. Klevity, if you've lost something, maybe I could look for it for you."

"You didn't find it last night," she said.

"Find what?"

She lumbered to her feet. "Let's look again. Everywhere. They'd surely be able to locate the house."

"What are we looking for?" I asked, searching the portable oven.

"You'll know it when we see it," she said.

And we searched the whole house. Oh, such nice things! Blankets, not tattered and worn, and even an extra one they didn't need. And towels with washrags that matched — and weren't rags. And uncracked dishes that matched! And glasses that weren't jars. And books. And money. Crisp new-looking bills in the little box in the bottom drawer — pushed back under some *extra* pillowcases. And clothes — lots and lots of clothes. All too big for any of us, of course, but my practiced eye had already visualized this, that, and the other cut down to dress us all like rich people.

I sighed as we sat wearily looking at one another. Imagine having so much and still looking for something else! It was bedtime and all we had for our pains were dirty hands and tired backs.

I scooted out to the bath house be-fore I undressed. I gingerly[7] washed the dirt off my hands under the cold of the shower and shook them dry on the way back to the house. Well, we had moved everything in the place, but nothing was what Mrs. Klevity looked for.

Back in the bedroom, I groped under the bed for my jamas and again had to lie flat and burrow under the bed for the tattered bag. Our moving around had wedged it back between two cardboard cartons. I squirmed under farther and tried to ease it out after shoving the two cartons a little farther apart. The bag tore, spilling out my jamas, so I grasped them in the bend of my elbow and started to back out.

Then the whole world seemed to ex-plode into brightness that pulsated and dazzled, that splashed brilliance into my astonished eyes until I winced them shut to rest their seeing and saw the dark inversions of the radiance behind my eyelids.[8]

I forced my eyes open again and looked sideways so the edge of my seeing was all I used until I got more accustomed to the glory.

Between the two cartons was an opening like a window would be, but lit-tle, little, into a wonderland of things I could never tell. Colors that had no names. Feelings that made windy moonlight a puddle of dust. I felt tears burn out of my eyes and start down my

---

7. **gingerly** (JIN•juhr•lee): very carefully; delicately.
8. **dark inversions . . . eyelids:** If you close your eyes after seeing a bright light (or **radiance**), you see dark spots where the brightest light was before.

cheeks, whether from brightness or wonder, I don't know. I blinked them away and looked again.

Someone was in the brightness, several someones. They were leaning out of the squareness, beckoning and calling — silver signals and silver sounds.

"Mrs. Klevity," I thought. "Something bright."

I took another good look at the shining people and the tree things that were like music bordering a road, and grass that was the song my evening grass hummed in the wind — a last, last look, and began to back out.

I scrambled to my feet, clutching my jamas. "Mrs. Klevity." She was still sitting at the table, as solid as a pile of bricks, the sketched face under the wild hair a sad, sad one.

"Yes, child." She hardly heard herself.

"Something bright —" I said.

⸻

Her heavy head lifted slowly, her blind face turned to me. "What, child?"

I felt my fingers bite into my jamas and the cords in my neck getting tight and my stomach clenching itself. "Something bright!" I thought I screamed. She didn't move. I grabbed her arm and dragged her off balance in her chair. "Something bright!"

"Anna." She righted herself on the chair. "Don't be mean."

I grabbed the bedspread and yanked it up. The light sprayed out like a sprinkler on a lawn.

Then *she* screamed. She put both hands up to her heavy face and screamed, "Leolienn! It's here! Hurry, hurry!"

"Mr. Klevity isn't here," I said. "He hasn't got back."

"I can't go without him! Leolienn!"

"Leave a note!" I cried. "If you're there, you can make them come back again and I can show him the right place!" The upsurge had passed make-believe and everything was realer than real.

Then, quicker than I thought she ever could move, she got paper and a pencil. She was scribbling away at the table as I stood there holding the spread. So I dropped to my knees and then to my stomach and crawled under the bed again. I filled my eyes with the brightness and beauty and saw, beyond it, serenity and orderliness and — and uncluttered cleanness. The miniature landscape was like a stage for a fairy tale — so small — so lovely.

And then Mrs. Klevity tugged at my ankle and I slid out, reluctantly, stretching my sight of the bright square until the falling of the spread broke it. Mrs. Klevity worked her way under the bed, her breath coming pantingly, her big,

226

ungainly body inching along awkwardly.

She crawled and crawled and crawled until she should have come up short against the wall, and I knew she must be funnelling down into the brightness, her face, head and shoulders so small, so lovely, like her silvery voice. But the rest of her, still gross and ugly, like a butterfly trying to skin out of its cocoon.

Finally only her feet were sticking out from under the bed and they thrashed and waved and didn't go anywhere, so I got down on the floor and put my feet against hers and braced myself against the dresser and pushed. And pushed and pushed. Suddenly there was a going, a finishing, and my feet dropped to the floor.

There, almost under the bed, lay Mrs. Klevity's shabby, black shoes, toes pointing away from each other. I picked them up in my hands, wanting, somehow, to cry. Her saggy lisle[9] stockings were still in the shoes.

Slowly I pulled all the clothes of Mrs. Klevity out from under the bed. They were held together by a thin skin, a sloughed off leftover of Mrs. Klevity that only showed, gray and lifeless, where her bare hands and face would have been, and her dull gray filmed eyes.

I let it crumple to the floor and sat there, holding one of her old shoes in my hand.

The door rattled, and it was gray, old, wrinkled Mr. Klevity.

"Hello, child," he said. "Where's my wife?"

"She's gone," I said, not looking at him. "She left you a note there on the table."

"Gone — ?" He left the word stranded in midair as he read Mrs. Klevity's note.

—◆◆◆—

The paper fluttered down. He yanked a dresser drawer open and snatched out spool-looking things, both hands full. Then he practically dived under the bed, his elbows thudding on the floor, to hurt hard. And there was only a wiggle or two, and *his* shoes slumped away from each other.

I pulled his cast[10] aside from under the bed and crawled under it myself. I saw the tiny picture frame — bright, bright, but so small.

I crept close to it, knowing I couldn't go in. I saw the tiny perfection of the road, the landscape, the people — the laughing people who crowded around the two new rejoicing figures — the two silvery, lovely young creatures who cried out in tiny voices as they danced. The girl one threw a kiss outward before they all turned away and ran up the winding white road together.

The frame began to   faster, faster, until it squeezed to a single bright bead and then blinked out.

---

9. **lisle** (LYL): knitted cotton.

10. **cast:** outer shell or covering. Mr. Klevity has shed his body the way a snake leaves its old skin.

All at once the house was empty and cold. The upsurge was gone. Nothing was real any more. All at once I whimpered, "My lunch money!"

I scrambled to my feet, tumbling Mrs. Klevity's clothes into a disconnected pile. I gathered up my jamas and leaned across the table to get my sweater. I saw my name on a piece of paper. I picked it up and read it.

Everything that is ours in this house now belongs to Anna-across-the-court, the little girl that's been staying with me at night.

Ahvlaree Klevity

I looked from the paper around the room. All for me? All for us? All this richness and wonder of good things? All this and the box in the bottom drawer, too? And a paper that said so, so that nobody could take them away from us.

A fluttering wonder filled my chest

and I walked stiffly around the three rooms, visualizing everything without opening a drawer or door. I stood by the stove and looked at the frying pan hanging above it. I opened the cupboard door. The paper bag of eggs was on the shelf. I reached for it, looking back over my shoulder almost guiltily.

The wonder drained out of me with a gulp. I ran back over to the bed and yanked up the spread. I knelt and hammered on the edge of the bed with my clenched fists. Then I leaned my forehead on my tight hands and felt my knuckles bruise me. My hands went limply to my lap, my head drooping.

I got up slowly and took the paper from the table, bundled my jamas under my arm and got the eggs from the cupboard. I turned the lights out and left.

I felt tears wash down from my eyes as I stumbled across the familiar yard in the dark. I don't know why I was crying — unless it was because I was homesick for something bright that I knew I would never have, and because I knew I could never tell Mom what really had happened.

Then the pale trail of light from our door caught me and I swept in on an astonished Mom, calling softly, because of the sleeping kids, "Mom! Mom! Guess what!"

——◆◆◆——

Yes, I remember Mrs. Klevity because she had eggs for *breakfast!* *Every day!* That's one of the reasons I remember her.

■ Understanding the Story

1. Why had the Klevitys left their homeland?

2. In what way is "Something Bright" a story about metamorphosis? Who changes, and what is the change?

3. Why do you think the author made Mrs. Klevity so physically unattractive?

4. At the end of the story, Anna says that she knew she "could never tell Mom what really had happened." What do you think she did tell her mother? Pretending to be Anna, write a brief dialogue that might follow after Anna says, "Mom! Guess what!" Write both what Anna said, and what her mother answered.

5. If you were Anna, would you have gone to the other world when you had the chance? Explain why or why not. Describe the kind of "other world" you would want to go to.

■ Understanding Literature

A skillful writer makes you eager to find out what will happen next. An exciting story contains *suspense,* uncertainty about how the story will end. *Suspense* comes from the Latin word *suspendere,* which means "to hang." A suspenseful story like "Something Bright" keeps you hanging on the next sentence, so curious that you can't help but read on.

An author builds suspense by keeping information from you and by dropping hints about what will happen later. Anna, the narrator, unfolds her story bit by bit. You see Mrs. Klevity through Anna's eyes as a slow-moving woman whose appearance and manner scare the children.

With Anna, you find out that Mrs. Klevity has some strange habits. She wants Anna to look under the bed every night, and she talks into the darkness. You become more interested in Mrs. Klevity as the author gives you clues that she is not at all what she seems to be. Clues or hints about what will happen later in the story are called *foreshadowings.* Part of the enjoyment in reading a suspenseful story comes from the rising and falling fear and hope you feel for characters whom you have come to know and like.

How do the following statements foreshadow the outcome of the story?

a. "It might be when you least expect, so you have to expect all the time."
b. "It was before I got used to Here."
c. "Anna, have you ever been in prison?"

■ Writing About the Story

Suppose that Ahvlaree Klevity managed to send Anna a postcard from her homeland. Design a postcard with a postage stamp that might be suitable for that land. Write Mrs. Klevity's message on the postcard.

Science fiction writers take science and mix it with a generous dash of imagination to create stories about the distant future. Perhaps because people are naturally curious about things to come, science fiction has become popular with readers of all ages. Science fiction stories may include characters, places, and events unlike anything in the world as we know it. However, every unusual element may be an extension of a scientific principle or the result of a possible scientific advancement. Science fiction stories usually appear to be educated guesses about the world of tomorrow.

Science fiction stories often reflect the extent of scientific knowledge at the time of their writing. For example, almost no recently published science fiction stories tell about life on Mars or Venus. This is because space probes have shown that surface conditions on these planets make the presence of any form of life extremely unlikely. Instead, today's science fiction writers usually set their stories on planets in other solar systems.

A problem for a scientist is not necessarily a problem for a science fiction writer. Most space scientists believe that the vast distances between stars make travel between solar systems impossible. Yet this kind of travel goes on all the time in science fiction.

To explain how spaceships can move faster than the speed of light (a feat most scientists doubt will ever be possible), science fiction writers have invented the idea of "hyperjump" (also called "stargate" or "space warp"). The writers suggest there are openings in space which spaceships can enter. Traveling faster than the speed of light, ships could pass through these openings to other points in the universe.

Asimov used in his Foundation novels. (For their book *Alien Landscapes,* Robert Holdstock and Malcolm Edwards prepared a "Galactic Time Chart" partially based on Asimov's predictions. A summary of this time chart appears on page 233.)

Sometimes science fiction writers think of inventions before scientists do. Rockets, submarines, radio communication, body-part transplants, moon landings, robots, and computerlike devices all appeared in science fiction before scientists made them realities.

Part of the fun of reading science fiction is deciding which unlikely occurrences will become possible or even probable with the passage of time. In the nineteenth century, several authors wrote about characters who visited the past. No one tried to explain how such a journey could be made, though, until H.G. Wells wrote *The Time Machine* in 1895. In this book Wells described a vehicle that moved both forward and backward in time. Still, most people continued to think of time travel as an impossibility.

However, scientists have now discovered that time apparently slows down when an object travels at speeds

These openings *could* exist, the writers say. In fact, they may be what we now call "black holes."

When one science fiction writer creates a particularly fascinating idea, later writers are likely to use the idea in their stories. In *The Foundation Trilogy,* three books written in the 1940s, author Isaac Asimov predicted that the future of the universe will be much like the past history of the earth, with empires rising and falling in cycles. Since then many writers have incorporated into their science fiction the time framework and sequence of events that

close to the speed of light. This opens up the possibility that a person in a spaceship traveling away from earth at nearly the speed of light could reach the center of the galaxy and return in one lifetime. Meanwhile, earth would have aged thousands of years.

Many science fiction stories deal with the possibility that hidden worlds exist parallel to our own. Some people believe that there may be a number of other worlds very near to us that we cannot perceive with our five senses. Furthermore, if such worlds exist, then a person could accidentally fall into one of these unseen worlds, perhaps never to be seen on earth again. (Many people say this is what has happened to ships and planes lost in the mysterious ''Bermuda Triangle.'')

Science fiction writer Zenna Henderson explores the opposite possibility in ''Something Bright.'' Two aliens, Mr. and Mrs. Klevity, find themselves trapped in our world, where they wait anxiously for a signal that will show them the way back to their own world.

Science fiction writers create worlds that reflect their own feelings about present-day life. Now and then a pessimistic writer takes readers to the end of the world: a terrible moment when our human shortcomings finally cause the total destruction of life as we know it. The great majority of writers, though, are sure enough of the basic goodness of people to show at least a partial victory for humanity—even in times and places that are light-years away. Perhaps the most consistent and gratifying message of science fiction stories is that there always will be a future for people to dream about.

Read the following summary of the ''Galactic Time Chart'' mentioned previously. Then imagine an event that takes place in one of the time periods listed. Write a description of the event, or join with other students to act it out. Do not specify the time of the event. Have other students guess the date by consulting the time chart.

1960–5000 A.D.: Humans land on moon. Space probes to planets and moons of our solar system. Contact with highly advanced beings from another planet.

5000–100,000 A.D.: Trade, treaties, and wars between planets. "Hyperjump" developed over 3000 years. Rapid galactic colonizing.

100,000 A.D.: Rise of First Galactic Empire.

200,000 A.D.: After many unsuccessful attempts to travel to neighboring galaxies, contact is finally made. Asimov's *Foundation* tales take place around this time.

500,000 A.D.: The Galactic Empire falls. Planets return to primitive conditions. Loss of contact between worlds. A few starships still travel between star systems.

600,000–1,000,000 A.D.: Rise of new galactic civilization after several cycles of rise and fall. Earth declared a forbidden zone (because of radiation), abandoned, and temporarily forgotten.

beware: do not read this poem

A poem by Ishmael Reed

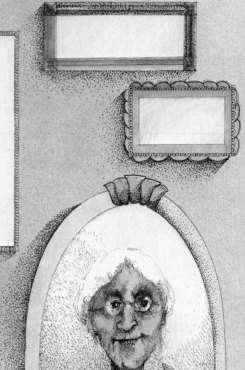

tonite , *thriller*[1] was
abt an ol woman , so vain she
surrounded her self w/
    many mirrors

it got so bad that finally she
locked herself indoors & her
whole life became the
    mirrors

one day the villagers broke
into her house , but she was too
swift for them . she disappeared
    into a mirror
each tenant who bought the house
after that , lost a loved one to
    the ol woman in the mirror:
    first a little girl
    then a young woman
    then the young woman/s husband

---

1. *thriller:* a television program in the 1960s that showed tales of terror.

Illustration by Al Lorenz

the hunger of this poem is legendary
it has taken in many victims
back off from this poem
it has drawn in yr feet
back off from this poem
it has drawn in yr legs
back off from this poem
it is a greedy mirror
you are into this poem . from
      the waist down
nobody can hear you can they ?
this poem has had you up to here
      belch
this poem aint got no manners
you cant call out frm this poem
relax now & go w/ this poem
move & roll on to this poem
do not resist this poem
this poem has yr eyes
this poem has his head
this poem has his arms
this poem has his fingers
this poem has his fingertips

this poem is the reader & the
reader this poem

statistic : the us bureau of missing persons reports
            that in 1968 over 100,000 people disappeared
            leaving no solid clues
                  nor trace   only
a space   in the lives of their friends

The Hatch

A poem by Norma Farber

I found myself one day
cracking the shell of sky,
peering into a place
beyond mere universe.

I broke from egg of here
into anotherwhere
wider than worldly home
I was emerging from.

I breathed, I took a step,
I looked around, and up,
and saw another lining
inside a further sky.

236   Illustration by Jaclyne Scardova

BOOKSHELF

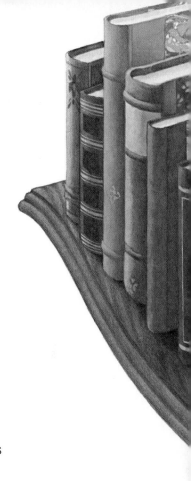

The Captive by Scott O'Dell. Houghton Mifflin, 1979. Young Julian, an idealistic student-priest in sixteenth-century Spain, is forced to voyage to the New World — a voyage that pits his wits against circumstance and disaster.

The Disappearance by Rosa Guy. Delacorte Press, 1979. Imamu Jones, though acquitted of one crime, must prove his innocence when he is implicated in another crime where the victim disappears.

I Am the Cheese by Robert Cormier. Random House, 1977. A psychological thriller told by the innocent young victim of a terrifying plot involving government corruption and espionage.

Slake's Limbo by Felice Holman. Charles Scribner's Sons, 1974. Aremis, thirteen and without a family, is harrassed by neighborhood gangs and takes his fear underground to live in the subway.

The Arm of the Starfish by Madeleine L'Engle. Farrar, Straus & Giroux, 1965. Adam enters a world of suspicion and international intrigue when he accepts a marine research assignment in Portugal.

Nettlewood by Mary Melwood. Seabury Press, 1974. Lacie comes to the English countryside to live with relatives and discovers that Nettlewood Manor, a nearby estate, is full of secrets.

A Midsummer Night's Death by K. M. Peyton. Collins & World, 1978. A young boy is stunned by the death of his English teacher and has reasons to doubt the verdict of suicide.

Remember Me When I Am Dead by Carol Beach York. Elsevier/Nelson, 1980. Sarah's mother is dead, yet her sister Jenny refuses to believe it. Sarah then puts a plan into action that brings suspense into their lives.

4 We, the People

I Hear America Singing

A poem by Walt Whitman

I hear America singing, the varied carols I hear,
Those of mechanics, each one singing his as it should be
    blithe and strong,
The carpenter singing his as he measures his plank or beam,
The mason singing his as he makes ready for work, or leaves
    off work,
The boatman singing what belongs to him in his boat, the
    deck-hand singing on the steamboat deck,
The shoemaker singing as he sits on his bench, the hatter
    singing as he stands,
The wood-cutter's song, the ploughboy's on his way in the
    morning, or at noon intermission or at sundown,
The delicious singing of the mother, or of the young wife at
    work, or of the girl sewing or washing,
Each singing what belongs to him or her and to none else,
The day what belongs to the day — at night the party of young
    fellows, robust, friendly,
Singing with open mouths their strong melodious songs.

Private Deborah

From the fictional biography *The Incredible Deborah* by Cora Cheney
Illustrated by Ronald Himler

The real founders of the U.S. were not the small group of "founding fathers" but the two million Americans who worked and fought for independence. Half of this founding generation were women. Daughters of Liberty led the boycott of British tea and cloth. Later, in addition to making clothes and ammunition for the troops, many women entered combat in the Revolutionary War against England. Some enlisted as regular soldiers who disguised their sex, others as civilian fighters in frontier militia units.

Private Deborah was a regular soldier, a woman who actually lived and fought in the American Revolution. One of seven children whose father had been lost at sea, Deborah Sampson grew up working in other people's homes to earn her keep. Despite the great kindness shown her by the Thomas family (with whom she lived for ten years), Deborah longed for independence. In 1782, vowing to "see the world and serve my country," she disguised herself as a man and ran off to join the Fourth Massachusetts Regiment of the Continental Army under the name Robert Shirtliff. She was twenty-one years old.

As this episode opens, "Bobby" (as soldier Deborah was called) "had fallen into place as a mild-mannered boy, a bit standoffish but ready enough to do his share or more. The older men looked out for him, thinking him the kind of lad they would like to have for their own son."

242

FOOD WAS ALWAYS A PROBLEM. As the soldiers had little to keep them busy in the summer of 1782, the local Patriot farmers hired them and paid them in food for the soldiers' mess. Deborah volunteered for farm duty. Except that she was dressed in comfortable pants, she might have been spending her usual summer day at the Thomas farm.

Working in the fields she found the privacy she missed in the camp. She even found a hide-out, a cave near the riverbank, that reminded her of her old eyrie[1] at Middleborough.[2] She could steal away there when she needed to be alone.

As winter approached, half the

---

1. **eyrie**: a treehouse (or a nest of a large bird).
2. **Middleborough**: a town in Massachusetts.

duties of the men were to find fuel. Deborah's company worked hard all day cutting and hauling wood and returned to the camp famished.

There was always grumbling about food, but one night it was worse than ever. "I'm fit to die with eating nothing but cow heels and tripe," snapped the corporal, rubbing his rumbling stomach.

The Captain agreed. The food didn't come because the contractors and the commissaries haggled and bickered while the soldiers starved. At least that was what the men said as they endlessly discussed their empty stomachs.

"The Captain is asking for volunteers for a foray on a Tory smokehouse that's loaded and waiting for the British Army," said the sergeant. "How about you, Bobby?"

Deborah ran to muster,[3] straightening her ragged cap and giving her baggy breeches an expert hitch.

"Let me go, sir," said Deborah eagerly. "I'm small and I can run fast too." This was her dish of tea, pitting her wits against the other side in a daring game.

"That's right, sir," said the sergeant. "Bobby here can run fast as a deer, and he knows how to keep himself hid when he wants. He can do things an older man can't."

The Captain looked at the slight boy. "Very well, Shirtliff, we'll count on you to bring us some bacon. You'll have a fight. The Tories are guarding that barn with all the men they can raise in the neighborhood, but we think the guards mostly sit around the kitchen fire."

The party of twelve men, their muskets on the ready, crept through the woods.

"Here's the plan, Bobby," whispered the sergeant when they reached the rendezvous point at dusk. "Leave your gun here, and at midnight you crawl in the smokehouse through the low window on the east. The rest of us will surround the place, keeping on our bellies, and take care of the guards outside."

"Aye, sir," said Deborah. The times she had crept through the smokehouse window at Deacon Thomas' on dares from the boys would pay off tonight.

"Cut down the hams and push the meat out the window, but set fire to the place before you escape."

"Set fire?" asked Deborah dubiously.

"Aye. In the confusion they might not even know we're stealing meat. We'll be out there pulling meat away as fast as you pass it out. Then we beat it to the rendezvous, loaded with meat. Ohhhh." The sergeant wiped the saliva from his lips with the back of his hand.

Deborah lay on her empty stomach until the October night was dark

---

3. to **muster**: to gather or assemble for service or review.

and still, waiting for the sergeant to give the signal.

She felt in her pocket for her tinderbox.[4] What wouldn't they think of her now, those people in Middleborough? Turned her out of the church, they had, because she put on men's clothes. She knew because she had heard it being told around the campfire last week when a scout who came through said they were looking for a girl from Massachusetts who was rumored to have tried to join the Army. Think of it, a woman wearing breeches. Deborah had roared with laughter along with the rest of them, especially when they told the part about that girl borrowing some fellow's clothes, and when he found out he swore never to wear them again.

She felt a light touch on her elbow, the sign to begin snaking her way across the open area around the smokehouse. She only hoped that the window would not be too securely bolted. She knew the kind of window it would be, a wooden shutter, probably held by a leather thong inside, a window that could be easily opened for regulating the smoke.

She was proud of how quietly she could move, even over the scratchy gravel. Once she crawled over a pile of cow dung and wished she could rip out swear words as easily as the

other soldiers did, but somehow the words wouldn't come, even in her mind.

She was at the window now. Across the yard she could faintly see a guard sitting against a tree, his musket over his knees. One of her party was creeping up behind him. She braced her foot against the shutter and pushed with all her muscle. The window gave way and fell to the dirt floor with a thud. Deborah squirmed into the opening like a nervous lizard and replaced the window after her.

The smokehouse was as dark as a well bottom. Should she strike her light now and run the risk of having a telltale streak of it show around the window or should she make her cat's eyes work in the dark? No, it was better to work fast and dangerously with the candle.

She struck a spark with her flint, lit the candle, and goggled at the meat hanging from rafters and set on shelves. She pulled out her knife and cut down the hams, stacking them by the window. Then, working with frantic energy, she pushed the meat through the opening.

There was a shout from the Tories in the house.

"Set it on fire, Bobby. Grab your sack and run for it," whispered the sergeant.

Deborah lit the straw piled by the door, scattered it a bit, and wriggled out of the small window. She

---

4. **tinderbox:** a box containing fire-starting material such as woodshavings and a flint.

grabbed as many hams as she could. Behind her the smell of burning straw filled the air. Men with their arms full of meat were running with her, the fire serving to confuse the Tories as the sergeant had predicted. She paused a moment to gloat,[5] and at that moment a shudder of pain that was far worse than all the pain she had ever imagined struck her. A musket ball had hit her thigh.

"Run for it! Bobby," shouted Ike, seeing her falter.

Deborah hung onto the hams in her arms, stumbled to the rendezvous, and picked up her musket.

The men were loading the provisions on their backs.

"Bobby's been shot," said Ike. "We've got to help him get out of here."

"I can make it," said Deborah through gritted teeth. She was hot and cold and faint, but she breathed deeply through her mouth and clenched her hands. She could feel the stream of blood running down her leg.

"The Tories are busy with their fire. We have two or three minutes start on them," said the sergeant. "If you can walk for a short spell, we'll carry you the rest of the way to the French camp and leave you there with the doctor."

---

5. **gloat**: to take delight in someone else's bad luck; to rejoice with evil satisfaction.

It was nearly dawn when the sergeant and Ike carried her into the encampment and left her with the French doctor. The sleepy surgeon looked at the blood-stained tear in the breeches and laid Deborah on a pallet. She cried out with pain when he probed the spot gently.

"The ball ees there, but we'll let the lad rest a while before we take those breeches off and dig it out. Here, let the brandy ease the pain."

Deborah gratefully swallowed some brandy and closed her eyes, trying to keep her mind in focus. She must get out of here, crawl away and get herself to her cave where she could lie down in privacy and sleep a while. Then she could take the bullet out herself. She would rather die in any case than face detection in this French Army camp. Why had she thought she wanted to be a soldier? Courage, courage, she told herself.

She could hear the doctor's snores resume from his cot. Biting her lips to keep from crying out, she got herself on her feet. She took the bottle of brandy, and, cautiously, as the good woodsperson she was, she got past the doctor, around the sentry, and into the woods as the first streaks of morning sun gave her the direction to follow to her cave.

In the cave were her woman's clean clothes. With her knife and the brandy and her tinderbox, canteen, and the butt of dried beef in her pocket, she could hide and survive a week.

She drank a little water from her canteen when she crawled into her cave. She rested on her bed of leaves until her strength rose a little, then took off her breeches and washed the wound with cold water and brandy. She lit a candle from her tinderbox and passed the knife through the flame. Mistress Thomas had taught her that if you must cut a person, first burn the knife to cut the pain.

When the knife was cool, she steadied her hand, took a swallow of brandy, gritted her teeth hard, and, leaning against the rock for strength, she dug out the musket ball.

With her ears ringing, she leaned her head forward to keep from fainting, poured brandy on the wound again, stanched the blood with the clean cloth, and pressed hard on it. Sometimes conscious, sometimes faint, she kept the pressure on the spot until she fell over into a deep sleep. When she woke, her head was momentarily clear and the bleeding had subsided.

Sleeping and rousing, sometimes crying out with pain, Deborah woke after three days and felt her strength returning. Her head felt clear, and she ate some of the meat. She pulled herself with stubborn determination to the nearby spring, where she washed herself and her bandages and refilled her canteen.

Luckily the ball had landed in the fleshy part of her thigh, and the healing was quick. But a second, smaller ball she discovered was deeply embedded further down her leg. It was impossible to remove it. I shall keep it for a souvenir, she decided grimly as she moved painfully around the cave. In a few days she could return to the camp.

Ike was overjoyed to see her. "We heard you had run away from the French. I feared you were dead."

"I was out of my head, wandering in the woods," said Deborah.

"You did a good job on the raid," said Ike. "You lie here and I'll take care of you."

"I'm fine. I can do my duty as well as ever," lied Deborah when the doctor looked at her. The doctor dismissed her without an examination, pressed by sicker patients. But when, ten days later, she was ordered to another foray, her stomach flipped.

Tramp, tramp, tramp, how her leg hurt. She paid scant attention to Richard Snow, who was marching beside her. Suddenly Richard stumbled and fell, and lay writhing on the ground.

The corporal in charge halted the men. "He's terrible sick," he said. "He can't go forward, and we can't leave him behind."

"There's a house nearby. I could stay and look after him," volunteered Deborah.

"Good boy, Bobby. We have to

keep moving or we'll all be targets in this Tory neighborhood. Good luck to you. Report back to headquarters when you get things under control."

Deborah, her leg on fire, dragged the desperately sick man to the nearest farmhouse. Old Mr. Van Tassel, the owner, let them in and grudgingly led them up to his bare attic.

"It's good enough for soldiers," he said meanly. "You can share it with the rats."

While Deborah rested her leg in

the cold attic, she cared tenderly for Richard with the secret help of Van Tassel's daughter.

"My father is a strong Tory," she whispered. "He would not want it known that he is housing Patriot soldiers. All my father cares for is food for his belly."

"Give me some for mine," begged Deborah. "I am like to starve."

Miss Van Tassel covertly brought them food, water, and cover, but by the end of ten days poor Snow died. Deborah wrapped him in a blanket, said a prayer over his body, and let herself out of the locked garret by a knotted rope from the window.

The ten heartbreaking days had given her leg a chance to heal. She walked back to West Point[6] ready for Army life again.

---

6. **West Point:** the United States Military Academy, located in southeastern New York State.

■ Understanding the Story

1. What did Deborah especially like about farm duty?

2. Deborah was chosen to sneak into the Tory smokehouse because she could "run fast as a deer." Find one other detail that tells why Deborah was well qualified for this particular mission.

3. Mistress Thomas had taught Deborah to burn a knife before using it in surgery. What reason did Mistress Thomas give for burning the knife? What real benefit did burning the knife have?

4. Most people think of a heroic person as someone who has a great deal of courage. Name two other "heroic" qualities that Deborah had.

5. Do you admire Deborah Sampson? Why or why not?

■ Understanding Literature

"Private Deborah" is part of a fictional biography based on the life of Deborah Sampson, a Massachusetts woman who served in the Continental Army. A *biography* is the history of one person's life. A biographer tries to use whatever facts are available. He or she invents only details, such as description and conversation, that will make the story more interesting and make the person seem more real. A *fictional biography* like "Private Deborah," however, does not claim to be an exact account of the person's life. Thus a fictional biography may contain a plot and characters that are made up. Everything the author makes up must be accurate for the time when the character lived. In order to insure this historical accuracy, all biographers have to do research.

Notice how details about life in the eighteenth century make Cheney's fictional biography seem more *authentic,* or real. For example, Deborah carries a tinderbox for starting a fire in the smokehouse. What other authentic details can you find?

■ Writing About the Story

By dressing and fighting as a Patriot, Deborah Sampson did something that was unusual for her time. Nowadays both women and men become doctors, nurses, secretaries, plumbers, teachers, and just about any occupation you can imagine. Think of what it would be like to do a job that in the past was usually done by someone of the opposite sex. For example, if you are a girl, what would it be like to be a taxi driver, and if you are a boy, what would it be like to be a nurse? Find out something about the job, and write a few paragraphs describing which daily activities you would most enjoy.

The Birth of a Nation: Amy's Version

Doonesbury cartoons by G. B. Trudeau

Copyright, 1975, G. B. Trudeau. Reprinted with permission of Universal Press Syndicate. All rights reserved.

From

The Other Pioneers

A poem by Roberto Felix Salazar

Now I must write
Of those of mine who rode these plains
Long years before the Saxon[1] and the Irish came.
Of those who plowed the land and built the towns
And gave the towns soft-woven Spanish names.
Of those who moved across the Rio Grande[2]
Toward the hiss of Texas snake and Indian yell.
Of men who from the earth made thick-walled homes
And from the earth raised churches to their God.
And of the wives who bore them sons
And smiled with knowing joy.

They saw the Texas sun rise golden-red with
        promised wealth
And saw the Texas sun sink golden yet, with
        wealth unspent.
"Here," they said. "Here to live and here to love."
"Here is the land for our sons and the sons of our
        sons."
And they sang the songs of ancient Spain
And they made new songs to fit new needs.
They cleared the brush and planted the corn
And saw green stalks turn black from lack of rain.

---

1. **Saxon**: English.
2. **Rio Grande**: the river that flows along the Texas–Mexico border.

And the years moved on.
Those who were first placed in graves
Beside the broad mesquite[3] and the tall nopal.[4]
Gentle mothers left their graces and their arts
And stalwart fathers pride and manly strength.
Salinas, de la Garza, Sánchez, García,
Uribe, González, Martínez, de León:[5]
Such were the names of the fathers.
Salinas, de la Garza, Sánchez, García,
Uribe, González, Martínez, de León:
Such are the names of the sons.

Illustration by Christa Kieffer

---

3. **mesquite** (mes·KEET): a small desert tree.
4. **nopal** (noh·PAHL, NOH·puhl): a type of cactus.
5. **Salinas . . . de Léon** (sah·LEE·nahs, day lah GAHR·sah, SAHN·ches, gahr·SEE·ah, oo·REE·bay, gohn·SAHL·es, mahr·TEEN·es, day lay·OHN).

The Battle of the Rosebud

From the novel *Only Earth and Sky Last Forever*
by Nathaniel Benchley
Illustrated by Arvis Stewart

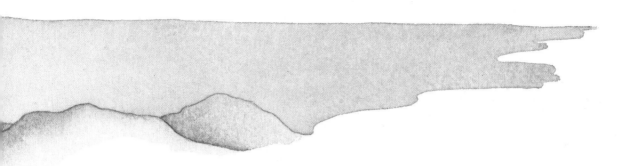

Dark Elk, a fictional character who narrates the true history of the Great Plains Indian War of 1876, was born a southern Cheyenne[1] but was adopted by the Oglala Sioux.[2] Of his youth, Dark Elk says, "My father was killed fighting the Bluecoats[3] in 1868, the year of the treaty that supposedly gave the Black Hills to the Indians for 'as long as the sun shines and the grass grows,' and my mother was killed later that year, when Long Hair Custer surprised our village. . . . So, from the time I was twelve, I lived with the Oglala Sioux, first at the Red Cloud Agency, and then, when that became unbearable, with Crazy Horse,[4] in rapidly dwindling freedom."

In March 1876, three companies of cavalry raided the Cheyenne camp of Chief Two Moon and burned what they couldn't steal. Two Moon, who had been about to surrender and return to the Red Cloud Agency, took his people to join Crazy Horse, who led them all to join Sitting Bull. These great chiefs tried to avoid war, but when gold was discovered in the Black Hills, the cavalry returned to take the area by force. The allied Indians soon moved their camp north, following the buffalo to Rosebud Creek, near the Little Bighorn River. They knew that the Bluecoats were nearby, but they didn't know where, so they sent scouts out in all directions.

While waiting for the battle that is sure to begin, Dark Elk longs for the chance to perform many coups[5] so that he will be invited to join one of the akicitas.[6]

---

1. **Cheyenne** (shy•AN).
2. **Oglala Sioux** (ohg•LAH•lah SOO).
3. **Bluecoats:** the U.S. Cavalry.
4. **Crazy Horse:** chief of the Oglala Sioux.
5. **coups** (KOOZ): brave deeds in battle.
6. *akicita* (AH•kih•SEE•tah): a warrior group.

A FEW DAYS LATER, when it was the Elk *akicita's* turn to do scouting duty, Little Hawk, one of their leaders, formed a party. He chose White Bird and his cousin Yellow Eagle and then, although I was not a member, he saw me standing by and said, "Dark Elk, will you come with us?"

I was astounded, because this was almost like being invited to join the *akicita,* and for a moment I couldn't find words. Then I said, "I would be happy to," trying to sound as though it was something I did every day, and went to get my pony.

We rode southward over the hills, toward the Rosebud. Little Hawk glanced at my pony, whose best days had long since passed, and said, "It would be good if we could get some horses from the white people. I think we could use a few."

"I know I could," I said, knowing what he meant. "My best pony was lost in Reynolds'[7] raid, and this was all I could find." I had a feeling we were out for something more important than a horse raid — and as it turned out I was right. But, just to go along with Little Hawk, I said, "My theory is a man can't have too many ponies."

Little Hawk laughed. "That's as true a statement as was ever made," he said.

We followed the Rosebud over rough terrain up to the head of the creek, then went back down the Tongue River to the north, and across to the Rosebud again. It was one of those clear days in spring, when the sky is bright and the wind gentle and warm, and we could smell the roses that bloomed by the thousands along the valley. When we reached the river we saw two other scouts, Crooked Nose and Little Shield, who was an Arapaho.[8] They joined us, and we all made camp for the night. So far, our scouting had been nothing but a pleasant ride.

Next day, at the big bend in the Rosebud, we saw some buffalo bulls, and Little Hawk killed one. It wasn't very fat but we skinned it, and started a fire, and we were cutting the meat into strips when Yellow Eagle said, "Look! There's better meat there!" We looked, and saw a herd of cows running over the hills to the south, running fast as though they'd been frightened.

Little Hawk watched them for a moment, then said, "Come on. Crooked Nose, you stay here and roast this meat. We'll see if we can't get something a little fatter."

We mounted our ponies and set off toward the cows, and had covered maybe half the distance when I happened to look around. Crooked

---

7. **Reynolds:** Colonel Joseph J. Reynolds led cavalry that burned Chief Two Moon's camp.

8. **Arapaho** (uh·RAP·uh·HOH): a Plains tribe related to the Cheyenne.

Nose was standing away from the fire and making frantic motions from side to side, which was the signal to come back. I told Little Hawk, and when he saw Crooked Nose's signals he turned his pony fast, and we all raced back to the fire. When we got there, Crooked Nose was excited. He pointed to a hill, where there were two red buttes outlined against the bright sky.

"I saw two men looking over there," he said. "They looked for a while, and then they rode up in plain sight. Each one was leading a horse. They went out of sight coming toward us — I think they're headed this way."

Little Hawk thought about this,

then smiled. "They must be Lakotas,"[9] he said. "Let's have some fun with them. We'll give them a fright." We headed for where the men had last been seen. Little Hawk's idea was to ambush them and pretend to capture them, and we rode along a gulch to keep out of sight. Then, when we'd gone a short distance, he got off his pony and crept to the crest of the hill and looked over. I saw his eyes widen, and he sucked in his breath and ducked back quickly. "Soldiers!" he hissed. "The country is alive with them!" He leaped on his pony,

9. Lakotas (lah•KOH•tuhz): members of a western Dakota tribe related to the Oglala Sioux.

257

and we galloped back to the fire and stamped it out. He lost his field glasses in the rush, but there was no time to stop for them now. We hurried down to the river bank, where there were trees and bushes to hide us, and then we rode as hard as we could up toward the head of the stream, the bushes whipping our faces and tearing at our hair.

We finally came out of the timber on a high butte about three miles away, and looked back on the mass of soldiers marching toward the river. There were pony soldiers and walking soldiers and wagons and pack mules; it was a whole expedition, and if we hadn't stopped to cook the buffalo we would have ridden right into them. Crooked Nose and Little Shield split off to alert their village, and the rest of us headed through the foothills of the Wolf Mountains toward ours.

We reached camp just as day was breaking, and we gave the wolf howl and swung our heads from side to side. People came running out to meet us, and the sides of the council lodge were rolled up so all could hear what we had to report. When Little Hawk told of the soldiers a great roar went up, and everyone began to make ready for war. Scouts were sent out to look for the soldiers and report their movements, and they galloped away, shouting and whipping their ponies in their excitement.

The rest of us went about the business of painting our bodies, sharpening our knives, and making whatever medicine we thought best for our own protection. In some cases older men instructed their sons in the medicine, showing them the proper procedure for such things as putting on the warbonnet. (You lift it from the ground, then face the sunrise singing, and three times bring the bonnet near your head, then on the fourth time put it on — all this, of course, if you've attained the maturity as a fighter to warrant wearing one.) There is also special

medicine that people work on their ponies, some throwing badger dust on their hooves, others standing them in water for a certain time, and also tying up their tails with eagle feathers and painting them with colored medicine stripes. Some like to run their ponies back and forth or around in circles, so they'll get their second wind before the fighting starts. Everyone has his own system, and there have been times when the preparations for a battle took longer than the battle itself.

When we were ready, we rode four times around the camp circle

while the women made their trilling noise, and then, with Little Hawk in charge of one party and young Two Moon in charge of another, we rode back into the Wolf Mountains. I was with Little Hawk's group, and among the two hundred or so with young Two Moon were a brother and sister, Chief Comes-in-Sight and Buffalo-Calf-Road-Woman. She prided herself on never having missed a battle. I vowed that on this day I'd do great deeds. For some reason I wasn't nervous; the old dry-mouth feeling was gone and I seemed to be moving without effort or conscious thought, as though I were dreaming. My friend Lone Wolf rode beside me as we went out, and his face was tense beneath his red-and-black war paint. I tried to cheer him, and said, "You know what the Lakotas say — 'This is a good day to die. Only the earth and the sky last forever.' "

"Thank you," said Lone Wolf.

"Do you feel well?"

"No."

I didn't want to ask if he was afraid, so I said, "What kind of sickness is it?"

"It's my crazy brother," he replied. "He's not quite thirteen, and he wants to fight."

I remembered his brother as the little boy who was always pestering us, and I couldn't imagine his being a warrior. We'd called him Fat Bug. "What's his name now?" I asked.

259

"We still call him Fat Bug," Lone Wolf replied. "But he doesn't like it. He wants to be called Bear-That-Roars-Like-a-Bull."

"He'll have to do something to deserve that name," I said.

"I know. And I'm afraid he's going to try." Lone Wolf looked around at the rear of the column, as though expecting his brother to be coming after us. "I told him someone had to stay in camp to guard the weak ones, but he said that was a job for the Big Bellies and old people."

"Can't your father make him stay?"

"I hope so."

"Well, if I see him I'll tell him to go home."

Lone Wolf smiled thinly. "It will take more than that," he said. "You'll have to tie him to a tree if you want to stop him."

"Then I'll do that." It made me feel good to think there was someone younger and less experienced than I, and it gave me a confidence in myself that made everything all right.

We rode for most of the night, and when we could smell the river we stopped, and rested our horses. Little Hawk had directed that everyone hold back, so as not to have wild young men go rushing out and alert the soldiers before we were ready, and a line of *akicita* warriors did what they could to maintain discipline. As the sky began to pale we heard a soft owl-hoot, and another war party moved up alongside us; I saw it was Crazy Horse and his Oglalas, and for a moment I wished I were with them. Then I told myself it didn't make any difference; we were all fighting the same enemy, and who was with whom mattered much less than who did what.

In the gray morning light I saw Crazy Horse untie his long braids, which came below his waist, and shake out his hair the way a stallion shakes his mane. He put on his cape, which he'd made from the skin of a calf he shot out of the soldiers' herd earlier that year. It was red with white spots. Even in the semidarkness, I could see the lightning slash on his cheek. Then he threw dust over the feet of his dappled war horse, and he was ready.

There was some firing as our scouts met with the Crow[10] scouts from the soldiers, and then we moved forward and saw the soldiers in the valley. There were so many they seemed to fill the entire valley, and looked like a large herd of buffalo. Crazy Horse held back, but Little Hawk and our group moved forward, and then things began to happen.

People who write about battles

---

10. **Crow:** a Plains Indian tribe from the Yellowstone River region in Wyoming: the Crow were great enemies of the Sioux and allies of the United States.

always make them look simple, saying these troops charged forward and these others retreated, and so the battle was won or lost, but when you're actually in one there is nothing but confusion. You see only what is in front of you at the moment, and you have no idea what is happening on the other parts of the field. I saw first a group of Crows charging at us, then something frightened them and they turned away, and through the dust and smoke I could see the Bluecoats. Some of them were mounted and some were afoot, and they were charging forward in short dashes, then lying down to fire. Crazy Horse and his warriors pulled back when the Bluecoats charged, and then all charged forward at once, shouting "Hoka hey!" and the soldiers broke and scattered. This was his plan, to work together instead of as individuals, and it seemed to work well.

The Cheyennes with whom I was fighting did it the old way, with warriors riding forward to count coup and show their bravery, and, while this suited me better, it was hard to be outstanding in all that confusion. I saw a lone trooper through the smoke and dust and charged at him with my lance, and just as he turned to face me there was a *thwik* and an arrow went into his open mouth, and out through the back of his neck. The look of surprise on his face was comical, and then blood poured out

of his mouth and he began to topple off his horse, still clutching the reins. I counted coup on his back with my lance, and turned away.

Off to one side, I saw Chief Comes-in-Sight riding out alone at the soldiers, waving his rifle and taunting them, and the bullets were kicking up puffs of dirt all around him. Then suddenly his horse reared and fell, and Comes-in-Sight sprang clear, took off the bridle to show he was unafraid, and began to dodge the bullets on foot. He seemed to be dancing in a cloud of dust. Here was a chance to show my courage; if I could save Comes-in-Sight from a spot like this, I'd be the hero of the battle. I urged my pony forward, lashing him with the rawhide quirt on my wrist, and, as I watched, another pony came out of the ranks, racing toward where Comes-in-Sight was zigzagging back and forth. It was Buffalo-Calf-Road-Woman, his sister, and she reached him, turned and presented her pony's rump to him, and he sprang up and they rode off together. Those of us who saw it set up a great shout and chanting, and even I, though disappointed, had to admire her. To the Cheyennes, the battle was thereafter known as The-Fight-Where-the-Girl-Saved-Her-Brother. (If you want to say it, it goes: "Kaē ē' sē wō ĭs tăn' ĭ wē ĭ tăt' ăn ē.") Other people called it the Battle of the Rosebud.

The main thing I remember, aside

from the various flashes of action, was the screaming noise of the eagle-bone whistles. It cut through the gunfire and shouts and cries and the swishing of arrows, and it made a thin, high background to everything that happened. I heard much later that soldiers who'd been in that fight used to wake up nights with the noise of the whistles in their ears, so I guess it had its effect on both sides.

The battle lasted almost the entire day. Crazy Horse's tactics seemed to work well, because each time the Lakotas made a mass charge they broke up the soldiers, and kept them from forming into one big battle line the way they usually did. Still, it would have been hard to tell the winner if the Bluecoats hadn't started to withdraw. In the late afternoon, when the sun was settling toward the hills, the bugles set up a snarling chorus, and the soldiers began to pull back. Now they formed into one front, but it was a defensive front, and after a few more skirmishes the action was broken off.

The field was littered with dead and wounded horses, soldiers, and Indians, and the noises made your stomach squirm. We gathered up our own and made travois[11] for the more severely wounded, and we were astonished to find out that,

after a full day of hard fighting, we had lost only eleven killed and five badly enough wounded to need help. Our scouts told us later that the soldiers had lost fifty-seven killed and wounded, including many of their Crow and Snake[12] scouts, so on this basis we were the winners. Also, the soldiers were almost out of ammunition and had to go back to Goose Creek and wait for reinforcements and supplies, so we accomplished our aim of protecting our camp. Their aim had been to attack us and wipe us out, and in that they failed. It was the first time we'd come out on top in a pitched battle with the soldiers, and to a great extent it was because of Crazy Horse's tactics. Three Stars Crook, who'd been in charge of the soldiers, had some new thoughts about fighting Indians.

When you say we had "only" eleven killed that sounds very good, unless one of your family happens to be among the eleven. As we were slowly leaving the field, after having picked up every rifle, cartridge, and saddle bag we could find, I saw Lone Wolf leading his pony, and behind him another pony with a travois, and on the travois was a long bundle wrapped in a blanket. One moccasined foot stuck out of the blanket, and I remember how absolutely still

---

11. **travois** (tra·VOI, trav·WAH): a carrier made up of two poles joined by a frame and pulled by an animal.

12. **Snake:** the name once used for the Shoshone (shoh·SHOH·nee) and Paiute (PY·yoot) tribes of Nevada and Utah.

it was, as though it was a part of the travois pole. I went alongside Lone Wolf, and saw his face: he was staring straight ahead, and his eyes were red and half-closed. His war paint was smeared, his face was streaked and dirty, and the muscles along the side of his jaw twitched. For a while neither of us spoke, and then I said, "How did he get here?"

"He must have followed us." Lone Wolf's eyes remained half-closed, unseeing.

"What happened?"

"I don't know. I didn't see him until they had him surrounded."

There was nothing I could say. The "only the earth and the sky last forever" line didn't seem particularly helpful at the moment, so I walked along in silence. The sky turned pink and then the light began to fade, and our whole war party straggled wearily back toward camp. There was some exultation, because we knew we'd done well, but a full day of fighting brought on such exhaustion that we had strength only to keep on moving. The time for celebration would come later, when we'd had some food and sleep. And in Lone Wolf's case, there would be no celebration. He had to present his father and mother with the body of their younger son.

Beside me, Lone Wolf walked along in silence, and the only sounds were the quiet thudding of many ponies' hooves, and the scraping of the travois poles across the earth.

Understanding the Story

1. How was Crazy Horse's battle plan different from the "old way" of fighting?

2. The Native American warriors fought with knives, arrows, and lances, but they also used some modern inventions. Name one modern weapon that they had.

3. Who won the Battle of the Rosebud? Why was it an important battle?

4. In literature, you find at least two very different attitudes toward war. Some writers celebrate the glory of war; others focus on its horrors. Which attitude seems stronger in "The Battle of the Rosebud"? Give a reason for your answer.

5. Had you been there, what would you have said to Lone Wolf's younger brother to convince him not to fight?

Understanding Literature

Dark Elk looked forward to the battle as a chance to "do great deeds" and thus prove himself a man. Many cultures have initiation *rites,* sacred ceremonies that a young person must go through before he or she can be called an adult. These rites often include *ordeals,* painful experiences that test the young person's ability to suffer mental and physical hardship. Many young people have an idealized view of these ordeals, as did Dark Elk. What rites of passage from childhood to adulthood does our culture have?

The battle enables Dark Elk to prove his courage, but it also forces him to look at war more realistically. After the battle, he realizes that for some people there will be no celebration. Lone Wolf's younger brother, who wanted to fight so that he could earn an adult name, has died. At the end of the story, Dark Elk and Lone Wolf walk beside the travois that carries the boy's body. They walk wearily and in silence, for they have learned one of the important lessons that often follows initiation rites: though the passage to adulthood is necessary, you may find that you have lost more and gained less than you expected.

Writing About the Story

Some Plains Indians made picture calendars on buffalo hide. Each year artists would select one outstanding event and paint a small picture to record it. If the hunting had been excellent that year, the artist might paint a buffalo on the hide. Try making a picture calendar for the past three years of your life. Choose one outstanding event from each year, and show that event in a single drawing or painting. Write a paragraph in which you explain each event and tell why it was important to you.

A Song of Greatness

A Chippewa song

Transcribed by Mary Austin

When I hear the old men
Telling of heroes,
Telling of great deeds
Of ancient days,
When I hear them telling,
Then I think within me
I too am one of these.

When I hear the people
Praising great ones,
Then I know that I too
Shall be esteemed,
I too when my time comes
Shall do mightily.

Illustration by Joel Snyder

A Wagon Load of Bricks

A chapter from the biography *Harriet Tubman: Conductor on the Underground Railroad* by Ann Petry

Illustrated by Kenneth Longtemps

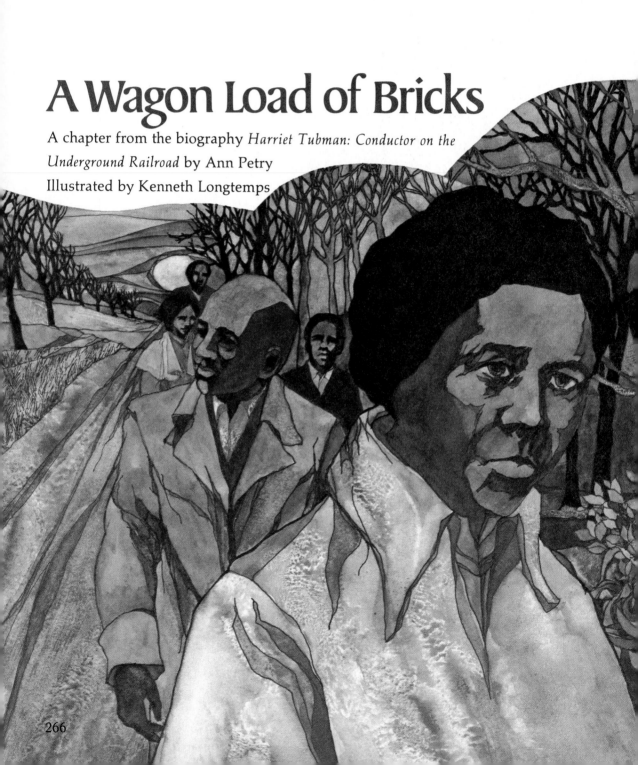

Harriet Tubman was a great leader in the fight against slavery in America. Born a slave in Maryland, she ran away and made the dangerous journey North in 1849, when she was twenty-nine. She returned South to conduct other slaves to freedom along the Underground Railroad. Her courage has inspired many writers, like Ann Petry who wrote the biography from which this excerpt is taken. Another such writer is Hildegarde Hoyt Swift, who wrote the following verse as part of a longer poem entitled "I brought to the New World the gift of devotion."

> I was Harriet Tubman, who would not stay in bondage.
> I followed the devious, uncharted trails to the North,
> I followed the light of the North Star,
>   I ran away to freedom in 1849.
> I was Harriet Tubman who could not stay in freedom,
>   While her brothers were enslaved.
>   . . . .
>   I was Harriet Tubman,
>   Who "never run my train off the track,
>   And never lost a passenger."

FROM 1851 TO 1857, the country moved closer to civil war. During these years Harriet Tubman made eleven trips into Maryland to bring out slaves.

In November, 1856, she rescued Joe Bailey. In the spring she had made two trips to the Eastern Shore.[1] The result of one of these trips is recorded in Still's *Underground Railroad:*[2] "April 1856. The next arrival numbered

---

1. **Eastern Shore:** the east side of Chesapeake Bay, where many slaves escaped from Virginia to Maryland, which was a free state.
2. **Still's *Underground Railroad:*** William Still's history of the secret network that helped slaves escape to the northern states and Canada.

four passengers, and came under the guidance of 'Moses' (Harriet Tubman) from Maryland. . . ."

The second trip, which took place in May, is mentioned in a letter that Thomas Garrett[3] wrote to J. Miller McKim and William Still of the Philadelphia Vigilance Committee:[4]

Wilmington, 5 mo. 11th, 1856

Esteemed Friends—McKim and Still:—
. . . . Those four I wrote thee about arrived safe up in the neighborhood of Longwood, and Harriet Tubman followed after in the stage yesterday. I shall expect five more from the same neighborhood next trip. . . .

As ever your friend,
THOS. GARRETT

The November trip started off inauspiciously.[5] There were three men in the group: Joe Bailey and his brother William, and a man named Peter Pennington. There was one woman, Eliza Nokey.

After Harriet heard Joe's story, her fear of immediate pursuit increased. Joe was a tall, dark man, muscular and handsome. His master had hired him out to another planter, William R. Hughlett, for six years. Finally, Hughlett decided to buy him, for Joe supervised the running of the plantation so well that Hughlett didn't have to pay an overseer.[6] He paid two thousand dollars for Joe.

Joe said the day Hughlett bought him, he beat him with a rawhide, to make certain Joe knew who was the master. Joe told them that he had said to himself, "This is the first and last time." That night he took a boat and rowed down the river to the plantation where Old Ben[7] lived. He told Ben, "The next time Moses comes, let me know."

---

3. **Thomas Garrett:** American abolitionist whose home in Wilmington, Delaware, was a refuge for runaway slaves and a station on the Underground Railroad.
4. **Philadelphia Vigilance Committee:** part of the Philadelphia Anti-Slavery Society.
5. **inauspiciously** (in·aw·SPISH·uhs·lee): unfavorably; with signs of bad luck.
6. **overseer:** a supervisor who made sure that the slaves did their work.
7. **Old Ben:** Harriet Tubman's father.

The scars on Joe's back weren't healed yet. Harriet worried about that. His height, the bloody stripes on his back, would make it easy to identify him. Perhaps it was the worry, the haste with which they had to move to get away, the fact that she felt impelled to urge them to move faster and faster; anyway, her head began to ache. She made them walk along the edge of the road, dangerous, but going through the woods was too slow. As she hurried them along, the scar from the old wound on her temple began to throb[8] like a toothache. The ache in her head increased. She could feel sleep creeping over her like a paralysis. She tried to sing, tried to fight off the sleep, and stumbled, went down on her knees. And was sound asleep.

When she awakened, she had no idea how long she had slept. She heard a man's voice saying, "You've got to trust her. When she has those sleeps you have to leave her alone till she wakes up, she'll wake up pretty soon."

It was Joe who had spoken. He was squatting on his heels, and Eliza and Bill and Peter were standing up, looking down at her. She was lying flat on the road. The sun was shining, sunlight so brilliant that she thought she could feel it warm on her eyelids. Yet the ground was cold, the air was cold.

She got to her feet quickly. Her heart seemed to be skipping beats; it was going so fast. They were out in plain sight, all of them; anyone who passed would recognize them for what they were—runaways, fugitives.

She ordered them to follow her and went into the woods that bordered the road, plunging into the woods, almost running. They came behind her, and it seemed to her their footsteps kept pace with the speed of her thoughts: should have been traveling at night, not in broad daylight; should have been concealed, not out in the open like that; got to go faster and faster, faster, faster.

Then she heard them muttering. One of the men said,

8. the scar . . . began to throb: Harriet Tubman was struck on the head when she was fifteen; thereafter she suffered sudden blackouts and unconsciousness.

"She's taking us back, I can tell, we're going back the same way we come, the woman's crazy —"

She led them on a zigzag course, up a hill and then down. At the foot of the hill there was a small river which followed a winding course. She went straight toward it.

Eliza Nokey said, panic in her voice, "You goin' wade that?"

Harriet said she had had a dream while she was sleeping. And in the dream she had seen this river.

Eliza said it was too deep to wade, they'd all drown.

Harriet said she was certain there was one place so shallow that they could wade it.

They stopped following her. All of them stopped. Bill asked her if she'd crossed this river before. She said no, but she'd seen it in her dream, that the Lord told her what to do, and running water leaves no trail. They would be safe on the other side.

Peter Pennington said, "I'll wade no freezin' water for no crazy woman," and started back toward the woods.

She raised the gun, pointed it, scowling. "Stand still," she ordered. "You try to go back, try to run back to the woods, and you'll never run any more. You go on with me or you die."

They went on. She didn't like it, the threat of violence always disturbed her. And she had never felt so unsure of herself, so desperate, so afraid. But her visions had never failed her.

She waded into the stream, water like ice was around her ankles, and as she went forward, it reached her thighs, and then her waist. She turned and looked back, and Joe was the only one who had followed her. The others were standing on the bank watching. Water reached to her shoulders and she kept going. She closed her eyes for a moment, in the grip of a despair as icy cold as the water.

She thought that if her belief were only strong enough, the waters of this stream would have parted, and they would all have walked across on dry land; instead the water rose higher, now it was above her shoulders, up to her chin. She kept going. She held the gun up out of the

water; at least Joe was still following; and she thought,
Wade in the water just like John,[9] and a feeling of confidence returned. When the Lord no longer wanted her —

The water began to recede. It was down to her shoulders. But it wasn't the water that was receding, the stream
was getting shallower. When the others saw this, they
started to wade the river, too. Then all of them reached
the opposite bank, dry land, a small island, or neck of
land. They were shivering, shocked by the cold, numb,
but otherwise unharmed.

They went through more woods and then they came to
a clearing. There was a cabin there. Harriet said she had
seen that in her dreams, too. They would be safe there.

---

9. **John:** John the Baptist, who, according to the Bible, taught Jesus and baptized
him in the Jordan River.

And they were. The cabin belonged to a family of free Negroes. They were made welcome, given food. Their wet clothing was dried in front of the open fire.

The next morning they set out again. They went back the same way they had come, but they did not have to wade through the river. Their host served as guide, and he led them by a long roundabout road.

When they reached the spot where Harriet had gone to sleep by the side of the road, the day before, they all shivered. The patrollers[10] had been there, had waited for them there. If they hadn't crossed the river at Harriet's direction, they would have been caught. The evidence was unmistakable: the grass had been trampled by horses' feet; the ground was littered with the stubs of half-smoked cigars.

A poster had been nailed to one of the trees. They recognized it immediately. In the upper left-hand corner there was a woodcut of a black man, a small running figure with a stick over his shoulder, and a bundle tied to the end of the stick, and another stick in his hand.

Harriet tore the poster down, and handed it to Joe. He read it aloud:

---

10. **patrollers** (puh·TROHL·uhrz); here, armed men who walked around hunting runaway slaves.

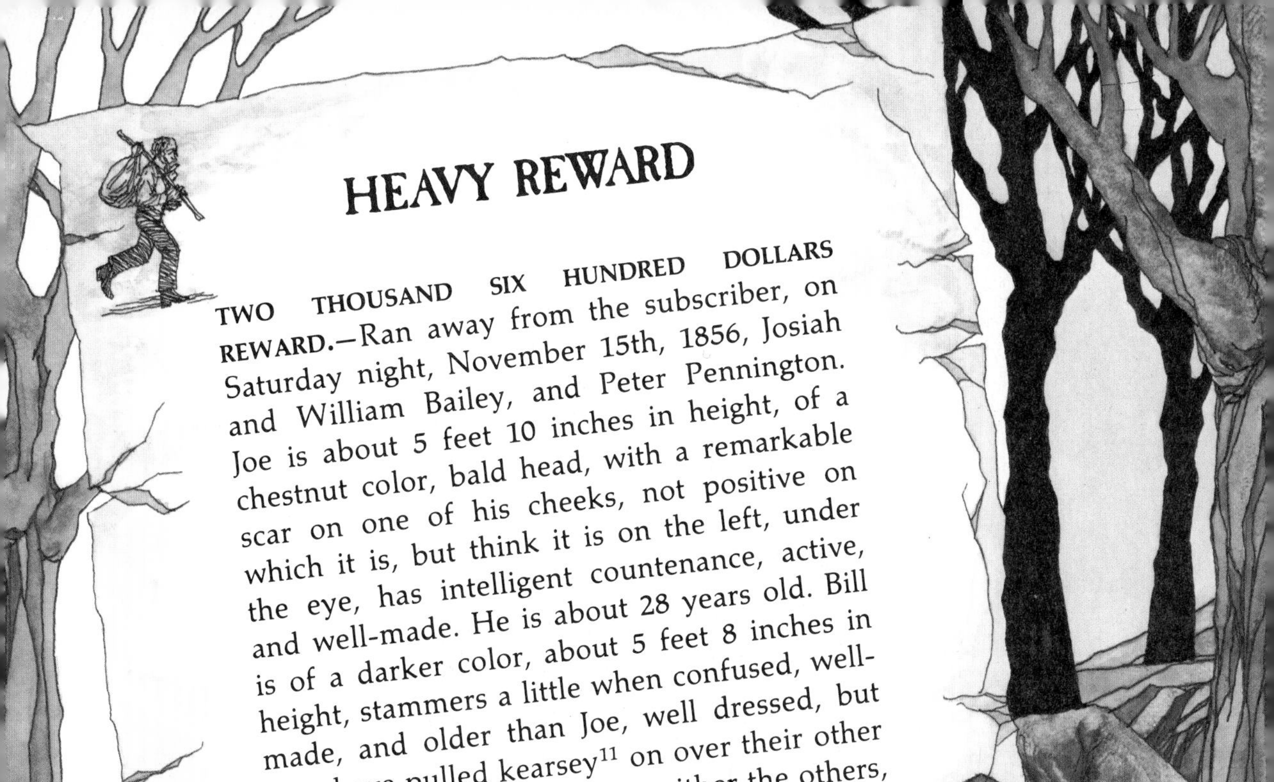

HEAVY REWARD

TWO THOUSAND SIX HUNDRED DOLLARS REWARD.—Ran away from the subscriber, on Saturday night, November 15th, 1856, Josiah and William Bailey, and Peter Pennington. Joe is about 5 feet 10 inches in height, of a chestnut color, bald head, with a remarkable scar on one of his cheeks, not positive on which it is, but think it is on the left, under the eye, has intelligent countenance, active, and well-made. He is about 28 years old. Bill is of a darker color, about 5 feet 8 inches in height, stammers a little when confused, well-made, and older than Joe, well dressed, but may have pulled kearsey[11] on over their other clothes. Peter is smaller than either the others, about 25 years of age, dark chestnut color, 5 feet 7 or 8 inches high.

A reward of fifteen hundred dollars will be given to any person who will apprehend the said Joe Bailey, and lodge him safely in the jail at Easton, Talbot Co., Md. and $300 for Bill and $800 for Peter.

W. R. HUGHLETT,
JOHN C. HENRY,
T. WRIGHT

When Joe finished reading, there was silence. Harriet tried to say something, and her voice was only a croaking sound in her throat. Again she tried to speak, and couldn't. She must have caught cold from the river. What would she do? Bill sighed. Then Peter groaned.

---

11. **kearsey** (KUR·zee): a heavy wool overcoat.

273

Eliza Nokey was angry. No one had offered any reward for her return. Then Joe started to sing. He looked at that poster which meant any man who read it would be tempted to start hunting for the slave who was worth fifteen hundred dollars to his master, crumpled it up in his hand, and started to sing.

They hurried in a northerly direction, and Joe kept singing, softly, under his breath:

> The little wheel run by faith,
>   And the big wheel run by the grace of God:
> A wheel within a wheel
>   Way in the middle of the air.

As they went along, Harriet sensed danger everywhere, smelled danger. They were not safe. She herded them along, sometimes going ahead of them, sometimes walking behind them, prodding them with the butt of the gun. The hoarseness prevented her from speaking.

It was Joe who talked, Joe who encouraged them, Joe who, as if by instinct, told the old stories about the slave ships, the torture, the irons and the whips. When he sang, they moved faster. Eliza Nokey fairly skipped along, as Joe sang, his voice almost a whisper:

> Who comes yonder all dressed in red?
> I heard the angels singing —
> It's all the children Moses led,
> I heard the angels singing.

They saw other places along the road where the patrollers had been, found one place where they must have waited for as much as an hour, in the hope that they would be able to find some trace of this party. The horses had been tied to the trees.

Joe shook his head and stopped singing.

It was daybreak when they reached the outskirts of Wilmington. Within sight of the long bridge Harriet called a halt. She told the runaways to hide in the woods, not to speak to anyone, not to make a sound, not to move.

She watched the bridge for a long time. It was guarded.

There were posters nailed to the trees all along the road. Stealthily, cautiously, she took two of the posters down, and went back to where she'd left the runaways. Joe said one of the posters was the one he'd read to them before and the reward for him had been increased to two thousand dollars.

But the other—the little running figure reproduced on the flimsy paper was that of a woman. The reward offered for her capture was twelve thousand dollars. The poster described her. It said she was dark, short, of a muscular build, with a deep voice, and that she had a scar on her left temple, scars on the back of her neck. Her name was Harriet Tubman. Sometimes she was called Moses.

Harriet laughed. She said nobody was going to catch her. She left them again and went as close to the bridge as she dared, waiting, watching. Thomas Garrett must know about those posters, must know the bridge was watched. He would try to get in touch with her. She was certain of it.

He did. Garrett sent his servant out to look for Harriet. When Harriet saw him, she signaled to him. They held a conference in the long grass by the side of the road. Then he went back to report to Garrett. Two hours later he was back again with Garrett's message.

It was dark when Harriet returned to the fugitives. As she went toward their hiding place, she signaled her approach by singing:

"Go down, Moses — "

Her voice was no longer beautiful. It was like the croaking of a frog, hoarse, tuneless.

She told them to follow her. She took them through the woods, and then along a road, heavy woods on each side of it, more like a country lane than a road. There was a long wagon there. And men. And the sound of horses, jingle of harness, stamping of feet, soft blowing out of breath.

They got in the wagon, one by one, and lay down flat. Harriet said the men were bricklayers. She said that the

men would cover them with bricks. When the men put boards over them, Eliza Nokey made a thin high sound of terror, and Harriet heard her whisper, "It's like being in a coffin." Then the bricks were placed on top of the boards. Harriet thought Eliza is right — it is as though we had died together and been buried in a common grave, and croaked, "We got to go free or die." The words were lost.

The wagon started. There was a sound of hoofbeats. The men on the wagon began to laugh and shout and sing. Then they were on the long bridge and someone cried, "Halt!"

The driver shouted, "Whoa! Whoa!"

When he was asked if he'd seen any runaway Negroes, he laughed and said with that kind of money being offered for them, he planned to start hunting for them as soon as he got home, right after supper.

When they got out of the wagon at Thomas Garrett's house in Wilmington, Garrett said of Harriet, "She was so hoarse she could hardly speak, and was also suffering with violent toothache."

Garrett forwarded them to Philadelphia where William Still wrote down their past history in his record book. From Philadelphia they were forwarded to the office of the Antislavery Society in New York.

When they reached New York, it was Joe who lost his courage. The moment they entered the office of Oliver Johnson, head of the New York Antislavery Society, Johnson glanced at Joe and said, "Well, Joe, I'm glad to see the man who is worth two thousand dollars to his master."

Joe looked as though he were going to faint. He said, "How did you know me, sir?"

"Here is the advertisement. From the description, no one could possibly mistake you."

"How far off is Canada?" Joe asked.

Oliver Johnson showed him a map. "It's more than three hundred miles, by railroad."

Joe said he wouldn't go any farther because he would be hunted every step of the way, and he couldn't stand it any longer. If a man who had never seen him could recognize him from the description, then the whole dream of freedom was hopeless. He told Harriet to take the others and go on. None of them would be safe as long as he was with them.

But Harriet said they would not go without him. Finally, reluctantly, he went with them. She said afterward, "From that time Joe was silent. He talked no more. He sang no more. He sat with his head on his hand, and nobody could rouse him, or make him take any interest in anything."

They were put aboard a train and they passed through
New York state without incident. The conductor had
hidden them in the baggage car, but when they approached Niagara Falls,[12] he took them into one of the
coaches.

Harriet tried to rouse Joe from his apathy, and urged
him to look at Niagara. But he still sat with his head in
his hands, refusing to look.

Then she shouted, "You've crossed the line! You're
free, Joe, you're free!"

The others shouted too. Still he sat, bent over, silent.
Harriet shook him. "Joe! Joe! You're a free man!"

Slowly he straightened up in his seat, and then stood
up, and lifted his hands, and began to sing. There were

---

12. **Niagara** (ny·AG·ruh) **Falls**: great waterfalls on the Niagara River at the United
States-Canada border.

tears streaming down his cheeks as he sang, louder and louder:

> *Glory to God and Jesus, too,*
> *One more soul got safe.*
> *Glory to God and Jesus, too,*
> *For all these souls got safe.*

His voice was like the sound of thunder. Harriet, listening, thought it put a glory over all of them.

About ANN PETRY

Ann Petry has maintained a lifelong interest in the history of slavery. Therefore, it is not surprising that she would write a book set in the Civil War period. Nor is it surprising that she would choose to write about Harriet Tubman, when you consider what Petry has to say about how she chooses subjects: "Having been born black and female, I regard myself as a survivor. And so I usually write about survivors."

Ann Petry was born in 1911 in Old Saybrook, Connecticut. Her father owned a drug store, and Ann decided that she too would become a pharmacist. After graduating in 1931 from the University of Connecticut, she returned to Old Saybrook and worked as a pharmacist for the next seven years. In 1938 she met George Petry, married him, and moved to New York City. There she began her writing career by working on newspapers — first the *Amsterdam News,* then the *People's Voice.* In 1945 Ann Petry won a Houghton Mifflin Literary Fellowship. With it she began to write her first novel, published in 1946. Since then she has written for adults, for young people, and for children.

Petry writes about contemporary as well as historical subjects. She believes that one cannot understand the present without understanding the past. Two of her most famous novels are *Tituba of Salem Village,* about a slave indicted for witchcraft, and *Legends of the Saints,* about people persecuted for their religious beliefs. Her other historical book, *Harriet Tubman: Conductor on the Underground Railroad,* was recognized for its excellence by the American Library Association.

Understanding the Story

1. In the Underground Railroad, railroad terms were used as a code. Who were the "passengers" on the train? What were the "stations"? How did Harriet Tubman serve as a "conductor"?

2. Why had Joe Bailey decided to run away?

3. One example of Harriet Tubman's great faith was that she led the slaves to a safe cabin that she had seen in a dream. Give one more example of Harriet's spiritual strength.

4. Would you have followed Harriet across the river if you were one of the slaves in the group? Why or why not?

5. Harriet Tubman is considered a hero for her courage and deeds. Name a person of today whom you consider a hero. Explain why you consider him or her heroic.

Understanding Literature

You have learned that stories and plays often contain a *theme.* A song also may express a theme, both in words and in music. Many spirituals, or religious songs, express a theme that is important not just to the oppressed people who created them, but to all of humanity. They express our universal longing for a better world, a place of peace and caring.

Many spirituals contain references to the Bible. Because the slaves identified themselves with the Israelites who were slaves in Egypt, the king of Egypt, Pharaoh, symbolized their slave masters. Slaveholders recognized and feared the power of the spirituals. In 1831, Nat Turner used the story of the Israelites' escape from Egypt to convince a group of slaves to rebel. After the uprising was put down, slaves were forbidden to sing certain spirituals, including "Go Down, Moses," which is about the Israelites' escape from Egypt.

Harriet Tubman, who had escaped from slavery in 1849, risked capture every time she returned to the South to find "passengers" for the Underground Railroad. At night she would signal her presence near the slave quarters of a plantation by singing softly the forbidden song "Go Down, Moses." It is little wonder that Harriet Tubman gained the title "Moses of her people." Just as Moses led the Israelites out of Egypt through the wilderness to the Promised Land, Harriet Tubman led the runaway slaves through the stations of the Underground Railroad to freedom.

Writing About the Story

Pretend you are a runaway slave on the Underground Railroad with Harriet Tubman. Write a diary entry for one of the days on the road. Try to include realistic details, as well as your feelings.

Women

A poem by Alice Walker

They were women then
My mama's generation
Husky of voice — Stout of
Step
With fists as well as
Hands
How they battered down
Doors
And ironed
Starched white
Shirts
How they led
Armies
Headragged[1] Generals
Across mined
Fields
Booby-trapped
Ditches
To discover books
Desks
A place for us
How they knew what we
Must know
Without knowing a page
Of it
Themselves.

---

1. **Headragged:** wearing a scarf on the head.

Illustration by Yoshi Miyake

★★★ The Bedquilt ★★★

A short story by Dorothy Canfield Fisher

Illustrated by Kinuko Craft

In nineteenth-century New England, few women had the chance to pursue a career or to set any goal in life other than marrying and raising a family. If she didn't marry, a woman had nowhere to go but to her relatives, who usually considered her a burden and put her to a lifetime of thankless tasks. Aunt Mehetabel was such a woman, a person whose days were empty and barren until, with the help of her one talent, the door to life opened just a crack — and she slipped in.

OF ALL THE ELWELL FAMILY Aunt Mehetabel was certainly the most unimportant member. It was in the old-time New England days, when an unmarried woman was an old maid at twenty, at forty was everyone's servant, and at sixty had gone through so much discipline that she could need no more in the next world. Aunt Mehetabel was sixty-eight.

She had never for a moment known the pleasure of being important to anyone. Not that she was useless in her brother's family; she was expected, as a matter of course, to take upon herself the most tedious[1] and uninteresting part of the household labors. On Mondays she accepted as her share the washing of the men's shirts, heavy with sweat and stiff with dirt from the fields and from their own hardworking bodies. Tuesdays she never dreamed of being allowed to iron anything pretty or even interesting, like the baby's white dresses or the fancy aprons of her young lady nieces. She

---

1. tedious (TEE·dee·uhs): tiring; long and boring.

stood all day pressing out a monotonous succession of dish cloths and towels and sheets.

In preserving-time she was allowed to have none of the pleasant responsibility of deciding when the fruit had cooked long enough, nor did she share in the little excitement of pouring the sweet-smelling stuff into stone jars. She sat in a corner with the children and stoned cherries incessantly,[2] or hulled strawberries until her fingers were dyed red.

The Elwells were not consciously unkind to their aunt, they were even in a vague way fond of her; but she was so insignificant a figure in their lives that she was almost invisible to them. Aunt Mehetabel did not resent this treatment; she took it quite as unconsciously as they gave it. It was to be expected when one was an old maid dependent in a busy family. She gathered what crumbs of comfort she could from their occasional careless kindnesses and tried to hide the hurt which even yet pierced her at her brother's rough joking. In the winter when they all sat before the big hearth, roasted apples, drank mulled cider, and teased the girls about their beaux[3] and the boys about their sweethearts, she shrank into a dusky corner with her knitting, happy if the evening passed without her brother saying, with a crude sarcasm, "Ask your Aunt Mehetabel about the beaux that used to come a-sparkin' her!" or, "Mehetabel, how was't when you was in love with Abel Cummings?" As a matter of fact, she had been the same at twenty as at sixty, a mouselike little creature, too shy for anyone to notice, or to raise her eyes for a moment and wish for a life of her own.

Her sister-in-law, a big hearty housewife, who ruled indoors with as autocratic a sway as did her husband on the farm, was rather kind in an absent, offhand way to the shrunken little old woman, and it was through her that Mehetabel was able to enjoy the one pleasure of her life. Even as a girl she had been clever with her needle in the way of patching bedquilts. More than that she could never learn to do. The garments which she made for herself were lamentable affairs,[4] and she was humbly grateful for any help in the bewildering business of putting them together. But in patchwork she enjoyed a tepid[5] importance. She could really do that as well as anyone else. During years of devotion to this one art she had accumulated a considerable store of quilting patterns. Sometimes the neighbors would send over and ask "Miss Mehetabel" for the loan of her sheaf-of-wheat design, or the double-star

---

2. **incessantly:** ceaselessly; without stopping.
3. **beaux** (BOHZ): boyfriends; suitors.

4. **lamentable affairs:** pitiful things.
5. **tepid** (TEP·id): moderate; slight (literally, *lukewarm*).

pattern. It was with an agreeable flutter at being able to help someone that she went to the dresser, in her bare little room under the eaves, and drew out from her crowded portfolio[6] the pattern desired.

⁂

She never knew how her great idea came to her. Sometimes she thought she must have dreamed it, sometimes she even wondered reverently, in the phraseology of the weekly prayer-meeting, if it had not been "sent" to her. She never admitted to herself that she could have thought of it without other help. It was too great, too ambitious, too lofty a project for her humble mind to have conceived. Even when she finished drawing the design with her own fingers, she gazed at it incredulously, not daring to believe that it could indeed be her handiwork. At first it seemed to her only like a lovely but unreal dream. For a long time she did not once think of putting an actual quilt together following that pattern, even though she herself had invented it. It was not that she feared the prodigious effort that would be needed to get those tiny, oddly shaped pieces of bright-colored material sewed together with the perfection of fine workmanship needed. No, she thought zestfully and eagerly of such endless effort, her heart

uplifted by her vision of the mosaic[7]-beauty of the whole creation as she saw it, when she shut her eyes to dream of it — that complicated, splendidly difficult pattern — good enough for the angels in heaven to quilt.

But as she dreamed, her nimble old fingers reached out longingly to turn her dream into reality. She began to think adventurously of trying it out — it would perhaps not be too selfish to make one square — just one unit of her design to see how it would look. She dared do nothing in the household where she was a dependent, without asking permission. With a heart full of hope and fear thumping furiously against her old ribs, she approached the mistress of the house on churning-day, knowing with the innocent guile[8] of a child that the country woman was apt to be in a good temper while working over the fragrant butter in the cool cellar.

Sophia listened absently to her sister-in-law's halting petition. "Why, yes, Mehetabel," she said, leaning far down into the huge churn for the last golden morsels — "why, yes, start another quilt if you want to. I've got a lot of pieces from the spring sewing that will work in real good." Mehetabel tried honestly

---

6. **portfolio:** a portable case for carrying papers.

7. **mosaic:** a picture made of small pieces of glass or stone.
8. **guile:** cunning; craftiness.

to make her see that this would be no common quilt, but her limited vocabulary and her emotion stood between her and expression. At last Sophia said, with a kindly impatience: "Oh, there! Don't bother me. I never could keep track of your quiltin' patterns, anyhow. I don't care what pattern you go by."

Mehetabel rushed back up the steep attic stairs to her room, and in a joyful agitation began preparations for the work of her life. Her very first stitches showed her that it was even better than she hoped. By some heaven-sent inspiration she had invented a pattern beyond which no patchwork quilt could go.

She had but little time during the daylight hours filled with the incessant household drudgery.[9] After dark she did not dare to sit up late at night lest she burn too much candle. It was weeks before the little square began to show the pattern. Then Mehetabel was in a fever to finish it. She was too conscientious to shirk even the smallest part of her share of the housework, but she rushed through it now so fast that she was panting as she climbed the stairs to her little room.

Every time she opened the door, no matter what weather hung outside the small window, she always saw the little room flooded with sunshine. She smiled to herself as she

bent over the innumerable scraps of cotton cloth on her work table. Already — to her — they were arranged in orderly, complex, mosaic-beauty.

Finally she could wait no longer, and one evening ventured to bring her work down beside the fire where the family sat, hoping that good fortune would give her a place near the tallow candles on the mantelpiece. She had reached the last corner of that first square and her needle flew in and out, in and out, with nervous speed. To her relief no one noticed her. By bedtime she had only a few more stitches to add.

9. **drudgery** (DRUJ•uh•ree): hard, dull work.

"Land's sakes!" cried her sister-in-law. "Why, Mehetabel Elwell, where did you git that pattern?"

"I made it up," said Mehetabel. She spoke quietly but she was trembling.

"No!" exclaimed Sophia. "Did you! Why, I never seen such a pattern in my life. Girls, come here and see what your Aunt Mehetabel is doing."

The three tall daughters turned back reluctantly from the stairs. "I never could seem to take much interest in patchwork quilts," said one. Already the old-time skill, born of early pioneer privation[10] and the craving for beauty, had gone out of style.

"No, nor I neither!" answered Sophia. "But a stone image would take an interest in this pattern. Honest, Mehetabel, did you really think of it yourself?" She held it up closer to her eyes and went on, "And how under the sun and stars did you ever git your courage up to start in a-making it? Land! Look at all those tiny squinchy little seams! Why, the wrong side ain't a thing *but* seams! Yet the good side's just like a picture, so smooth you'd think 'twas woven that way. Only nobody could."

The girls looked at it right side, wrong side, and echoed their mother's exclamations. Mr. Elwell

As she stood up with the others, the square fell from her trembling old hands and fluttered to the table. Sophia glanced at it carelessly. "Is that the new quilt you said you wanted to start?" she asked, yawning. "Looks like a real pretty pattern. Let's see it."

Up to that moment Mehetabel had labored in the purest spirit of selfless adoration of an ideal. The emotional shock given her by Sophia's cry of admiration as she held the work towards the candle to examine it, was as much astonishment as joy to Mehetabel.

---

10. **privation:** poverty; a lack of something.

himself came over to see what they were discussing. "Well, I declare!" he said, looking at his sister with eyes more approving than she could ever remember. "I don't know a thing about patchwork quilts, but to my eye that beats old Mis' Andrew's quilt that got the blue ribbon so many times at the County Fair."

As she lay that night in her narrow hard bed, too proud, too excited to sleep, Mehetabel's heart swelled and tears of joy ran down from her old eyes.

The next day her sister-in-law astonished her by taking the huge pan of potatoes out of her lap and setting one of the younger children to peeling them. "Don't you want to go on with that quiltin' pattern?" she said. "I'd kind o' like to see how you're goin' to make the grapevine design come out on the corner."

For the first time in her life the dependent old maid contradicted her powerful sister-in-law. Quickly and jealously she said, "It's not a grapevine. It's a sort of curlicue I made up."

"Well, it's nice-looking anyhow," said Sophia pacifyingly. "I never could have made it up."

By the end of the summer the family interest had risen so high that Mehetabel was given for herself a little round table in the sitting room, for *her*, where she could keep her pieces and use odd minutes for her work. She almost wept over such kindness and resolved firmly not to take advantage of it. She went on faithfully with her monotonous housework, not neglecting a corner. But the atmosphere of her world was changed. Now things had a meaning. Through the longest task of washing milk-pans, there rose a rainbow of promise. She took her place by the little table and put the thimble on her knotted, hard finger with the solemnity of a priestess performing a rite.

She was even able to bear with some degree of dignity the honor of having the minister and the minister's wife comment admiringly on her great project. The family felt quite proud of Aunt Mehetabel as Minister Bowman had said it was work as fine as any he had ever seen, "and he didn't know but finer!" The remark was repeated verbatim to the neighbors in the following weeks when they dropped in and examined in a perverse Vermontish silence some astonishingly difficult tour de force[11] which Mehetabel had just finished.

The Elwells especially plumed[12] themselves on the slow progress of the quilt. "Mehetabel has been to work on that corner for six weeks, come Tuesday, and she ain't half done yet," they explained to visitors. They fell out of the way of always expecting her to be the one to run on errands, even for the children. "Don't bother your Aunt Mehetabel," Sophia would call. "Can't you see she's got to a ticklish place on the quilt?" The old woman sat straighter in her chair, held up her head. She was a part of the world at last. She joined in the conversation and her remarks were listened to. The children were even told to mind her when she asked them to do some service for her, although this she ventured to do but seldom.

One day some people from the next town, total strangers, drove up to the Elwell house and asked if they could inspect the wonderful quilt which they had heard about even down in their end of the valley. After that Mehetabel's quilt came little by little to be one of the local sights. No visitor to town, whether he knew the Elwells or not, went away without having been to look at it. To make her presentable to strangers, the Elwells saw to it that their aunt was better dressed than she had ever been before. One of the girls made her a pretty little cap to wear on her thin white hair.

A year went by and a quarter of the quilt was finished. A second year passed and half was done. The third year Mehetabel had pneumonia and lay ill for weeks and weeks, horrified

---

11. **tour de force**: a feat of remarkable strength or skill (from the French).
12. **plumed**: prided.

by the idea that she might die before her work was completed. A fourth year and one could really see the grandeur of the whole design. In September of the fifth year, the entire family gathered around her to watch eagerly, as Mehetabel quilted the last stitches. The girls held it up by the four corners and they all looked at it in hushed silence.

Then Mr. Elwell cried as one speaking with authority, "By ginger! That's goin' to the County Fair!"

Mehetabel blushed a deep red. She had thought of this herself, but never would have spoken aloud of it.

"Yes indeed!" cried the family. One of the boys was dispatched to the house of a neighbor who was Chairman of the Fair Committee for their village. He came back beaming, "Of course he'll take it. Like's not it may git a prize, he says. But he's got to have it right off because all the things from our town are going tomorrow morning."

Even in her pride Mehetabel felt a pang as the bulky package was carried out of the house. As the days went on she felt lost. For years it had been her one thought. The little round stand had been heaped with a litter of bright-colored scraps. Now it was desolately bare. One of the neighbors who took the long journey to the Fair reported when he came back that the quilt was hung in a good place in a glass case in "Agricultural Hall." But that meant little

to Mehetabel's ignorance of everything outside her brother's home. She drooped. The family noticed it. One day Sophia said kindly, "You feel sort o' lost without the quilt, don't you Mehetabel?"

"They took it away so quick!" she said wistfully. "I hadn't hardly had one good look at it myself."

The Fair was to last a fortnight. At the beginning of the second week Mr. Elwell asked his sister how early she could get up in the morning.

"I dunno. Why?" she asked.

"Well, Thomas Ralston has got to drive to West Oldton to see a lawyer. That's four miles beyond the Fair. He says if you can git up so's to leave here at four in the morning he'll drive you to the Fair, leave you there for the day, and bring you back again at night." Mehetabel's face turned very white. Her eyes filled with tears. It was as though someone had offered her a ride in a golden chariot up to the gates of heaven. "Why, you can't *mean* it!" she cried wildly. Her brother laughed. He could not meet her eyes. Even to his easy-going unimaginative indifference to his sister this was a revelation of the narrowness of her life in his home. "Oh, 'tain't so much — just to go to the Fair," he told her in some confusion, and then "Yes, sure I mean it. Go git your things ready, for it's tomorrow morning he wants to start."

A trembling, excited old woman

stared all that night at the rafters. She who had never been more than six miles from home — it was to her like going into another world. She who had never seen anything more exciting than a church supper was to see the County Fair. She had never dreamed of doing it. She could not at all imagine what it would be like.

The next morning all the family rose early to see her off. Perhaps her brother had not been the only one to be shocked by her happiness. As she tried to eat her breakfast they called out conflicting advice to her about what to see. Her brother said not to miss inspecting the stock, her nieces said the fancywork was the only thing worth looking at, Sophia told her to be sure to look at the display of preserves. Her nephews asked her to bring home an account of the trotting races.

The buggy drove up to the door, and she was helped in. The family ran to and fro with blankets, woolen tippet, a hot soapstone from the kitchen range.[13] Her wraps were tucked about her. They all stood together and waved good-bye as she drove out of the yard. She waved back, but she scarcely saw them. On her return home that evening she was ashy pale, and so still that her brother had to lift her out bodily.

---

13. woolen tippet, a hot soapstone from the kitchen range: a scarf, and a stone that was heated in the oven, usually used for heating cold beds.

But her lips were set in a blissful smile. They crowded around her with questions until Sophia pushed them all aside. She told them Aunt Mehetabel was too tired to speak until she had had her supper. The young people held their tongues while she drank her tea, and absent-mindedly ate a scrap of toast with an egg. Then the old woman was helped into an easy chair before the fire. They gathered around her, eager for news of the great world, and Sophia said, "Now, come, Mehetabel, tell us all about it!"

Mehetabel drew a long breath. "It was just perfect!" she said. "Finer even than I thought. They've got it hanging up in the very middle of a sort o' closet made of glass, and one of the lower corners is ripped and turned back so's to show the seams on the wrong side."

"What?" asked Sophia, a little blankly.

"Why, the quilt!" said Mehetabel in surprise. "There are a whole lot of other ones in that room, but not one that can hold a candle to it, if I do say it who shouldn't. I heard lots of people say the same thing. You ought to have heard what the women said about that corner, Sophia. They said — well, I'd be ashamed to *tell* you what they said. I declare if I wouldn't!"

Mr. Elwell asked, "What did you think of that big ox we've heard so much about?"

"I didn't look at the stock," returned his sister indifferently. She turned to one of her nieces. "That set of pieces you gave me, Maria, from your red waist, come out just lovely! I heard one woman say you could 'most smell the red roses."

"How did Jed Burgess' bay horse place in the mile trot?" asked Thomas.

"I didn't see the races."

"How about the preserves?" asked Sophia.

"I didn't see the preserves," said Mehetabel calmly.

Seeing that they were gazing at her with astonished faces she went on, to give them a reasonable explanation, "You see I went right to the room where the quilt was, and then I didn't want to leave it. It had been so long since I'd seen it. I had to look at it first real good myself, and then I looked at the others to see if there was any that could come up to it. Then the people begun comin' in and I got so interested in hearin' what they had to say I couldn't think of goin' anywheres else. I ate my lunch right there too, and I'm glad as can be I did, too; for what do you think?" — she gazed about her with kindling eyes. "While I stood there with a sandwich in one hand, didn't the head of the hull concern[14] come in and open the glass door and pin a big bow of blue ribbon right in the

_____

14. hull concern: the whole business (that is, the fair).

292

middle of the quilt with a label on it, 'First Prize.' "

There was a stir of proud congratulation. Then Sophia returned to questioning, "Didn't you go to see anything else?"

"Why, no," said Mehetabel. "Only the quilt. Why should I?"

She fell into a reverie. As if it hung again before her eyes she saw the glory that shone around the creation of her hand and brain. She longed to make her listeners share the golden vision with her. She struggled for words. She fumbled blindly for unknown superlatives. "I tell you it looked like — " she began, and paused.

Vague recollections of hymnbook phrases came into her mind. They were the only kind of poetic expression she knew. But they were dismissed as being sacrilegious to use for something in real life. Also as not being nearly striking enough.

Finally, "I tell you it looked real *good*," she assured them and sat staring into the fire, on her tired old face the supreme content of an artist who has realized her ideal.

■ Understanding the Story

1. Mehetabel had to do the most tedious and uninteresting work in her brother's house. Why did she stay there?

2. How did making the bedquilt change Mehetabel's feelings about herself and her life?

3. Mehetabel made something that was, in her opinion, perfect. Have you ever felt completely satisfied about something you did or made? Tell what it was and describe how you felt.

■ Understanding Literature

In different parts of the United States, the toys, clothing, furniture, tools, and other household objects used in daily life were made from and decorated with designs traditionally used in that particular region. Patchwork quilts, the kind that Mehetabel made in "The Bedquilt," are uniquely American, and their designs varied from region to region. Many quilts made in New England were made from cloth with dark, subdued colors, while quilts made in the Appalachian mountains of West Virginia were bright and colorful.

Language, like quilts or other forms of artistic expression, reflects and preserves the culture of a region. Like a patchwork quilt, language can be practical and simple or, if it is full of figurative language, colorful and fun. The regional flavor of the Elwells' speech adds liveliness to the story. Rewrite the following sentences in your own words and notice how they lose their flavor: (a) "Like as not it may git a prize"; (b) "Ask your Aunt Mehetabel about the beaux that used to come a-sparkin' her."

■ Writing About the Story

Pretend that you are making a patchwork quilt using words. Take a large piece of paper and fold it in half four times, so that when you unfold it you have sixteen boxes, four in each row and in each column. In each of the four boxes in the first column, write a phrase like *I am inspired to* or *I hope to.* In the next column, write in each box the present tense of a verb like *catapult* or *explode.* In each box in the third column, write a noun with the article *the* in front of it, such as *the chicken* or *the planets.* In each box in the last column, write an unusual color that you might take from a box of sixty-four crayons, like *magenta* or *avocado.*

Now tear or cut the paper on the fold lines so that you have sixteen pieces of paper, being careful to keep the columns in the same order as you wrote them. Rearrange the words in each column and read across.

What does your patchwork poem say? Does it make any sense?

Thumbprint

A poem by Eve Merriam

In the heel of my thumb
are whorls, whirls, wheels
in a unique design:
mine alone.
What a treasure to own!
My own flesh, my own feelings.
No other, however grand or base,
can ever contain the same.
My signature,
thumbing the pages of my time.
My universe key,
my singularity.
Impress, implant,
I am myself,
of all my atom parts I am the sum.
And out of my blood and my brain
I make my own interior weather,
my own sun and rain.
Imprint my mark upon the world,
whatever I shall become.

Illustration by Gary Van Der Steur

LINCOLN SCHOOL

From the autobiography *Barrio Boy* by Ernesto Galarza

Illustrated by Bert Dodson

In 1913, after three years of searching for work in northern Mexico during the revolution, Henriqueta[1] Galarza brought her young son Ernesto north to Sacramento, California. Like most other immigrants who came from all over the world to this busy agricultural port, they moved into the lower part of town. Lower Sacramento was a mix of many nationalities. As Ernesto describes it, "it was a kaleidoscope of colors and languages and customs that surprised and absorbed me at every turn." Two blocks from the Galarzas was a Japanese neighborhood, and beyond that lay Chinatown. Portuguese and Italian families gathered in their own neighborhoods along the river. The adult immigrants tended to keep to the security of their own people, and many lived their whole lives without learning English. For their children, however, it was another story. No matter where they came from, they all wound up at Lincoln School.

---

1. **Henriqueta** (EN·ree·KAY·tah).

AMERICA WAS ALL AROUND US, in and out of the *barrio*.[2] Abruptly we had to forget the ways of shopping in a *mercado*[3] and learn those of shopping in a corner grocery or in a department store. The Americans paid no attention to the Sixteenth of September,[4] but they made a great commotion about the Fourth of July. In Mazatlán[5] our teacher Don Salvador had told us, saluting and marching as he talked to our class, that the *Cinco de Mayo*[6] was the most glorious date in human history. The Americans had not even heard about it.

In Tucson, when I had asked my mother if the Americans were having a revolution like the Mexicans, the answer was: "No, but they have good schools, and you are going to one of them." We were by now settled at 418 L Street and the time had come for me to exchange a revolution for an American education.

The two of us walked south on Fifth Street one morning to the corner of Q Street and turned right. Half of the block was occupied by the Lincoln School. It was a three-story wooden building, with two wings that gave it the shape of a double-T connected by a central hall. It was a new building, painted yellow, with a shingled roof that was not like the red tile of the

school in Mazatlán. I noticed other differences, none of them very reassuring.

We walked up the wide staircase hand in hand and through the door, which closed by itself. A mechanical contraption screwed to the top shut it behind us quietly.

Up to this point the adventure of enrolling me in the school had been carefully rehearsed. Mrs. Dodson, our landlady, had told us how to find it and we had circled it several times on our walks. Friends in the *barrio* explained that the director was called a principal, and that it was a lady and not a man. They assured us that there was always a person at the school who could speak Spanish.

Exactly as we had been told, there was a sign on the door in both Spanish and English: "Principal." We crossed the hall and entered the office of Miss Nettie Hopley.

Miss Hopley was at a roll-top desk to one side, sitting in a swivel chair that moved on wheels. There was a sofa against the opposite wall, flanked by two windows and a door that opened on a small balcony. Chairs were set around a table and framed pictures hung on the walls of a man with long white hair and another with a sad face and a black beard.

The principal half turned in the swivel chair to look at us over the pinch glasses crossed on the ridge of her nose. To do this she had to duck her head slightly as if she were about to step through a low doorway.

---

2. *barrio* (BAHR‧ree‧oh): Spanish for *urban district*.
3. *mercado* (MER‧KAH‧doh): a Mexican market.
4. **Sixteenth of September**: Mexican Independence Day.
5. **Mazatlán** (mah‧saht‧LAHN): a city in Mexico.
6. *Cinco de Mayo* (SIN‧koh day MY‧oh): Fifth of May, an important Mexican holiday.

What Miss Hopley said to us we did not know but we saw in her eyes a warm welcome and when she took off her glasses and straightened up she smiled wholeheartedly, like Mrs. Dodson. We were, of course, saying nothing, only catching the friendliness of her voice and the sparkle in her eyes while she said words we did not understand. She signaled us to the table. Almost tiptoeing across the office, I maneuvered myself to keep my mother between me and the lady. In a matter of seconds I had to decide whether she was a possible friend or a menace. We sat down.

Then Miss Hopley did a formidable thing. She stood up. Had she been standing when we entered she would have seemed tall. But rising from her chair she soared. And what she carried up and up with her were firm shoulders, a straight sharp nose, full cheeks slightly molded by a curved line along the nostrils, thin lips that moved like steel springs, and a high forehead topped by hair gathered in a bun. Miss Hopley was not a giant in body but when she mobilized it to a standing position she seemed a match for giants. I decided I liked her.

She strode to a door in the far corner of the office, opened it and called a name. A boy of about ten

years appeared in the doorway. He sat down at one end of the table. He was brown like us, a plump kid with shiny black hair combed straight back, neat, cool, and faintly obnoxious.

Miss Hopley joined us with a large book and some papers in her hand. She, too, sat down and the questions and answers began by way of our interpreter. My name was Ernesto. My mother's name was Henriqueta. My birth certificate was in San Blas.[7] Here was my last report card from the Escuela Municipal Numero 3 para Varones[8] of Mazatlán, and so forth. Miss Hopley put things down in the book and my mother signed a card.

As long as the questions continued, Doña Henriqueta could stay and I was secure. Now that they were over, Miss Hopley saw her to the door, dismissed our interpreter and without further ado took me by the hand and strode down the hall to Miss Ryan's first grade.

Miss Ryan took me to a seat at the front of the room, into which I shrank — the better to survey her. She was, to skinny, somewhat runty me, of a withering[9] height when she patrolled the class. And when I least expected it, there she was, crouching by my desk, her blond radiant face level with mine, her voice patiently maneuvering me over the awful idiocies of the English language.

During the next few weeks Miss Ryan overcame my fears of tall, energetic teachers as she bent over my desk to help me with a word in the pre-primer. Step by step, she loosened me and my classmates from the safe anchorage of the desks for recitations at the blackboard and consultations at her desk. Frequently she burst into happy announcements to the whole class. "Ito[10] can read a sentence," and small, shy Japanese Ito slowly read aloud while the class listened in wonder: "Come, Skipper, come. Come and run." The Korean, Portuguese, Italian, and Polish first graders had similar moments of glory, no less shining than mine the day I conquered *butterfly,* which I had been persistently pronouncing in standard Spanish as "boo-ter-flee." "Children," Miss Ryan called for attention. "Ernesto has learned how to pronounce *butterfly!"* And I proved it with a perfect imitation of Miss Ryan. From that celebrated success, I was soon able to match Ito's progress as a sentence reader with "Come, butterfly, come fly with me."

Like Ito and several other first graders who did not know English, I received private lessons from Miss Ryan in the closet, a narrow hall off the classroom with a door at each end. Next to one of these doors Miss Ryan placed a large chair for herself and a small one for me. Keeping an eye on the class through the open door she

---

7. **San Blas** (san BLAS): a Mexican village.
8. **Escuela Municipal Numero 3 para Varones:** Municipal (City) School Number 3 for Males.
9. **withering:** here, intimidating; frightening.

---

10. **Ito** (EE·toh).

read with me about sheep in the meadow and a frightened chicken going to see the king, coaching me out of my phonetic ruts[11] in words like *pasture, bow-wow-wow, hay,* and *pretty,* which to my Mexican ear and eye had so many unnecessary sounds and letters. She made me watch her lips and then close my eyes as she repeated words I found hard to read.

When we came to know each other better, I tried interrupting to tell Miss Ryan how we said it in Spanish. It didn't work. She only said "oh" and

went on with *pasture, bow-wow-wow,* and *pretty.* It was as if in that closet we were both discovering together the secrets of the English language and grieving together over the tragedies of Bo-Peep. The main reason I was graduated with honors from the first grade was that I had fallen in love with Miss Ryan. Her radiant, no-nonsense character made us either afraid not to love her or love her so we would not be afraid, I am not sure which. It was not only that we sensed she was with it, but also that she was with us.

Like the first grade, the rest of the Lincoln School was a sampling of the lower part of town where many races

---

11. **phonetic** (foh•NET•ik) **ruts**: discouraging difficulties with pronunciation (phonetics).

made their home. My pals in the second grade were Kazushi,[12] whose parents spoke only Japanese; Matti, a skinny Italian boy; and Manuel, a fat Portuguese who would never get into a fight but wrestled you to the ground and just sat on you. Our assortment of nationalities included Koreans, Yugoslavs, Poles, Irish, and home-grown Americans.

Miss Hopley and her teachers never let us forget why we were at Lincoln: for those who were alien,[13] to become good Americans; for those who were so born, to accept the rest of us. Off the school grounds we traded the same insults we heard from our elders. On the playground we were sure to be marched up to the principal's office for calling someone an insulting name. The school was not so much a melting pot as a griddle where Miss Hopley and her helpers warmed knowledge into us and roasted racial hatreds out of us.

At Lincoln, making us into Americans did not mean scrubbing away what made us originally foreign. The teachers called us as our parents did, or as close as they could pronounce our names in Spanish or Japanese. No one was ever scolded or punished for speaking in his native tongue on the playground. Matti told the class about his mother's down quilt, which she had made in Italy with the fine feathers of a thousand geese.

Encarnación[14] acted out how boys learned to fish in the Philippines. I astounded the third grade with the story of my travels on a stagecoach, which nobody else in the class had seen except in the museum at Sutter's Fort. After a visit to the Crocker Art Gallery and its collection of heroic paintings of the golden age of California, someone showed a silk scroll with a Chinese painting. Miss Hopley herself had a way of expressing wonder over these matters before a class, her eyes wide open until they popped slightly. It was easy for me to feel that becoming a proud

---

12. **Kazushi** (kah·ZOO·shee).
13. **alien:** foreign born; not citizens.

14. **Encarnación** (EN·kahr·nah·SYOHN).

American, as she said we should, did not mean feeling ashamed of being a Mexican.

The Americanization of Mexican me was no smooth matter. I had to fight one lout who made fun of my travels on the *diligencia,*[15] and my barbaric translation of the word into "diligence." He doubled up with laughter over the word until I straightened him out with a kick. In class I made points explaining that in Mexico roosters said "qui-qui-ri-qui" and not "cock-a-doodle-doo," but after school I had to put up with the taunts of a big Yugoslav who said Mexican roosters were crazy.

But it was Homer who gave me the most lasting lesson for a future American.

Homer was a chunky Irishman who dressed as if every day was Sunday. He slicked his hair between a crew cut and a pompadour.[16] And Homer was smart, as he clearly showed when he and I ran for president of the third grade.

Everyone understood that this was to be a demonstration of how the American people vote for president. In an election, the teacher explained, the candidates could be generous and vote for each other. We cast our ballots in a shoe box and Homer won by two votes. I polled my supporters and came to the conclusion that I had voted for Homer and so had he. After class he didn't deny it, reminding me of what the teacher had said — we could vote for each other but didn't have to.

The lower part of town was a collage of nationalities in the middle of which Miss Nettie Hopley kept school with discipline and compassion. She called assemblies in the upper hall to introduce celebrities like the police sergeant or the fire chief, to lay down the law of the school, to present awards to our athletic champions, and to make important announcements. One of these was that I had been proposed by my school and accepted as a

---

15. *diligencia* (dee·lee·HEN·syah): Spanish for *stage-coach.*

16. **pompadour** (POM·puh·dawr): a hairstyle in which the hair is combed up high from the forehead.

member of the newly formed Sacramento Boys Band. "Now, isn't that a wonderful thing?" Miss Hopley asked the assembled school, all eyes on me. And everyone answered in chorus, including myself, "Yes, Miss Hopley."

It was not only the parents who were summoned to her office and boys and girls who served sentences there who knew that Nettie Hopley meant business. The entire school witnessed her sizzling Americanism in its awful majesty one morning at flag salute.

All the grades, as usual, were lined up in the courtyard between the wings of the building, ready to march to classes after the opening bell. Miss Shand was on the balcony of the second floor off Miss Hopley's office, conducting us in our lusty singing of "My Country tiz-a-thee." Our principal, as always, stood there like us, at attention, her right hand over her heart, joining in the song.

Halfway through the second stanza she stepped forward, held up her arm in a sign of command, and called loud and clear: "Stop the singing." Miss Shand looked flabbergasted. We were frozen with shock.

Miss Hopley was now standing at the rail of the balcony, her eyes sparking, her voice low and resonant, the words coming down to us distinctly and loaded with indignation.

"There are two gentlemen walking on the school grounds with their hats on while we are singing," she said, sweeping our ranks with her eyes. "We will remain silent until the gentlemen come to attention and remove their hats." A minute of awful silence ended when Miss Hopley, her gaze fixed on something behind us, signaled Miss Shand and we began once more the familiar hymn. That afternoon, when school was out, the word spread. The two gentlemen were the Superintendent of Schools and an important guest on an inspection.

I came back to the Lincoln School after every summer, moving up through the grades with Miss Campbell, Miss Beakey, Mrs. Wood, Miss Applegate, and Miss Delahunty. I sat in the classroom adjoining the principal's office and had my turn answering her telephone when she was about the building repeating the message to the teacher, who made a note of it. Miss Campbell read to us during the last period of the week about King Arthur, Columbus, Buffalo Bill, and Daniel Boone, who came to life in the reverie of the class through the magic of her voice. And it was Miss Campbell who introduced me to the public library on Eye Street, where I became a regular customer.

All of Lincoln School assembled to say good-bye to Miss Applegate, who was off to Alaska to be married. Now it was my turn to be excused from class to interpret for a parent enrolling a new student fresh from Mexico. Graduates from Lincoln came back now and then to tell us about high school. A naturalist entertained us in assembly, imitating the calls of the meadow lark, the water ouzel, the oriole, and the killdeer. I decided to become a bird man after I left Lincoln.

In the years we lived in the lower part of town, La Leen-Con, as my family called it, became a benchmark[17] in our lives.

---

17. **benchmark:** a landmark; a high point.

About ERNESTO GALARZA

Sometimes it seems to students that teachers spend their lives in classrooms and teach only what they learn in books. Ernesto Galarza has taught people of all ages, from elementary-school children to university students, and is a teacher of a different sort. Galarza, an activist and a writer, has been as involved in the world as he has been in the classroom.

Ernesto Galarza was born in Mexico. About his childhood Galarza has said, "We had no radio or television or movies. We had nature. . . . We learned to use all our senses to hear, feel, smell, and taste all of nature's performance around us. . . . We put all this together in ways that pleased our fancy. We were poets." Later in his life, Galarza would use his sensitivity to nature in writing poems for children. His family fled during the 1910 Mexican Revolution, and Galarza grew up in California. As a teenager he worked on the farms of the hot Central Valley in California and learned firsthand about the hard lives of farm laborers.

When he left for school, teaching, and a job in Washington, D.C., he kept in mind the problems he had seen. He soon became involved in the struggle to gain respect and decent conditions for farm workers. He argued his position in the fields and also wrote several books and many articles and pamphlets. His autobiography, *Barrio Boy,* first began as a series of stories he told his family and friends, stories that related the difficulties and successes of growing up in a new land among new people. "There is no more interesting history than that in which one has taken part," he once said, "and no better reward than the opportunity to write it."

■ Understanding the Story

1. Miss Hopley could not speak Spanish, but she made Ernesto Galarza and his mother feel welcome at her school. Galarza remembers that "she smiled wholeheartedly." Find one other detail about Miss Hopley that helped Ernesto decide that she was a friend.

2. Miss Ryan gave several first-graders private lessons in English. Name one other way in which she helped the children learn English.

3. How did the teachers at Lincoln School encourage students to be proud of their different backgrounds?

4. In the third grade, Ernesto ran for president of his class. Find another detail that tells you Ernesto's years at Lincoln were successful.

5. What was the most lasting lesson that you think you learned in elementary school?

■ Understanding Literature

"Lincoln School" comes from Ernesto Galarza's autobiography, *Barrio Boy*. An *autobiography* is a person's written account of his or her own life, whereas a *biography* is a person's life story written by someone else. Both are forms of *nonfiction:* writing that records actual events or presents facts.

Most autobiographers write from the first-person point of view. They recount incidents they recall from various times in their lives. Sometimes well-known personalities write about their life experiences in a type of autobiography called a *memoir.* A memoir will often contain interesting anecdotes that come from the author's varied experiences with famous people.

Ernesto Galarza writes about the incidents he remembers from Lincoln School. You will notice that he makes a point of telling how he felt about the people and events at his elementary school. He also includes numerous details to help us "see" his days at Lincoln School the way he saw them. For example, on page 298, he describes Miss Hopley's office: "There was a sofa against the opposite wall, flanked by two windows and a door that opened on a small balcony." Galarza had to search his memory carefully for the image of that morning to give his readers these vivid impressions.

■ Writing About the Story

What do you recall of your first day in elementary school? What did you think of your teacher? Were you frightened? Write a page or so in which you tell what you remember about that important day. If you do not remember your first school day, write about some other event from your elementary-school days. Write this account in the form of advice for a real or imaginary young friend who is about to begin school.

Those Winter Sundays

A poem by Robert Hayden

Illustration by Clifford Timm

Sundays too my father got up early
and put his clothes on in the blueblack cold,
then with cracked hands that ached
from labor in the weekday weather made
banked fires blaze. No one ever thanked him.

I'd wake and hear the cold splintering, breaking.
When the rooms were warm, he'd call,
and slowly I would rise and dress,
fearing the chronic angers of that house,

Speaking indifferently to him,
who had driven out the cold
and polished my good shoes as well.
What did I know, what did I know
of love's austere[1] and lonely offices?[2]

---

1. **austere** (aw•STEER): simple, serious, and severe.
2. **offices**: services; chores.

GRADUATION

From the teleplay *I Know Why the Caged Bird Sings*
by Leonora Thuna and Maya Angelou
Illustrated by Diane De Groat

*This television play was adapted from poet Maya Angelou's[1] auto-
biography,* I Know Why the Caged Bird Sings. *As in a stage
play, the script contains guides for the actors' speech and movements; it also includes directions for camera shots, scenery, and
lighting, which help the reader to visualize the action.*

*In the Depression years of the 1930s, when she was four years
old, Marguerite Johnson (better known as Maya) and her older
brother Bailey went to live with their grandmother (Momma) and
their uncle Willie in the rural town of Stamps, Arkansas. Maya
had a painful childhood, but with the loving support of her family
and her teacher, Miss Flowers, the timid girl blossomed into the
bright, confident teenager who is about to give the main address at
the Lafayette County Training School graduation. Like most
schools in the 1940s, Maya's school is segregated: all the students
and teachers are Black. The school district officials, however, are
white, and they have just prohibited the singing of "Lift Every
Voice and Sing," better known as the "Negro National Anthem."*

---

1. **Maya Angelou** (MY·uh AN·juh·loo).

Characters

Maya
Bailey
Uncle Willie
Momma
Principal
Minister

Tommy Valdon, another student
Mr. Donleavy
Miss Flowers, Maya's teacher
Male and female graduates
Families and friends of the
    graduates

Setting: The location is Stamps, Arkansas; the time is the 1940s. The scenes take place in front of Momma's country general store, in Momma's house, and in the school auditorium.

Long shot of a small, country general store — day. Close up of hammering a sign on the door. It reads:
CLOSED FOR GRADUATION
We pull back to see Maya *and* Uncle Willie *on the porch.* (Uncle Willie *is hammering the sign, and* Maya, *in her pajamas, is watching him. He finishes and turns to her.)*

Uncle Willie: Well? How's it look?

Maya *(Trembling with excitement):* I have to tell you something. I have to tell you I never really believed I would live to see this day. And I still can't believe it. I'm thirteen! And it's graduation day!

Uncle Willie: Start believing it. The day'll be over soon. *(He goes inside the store.* Bailey *comes out.)*

Bailey: Maya, here's your graduation present. *(He hands her a present wrapped in brown paper.)* I hope you like it. *(As she unwraps it)* You better like it. I saved for three months to buy it. (Maya *takes the gift out. It is a beautifully bound book.)*

Maya *(Reading):* Poems by Edgar Allan Poe.[2] *(Touching it)* Thank you! I

never had a book like this before! *(She opens it, and she and* Bailey *start walking.)*

Long shot — the yard. (Bailey *and* Maya, *in their nightclothes, walk around the yard, reading, alternating the lines.)*

Maya: "It was many and many a year ago,

Bailey: "In a kingdom by the sea,

Maya: "That a maiden there lived, whom you may know,

Bailey: "By the name of Annabel Lee — "

Dissolve to: Interior: the table — same day (Momma *is in her Sunday dress.* Uncle Willie *has a starched white shirt, tie and a dark suit on. They have just eaten an enormous breakfast.* Uncle Willie *and* Momma *look at each other, smiling.* Uncle Willie *passes a plate to* Maya *with a napkin over it.)*

Uncle Willie: Sister, you taste this yet?

Maya: Oh, Momma, I just don't think I can eat anymore.

Momma: Well, maybe if you just take a little peek, it might perk up your appetite. (Maya *takes the plate. Lifts the napkin. Her mouth drops open. A "Mickey Mouse" watch is lying across the plate.)*

Maya: Oh, Momma! A Mickey Mouse watch! Oh, Momma! Oh,

---

2. Edgar Allan Poe (1809–1849): American poet, short-story writer, and critic.

Uncle Willie, thank you! Thank you! *(She jumps up, kisses* Uncle Willie, *who pats her shoulder, then she hugs* Momma.*)*

Cut to: Interior: auditorium — day. (The chorus is singing in energetic harmony. As they sing, the rest of the class marches in and sits down. The small auditorium is filled with parents and guests. On the platform stands the chorus, their teachers — including Miss Flowers — *the* Principal *and* Minister. *The rest of the school sits in the auditorium. The march over, the* Principal *steps to the podium.)*

Principal: Welcome, parents and friends. I'd like to ask Reverend Davis to lead us in a prayer. *(The* Minister *steps up.)*

Minister: Bow our heads in prayer. *(Everyone bows their heads.) Close up of* Maya.

Minister *(Offstage):* Our Father, God, we thank thee for our assembly here, for this graduation. We thank thee for the parents of these children. *(*Maya *is sitting in front of tall* Tommy Valdon, *who leans forward to talk to her.)*

Tommy: You look real nice.

Maya *(Surprised, continues to look forward):* Who? Me?

Tommy: Yeah.

Maya *(Pleased but still not turning around):* So do you.

Minister: . . . and be more productive citizens. Amen.

(The Principal *returns to the podium. He looks embarrassed and uncomfortable.)*

Principal: We are . . . er . . . departing a bit from our prepared program because . . . er . . . our guest speaker today, who is also our friend, came from Texarkana to deliver the commencement address. But due to the irregularity of the train schedule, he's going to, as they say, "speak and run." *(He laughs nervously.)* And without further ado, I would like to introduce you to Mr. Edward Donleavy.

*(*Donleavy, *a thick, heavy-set white man with horn-rimmed glasses, gets up from his seat on the platform and goes to the podium. He is the only white person in the room. He takes some papers from his pocket and spreads them on the podium. He speaks in a dull, sonorous[3] tone.)*

Donleavy: Good morning. I am glad to be here and see the things going on here at this school just as they are at the other schools. As some of you may know — and I hope all of you will know — *(He smiles)* . . . I am running for elective office in this county. And one of my platforms is to improve the education of our children — white and Negro.

---

3. **sonorous** (suh·NAWR·uhs, SON·uh·ruhs): loud and deep.

(As he speaks the camera pans the audience looking very bored.)

Donleavy *(Cont.):* Now. I believe we are giving our Negro children a first-class education for those who want to take advantage of it. Now, if you look out that window, you see weeds and you see all the bushes. But I am proud to stand here in front of you today and to tell you that before long, when you look out that window, you're going to see not a whole lot of weeds and bushes . . . but you gonna see a paved playing field!

Angle — boy graduates (The erect bearing they had at the beginning of the ceremony has dissipated,[4] and shoulders slump, heads droop.)

Donleavy *(Offstage):* You know what that means, don't you? That means that our boys at Lafayette have a . . . chance to have a full-fledged development of their athletics. (As he speaks, Miss Flowers puts on her glasses and starts to read a book.)*

Donleavy *(Offstage cont.):* We can't forget that Paul Triskle, one of the first-line football tackles at Arkansas Agricultural and Mechanical College . . . came from right here at Lafayette! And now for the girls, we're not forgetting you.

Angle — girl graduates (Some have their eyes fastened on the small bouquets of flowers they hold in their hands. Some are twisting and folding their white handkerchiefs into tiny squares.)

Donleavy *(Offstage):* I can't give you the exact dates, but I'm pretty sure that you're bound to get some new equipment for your home economics building. No reason why you shouldn't be the best cooks and housekeepers in the whole country!

(Miss Flowers is reading her book while the Principal has his hands to his eyes.)

Donleavy *(Offstage cont.):* Now these improvements are due in no small way to my efforts to improve . . .

Donleavy *(Cont.):* . . . the educational facilities in Stamps. And I want to tell you that I didn't forget the Lafayette County Training School. *(The audience is half asleep.)*

Donleavy *(Offstage):* I thank you all very much. *(He steps down, takes his sheaf of papers and walks out, not even waiting for the perfunctory applause. All is still. The atmosphere is heavy. Quiet. The buzzing of flies can be heard. Slowly, the Principal gets up. Goes to the podium.)*

Principal *(Clears his throat):* Our valedictorian[5] — Marguerite Johnson.

---

4. **dissipated:** vanished; fallen apart, disintegrated.

5. **valedictorian:** a student who gives the main speech at a graduation ceremony.

(*He walks away.* Momma, *sitting in the audience, is smiling broadly. Sitting next to her are* Bailey *and* Uncle Willie. *At the podium,* Maya *stands up tall and straight.*)

Maya: Mr. Principal, dear teachers, fellow graduates, dear parents and friends. Our speaker just told us that he was improving the educational facilities in Stamps. He's giving us a chance to become basketball players and cooks. Well, I want to thank Mr. Donleavy for this chance, but I don't think I'm going to take it. I didn't memorize the whole of "The Rape of Lucrece"[6] so I could be a cook, or a cleaning lady.

_____

6. "The Rape of Lucrece" (loo·KREES): a narrative poem by William Shakespeare.

(*Close up of* Miss Flowers, *who has closed her book and is looking at* Maya, *listening avidly. The* Principal *looks uncomfortable next to her.*)

Maya (*Cont.*): See, I give Mr. Donleavy all the rights he wants. But I don't believe he has the right to decide that my only hero has got to be a first-line football tackle. I got other heroes. For example, Edgar Allan Poe because I like what he said. And I like the way he said it. My teachers, because they showed me a map and on that map I saw that the world went beyond Stamps, Arkansas, United States of America, North American Continent. And I got another hero. Me. And me is not just a proud member of the graduating class of Lafayette County Training School.

Me is a proud member of the Negro race. The wonderful, beautiful Negro race.

Angle — the audience (They're not quite sure what's happening, but they know the atmosphere in the auditorium has changed.)

Maya *(Cont.)*: Well, I want to thank Mr. Donleavy for the paved playing field, but I'm not going to run

on it. I got other things to do. *(Maya turns and looks at Momma.) Close up —* Momma *(She looks placid and serene as she watches Maya — as though nothing Maya says can surprise her.)*

Maya *(Cont.)*: And I want to thank my grandmother who taught me how to sing. She said that in order to lift your voice, you have to lift your head. And when you lift your head — you're looking at heaven. *(Momma's head lifts a bit at these words. Maya turns to the graduates.)*

Maya *(Cont.)*: So I'm going to ask my fellow graduates to sing with me — the Negro National Anthem. *(Singing)*
TILL EARTH AND HEAVEN RING
RING WITH THE HARMONIES OF LIBERTY.

Principal *(To Miss Flowers)*: What is she doing? That song is not allowed.

Miss Flowers: It's too late now. *(Tommy Valdon stands, followed by Miss Flowers.)*

Maya:
LET OUR REJOICING RISE
HIGH AS THE LISTENING SKIES

(And now, the graduates start to sing with her, rising to their feet, one by one, three by three until all are standing, including the adults, and teachers. The Principal gives up, and signals the pianist to accompany them.)

Maya and graduates:
LET IT RESOUND LOUD AS
THE ROLLING SEA
SING A SONG FULL OF THE
FAITH
THAT THE DARK PAST HAS
TAUGHT US
SING A SONG FULL OF THE
HOPE
THAT THE PRESENT HAS
BROUGHT US —

(As they sing we see flashbacks of
Maya's *life from the beginning of the*
story to the end.)

All Singing *(With real feeling now)*:
PRAISING THE RISING SUN
WHEN EVERY DAY BE DONE,
LET US MARCH ON
TILL VICTORY IS WON!
PRAISING THE RISING SUN
WHEN EVERY DAY BE DONE,
LET US MARCH ON
TILL VICTORY IS WON!

About MAYA ANGELOU

"I was a Black girl in the South, six feet tall and not pretty. . . . I was told by everyone . . . that I could never amount to anything," Maya Angelou recalls. "But then I wondered: hey, who made that rule? I'm a human being! I realized that no one else could tell me what I could or couldn't do." Maya Angelou has become a successful writer, poet, actress, songwriter, singer, dancer, producer, director, journalist, playwright, choreographer, wife, and mother. She is always pushing herself — to learn more, do more, try more. "Not bad, Maya," she tells herself, "you can do it all — and more."

Maya Angelou feels that the more you learn and the more active you are, the more you can do. She is convinced that anyone can be almost anything, because she believes there are no limits to potential. "It's dangerous and limiting," she explains, "for people to assume . . . that because you are one thing you can't be something else."

Maya Angelou's formal education stopped when she finished high school, but she has never stopped learning or dreaming. "Dreams," she says, "are wonderful — private, delicate, tender wishes that can be achieved."

The Bracelet

A short story by Yoshiko Uchida
Illustrated by Hal Frenck

*After the Japanese attack on Pearl Harbor (December 7, 1941),
the American government panicked. Under President Roosevelt's
infamous Executive Order 9066, all persons of Japanese ancestry
on the West Coast were forcibly evacuated from their homes and
relocated in ten inland detention centers. Despite overwhelming evidence of their loyalty to the United States, over 100,000 Japanese
Americans (two-thirds of them citizens) were imprisoned under
miserable conditions until 1945. At the end of the war, they found
their homes and land — which included ten percent of all farms
in California — sold for taxes and "storage fees."*

*"The Bracelet" is a story of the special courage of a young girl
of Japanese ancestry — no different from any other American girl —
and a special gift of friendship.*

"Mama, is it time to go?"

I hadn't planned to cry, but the tears came suddenly,
and I wiped them away with the back of my hand. I
didn't want my older sister to see me crying.

"It's almost time, Ruri," my mother said gently. Her
face was filled with a kind of sadness I had never seen
before.

I looked around at my empty room. The clothes that
Mama always told me to hang up in the closet, the junk
piled on my dresser, the old rag doll I could never bear to
part with; they were all gone. There was nothing left in
my room, and there was nothing left in the rest of the
house. The rugs and furniture were gone, the pictures and

317

drapes were down, and the closets and cupboards were empty. The house was like a gift box after the nice thing inside was gone; just a lot of nothingness.

It was almost time to leave our home, but we weren't moving to a nicer house or to a new town. It was April 21, 1942. The United States and Japan were at war, and every Japanese person on the West Coast was being evacuated by the government to an internment camp. Mama, my sister Keiko,[1] and I were being sent from our home, and out of Berkeley,[2] and eventually, out of California.

The doorbell rang, and I ran to answer it before my sister could. I thought maybe by some miracle a messenger from the government might be standing there, tall and proper and buttoned into a uniform, come to tell us it was all a terrible mistake; that we wouldn't have to leave after all. Or maybe the messenger would have a telegram from Papa, who was interned in a prisoner-of-war camp in Montana because he had worked for a Japanese business firm.

The FBI had come to pick up Papa and hundreds of other Japanese community leaders on the very day that Japanese planes had bombed Pearl Harbor. The government thought they were dangerous enemy aliens. If it weren't so sad, it would have been funny. Papa could no more be dangerous than the mayor of our city, and he was every bit as loyal to the United States. He had lived here since 1917.

When I opened the door, it wasn't a messenger from anywhere. It was my best friend, Laurie Madison, from next door. She was holding a package wrapped up like a birthday present, but she wasn't wearing her party dress, and her face drooped like a wilted tulip.

"Hi," she said. "I came to say good-bye."

She thrust the present at me and told me it was something to take to camp. "It's a bracelet," she said before I could open the package. "Put it on so you won't have to

---

1. **Keiko** (KAY·koh).
2. **Berkeley**: a city in California, on San Francisco Bay.

pack it." She knew I didn't have one inch of space left in my suitcase. We had been instructed to take only what we could carry into camp, and Mama had told us that we could each take only two suitcases.

"Then how are we ever going to pack the dishes and blankets and sheets they've told us to bring with us?" Keiko worried.

"I don't really know," Mama said, and she simply began packing those big impossible things into an enormous duffel bag — along with umbrellas, boots, a kettle, hot plate,[3] and flashlight.

"Who's going to carry that huge sack?" I asked.

But Mama didn't worry about things like that. "Someone will help us," she said. "Don't worry." So I didn't.

Laurie wanted me to open her package and put on the bracelet before she left. It was a thin gold chain with a heart dangling on it. She helped me put it on, and I told her I'd never take it off, ever.

"Well, good-bye then," Laurie said awkwardly. "Come home soon."

"I will," I said, although I didn't know if I would ever get back to Berkeley again.

I watched Laurie go down the block, her long blond pigtails bouncing as she walked. I wondered who would be sitting in my desk at Lincoln Junior High now that I was gone. Laurie kept turning and waving, even walking backwards for a while, until she got to the corner. I didn't want to watch anymore, and I slammed the door shut.

The next time the doorbell rang, it was Mrs. Simpson, our other neighbor. She was going to drive us to the Congregational church, which was the Civil Control Station where all the Japanese of Berkeley were supposed to report.

It was time to go. "Come on, Ruri. Get your things," my sister called to me.

It was a warm day, but I put on a sweater and my coat so I wouldn't have to carry them, and I picked up my two

---

3. **hot plate**: a small, portable electric stove.

suitcases. Each one had a tag with my name and our family number on it. Every Japanese family had to register and get a number. We were Family Number 13453.

Mama was taking one last look around our house. She was going from room to room, as though she were trying to take a mental picture of the house she had lived in for fifteen years, so she would never forget it.

I saw her take a long last look at the garden that Papa loved. The irises beside the fish pond were just beginning to bloom. If Papa had been home, he would have cut the first iris blossom and brought it inside to Mama. "This one is for you," he would have said. And Mama would have smiled and said, "Thank you, Papa," and put it in her favorite cut-glass vase.

But the garden looked shabby and forsaken now that Papa was gone and Mama was too busy to take care of it. It looked the way I felt, sort of empty and lonely and abandoned.

When Mrs. Simpson took us to the Civil Control Station, I felt even worse. I was scared, and for a minute I thought I was going to lose my breakfast right in front of everybody. There must have been over a thousand Japanese people gathered at the church. Some were old and some were young. Some were talking and laughing, and some were crying. I guess everybody else was scared too. No one knew exactly what was going to happen to us. We just knew we were being taken to the Tanforan Race-tracks, which the army had turned into a camp for the Japanese. There were fourteen other camps like ours along the West Coast.

What scared me most were the soldiers standing at the doorway of the church hall. They were carrying guns with mounted bayonets. I wondered if they thought we would try to run away, and whether they'd shoot us or come after us with their bayonets if we did.

A long line of buses waited to take us to camp. There were trucks, too, for our baggage. And Mama was right; some men were there to help us load our duffel bag. When it was time to board the buses, I sat with Keiko

and Mama sat behind us. The bus went down Grove Street and passed the small Japanese food store where Mama used to order her bean-curd cakes and pickled radish. The windows were all boarded up, but there was a sign still hanging on the door that read, "We are loyal Americans."

The crazy thing about the whole evacuation was that we were all loyal Americans. Most of us were citizens because we had been born here. But our parents, who had come from Japan, couldn't become citizens because there was a law that prevented any Asian from becoming a citizen. Now everybody with a Japanese face was being shipped off to internment camps.

"It's stupid," Keiko muttered as we saw the racetrack looming up beside the highway. "If there were any Japanese spies around, they'd have gone back to Japan long ago."

"I'll say," I agreed. My sister was in high school and she ought to know, I thought.

When the bus turned into Tanforan, there were more armed guards at the gate, and I saw barbed wire strung

around the entire grounds. I felt as though I were going into a prison, but I hadn't done anything wrong.

We streamed off the buses and poured into a huge room, where doctors looked down our throats and peeled back our eyelids to see if we had any diseases. Then we were given our housing assignments. The man in charge gave Mama a slip of paper. We were in Barrack 16, Apartment 40.

"Mama!" I said. "We're going to live in an apartment!" The only apartment I had ever seen was the one my piano teacher lived in. It was in an enormous building in San Francisco with an elevator and thick carpeted hallways. I thought how wonderful it would be to have our own elevator. A house was all right, but an apartment seemed elegant and special.

We walked down the racetrack looking for Barrack 16. Mr. Noma, a friend of Papa's, helped us carry our bags. I was so busy looking around, I slipped and almost fell on the muddy track. Army barracks had been built everywhere, all around the racetrack and even in the center oval.

Mr. Noma pointed beyond the track toward the horse stables. "I think your barrack is out there."

He was right. We came to a long stable that had once housed the horses of Tanforan, and we climbed up the wide ramp. Each stall had a number painted on it, and when we got to 40, Mr. Noma pushed open the door.

"Well, here it is," he said, "Apartment 40."

The stall was narrow and empty and dark. There were two small windows on each side of the door. Three folded army cots were on the dust-covered floor and one light bulb dangled from the ceiling. That was all. This was our apartment, and it still smelled of horses.

Mama looked at my sister and then at me. "It won't be so bad when we fix it up," she began. "I'll ask Mrs. Simpson to send me some material for curtains. I could make some cushions too, and . . . well. . . ." She stopped. She couldn't think of anything more to say.

Mr. Noma said he'd go get some mattresses for us. "I'd

better hurry before they're all gone." He rushed off. I think he wanted to leave so that he wouldn't have to see Mama cry. But he needn't have run off, because Mama didn't cry. She just went out to borrow a broom and began sweeping out the dust and dirt. "Will you girls set up the cots?" she asked.

It was only after we'd put up the last cot that I noticed my bracelet was gone. "I've lost Laurie's bracelet!" I screamed. "My bracelet's gone!"

We looked all over the stall and even down the ramp. I wanted to run back down the track and go over every inch of ground we'd walked on, but it was getting dark and Mama wouldn't let me.

I thought of what I'd promised Laurie. I wasn't ever going to take the bracelet off, not even when I went to take a shower. And now I had lost it on my very first day in camp. I wanted to cry.

I kept looking for it all the time we were in Tanforan. I didn't stop looking until the day we were sent to another camp, called Topaz, in the middle of a desert in Utah. And then I gave up.

But Mama told me never mind. She said I didn't need a bracelet to remember Laurie, just as I didn't need anything to remember Papa or our home in Berkeley or all the people and things we loved and had left behind.

"Those are things we can carry in our hearts and take with us no matter where we are sent," she said.

And I guess she was right. I've never forgotten Laurie, even now.

About YOSHIKO UCHIDA

Yoshiko Uchida always wanted to write. When she was a very young child in California, she made books out of brown wrapping paper and filled them with her stories. Years later, she published her first real book, *The Dancing Kettle,* a collection of Japanese folk tales.

Yoshiko Uchida has also always loved arts and crafts. She often combines this interest with her writing. She has written several articles on craftspeople, and many of the characters in her books are Japanese potters.

When she decided to write fiction, Yoshiko Uchida knew that she wanted to write about the experience of being Japanese American. She hoped to help people of Japanese descent in their search for identity as Asian Americans. "I am hoping," she says, "to examine further the relatively unexplored history of the Japanese in America. . . ."

During World War II, Yoshiko Uchida and her family, like most Japanese Americans, were sent to internment camps. The camps were a great hardship, and after the war many of those people who had been imprisoned found it difficult to return to their former lives. Several of Uchida's books are about the struggle of Japanese Americans to survive during that difficult period.

Understanding the Story

1. Why were Ruri and her family leaving their home?

2. The barbed wire around Tanforan made Ruri feel as if she were going to prison. Find one other detail that shows Japanese Americans were treated as prisoners.

3. Ruri's mother is a strong woman who looks to the future with courage. Find one detail that shows her basic optimism, her generally cheerful outlook on the future.

4. A *symbol* is a place, person, object, or action that stands for something else. A dove, for example, is a symbol of peace. What does the bracelet symbolize in the story?

5. Do you sympathize with Ruri? Why? If you were forced to leave your home and your school, what are some of the things you would miss the most?

Understanding Literature

In listening and in reading, the goal is to discover what the speaker or writer means. Thus, in language and in literature, people create methods for extending and emphasizing meaning. The use of *irony* extends meaning by giving words and events more than one level of significance. In general, irony is a contrast between what appears to be and what actually is.

When you look out at a messy, rainy day and say, "What a beautiful day," you are using *verbal irony.* In verbal irony, a speaker or writer says one thing and means the opposite.

In stories and plays, you will often encounter *dramatic irony,* which means that the reader or audience knows something that one of the characters does not know.

In literature, authors often use yet another type of irony, *irony of situation,* in which what is expected contrasts with what actually occurs. For example, on page 322 in "The Bracelet," Ruri becomes excited when their housing assignment says they are to be in Apartment 40. She remembers her piano teacher's apartment and thinks, "A house was alright, but an apartment seemed elegant and special." Ruri expects an apartment like her piano teacher's, but instead she gets a horse stall. The fact that she gets the opposite of what she expects makes the situation ironic.

Writing About the Story

Americans may influence their government in many ways. One way is to write letters to the president, to congressional representatives, or even to local newspapers. Pretend that you are Ruri's classmate and write a letter expressing your feelings about what is happening to Ruri.

Studs Terkel, a veteran Chicago radio reporter, spent three years talking to scores of people about what they do all day and how they feel about it. He found that, as one woman put it, "most of us have jobs that are too small for our spirit. Jobs are not big enough for people."

Three of the four people interviewed in this selection are among "the happy few who find a savor in their daily job: the Indiana stonemason, who looks upon his work and sees that it is good; the bookbinder, who saves a piece of history"; and the organizer, who works trying to change history. The other, a part-time welfare worker, takes pride in her goal of supporting herself and her children.

From
Working

Interviews adapted from the book by Studs Terkel

Illustrated by Sue Rother

 **Stonemason**
Carl Murray Bates

We're in a tavern no more than thirty yards from the banks of the Ohio. He is fifty-seven years old. He's a stonemason who has pursued his craft since he was seventeen. None of his three sons is in his trade.

As far as I know, masonry is older than carpentry, which goes clear back to Bible times. Stone mason goes back way *before* Bible time: the pyramids of Egypt, things of that sort. Anybody that starts to build anything, stone, rock, or brick, start on the northeast corner. Because when they built King Solomon's Temple,[1] they started on the northeast corner. To this day, you look at your courthouses, your big public buildings, you look at the cornerstone, when it was created, what year, it will be on the northeast corner. If I was gonna build a septic tank, I would start on the northeast corner. (Laughs.) Superstition, I suppose.

With stone we build just about anything. Stone is the oldest and best building material that ever was. Stone was being

---

1. **King Solomon's Temple:** the great First Temple of the Jews, built by King Solomon in 950 B.C.

used even by the cavemen that put it together with mud. They built out of stone before they even used logs. He got him a cave, he built stone across the front. And he learned to use dirt, mud, to make the stones lay there without sliding around — which was the beginnings of mortar, which we still call mud. The Romans used mortar that's almost as good as we have today.

Every piece of stone you pick up is different, the grain's a little different and this and that. It'll split one way and break the other. You pick up your stone and look at it and make an educated guess. It's a pretty good day layin' stone or brick. Not tiring. Anything you like to do isn't tiresome. It's hard work; stone is heavy. At the same time, you get interested in what you're doing and you usually fight the clock the other way. You're not lookin' for quittin'. You're wondering you haven't got enough done and it's almost quittin' time. (Laughs.) I ask the hod carrier[2] what time it is and he says two thirty. I say, "Oh, my, I was gonna get a whole lot more than this."

Stone's my life. I daydream all the time, most times it's on stone. Oh, I'm gonna build me a stone cabin down on the Green River. I'm gonna build stone cabinets in the kitchen. That stone door's gonna be awful heavy and I don't know how to attach the hinges. I've got to figure out how to make a stone roof. That's the kind of thing. All my dreams, it seems like it's got to have a piece of rock mixed in it.

There's not a house in this country that I haven't built that I don't look at every time I go by. (Laughs.) I can set here now and actually in my mind see so many that you wouldn't believe. If there's one stone in there crooked, I know where it's at and I'll never forget it. Maybe thirty years, I'll know a place where I should have took that stone out and redone it but I didn't. I still notice it. The people who live there might not notice it, but I notice it. I never pass that house that I don't think of it. I've got one house in mind right now. (Laughs.) That's the work of my hands. 'Cause you see,

---

2. **hod carrier:** a stonemason's assistant whose job is to carry hods (portable troughs) of materials.

stone, you don't prepaint it, you don't camouflage it. It's there, just like I left it forty years ago.

I can't imagine a job where you go home and maybe go by a year later and you don't know what you've done. My work, I can see what I did the first day I started. All my work is set right out there in the open and I can look at it as I go by. It's something I can see the rest of my life. Forty years ago, the first blocks I ever laid in my life, when I was seventeen years old. I never go through Eureka — a little town down there on the river — that I don't look thataway. It's always there.

Immortality as far as we're concerned. Nothin' in this world lasts forever, but did you know that stone — Bedford limestone, they claim — deteriorates one-sixteenth of an inch every hundred years? And it's around four or five inches for a house. So that's gettin' awful close. (Laughs.)

 Bookbinder
Donna Murray

She has been binding books for twenty-five years. "I didn't even really become a bookbinder. It happened because we had so many books. I inherited this great big library from my father, and my husband, John, had many, many art books that were falling apart. We had acres of books, and I thought this was the thing to do: I'll put these books together and make them fit. So I began a sort of experiment and I enjoyed it very much."

At first no one taught me. I wasn't doing much of anything. Then a *marvelous* woman, who's a brilliant artist, gave me a *marvelous* frame that her father made for her, for sewing books and that sort of thing. So I learned to sew books. They're really good books, it's just the covers that are rotten. You take them apart and you make them sound and you smash them in and sew them up. That's all there is to it.

I have a bindery at home, it's kind of a cave, really. It's where you have your gear — a table where you work, a cutter, a press, and those kinds of things. You have a good screw press, a heavy one that presses the books down. A binder's gear is principally his thumbnail. You push, you use your thumbnail more than anything else.

I mustn't pose as a fine binder because I'm not. That's exhibition binding, gold tooling. You roll out this design and you fill it with egg white. Then you cover it with pure gold leaf. I enjoy restoration very much — when you restore an old book that's all ragged at the back. You must make a rubbing of the spine. The spine's all rotten, so you put that aside and you turn back the pages *very carefully.* That's what I enjoy most of all.

I go to the house and take my equipment, oils and paints and a certain binder's paste. And a painter's drop cloth. There's a beautiful Oriental rug, and indeed you may not drop anything on it. You set up a card table and book ends and that's about it, really.

We calculate the books. We make a point of being sure that the books go back exactly where they were before. We look at each book and pull it out and test it for tears. Almost everybody pulls books out by their tops, and they're always broken. Torn from beautiful leather bindings. In dusting books, you never touch them inside. The dust only goes to the top. People who pull them out with the idea of dusting them — it's just ridiculous. It only destroys the book.

My assistant takes the cloth for me, and then we line up the books. She dusts the tops. You always dust from the spine out, cleaning the book. Then you use the *marvelous* British Museum formula, potassium lactate. It's swabbed on the books to put back in the leather the acids that were taken out, that were in the hide in the beginning. They've been dried out completely and all the salts have been destroyed. So we swab all the leather goods with this potassium lactate. A very little swab, and let it sink in. Then these books are polished and put back on the shelves. It preserves books that could never exist in this climate after five years.

It's an arduous thing, but I suppose it's important because if that kind of thing didn't happen, the books would just disintegrate. Father's library did. Especially in the city with its very high potency of sulphur dioxide, which eats up the books.

The hideous air, the poisonous air of the city. It destroys them. It eats them up. Terrible.

I adore the work. It's very comforting. The only thing that makes me angry is that I'm almost all the time on the outside rather than on the inside. I'd like to be reading them. But I do think working in my house and being comfortable and doing something you feel is beneficial — it is important, isn't it?

I'm just a swabber. (Laughs.) I'm not an artist. I just use aniline dyes, so they won't be hurting the leather. Aniline's a natural dye, and that's about it. It isn't very skilled work. It's just knowing what books need, if you want to preserve them. It's just something you do. A mechanic takes care of a tire, and he knows . . .

Oh, I think it's important. Books are things that keep us going. Books — I haven't got much feeling about many other things. I adore the work. Except sometimes it becomes very lonesome. It's nice to sit beside somebody, whether it's somebody who works with you or whether it's your husband or your friend. It's just lovely, just like a whisper, always . . . But if you bind good books, you make something good, really and truly good. Yes, I would like to make a good book hold good and I would like to be involved in a pact that will not be broken, that holds good, which would really be as solid as the book.

Keeping a four-hundred-year-old book together keeps that spirit alive. It's an alluring kind of thing, lovely, because you know that belongs to us. Because a book is a life, like one man is a life. Yes, yes, this work is good for me.

Housewife
Jesusita Novarro

She is a mother of five children: the oldest twelve, the youngest two. She is working part-time as an assistant case aide at a settlement house in the neighborhood. The director "says I'm doing real good and can have a job upstairs with a little bit more money. It's only four hours, because in the afternoon I want to be with my children. They're still small."

I start my day here at five o'clock. I get up and prepare all the children's clothes. If there's shoes to shine, I do it in the morning. About seven o'clock I bathe the children. I leave my baby with the baby sitter and I go to work at the settlement house. I work until twelve o'clock. Sometimes I'll work longer if I have to go to welfare and get a check for somebody. When I get back, I try to make hot food for the kids to eat. In the afternoon it's pretty well on my own. I scrub and can and cook and do whatever I have to do.

Welfare makes you feel like you're nothing. Like you're laying back and not doing anything and it's falling in your lap. But you must understand, mothers, too, work. My house is clean. I've been scrubbing since this morning. You could check my clothes, all washed and ironed. I'm home and I'm working. I am a working mother.

A job that a woman in a house is doing is a tedious job — especially if you want to do it right. If you do it slipshod, then it's not so bad. I'm pretty much of a perfectionist. I tell my kids, hang a towel. I don't want it thrown away. That is very hard. It's a constant game of picking up this, picking up that. And putting this away, so the house'll be clean.

Some men work eight hours a day. There are mothers that work eleven, twelve hours a day. We get up at night, a baby vomits, you have to be calling the doctor, you have to be changing the baby. When do you get a break, really? You don't. This is an all-around job, day and night. Why do they say it's charity? It is not charity. We are giving some kind of home to these children.

The head of the settlement house wants me to take the social worker's job. I visit homes, I talk to mothers. I try to make them aware that they got something to give. I don't try to work out the problems. This is no good. I try to help them come to some kind of a decision. If there's no decision, to live with it, because some problem doesn't have any answer.

There was one mother that needed shoes. I found shoes for her. There was another mother that needed money because her check was late. I found someplace for her to borrow a couple of dollars. It's like a fund. I could borrow a couple of dollars until my check comes, then when my check comes I give it back. How much time have mothers left to go out and do this? How many of us have given time so other mothers could learn to speak English, so they'll be able to go to work.

I went to one woman's house and she's Spanish speaking. I was talking to her in English and she wouldn't unbend. I could see the fear in her eyes. So I started talking Spanish. Right away, she invited me for coffee and she was telling me the latest news . . .

I would like to help mothers be aware of how they can give to the community. Not the whole day — maybe three, four hours. And get paid for it. There's nothing more proud.

 Organizer
Bill Talcott

My work is trying to change this country. This is the job I've chosen. I try to bring people together who are being put down by the system, left out. You try to build an organization that will give them power to make the changes.

I put together a fairly solid organization of Appalachian people[3] in Pike County. It's a single industry area, coal. You either work for the coal company or you don't work.

The word *organizer* has been romanticized. You get the vision of a mystical being doing magical things. An organizer is a guy who brings in new members. I don't feel I've had a good day unless I've talked with at least one new person. We have a meeting, make space for new people to come in. The organizer sits next to the new guy, so everybody has to take the new guy as an equal. You do that a couple of times and the guy's got strength enough to become part of the group.

You must listen to them and tell them again and again they are important, that they have the stuff to do the job. They don't have to shuck themselves about not being good enough, not worthy. Most people were raised to think they

---

3. **Appalachian people:** people from the Appalachian Mountains of eastern Kentucky.

are not worthy. That's as true of a twenty-five-thousand-dollar a year executive as it is for the poorest. People become afraid of each other. They're convinced there's nothing they can do. I think we have it inside us to change things. We need the courage. It's a scary thing. Because we've been told from the time we were born that what we have inside us is bad and useless. What's true is what we have inside us is good and useful.

I work all the way from two in the morning until two the next morning seven days a week. (Laughs.) I'm not a martyr.[4] I'm one of the few people I know who was lucky in life to find out what he really wanted to do. I'm just havin' a ball, the time of my life. I feel sorry for all these people I run across all the time who aren't doing what they want to do. I think everybody ought to quit their job and do what they want to do. You've got one life. You've got, say, sixty-five years. How on earth can you blow forty-five years of that doing something you hate?

I have a wife and three children. I've managed to support them for six years doing this kind of work. We don't live fat. I have enough money to buy books and records. The kids have as good an education as anybody in this country. My kids know the name of the game: living your life up to the end.

All human recorded history is about five thousand years old. How many people in all that time have made an overwhelming difference? Twenty? Thirty? Most of us spend our lives trying to achieve some things. But we're not going to make an overwhelming difference. We do the best we can. That's enough.

The problem with history is that it's written by college professors about great men. That's not what history is. History's a lot of little people getting together and deciding they want a better life for themselves and their kids.

---

4. **martyr** (MAHR·tuhr): someone who dies or suffers for the good of a cause or belief.

■ Understanding the Story

1. The stonemason and the bookbinder are alike in that they both value the materials they work with and the finished product. What do the welfare worker and the organizer seem to value most?

2. As they tell about their jobs, the people interviewed reveal their characters and personalities. Choose one of the four workers and describe him or her briefly.

3. Forecasters say that in the next ten years the following jobs will probably pay the highest salaries: computer operator, doctor, health service administrator, engineer, and dentist. Some jobs that may have lower salaries than at present are teacher, soldier, newspaper reporter, lawyer, and architect. Of these jobs, which appeals to you most? Why?

■ Understanding Literature

For his book *Working,* Studs Terkel transcribed, or wrote down, from tape recordings what workers said almost exactly the way they said it. Because they were recorded, these interviews reflect as accurately as possible the oral language of ordinary American men and women.

Oral language differs from written language because different processes are involved in speaking and writing. Language changes constantly, but spoken English changes much more rapidly than written English. Also, the rules for written English are much more rigid than the rules for spoken English. When we write, we are expected to use *standard English,* the written language we learn in school and find in textbooks. When we speak, we often use incomplete sentences and slang expressions. We don't worry as much about correctness when we speak as we do when we write because there are so many acceptable variations in speech.

Because Terkel wanted to capture the spoken language of ordinary Americans, he did not rewrite the workers' conversations to conform to standard written English. But, interestingly enough, many of the passages in these interviews have a beauty equal to that of carefully crafted literature. Look at the speech by stonemason Carl Murray Bates on page 328. He expresses his feelings poetically when he says: "All my dreams, seems like it's got to have a piece of rock in it."

Look through the four interviews again. Find two other passages that you think use language in an interesting or poetic way.

■ Writing About the Story

What is your idea of a good job? Write the kind of "Help Wanted" newspaper advertisement that you would someday like to answer. Your ad should be about one hundred words.

The English word "interview" comes from the French word *entrevoir,* which means "to see one another." A well-conducted interview brings out a person's thoughts, experiences, and opinions. An interview thus reveals more about a person than is apparent on the surface.

You can find interviews on radio and television, and in magazines, newspapers, and books. Published interviews, such as those in news magazines and nonfiction books, tend to be longer and more detailed than those on the air. These interviews often go beyond what is of current interest; they try to provide information that will be of use in years to come.

A relatively new field of history, called *oral history,* has grown up as a result of the availability of portable tape recorders. Historians collect bits of oral history by recording conversations with selected individuals about experiences and customs. These interview tapes are usually transcribed into typed manuscript so the information can be easily used by other researchers.

Foxfire magazine publishes transcriptions of interviews with the mountain people of Georgia. The interviews include the songs, stories, history, craft lore, and practical knowledge of a generation that kept few written records. The project began as a way to get junior high and high school students more involved in English and journalism. The interviews, done by the students, proved to be so fascinating that the magazine now enjoys international distribution.

Real words from real people can also help to give an accurate picture of

how people in faraway places live their lives. Today anthropologists frequently tape-record interviews with members of the societies they study, and they often use parts of the interviews in the articles they write.

Perhaps the best-known interviewer-writer today is Chicago's Studs Terkel. Terkel has put together several books of interviews with ordinary Americans, and two of his books have risen to the top of the best-seller lists. One reason

Terkel's work has found such a large readership is that he makes each person live and breathe on the pages of his books. He does this by choosing only the most vital, expressive parts of each interview to include. This often means that he tape-records two or three hours of conversation and then searches through it for two or three minutes' worth of good material.

Perhaps you would like to interview someone whose thoughts and experiences are of interest to you. You may want to interview an elderly person in your family or neighborhood. Perhaps you would prefer to talk with an elected official or a candidate for office. You might want to interview someone who has the kind of job you would like to have someday. Take a moment now to decide on both the kind of person you want to interview and the subject you want to explore. For example, if you decide to interview a teacher, here are some topics you might want to discuss: changes in teaching methods, training for teaching, rewards and disadvantages of a teaching career. After you choose a person and a topic, prepare questions, conduct the interview, and then write up the results.

Here is a plan of action you might want to follow:

1. *Make an appointment to see the person you want to interview.* If the person you want to interview is well known, you may want to write a letter before telephoning. Introduce yourself and tell why you want to conduct an interview.

2. *Find out as much as you can about the person and the subject you have chosen.* If you are going to interview an elderly person, for example, and you want to find out about that person's early life, do some background reading to find out about that time period. Knowing something about your subject will help you find good questions to ask.

3. *Make a list of several questions for use in the interview.* Try to make each question a springboard for ideas and feelings.

4. *During the interview, take notes while the person answers questions, but don't try to write down every word.* Listen carefully and respond to the person as he or she talks. Encourage the speaker to continue with interesting stories by asking questions such as "What happened then?" and "How did you feel about that?" If you plan to use a tape recorder, be sure to get permission from the person you are interviewing before you turn the recorder on.

5. *Transcribe the tape or your notes into paragraphs that you can edit.* If you know how to type, you can type a transcription. Otherwise, listen to the tape several times and take notes. Then edit the material. Terkel describes the editing process as "panning for gold." A one-hundred-page transcript may be edited to four or five pages of material.
6. *Write a final version of the interview.* This should first identify the person and then explain why you chose that person and the particular topic. Then it should list your questions and the answers you received.

You can get more ideas on how to conduct an interview by watching television news programs or listening to talk shows on the radio. Here, cartoonist G.B. Trudeau, whose *Doonesbury* cartoons appear in newspapers throughout the country, shows how *not* to conduct an interview.

Copyright, 1978, G. B. Trudeau. Reprinted with permission of Universal Press Syndicate. All rights reserved.

BOOKSHELF

Forten the Sailmaker: Pioneer Champion of Negro Rights
by Esther M. Douty. Rand McNally, 1968. The true story of
James Forten, who spent his life and his hard-earned fortune fighting for freedom and equality for Black people.

Johnny Tremain by Esther Forbes. Houghton Mifflin, 1943.
The award-winning story of a young boy's involvement in
the American War of Independence.

1776: A Musical Play by Peter Stone and Sherman Edwards.
Viking Press, 1970. This re-creation of the days of the Second Continental Congress is rich with emotional depth and
drama.

My Brother Sam Is Dead by James Lincoln Collier and Chris-
topher Collier. Four Winds Press, 1974. Tim Meeker sees
the American War of Independence as a destructive force
that brings tragedy into his life.

To Spoil the Sun by Joyce Rockwood. Holt, Rinehart & Winston, 1976. Forewarned by omens, a Cherokee village is
struck by an ''invisible fire'' — smallpox brought to
America by European explorers.

The Light in the Forest by Conrad Richter. Alfred A. Knopf,
1966. True Son, captured and raised by Delaware Indians,
is rescued and returned to his family where his life becomes laden with conflict.

**Journey to Topaz: A Story of the Japanese-American
Evacuation** by Yoshiko Uchida. Charles Scribner's Sons,
1971. After the Japanese attack on Pearl Harbor, the Sa-
kane family is sent to an internment camp in Utah where
Yuki finds a friend and adjusts to the changes in her life.

The Summer of My German Soldier by Bette Greene. Dial
Press, 1973. After befriending a German POW and helping
him escape from a prison in Arkansas, Patty endures ridicule and condemnation.

342

5 Secrets

THE SECRET OF BLUE BEACH

From the novel *Carlota* by Scott O'Dell

Illustrated by Ted Rand

For the Spanish ranchers of southern California, 1846 was a year of financial problems. In these last days before the Mexican War, Don Saturnino's[1] huge rancho would have suffered had it not been for a gift from the sea. Whenever his family needed money, Don Saturnino took his sixteen-year-old daughter, Carlota,[2] to the Blue Beach "to dip out a bucket of water." As Carlota explains, these were no ordinary waters — nature kept a secret at Blue Beach.

---

1. **Don Saturnino** (dohn sah·toor·NEE·noh).
2. **Carlota** (kahr·LOH·tah).

MY FATHER AND I had been coming to Blue Beach for two years. On the three journeys we had made, we had always been followed. Sometimes by one or two Indians, sometimes by more. But to this day, no one had followed us farther than this spot where we crossed the river. Here we had managed to elude them.

One thing that helped was that we never told anyone our secret — the story of the Blue Beach.

We told none of the vaqueros[3] or the *mayordomo*.[4] Nor even Doña Dolores,[5] whom we could trust most of all. Dolores you could hang by her thumbs and still not hear one word that she did not wish to speak.

There was no way to find the Blue Beach except by following the river,

---

3. vaqueros (bah·KAY·rohs, vah·KAYR·ohs): cowboys.
4. *mayordomo* (MY·awr·DOH·moh): a foreman.
5. Doña Dolores: Carlota's grandmother.

either down from the mountains or up from the sea. From the sea no one would ever find it because of a series of lagoons. From the direction of the mountains you would need to be very lucky, as lucky as we had been in the beginning.

The river at this point, where it fanned out into the deep lagoons, ran narrow, between two sheer walls of granite, where even a mountain goat would be lost. At the bottom of these cliffs were two beaches, one facing the other across a distance of a hundred steps.

The beaches were strips of fine sand, finer than the sand you find on the sea beach itself. Both had a bluish cast, like pebbles you see through clear-running water. But they also had another color, a lighter blue that had a look of metal, as if there were copper deposits in the cliffs that had been washed down by the river and the rain and had mixed with the lighter color.

Someone might call the beaches green or the color of turquoise, but to us they were blue and this is what we called them — the Blue Beaches, more often, the Blue Beach.

On this day, as on the three other journeys we had made to the Blue Beach, we tied our horses and climbed up from the stream to a towering rock. From this high place we could survey the trails, one com-ing along the river, and one from the sea.

"What do you see?" my father said. He liked to test my eyesight. "Are we followed?"

"I see nothing on the trail," I said, "either from the river or from the sea."

"What is the brown spot among the oaks?"

"Where?"

"Up the river about a hundred *varas.*"[6]

"I see nothing."

"Look once more."

"Does it move?"

"Judge for yourself. But first you need to find it."

I looked hard and at last made out

---

6. *varas* (BAH·rahs): yards (1 *vara* = 2.78 feet).

the brown spot among the oaks. "It is a cow grazing," I said.

"There are two, and one is not a cow but a yearling fawn. What do you hear?"

"The stream."

"What else?"

"A crow somewhere."

"Is that all?"

"Yes."

"Listen."

"A woodpecker behind us."

"Yes. And what else do you hear?"

"Nothing."

"Besides the stream and the surf at the mouth of the river and gulls fishing?"

"You have good ears."

"And you will have them someday."

"Never so good as yours."

"Better. *Mucho más.*"[7]

Don Saturnino was silent for a while. Then he said, "Tomorrow is Carlos's birthday. He would have been eighteen had he lived."

"He would have liked these journeys," I answered.

"Perhaps. Perhaps not. Who knows? It is sufficient that you like them. You do like them, Carlota?"

"Everything, Father," I said. "Everything."

Here we sat for an hour, to make sure that we had not been followed.

When the sun was overhead, we crawled down from the pinnacle. We reached the Blue Beach and took off our boots and stepped out into the middle of the stream. We made our way for a distance of some fifty paces, leaving no tracks behind us. A clump of willows grew amidst a pile of driftwood and boulders at this place. Here the river divided and ran in two smaller streams on both sides of the willows.

The boulders could not be seen at high tide. But the tide was low now and they stuck up in two crescents, facing each other and leaving a clear space between them. The water was cold, both the sea water that met the river at this point and likewise the river water itself.

---

7. *Mucho más* (MOO·choh MAHS): much more.

Stripped to my singlet,[8] I splashed water on my legs, on my arms and chest. I had found that the best way to approach cold water was by small shivers, suffered one at a time.

Throwing out my arms, I took in a great gulp of air, held it for a minute, counting each second. Then I let out all the air in a quick whoosh. Then I raised my arms and took in a greater gulp.

This air I held for two minutes, still counting the seconds in my mind — one second, two seconds, and so forth. I repeated this three times. The third time I counted up to four minutes.

It had taken me two years to build up to where I could hold my breath for this length of time. My father had heard of pearl divers in La Paz[9] who could hold their breath for five minutes and even longer. I had tried this but had fainted.

Carefully we stepped into the wide pool between the two crescents of stone, beneath the canopy of willows. We inched our way to the center of the pool, cautious not to rile the sand.

As my foot touched a smooth slab of stone, I stooped down, lifted it with much care, and set it to one side. Beneath it was a rock-lined hole filled with water, the size of my body and twice its height.

At the bottom of this hole was something that, when we first saw it,

8. **singlet:** an undershirt.

9. **La Paz** (LAH PAHS): a Mexican port city.

seemed to be the trunk of a tree — a tree washed down from the mountains. Undoubtedly, it once had risen above the water, but over the years floods had worn it away to a worm-eaten stump.

It had been the mainmast of a ship, which my father said was some seventy feet in length. It had the wide beam, the high stern, of the galleons that two centuries before had sailed the seas between China and the coast of California and Mexico.

These ships, my father said, came on favorable winds and currents to northern California, then along the coast south to the ports of San Blas[10] and Acapulco.[11] They carried great treasures from the Indies,[12] these galleons, so great that they became the prey of American and English pirates.

Some of these treasure ships had been captured. On some, their crews had died of scurvy.[13] Others had run aground through careless navigation. Others were driven ashore by storms. Still others had sought refuge from their pursuers by hiding in lagoons such as the one at Blue Beach.

10. **San Blas** (san BLAS): a Mexican village and seaport, once used by the Spanish.
11. **Acapulco** (AH·kah·POOL·koh): now, a famous Mexican resort; then, a major seaport and trade center.
12. **Indies**: here, the East Indies — India, Indonesia, and the islands of Southeast Asia.
13. **scurvy**: a disease once very common at sea, marked by bleeding gums, fatigue, and spotted skin; caused by a diet lacking in vitamin C (fresh fruits and vegetables).

"This must have been a large lagoon at one time," my father said when we first discovered the galleon. "A good place to hide a ship. But when it was once inside, something happened to the ship and it never returned to the sea."

Hidden in the galleon's hold, near the stump of the mainmast, were two chests filled with coins. The coins were of pure gold. They showed three castles and the two flying doves that meant they had been struck in the mint at Lima,[14] Peru. The date marked upon each coin that we carried away on the trips we had made was the year of Our Lord 1612.

The two chests — each made of hard wood banded with iron straps and sealed with a hasp that had rusted and fallen off — were well beneath the surface of the water, whether at low tide or in the summer, when the stream ran low. This was fortunate, for had the chests been exposed, some passing Indian or vaquero would have discovered them.

There were many things to do before the chests could be reached. Usually it took me half a day to bring up a pouch of coins from the sunken ship.

The place where I dove, which was surrounded by jagged rocks and

14. **Lima** (LEE·mah): capital of Peru.

driftwood, was too narrow for my father. He had tried to squeeze through when we first discovered the galleon, but partway down he got stuck and I had to pull him back. It was my task, therefore, to go into the cavelike hole. My father stood beside it and helped me to go down and to come up.

I buckled a strong belt around my waist and to it tied a riata[15] that was ten *varas* long and stout enough to hold a stallion. I fastened my knife to my wrist — a two-edged blade made especially for me by our blacksmith — to protect myself against spiny rays and the big eels that could sting you to death. In the many dives I had made, I never had seen a shark.

Taking three deep breaths, I prepared to let myself down into the hole. In one hand I held a sink-stone, heavy enough to weigh me down. I let out all the air in my chest, took a deep breath, and held it. Then I began the descent.

The sink-stone would have taken me down fast, but the edges of the rocky hole were sharp. I let myself down carefully, one handhold at a time. It took me about a minute to reach the rotted deck where the chests lay. I now had two minutes to pry the coins loose and carry them to the surface. We had tried putting the coins in a leather sack and hoist-

ing them to the surface. But we had trouble with this because of the currents that swept around the wreck.

The coins lay in a mass, stuck together, lapping over each other and solid as rock. They looked, when I first saw them, like something left on the stove too long. I always expected to find them gone, but now as I walked toward the chests, with the stone holding me down, I saw that they were still there. No one had come upon them during the seven months since our last visit.

The first time I had dived and brought up a handful of coins, I said to my father that we should empty both chests and take the coins home.

"Then everyone would talk," Don Saturnino said. "As soon as they saw the gold coins the news would spread the length of California."

"We don't need to tell anyone. I can hide them in my chest at home."

"The news would fly out before the sun set. At the ranch there are many eyes."

I still thought it was a better idea to empty the chests before someone else did, but I could see that my father enjoyed these days, when the two of us went to the Blue Beach, so I said no more.

The sun was overhead and its rays slanted down through the narrow crevice. There were many pieces of debris on the deck and I had to step carefully. With my knife I pried loose a handful of coins. They were

---

15. **riata** (ree·AH·tah): a lariat.

of a dark green color and speckled here and there with small barnacles. I set the coins aside.

My lungs were beginning to hurt, but I had not felt the tug of the riata yet, the signal from my father that I had been down three minutes. I pried loose a second handful and put my knife away. Before the tug came I dropped my sink-stone and took up the coins. Gold is very heavy, much heavier than stones of the same size.

Fish were swimming around me as I went up through the hole of rocks and tree trunks, but I saw no sting rays or eels. I did see a shark lying back on a ledge, but he was small and gray, a sandshark, which is not dangerous.

On my third trip down, I hauled up about the same number of coins as the other times. The pouch we had brought was now full. I asked my father if we had enough.

"Are you tired?" he said.

"Yes, a little."

"Can you go down again?"

"Yes."

"Then go."

I dived twice more. It was on the last dive that I had the trouble. The

tug on the riata had not come, but I was tired, so I started away from the chest with one handful of coins. Close to the chests, between them and the hole, I had noticed what seemed to be two pieces of timber covered with barnacles. They looked as if they might be a part of a third and larger chest.

I still held my knife and I thrust it at a place where the two gray timbers seemed to join. It was possible that I had found another chest filled with coins.

As the knife touched them, the two timbers moved a little. Instantly, I felt pressure upon my wrist. I drew back the hand that held the knife. Rather, I tried to draw it back, but it would not move. The tide had shifted the timbers somehow and I was caught. So I thought.

I felt a tug upon the riata fastened to my waist. It was the signal from my father to come to the surface. I answered him with two quick tugs of the leather rope.

Now I felt a hot pain run up my arm. I tried to open my fingers to drop the knife, but my hand was numb. Then as I stared down into the murky water I saw a slight movement where my hand was caught. At the same moment I saw a flash of pink, a long fleshy tongue sliding along my wrist.

I had never seen a burro clam, but I had heard the tales about them, for there were many on our coast.

Attached to rocks or timbers, they grew to half the height of a man, these gray, silent monsters. Many unwary fishermen had lost their lives in the burros' jaws.

The pain in my arm was not so great now as the hot pains in my chest. I gave a long, hard tug on the riata to let my father know that I was in trouble. Again I saw a flash of pink as the burro opened its lips a little, and the fat tongue slid back and forth.

I dropped the coins I held in my other hand. The burro had closed once more on my wrist. But shortly it began to open again, and I felt a sucking pressure, as if the jaws were trying to draw me inside the giant maw.[16]

Putting my knees against the rough bulge of the shell, as the jaws opened and then began to close, I jerked with all my strength. I fell slowly backward upon the ship's deck. My hand was free. With what breath I had I moved toward the hole. I saw the sun shining above and climbed toward it. The next thing I saw was my father's face and I was lying on the river's sandy bank. He took my knife in his hand.

After I told him what had happened, my father said, "The knife saved your life. The burro clamped down upon it. See the mark here. The steel blade kept its jaws open.

---

16. **maw**: mouth.

Enough to let you wrench yourself free."

He pulled me to my feet and I put on my leather pants and coat.

"Here," he said, passing the reins of his bay gelding to me, "ride Santana. He goes gentler than your Tiburón."

"I'll ride my own horse," I said.

"Good, if you wish it."

"I wish it," I said, knowing that he didn't want me to say that my hand was numb.

"Does the hand hurt?"

"No."

"Some?"

"No."

"You were very brave," he said.

My father wanted me to be braver than I was. I wanted to say I was scared, both when the burro had hold of me and now, at this moment, but I didn't because he expected me to be as brave as Carlos. It was at times like this that I was angry at my father and at my dead brother, too.

"It was good fortune," I said.

"Fortune and bravery often together," Don Saturnino said. "If you do not hurt, let us go."

I got on the stallion and settled myself in the saddle. "Yes, let us go," I said.

Understanding the Story

1. What was the secret of Blue Beach?

2. How was Carlota trapped under-water? What saved her life?

3. Why does Carlota pretend to her father that she is braver than she is?

4. One external conflict in this story is Carlota's struggle against her need for air when she is underwater. What is another external conflict?

5. Had you been in Carlota's place, would you have hidden your fear or admitted it? Why?

Understanding Literature

As you know, *conflict* is an important element in plot. Conflict refers to a character's struggle with opposing forces. Conflict can be *external,* in which case the character struggles with nature or with another character, animal or human. The conflict between two characters may be physical, or it may be a nonphysical battle of words or wills. Conflict also may be *internal,* when a character struggles against his or her own feelings.

A story often contains both kinds of conflict. In "The Secret of Blue Beach," the struggle between Carlota and the burro clam is central to the plot, but there are several other conflicts in the story. These conflicts occur because of the kind of person Carlota is. She is always pushing and testing herself, trying to prove to her father that she is as strong and as brave as her brother, Carlos, was. Don Saturnino also pushes her to see more, to listen more carefully, to hold her breath longer. Because of this constant pushing from herself and her father, Carlota is continually in conflict with her own physical limits. Another external conflict is the unspoken conflict between Carlota and her father. He expects her "to be as brave as Carlos," and she fears that if she is not as brave, her father will not love her. The internal conflict is Carlota's fight to control her feelings of resentment and anger at her father for expecting her to be someone she can never be.

Writing About the Story

Suppose "The Secret of Blue Beach" has been made into a film and you are in charge of the advertising campaign to get people to see the film. Write a television or radio advertisement for "The Secret of Blue Beach." Remember to include descriptions of the visual and/or sound effects in your script. You'll also need directions for the announcer.

Nahuatl:[1] A Song of Nezahualcoyotl[2]

A poem translated from the Nahuatl

the riches of this world are only lent to us

the things that are so good to enjoy we do not own

the sun pours down gold
fountains pour out green water
colors touch us like fingers
of green quetzal[3] wings

none of this can we own for more than a day

none of these beautiful things can we keep for more than an
   hour

one thing alone we can own forever
the memory of the just
the remembrance of a good act
the good remembrance of a just man

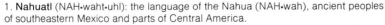

this one thing alone will never be taken away from us

will never die

---

1. **Nahuatl** (NAH·waht·uhl): the language of the Nahua (NAH·wah), ancient peoples of southeastern Mexico and parts of Central America.
2. **Nezahualcoyotl** (NEZ·wah·KOH-AH·tuhl): a fifteenth-century Nahuatl poet-king.
3. **quetzal** (ket·SAHL): a beautiful Central American bird with bright red and golden green feathers.

Illustration by Jane Oka

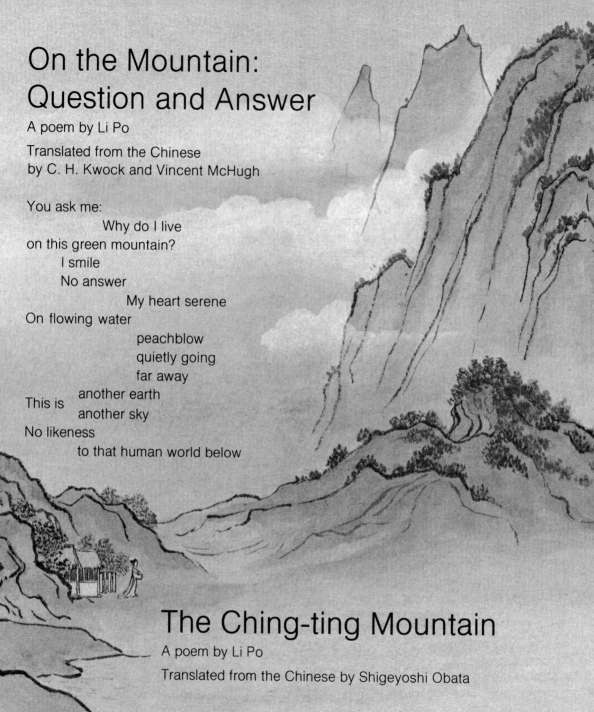

On the Mountain:
Question and Answer

A poem by Li Po

Translated from the Chinese
by C. H. Kwock and Vincent McHugh

You ask me:
      Why do I live
on this green mountain?
   I smile
   No answer
      My heart serene
On flowing water
     peachblow
     quietly going
     far away
This is another earth
    another sky
No likeness
   to that human world below

The Ching-ting Mountain

A poem by Li Po

Translated from the Chinese by Shigeyoshi Obata

Flocks of birds have flown high and away;
A solitary drift of cloud, too, has gone, wandering on.
And I sit alone with the Ching-ting Peak, towering beyond.
We never grow tired of each other, the mountain and I.

356

Illustration by Kinuko Craft

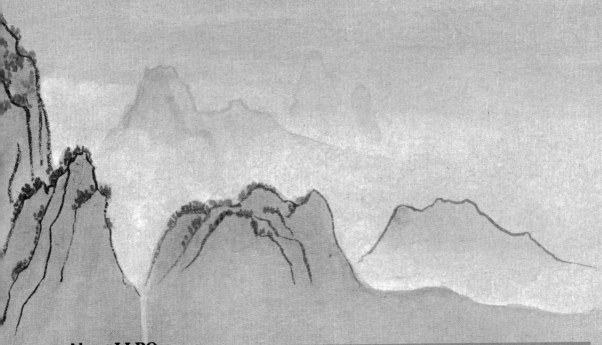

About LI PO

Li Po lived and wrote almost thirteen centuries ago and is still regarded as one of China's greatest poets. He wrote of universal themes that appeal to people today as much as they did to people living many years ago: the beauty of nature, the sorrows of separation, and the joys of love.

If Li Po were living today, he would probably be considered a colorful character, for he spent most of his life roaming the countryside, stopping briefly if someone invited him to stay. For a time he lived at the royal court, where, as an official poet, he was expected to write verse on command. Such an ordered life gave him little pleasure, and soon he resumed traveling.

Eventually he joined an expedition with one of the emperor's sons as a sort of poet-in-residence. However, this prince was accused of treason and executed; Li Po was imprisoned. Fortunately a general pardon was declared, and he was released.

He never again stayed in any one place for long, preferring to live a free and simple life. Legend has it that he drowned while trying to embrace the moon's reflection in a river. Other accounts say that he died peacefully at the home of a relative. However he died, his poetry lives on as it is still read by people around the world.

357

maggie and milly and molly and may

A poem by e. e. cummings

maggie and milly and molly and may
went down to the beach(to play one day)

and maggie discovered a shell that sang
so sweetly she couldn't remember her troubles,and

milly befriended a stranded star
whose rays five languid fingers were;

and molly was chased by a horrible thing
which raced sideways while blowing bubbles:and

may came home with a smooth round stone
as small as a world and as large as alone.

For whatever we lose(like a you or a me)
it's always ourselves we find in the sea

Illustration by Angela Adams

About E. E. CUMMINGS

The poet E. E. Cummings was concerned both with how words sounded and with how they looked on the page. A good example is the opening line of his volume *No Thanks:* "mOOn Over tOwns mOOn."

E. E. Cummings was a painter as well as a writer, and all his life he devoted equal time to his painting and to his writing. For years, he painted in the afternoons and wrote at night. His paintings may have contributed to what many critics feel was an unusual sense of poetry, but then Cummings had a unique sense of everything. He was a strong individualist who said of artists, "The artist's country is inside him."

"If poetry is your goal," he said, "you've got to forget all about punishments and all about rewards and all about selfstyled obligations and duties and responsibilities etcetera ad infinitum and remember one thing only: that it's you — nobody else — who determine your destiny and decide your fate."

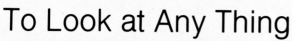

To Look at Any Thing

A poem by John Moffitt

To look at any thing,
If you would know that thing,
You must look at it long:
To look at this green and say,
'I have seen spring in these
Woods,' will not do — you must
Be the thing you see:
You must be the dark snakes of
Stems and ferny plumes of leaves,
You must enter in
To the small silences between
The leaves,
You must take your time
And touch the very peace
They issue from.[1]

---

1. **issue from:** come from; are a product of; are born of.

Illustration by Trudy Smith

Winter Poem

A poem by Nikki Giovanni

once a snowflake fell
on my brow and i loved
it so much and i kissed
it and it was happy and called its cousins
and brothers and a web
of snow engulfed me then
i reached to love them all
and i squeezed them and they became
a spring rain and i stood perfectly
still and was a flower.

Illustration by Kitty Diamantis

Learn About

Poetry

by Myra Cohn Livingston

An invitation brings the promise of excitement. Its words are few, but its message stirs your thoughts: *What will happen? Who will be there? Where are we going? What will I see? What surprises will there be?*

If you think of a poem as an invitation, you begin to understand that the reader of poetry is as important to a poem as a guest is to a party. Poets, through their words and rhythms, extend an invitation to you, to be where they have been, to see what they have seen — or imagined. Sometimes it is a story they tell, with or without rhyme, to entertain you. Often they ask you to participate with all your senses — to see, to hear, to perceive a texture or a movement communicated by their musical phrases.

In many poems the involvement is direct. Miroslav Holub begins his poem "The Door" with:

> Go and open the door.
>   Maybe outside there's
>   a tree, or a wood,
>   a garden,
>   or a magic city.

Such an invitation asks you, the reader, to let your mind run free, to consider what fantastic sights you would like to see. A poem need not be fanciful, however, to get you involved. Frequently, poets simply tell what they have done or seen; they choose words and details so carefully that the poem triggers forgotten memories, or perhaps makes you feel that you have shared a profound experience.

Even a poem that appears in its opening lines to be talking about other people may draw you in as you read along:

> maggie and milly and molly and may
> went down to the beach (to play
>   one day)

Here E.E. Cummings seems to be writing about four girls who went to play at the beach. Yet by later mentioning a "shell that sang," a "stranded star," a "horrible thing," and a "smooth round stone," he calls upon you, the reader, to recall what you may have found at the beach—or elsewhere. The last line, "it's always ourselves we find in the sea," invites you to discover some part of yourself in a shell, or a stone, or a starfish, or a "horrible thing"—not only at the beach but wherever you might venture.

362

In "Winter Poem," Nikki Giovanni invites you to join her in the snow. As you do, you may begin to use your sense of feeling, imagining, and touching so that falling snow becomes spring rain, which in turn transforms you into a budding flower. This opportunity to pretend is somewhat like an invitation to a costume party, where you can briefly be something other than yourself. Most of all, though, it is an invitation to use your imagination!

Maxine Kumin suggests another way to use imagination in her poem "The Presence":

> Something went crabwise
> across the snow this morning
> . . . .
> It could have been. . . .

Here she is imagining, as winter travelers often do, what makes certain tracks in the snow. Her guesses may help you to see new images or pictures as you read, but more importantly, she invites you to stretch your perception of things you encounter.

When people stop and stare at clouds, they frequently find animals or faces of people in the cloud shapes.

Often deeper things follow. In his poem "The Ching-ting Mountain," Li Po thinks of the mountain as his friend beneath a solitary cloud. By sharing his unusual thoughts on friendship, the poet invites you to think further about personal friends. Similarly, the unnamed speaker in "A Song of Nezahualcoyotl" is moved by the sun, fountains, and colors to think about what things have lasting values.

As a rule, people do not like to be told what to do. Sometimes, however, following a wise command helps a person make new discoveries. The poet John Moffitt tells readers they must look at things for a long time in order to know them:

> you must
> Be the thing you see.

With these words he is suggesting that your imagination is at its height when you begin to feel like the thing you see.

If you have portrayed a character in a play or worked at pantomime, you may already understand what he means.

Robert Watson's poem "Victory" begins with the following lines:

> Moving furniture around my room
> I can move stars, the streetlights and
>   the dust
> In rolls below our chairs. I can change
>   weather
> If I want.

Although this may sound like wild imagining, the poet brings his message into sharp focus as he ends his poem with these thoughts:

> But you, like a frozen tree in frozen
>   ground,
> I'll walk around, I'll walk around the
>   block,
> I'll shift all the furniture in my room.
> I'll move you yet.

Here is the best invitation of all, although it may not use words to which we are accustomed. Here the poet invites readers to move, to change, to open doors, to thaw and remain open to the possibilities of life. It is in this way that Robert Watson, and all poets, extend their invitations to make a leap of the imagination, to be aware of ev-erything in the world, to make use of the experiences and stories of others, and to make things happen. "A frozen tree in frozen ground" cannot do that. A reader who accepts a poet's invitation can.

Close your eyes and imagine that you are looking at a door. Concentrate on the door for a long time. Then fling it open to see what is beyond it. Write at least five sentences about what you see.

Read the poem "Victory" on page 149. List the actions mentioned in the poem that a person could really do, such as move furniture. Then list the things no one could do, such as move stars. Think about why the poet might have felt like doing the impossible things. Then list three impossible things you would like to do.

365

The Purple Moccasin

A short story by MacKinlay Kantor

Illustrated by V. Douglas Snow

ONCE UPON A TIME there was a boy who had run away from home, and he said that he was going up into northern Missouri to find Jesse James.[1]

The runaway traveled all day on unfamiliar roads, and his legs grew powerful weary; but still he kept on traveling, because he was in anger with his pappy. The bunting birds sang constantly, and I reckon they were surprised to see him loping down the rocky twists and turns that led into valleys he had never walked before.

It seemed as if the devil himself was pursuing, and nagging, and saying, "Hasten up, bubby. You've got a long ways to go, and you don't want Jesse James to be vanished when you get there."

And at sunset the boy came to a secret place beside a brown river. It was cool there, and you could smell the sweet marsh that neighbored the stream. A hot day's journey had brought that boy nigh the point where he was ready to fling himself down and cry his heart empty and dry. I have knowledge how he was feeling, for I was that boy.

I sat me down on an old log bridge across the stream; I let my sore feet swing close to the water, and I put my little bundle of possessions beside me. I wondered if my sisters were crying, because I hadn't come back to take supper at home.

And then, the next moment, I was standing square erect as any cat — for the sound of a shotgun takes an exhausted person by surprise.

Over in those woods I had just passed was where the shot came from. And now I could hear voices, a

---

1. **Jesse James** (1847–1882): American outlaw and folk hero.

clear, high-pitched voice, and one that was deeper, but more threatening. I legged it across the bridge, because I was plumb certain that the Pinkerton men[2] had sighted me, and that somehow they had got wind of my intentions about Jesse James.

But by the time I got to the far shore, my curious nature had come alive; I couldn't have stirred another step until I saw just what was in those woods, and who had fired the shotgun, and who was roaring like the bull of Bashan.[3]

Then they came out of the brush, moving mighty quick. The first was a little girl, and she went through the rails of that old fence like a garter snake. The second was a man, a tall one, with a shabby coat flapping about his thighs. He'd lost his hat sure enough, for his hair shone white and silvery in the dusk. He crossed the fence, but more dignified than the little girl. At first I thought he was toting a rifle along with him, but in the next moment, even through the gloom, I could see that it was only a spade.

There were firearms abroad, though; I hadn't mistrusted my ears. The bushes began to wave, and a strong-built man stepped into the open space behind the fence. He carried his weapon so that the muzzle was aimed threateningly at those two figures in the road. I scrooched low, but I was mighty near all eyes and ears.

"This is the second offense," said the man with the gun. "I warn you, mister, that the third offense will prove fatal."

The white-haired gentleman in the road kind of pulled himself together and straightened his coattails. "My friend," he said, "your boast is hollow unless you improve your marksmanship."

"The goodness of my aim hain't never been questioned," replied he who held the shotgun. "That time I fired into a buttonball tree, so as not to orphan this kid of yourn."

"Orphan or not," the older man told him, kind of loftily, "she'll acquit herself skillfully in the world. But I insist that you listen to reason, my good sir! I have only one purpose in visiting your property, and. . . ."

The armed man swung back into the bushes. "Good enough purpose, too, I'll be bound!" he yelled over his shoulder. "You want that gold and you want that silverware. But if there's any digging to be done on this property, I reckon I'll hoist the shovel myself!" Then, before there could be a reply, he had gone crackling through the bushes.

I heard that tall bareheaded man say distinctly, "Flower of My Life, I shall yet lift the purple moccasin

---

2. **Pinkerton men:** detectives from the Pinkerton Agency.
3. **bull of Bashan** (BAY·shuhn): from the Bible; a symbol of size and strength.

from alien soil!" The little girl laughed with a terrified voice. Then the two of them came toward me, and they were halfway across the bridge before they saw the kind of lump I made, squatting there in the twilight.

He pulled up right smart, and the girl with him. They eyed me for a spell, and I managed to stand erect, though me knees were palsied.[4] "Another wayfarer is present," cried the old man. "Kitty Cat, do you think he intends to dispute our crossing?"

The little girl made a few steps forward and peered at me. The sun-

set was far distant beyond that valley and the trees that rimmed it, but I swear it was reflected in the mane of hair that dressed her head, and I'll think about her every time I see embers glowing in the night.

"Why, Daddy," she yelped, "he's just a little boy!"

I was jealous of my age and didn't admire to be called a little boy. "Howdy," I said, but my voice did sound mighty piping.

He came closer, until he could look down into my face. "My son," he said, "you seem to be unhappy about something."

"No," I whispered, "I've just been traveling."

"Where from?"

---

4. **palsied** (PAWL·zeed): here, weak and shaking.

An idea snapped into my head, quick as lightning. "Arkansas," I told him.

"Arkansas," repeated the stranger. He took note of my bare feet and the bundle in my hand, and he kind of chuckled. "My young friend, I assume from your demeanor and from the state of your attire, that you are a wanderer drifting abroad like the tumbleweed blown from its native heath."

Well, I was flabbergasted by his speech, because folks didn't talk that way in our neighborhood. But I did manage to mumble out something about how I was going to attach myself to Jesse James, and Cole Younger,[5] too, as soon as he got out of Stillwater.[6]

"Ah," said this man, "Jesse James indeed! A ruthless man, no doubt, and given to incursions and forays."

"Mister," I said, "he robs banks and trains, and he don't give a hoot about Pinkerton men."

The little girl said, kind of pert, "I bet, little boy, he'd eat you up in one bite, if you came nigh to him."

"*Near*, Kitty Cat," cried the tall

5. **Cole Younger** (1844–1916): a leading member of the James gang.
6. **Stillwater**: the Minnesota State Prison at Stillwater.

man. "The word is *near*. I resent your adoption of the colloquial phrase." He kept fondling that spade, with the dusk growing thicker at every breath. He seemed powerful old, to have a daughter smaller than me.

The girl called Kitty Cat or Flower of My Life, as the case may be, came real close and poked her finger at my chest. "Boy," she said, "how old are you?"

"Mighty nigh onto thirteen," said I, kind of fuming, "and I'm no little boy, either."

"Oh," said Kitty Cat, "you're scarcely older than I, because I'm just twelve myself! Daddy, I guess he's the dirtiest boy I've ever seen."

The old man shook his head at her, and his long locks danced about his ears. "Impolite, Flora Katherine, highly impolite. Your own appearance is scarcely impeccable."

"Boy," she demanded to know, "what's your name?"

"Jesse," I said, "same as Jesse James. And I've got a weapon too. It's a pepperbox revolver that my Uncle Andrew gave me last year, and I've got it right here in this bundle." And then I added, in proud manner, "I'll show it to you, if you want me to."

"No," she said, "I don't like guns. That old man Travis just fired off his shotgun to scare us. And I was scared, and I bet you'd be scared too."

"I wager I wouldn't," I said. We glared at each other, though the gloom was getting so thick you could cut it with a knife.

All this time her father had been dreaming to himself — sighing, and saying over and over again, "Alien soil. Alien soil." But now he shook his head and clucked like a hen coming off her nest, and he poked his finger at me. "Jesse," he said, "fellow traveler of the unfriendly byways, have you broken bread of late?"

Though folks didn't talk that way in our neck of the woods, my father used to read aloud out of books; I wasn't the ignorant little boy that I looked to be. "Mister," I said, "I reckon I could eat a polecat."

"Inedible," he cried. "Absolutely inedible! Carnivorous mammal. *Mephitis mephitica*, wholly unfit for food. But, to return to my invitation, our stores are ample for our simple needs. I can sup very eagerly myself, despite my disappointment," and then he went to mumbling, uttering again that strange remark about the purple moccasin.

He led the way along the road past the bridge, and the little girl and I scampered after him. A kind of cavern opened up beside us, and it was a lane leading down to a forgotten ford[7] by the brookside. The man went ahead, tall and straight and dreamy, with his silvery hair shaking

---

7. ford: a shallow crossing.

in a little breeze that had sprung up with the falling of night.

But now it was dark in that tunnel through the trees, and I stumbled in all directions. Next thing I knew, Flora Katherine had reached out her hand; she pulled me along, because she knew the way over these roots and boulders, and it was kind of comforting to have her holding on to me. I thought of my sisters Melissa and Algy, and I kept blinking my eyes.

When I had blinked the wetness out of them, I could see a fire burning low, as if it hadn't been tended for an hour or two. There was a wagon with a canvas top, like movers rode in when they passed our house, but smaller, and there was an old white horse that nickered his head off when he heard us.

They had camped here for days and days. The grass was all tromped down, and there was a scattering of little things underfoot, and there was a tent set up beside the wagon. Not far away, the river chattered among its rocks and told a good and comforting message about the black bass and the little nibbling suckers that lived there.

"Kitty Cat," said the man, "do you put that skillet on the coals. And possibly our young visitor can fetch some wood from the pile. Unless I am gravely mistaken, a reluctant visitor or two may be quivering on our line."

So he vanished toward the river, and I went smelling around for wood. As for Flora Kitty Cat, she spread herself high, wide, and handsome around that clearing. She scooped the coals together and set the frying pan level and true; next minute she had dropped in some bacon. And after that, she was getting out a sack of fodder and shaking some loose for the old white horse, though anybody could see that he was fat as a pig already. And she called him Linnaeus, which was a mighty strange name for a horse.

"Why do you call him Linnaeus?" I demanded to know.

"Because that's his name."

"It's a crazy variety of name, if you ask me," I told her.

Kitty Cat said, "Well, I didn't ask you," and went right on feeding him.

"At home," I made bold to say, "a horse critter is named Dobbin or Maud or Betsy or Bill, or some decent-sounding name."

She snapped at me, "At home — where's that?" I came close to saying "Rosy Ridge," but I thought twice and gulped out "Arkansas."

"Linnaeus was a great man," she said. "He defined genera and species.[8] He deserves to have a horse named after him."

I tell you she made me boil,

---

8. **genera and species**: terms used in a system of plant and animal identification invented by the Swedish scientist Linnaeus.

because I didn't admire having any girl fling that variety of language at me. But I swallowed my pride and went on building one side of the fire, while the bacon stewed and smoked and frizzled on the other side. Next moment we heard a kind of yell, which I reckoned was happiness, from the direction of the river. It was plumb certain that we wouldn't have to content ourselves with side meat.

"What's his name?" I asked.

"Who?"

"Your pappy."

"He's Doctor Samuel Sickles, Mister Jesse, and I'll thank you not to push those coals into the bacon."

Well, I got the coals out, but burned my fingers doing it. And I wanted to know whether he doctored horses or people, for those were the only two kinds of doctors that I knew anything about; no other kind had ever come a-visiting us.

"He's a doctor of science," she chirped, "and I guess that's what I'll be, too, when I grow up. You're very clumsy, boy. Will you please get your legs out of the way, so that I can put this corn pone[9] to get hot?"

Her manner was driving me wild; but Doctor Samuel Sickles came back, and he had two catfish, not big enough to be coarse and strong, but

---

9. corn pone: corn bread.

373

big enough to be worth eating. And that supper which we ate — there was a jar of pickles to go with it, and some apples, and peach preserves that had never been stewed over that fire — was something to remember. I reckon I'll remember it until I give up the ghost,[10] no matter how tart and ornery Flora Katherine acted.

There are strange miseries that enter the heads and hearts of older folks, which young'uns know nothing about. Doctor Samuel Sickles was now besieged by an ailment of that kind. For he did not eat sufficient to keep him alive. Soon he was silent and melancholy, over by his side of the fire, and the little girl undertook to nurse him. She offered him the finest morsels of catfish and pone and pickles, but he didn't pay heed. He hunched down lower and lower, with the points of his shoulders going up against his ears, and every now and then his voice would exclaim in sadness or contempt.

"What ails him anyway?" I managed to whisper to Kitty Cat, when she gave me my last slab of fish.

"He's feeling bad about the purple moccasin."

"Can't he make one for his own self?" I wanted to know.

She looked reproving, and she told me that God had made this purple moccasin, and it was the only one in the world, so far as she knew.

_____

10. give up the ghost: to die.

I asked, "Is it a snake?"

"Oh, no!" she said shivering. "I don't like snakes a bit. But this is beautiful."

By this time she was talking as loud as you please. Still, Doctor Sickles gave us no attention. He looked moody as a ghost that couldn't get back to his tomb, and when he stood up, he walked right into the frying pan, and he had no swear word to utter about it. The fire was low again, so it was hard to make out the figure of this old man, once he had wandered away from the embers. Though I could follow the red glow on his gleaming hair, and I saw him go to the tail of the wagon; then, from somewhere, he had drug out a tin lamp and a watering pot.

He lighted the lamp and clumb up over the tailboard. For a while we could watch his tall shape shadowing around inside the canvas, all lit up, like a big black ghost, by the lamp glow. He was doing strange things inside that wagon, and I reckoned I'd die of curiosity.

"Is your pap going to bed?" I asked Kitty Cat.

"We don't sleep there," she said. "He's just seeing after things."

"People always sleep in wagons," I told her, for plenty of movers had gone by our house, bound for Texas and the Indian country, and I knew their habits.

But Flora Katherine Sickles was as

sharp as her name, and she told me to be more polite. She said that she wasn't allowed to sleep in the wagon, nor did Doctor Sickles allow himself to do it, and there wasn't room for them anyway.

We were fussing and fuming at each other again, and our angriness got the better of us both, and then we didn't talk again for a long time.

I sat there cross-legged by the fire, and thought how many miles away my home was lying and how badly I had been mistreated. And finally I was feeling lonesome and bereft, and I couldn't see the fire at all because my eyes were so blurry. Then, just when the spasms were rising and I thought they'd slay me in my throat, I felt a hard little hand take hold of mine, and there was Kitty Cat kneeling beside me.

In the low firelight, her hair seemed too wonderful to adorn any living head, and it overcome my breath. For she did look like a kind of angel, although one that had been running loose in the woods and tearing her dress when she did it.

"Jesse," she said, "you seem to be feeling miserable. I feel sorry for you, Jesse."

I contrived[11] to tell her that she didn't need to and that pretty soon I'd go on looking for Jesse James.

"I'll bet you ran away from home," she murmured. But I said it wasn't none of her business if I had.

---

11. **contrived:** planned; had in mind.

She asked, "Haven't you got a mother or a sister?"

I told her that I had two sisters and a mighty handsome mother, but that my father had been meaner than Satan, and he had whipped me out, though it was only the third time in my life I had ever been licked. He whipped me because I hit the red cow with a wagon spoke, and he said it wasn't her fault that the milk pail was upset, though I reckoned it was.

"I won't stay around home to be whipped on account of red cows," I cried to Flora Katherine. "And they're all going to feel mighty discontented if I get caught by the Pinkerton men and get shut up in Stillwater Penitentiary."

But all this time she was looking at me, and her eyes, which had seemed like the eyes of a deer when first I saw her, and like the eyes of an angry tomcat sometime later, were now pitying and motherly; and I let her hang onto my hand as much as she liked, and I wondered what it would feel like to kiss a girl who wasn't your sister.

"You can't go wandering off after Jesse James tonight," she said. "Daddy wouldn't let you. You might get caught by robbers, or something."

"No, I wouldn't," I said. "I'd shoot them quick as scat," and I forgot my sadness in opening up my bundle, to show her the pepperbox revolver that Uncle Andrew had given me.

"Why," said Flora Katherine, "it's all rusty! You couldn't shoot any robbers."

I was on the point of telling her that someday I'd get the revolver fixed up, and have caps and cartridges for it, when Doctor Samuel Sickles came back to the fire and kicked some ends of charred logs onto the coals. The flames shot up immediately, and then we could see his face, grave and furrowed and imposing in the red light, and his thin mane of hair curling around his neck.

"Kitty Cat," he said, "Torrey and Gray[12] make no mention whatsoever of the purple moccasin." He had a thick book in his hands, but it didn't look like any Bible I ever saw.

"The ecologists do not suspect its existence," the old man continued, ruffling the pages with his hand. "They list many others, but none resembles it." He closed the book with a bang and went back to the wagon and put the book inside. He blew out the tin lamp, too, which he had left standing on the tailboard with little betty-millers flittering around it. Then he returned to us, and I was standing up by this time, for I had never seen such goings-on in all my born days.

Doctor Sickles planted his shabby boots wide apart, and he slid one hand inside his coat like a lawyer in

---

12. **Torrey and Gray:** *A Flora of North America*, a pioneering description of American plant life by the botanists John Torrey and Asa Gray (1838).

court. "Our woodlands have been ravaged," he said. "The fairest flowers have been plucked from full many a tree, until the branches hang withered and barren. God's creatures have been scourged out of the underbrush and slaughtered without discrimination. With my own eyes I have seen the wild pigeons dashed to the ground, an acre at a time. They tell me, too, that the lordly bison are fading before the hunters' guns. Do you remember those stacks of hides we saw in St. Jo, Kitty Cat?"

Kitty Cat nodded and clapped her hands, and I thought I ought to clap, because this was marvellous speechifying.

The old man kind of nodded, as if we had pleased him. He picked up the spade, which was lying on the ground. "The Lord himself only knows," he said. "I may be an instrument of regeneration, and I may be holding one of the very tools in my hand! Who am I to be balked by a mere Travis and a mere shotgun?"

Flora Katherine was dancing up and down with excitement; I tell you, he shed excitement like a sunset

sheds paint, the way he stood there so gaunt and grand. "He said he'd shoot you next time, Daddy," the girl cried. "Do you really think he would? Do you really think he'll shoot?"

"He had murder in his eyes," said Doctor Sickles solemnly.

Her red hair fairly curled with the flames in it. She gasped, "He'll think you came after all that gold, and after the silver spoons. Maybe. . . ."

Her father declared, "Stealth, Kitty Cat! We can circumvent murder by stealth. We will go by night, now, this very night, when the ignorant are slumbering and their guns are behind the doors."

Well, she screamed with joy, and then she said, "Can Jesse come along with us?" and my heart was heated in my mouth.

"Jesse can come, if he will." He came around the fire and put his long bony hand under my chin and turned my face up until it looked square into his. "My son," he said, and I had the ague[13] down into my toes, "my son, your ambition is to become an outlaw. Will you be content with this strange outlawry of ours?"

I mumbled that I'd like to go with them.

"We'll need the spade," Doctor Sickles decided, "and the bucket and the lantern, and we'll need three pairs of hands to manage the deed with due safety and dispatch. Come along," he said, "both of you, and we'll prepare ourselves."

Sometimes it seems as if the deepest shades of night are those in the earliest hours, with the horn calls of whippoorwills sounding mournful in every brake, and the air fuzzy with June bugs and flying beetles and the plump gray moths that come to the kitchen window when a lamp is there. This is no occasion for ghosts, but a time for human beings to be faring abroad on most mysterious errands.

The bridge sounded like a hollow drum under our feet, no matter how dainty we walked. We went into Mr. Travis's timber at about the point where he had chased the Sickleses out with his shotgun; Doctor Sickles led the way, with a sooty lantern in his hand, and little daggers of light pointed hot into the underbrush on every side. Kitty Cat and I stayed to hand, but still we were behind him, and there was chance for me to question her about Mr. Travis again, and about all the excitement he had bespoken when he talked of silverware and gold.

What she told me set the skin to puckering over my shoulder blades. They had questioned some folks in the neighbourhood, and they knew why Mr. Travis hated to have other people step upon his soil. Because it was a soil that he believed to be

---

13. **ague** (AY·gyoo): a chill.

filled with fortunes, and folks declared him to be a no-account farmer, but a savage man with a gun. During the war, that land had belonged to somebody else, and the somebody else who owned it was rich, and all his money and the costly silverware from his house were hidden away when the Yankees came nigh. It still lay, the story said, buried, unknown, and neglected, in some corner of the farm. And Mr. Travis demanded to be left in peace to dig it up, and then he'd be rich himself and beholden to no one.

It wasn't disturbing of rabbits and muskrats that dwelt in his underbrush, which he dreaded, but the prowling foot, and the hand reaching out for money; and most of all he hated anybody who carried a spade. Already he had dug a hundred holes around his farm, and he concluded that he might have to dig the whole place up, but he was more than willing to do it.

Like enough, he never knew that the purple moccasin was there until the day when Doctor Sickles saw it with his own eyes, and Flora Katherine saw it with hers. And maybe he wasn't even aware of it now. He had ordered them off his property with his gun ready cocked, and the second time, as I knew, he plotted to scare them by firing.

I kept imagining how the purple moccasin would look, as we circulated through the thickets. I wondered why it hadn't rotted away long before. Probably the Indians had left it behind them when they were persecuted down into the Ouachita Mountains;[14] I had never heard of anybody finding one of their moccasins before. But I had found arrowheads myself, and Uncle Andrew dug up part of a stone axe when he was punching post holes for his new gate. So it was plumb sensible to consider that a purple moccasin might be important, and with my own ears I had heard Mr. Yeary offer Uncle Andrew thirty cents for the axe. Still, Doctor Sickles wasn't one to go hog-wild over money; the whole thing had me perplexed to death.

We went astray a dozen times. The hazel brush scratched our faces, and the berry vines did things to our clothes. "We're off the track, Kitty Cat," the old man would whisper. "We've gone far afield. Stand by until I survey the route again." And then he'd prowl ahead, holding the lantern in front of him and bending his shoulders low, until he thought he saw a familiar trunk or a combination of trees to guide him.

"Are you fearful?" he'd want to know, time and again. "My children, keep your ears receptive for the approach of Mr. Travis."

So we'd listen, and all we could hear was the fluttering of catbirds

---

14. Ouachita (WOSH·i·taw) Mountains.

that we disturbed off their roosts, and the buzzing of unknown critters in the air; and our frightened eyes would start out of our heads whenever we walked into webs of the big black-and-gold spiders that lived there. All the time, we were going deeper and deeper into the hollows; once a fox yapped on the hill above, and I jumped out of my skin.

Then, when at last the talking of the river had faded plumb into the past, we found ourselves at the rim of a twisting gully, and Kitty Cat's hand was perspiring instead of cold, when it clutched mine. "We're here," she whispered. "This is the place, Jesse. This is where we found the purple moccasin." Doctor Sickles was breathing hard as he tumbled down the steepness ahead of us. We brought up amongst basswood trunks that shone pearl gray in the lantern light, and I felt my feet go deeper and deeper into the mold of forgotten leaves.

Doctor Sickles was squatting now. His hand shook so that he seemed ready to upset the lantern and maybe burn those woods to ash, and the purple moccasin too. For there it was directly under our eyes, and at the first second I felt a shiver of disappointment inside me. But the next minute I reckoned that here was something kind of holy, if it could make Doctor Sickles cry the way he was doing.

It was a flower, and it grew tall and straight in its solitary little pocket of wilderness. It was like the lady's slippers I had picked so many times, but instead of being yellow or being pinkish or white, the swollen petals of this flower were as purple as the purplest dress that any lady ever wore. They seemed fashioned of silk and velvet, and numerous fabrics out of fairy tales; the color was as rich as a crow's-foot violet, and when a little wind came down the hollow, the long pointed leaves seemed to sway with pride.

Doctor Sickles sucked in his breath until it made a steamy sound through his teeth. "*Cypripedium*," he said. I reckoned that was a new kind of prayer, like the French Catholic said who came to work for my pap one time. "*Cypripedium* most certainly, Kitty Cat. And I would have said *hirsutum* from the beginning, but I had no chance to observe the corolla before Travis was upon us. Look! Look!" He was fair shouting with delight and astonishment, and the noise he made would have tweaked a dozen Mr. Travises out of their slumbers.

"*Acaule*," he said, "*Cypripedium acaule*. Certainly there must be a close alliance. Winthrop may say that this is aberration, Kitty Cat, and he may be correct. But I believe that here is treasure of the rarest tincture."

And then he sort of sighed and lifted up his head and surveyed the barrier of darkness. "If I only knew, my children, what other beauties lie buried in yonder fastnesses. . . . Young Jesse, give me the spade."

He cut deep into the rich, clinging soil, and he took out a generous circle all around that plant. He worked carefully with fingers and blade, and I saw that he had intention of filling the wooden bucket we had brought, with all the earth that had nourished that most peculiar flower. And maybe that same earth would nourish it in the future and let it grow to be a joy forever.

It seemed hours. My throat was dry, a-watching and a-waiting, but there wasn't much that Kitty Cat and I could do, except to hold the lantern and fetch the bucket close when he

wanted it. He brought up the whole enormous beauty of the soil in one cake, and it couldn't have been more than the passage of a few moments before the purple moccasin was growing from the bucket as if it had always grown there. Then we crept out of the gully, and this time Kitty Cat was carrying the lantern and I had the spade, and Doctor Samuel Sickles nursed the bucket like it was a cradle with a two days' babe inside.

But the fortune that had attended us began to slip and yield; far away we caught a flicker of light, and a dog barked even closer.

"Daddy," asked Flora Katherine, in a weak little voice, "shall I blow out the lantern?"

The old man stood stock-still. He didn't seem to breathe. "Heaven forgive me," I heard him murmur, "if my avarice has brought harm to you." And then he whispered sharply, "No! We must run. The dog would find us, even if we lay in the dark."

We went through that brush as hard as we could pelt.[15] The vines harried us, and I reckon we weren't following the path by which we had come in, for it was no path at all. But we did know our directions; we could catch sight of the Big Dipper high ahead of us, and other stars that anybody might know. The dog

bayed and barked, and once he was silent for a long time, so long that he seemed lost in the brambles. But he came forth again, nearer at hand, and we heard the voice of Mr. Travis, urging him on.

It wasn't rapid fleeing that we did. The bucket hung heavy in the old man's hands, and he had to shield the tall flower from dead limbs that reached out and tried to smash it. I tripped twice and went flat, but was on my feet spunky enough thereafter; and Kitty Cat was the fastest runaway ever I saw, to escape through unfamiliar forests in this fashion. But the dog and the man were coming closer behind us.

I reckon some kind of angels opened up the underbrush, for it's certain we made more rapid journeying coming out than we had made going in. . . . Rays of the lantern flew helter-skelter across the rail fence that lined the road. Horses were gallivanting beyond; the light caught their legs; and in all our breathlessness and fear, we could seek dark forms of riders atop them.

By this time Mr. Travis's dog was close amongst us, and though he didn't snap or bite, he outcried in a way to drive us distracted; and Mr. Travis himself was crashing through the final thicket, and I wondered in my agony why he didn't shoot.

A rail scraped my shin. Another took a bite out of my shoulder, and then I was through the fence, and so

---

15. **pelt**: to hurry.

was Kitty Cat. But poor Doctor Sickles couldn't fly through any fence — not with that bucket, and all the stiffness of his limbs, and his intention of guarding the purple moccasin that nodded and swayed under the bucket's bail.

He swung around to face his pursuer, and he held up one hand. "Mr. Travis," he cried, "be wary with your shotgun! Don't stain your hands with the blood of these innocent young!"

"They're no more innocent than you be!" yelled Mr. Travis, bursting from the hazel brush like a bear from his den. "I see you've got a bucket full, but you'll never cross that fence with it!" The barrel of the shotgun poked out long and vicious in the dull light.

Those horses in the road had the bits drawn tight in their mouths, and they were rearing with astonishment, and the men who rode them were mighty well astonished too.

"Stop that!" came a voice. "Put down that gun, or I'll drill you quick!" and the rider who had spoken talked as if he had a revolver in his hand.

Slow and uncertain, the barrel of the shotgun went down; I heard Mr. Travis a-growling.

Doctor Sickles stood there, facing him steadily, with the bucket handle gripped tight. Then a horse crowded against me so close that I could smell his hair, and a wonderful voice cried out, "Jesse! What in time are you doing here!" My knees turned to dough all on a sudden for I knew that voice, it was my pap, and he was close to hand.

They got down from their horses—three men — and they took the lantern from Flora Katherine. Sure enough, here was Pap, and he took hold of my arm, and I liked to feel him doing it.

And nigh to him was Uncle Andrew, and a third man that I couldn't recognize for a moment, as I'd never seen him frequent. He was tall and dark and young, and he had a handsome black mustache that hung low on either side of his mouth. And then I knew him for Mr. Charley Gaffney. Even with the frail light making patterns on his face, I should have been able to recognize him before this: he was sheriff of Barbary County, and a right mean man to come against.

"Ben Travis," he said, "you won't commit murder in my presence."

"He's got the gold off of my land!" cried Mr. Travis, pointing at the bucket. "They've been coming after it for days, and they'll only carry it off over my dead body!"

The sheriff chuckled, and then he climbed over the fence most speedily and bent down to glimpse the burden that Doctor Sickles was carrying. "He's got a plant, Ben Travis. Some kind of flower. And that's all he seems to have, and a lot of dirt with it. . . . I reckon it's mighty lucky we happened by here a-searching for this young'un of Henry Bohun's."

Well, the explaining started up, and for a while they couldn't make much out of Doctor Sickles's talk, with all his praise and wonderment about the purple moccasin; and through the whole rigmarole, Ben Travis was still demanding Doctor Sickles's blood, but the sheriff took his shotgun away.

Sheriff Gaffney laughed his head off, and he said that it was astonishing how crazy Mr. Travis acted about that land of his, and he had better look out or they'd lock him up for a lunatic. "Who owned this land during the war, Ben Travis?" he kept demanding.

"Your pappy!" said Travis. "But everybody knows that his slaves buried the treasure at a point unknown to him, and then they skun out when the Yankees rode up, and they never come back. And with my own ears I heard your pap say that there was gold and silver in this soil, long before he died and long before I ever bought this farm."

But Mr. Sheriff Gaffney just put his arm on Ben's shoulder and begged him to consider reason. "It may be," he said, "that there's a dozen or two teaspoons and a hundred dollars in gold stowed under a stump somewhere. But there's no great wealth, Ben Travis. If my father spoke of gold and silver in this earth, he meant the kind that comes from grain and hogs and apple trees, from toil well performed and duties done honest. That's what he meant, and you'd better put in some crops instead of raring around with a shooting iron."

They had to hear all about Doctor Sickles, too, and whence he came. He told them his wagon was filled with plants, but none so wonderful as the purple moccasin, and he reckoned folks wouldn't believe he had it, when sometime he wandered back to the cities with his little girl and stopped at the dooryards of men who took interest in such things. He wanted all of us to come to his camp, and we did have to go for my bundle. Doctor Sickles wanted us to see his herbs and posies, and others that were squashed flat in big books, and I guess he had written a few books himself. And most of all, when they could pull him away from his plants, he marveled at how my pap had ridden from Arkansas to find me.

"Arkansas!" cried out Uncle Andrew, and I had to hang my head. "Why this boy ain't no more than fourteen mile from home this minute. He was born right here in Barbary County, and we all live on Rosy Ridge, and we'd admire to have you come a-visiting us." He put his hands down and played with Flora Katherine's hair, though I was annoyed with him for doing so.

But Doctor Sickles made another wonderful speech in which he talked about the pigeons and the lordly bison, and the flora that had been despoiled. He said that he had right smart of journeying to do this season, and many more flowers to stow away in his wagon, and that there might be wondrous things as pleasurable to find as a purple moccasin.

So now the time was come when I must say good-bye to the purple moccasin and to Doctor Sickles, and, most of all, to Flora Katherine. I sort of mumbled around; then, quick, I thought how I'd like to kiss her. And I did it, too, before my pap took me up on his horse to ride home through the night.

■ Understanding the Story

1. Why had the narrator run away from home?

2. By having Jesse misunderstand the kind of treasure Dr. Sickles is looking for, author MacKinlay Kantor increases both suspense and humor in the story. The author gives you a clue that the purple moccasin is a flower when Dr. Sickles calls his daughter "Flower of My Life." Find one other clue.

3. When the author begins this story, it sounds as if it will be told from the third-person point of view. What sentence changes the story from third person (he) to first person (I)?

4. In the United States today, thousands of plants and animals are classified as *endangered,* that is, close to disappearing forever from the world. Do you believe that these plants and animals should be protected? Explain how and why. Name one endangered species that you are concerned about.

■ Understanding Literature

MacKinlay Kantor captures the flavor of rural Missouri just after the Civil War by having his narrator speak its unique regional *dialect.* Dialect is a variation of English spoken by a particular group of people. Different dialects often are identified by the way people pronounce words. But most dialects also have certain words unique to that region.

Much of the humor in this story comes from the difficulty the characters have in understanding one another's language. All of the characters speak English, but Dr. Sickles's language is extremely formal, the kind of English that a college professor might use in giving a lecture on plants. The narrator says he is "flabbergasted" by Dr. Sickles's speech "because folks didn't talk that way in our neighborhood." How do people talk in your neighborhood? Ask friends and neighbors what words they use for the following objects: paper container for groceries; lever with which you turn on water; metal utensil used to fry food in; a carbonated drink; bread made of cornmeal.

■ Writing About the Story

Draw or paint a picture of the rarest flowering plant, one that you have seen only in your imagination. Write a paragraph naming your plant, telling where it might grow (for example, desert, seashore, forest, garden, Mars), and what it might be used for if it has a value other than beauty.

Creature of the Snows

A short story by William Sambrot

Illustrated by Jon Friedman

ED MCKALE STRAIGHTENED UP under his load of cameras and equipment, squinting against the blasting wind, peering, staring, sweeping the jagged, unending expanse of snow and wind-scoured rock. Looking, searching, as he'd been doing now for two months, cameras at the ready.

Nothing. Nothing but the towering Himalayas,[1] thrusting miles high on all sides. Two months of nothing. Big, fat nothing.

The expedition was a bust. The goofiest assignment of this or any other century, as Ed felt it would be from the moment he'd sat across a desk from the big boss in the picture magazine's New York office, two months ago, looking at the blurred photograph, while the boss filled him in on the weird details.

The photograph, his boss had told him gravely, had been taken in the Himalaya Mountains, at an altitude of twenty-one thousand feet, by a man soaring overhead in a motorless glider.

"A glider," Ed had said noncommittally, staring at the fuzzy enlarged snapshot of a great expanse of snow and rocky ledges, full of harsh light and shadows, a sort of roughly bowl-shaped plateau apparently, and in the middle of it a group of indistinct figures, tiny, lost against the immensity of great ice pinnacles. Ed looked closer. Were the figures people? If so, what had happened to their clothes?

"A glider," his boss reiterated firmly. The glider pilot, the boss said, was maneuvering in an updraft, attempting to do the incredible, soar over Mount Everest[2] in a homemade glider. The wide-winged glider had been unable to achieve the flight over Everest, but, flitting silently about seeking updrafts, it cleared a jagged pinnacle and there, less than a thousand feet below, the pilot saw movement where none should have been. And dropping lower, startled, he'd seen, the boss said dryly, "Creatures — creatures that looked exactly like a group of naked men and women and kids, playing in the snow, at an altitude of twenty thousand five hundred feet." He'd had the presence of mind to take a few hasty snapshots before the group disappeared. Only one of the pictures had developed.

---

1. **Himalayas** (HIM·uh·LAY·uhz, hi·MAHL·yuhz): a high mountain range in southern Asia (India, Tibet, and Nepal).

2. **Mount Everest**: in the Himalayas, the highest mountain in the world (29,028 feet).

Looking at the snapshot with professional scorn, Ed had said, "These things are indistinct. I think he's selling you a bill of goods."

"No," the boss said, "we checked on the guy. He really did make the glider flight. We've had experts go over that blowup. The picture's genuine. Those are naked biped,[3] erect-walking creatures." He flipped the picture irritably. "I can't publish this thing; I want close-ups, action shots, the sort of thing our subscribers have come to expect of us."

He'd lighted a cigar slowly. "Bring me back some pictures I can publish, Ed, and you can write your own ticket."

"You're asking me to climb Mount Everest," Ed said, carefully keeping the sarcasm out of his voice. "To search for this plateau here" — he tapped the shoddy photograph — "and take pix of — what are they, biped, erect-walking creatures, you say?"

The boss cleared his throat. "Not Mount Everest, Ed. It's Gauri Sankar, one of the peaks near Mount Everest. Roughly, it's only about twenty-three thousand feet or so high."

"That's pretty rough," Ed said.

The boss looked pained. "Actually it's not Gauri Sankar either. Just one of the lesser peaks of the Gauri Sankar massif.[4] Well under twenty-three thou-

sand. Certainly nothing to bother a hotshot ex-paratrooper like you, Ed."

Ed winced, and the boss continued, "This guy, this glider pilot, wasn't able to pinpoint the spot, but he did come up with a pretty fair map of the terrain, for a pretty fair price. We've checked it out with the American Alpine Club; it conforms well with their own charts of the general area. Several expeditions have been in the vicinity, but not this exact spot, they tell me. It's not a piece of cake by any means, but it's far from being another Annapurna, or K-2."[5]

He sucked at his cigar thoughtfully. "The Alpine Club says we've got only about two months of good weather before the inevitable monsoons[6] hit that area, so time, as they say, is of the essence, Ed. But two months for this kind of thing ought to be plenty. Everything will be first class; we're even including these new gas guns that shoot hypodermic needles, or something similar. We'll fly the essentials in to Katmandu[7] and airdrop everything possible along the route up to your base at" — he squinted at a map — "Namche Bazar. A Sherpa[8] village which is twelve thousand feet high."

He smiled amiably at Ed. "That's a couple of weeks' march up from the nearest railroad, and ought to get you acclimatized nicely. Plenty of experienced porters at Namche, all Sherpas.

---

3. **biped** (BY•ped): two-footed (having two feet).
4. **massif** (MAS•if, mah•SEEF): a compact section of a mountain range, with one or more peaks.

5. **Annapurna; K-2:** two of the world's highest peaks.
6. **monsoons:** seasonal winds that bring heavy rains.
7. **Katmandu:** the capital city of Nepal.
8. **Sherpa:** Tibetan people of the Nepalese Himalayas.

We've lined up a couple of expert mountain climbers with Himalayan background. And expedition leader will be Doctor Schenk, top man in his field.''

"What is his field?'' Ed asked gloomily.

"Zoology. Whatever these things are in this picture, they're animal, which is his field. Everyone will be sworn to secrecy; you'll be the only one permitted to use a camera, Ed. This could be the biggest thing you'll ever cover, if these things are what I think they are.''

"What do you think they are?''

"An unknown species of human, or subhuman,'' his boss said and prudently Ed remained silent. Two months would tell the tale.

But two months didn't tell. Oh, there were plenty of wild rumors by the Nepalese all along the upper route. Hushed stories of the two-legged creature that walked like a man. A monster the Sherpas called *yeti*. Legends: Strange encounters, drums sounding from snow-swept heights, wild snatches of song drifting down from peaks that were inaccessible to ordinary men. And one concrete fact — a ban, laid on by the Buddhist monks, against the taking of any life in the high Himalayas. What life? Ed wondered.

Stories, legends, but nothing else.

Two months of it. Starting from the tropical flatlands, up through the lush, exotic rain forest, where sun struggled through immense trees festooned with

orchids. Two months, moving up into the arid foothills, where foliage abruptly ceased and the rocks and wind took over. Up and ever up, to where the first heavy snowpack lay. And higher still, following the trail laid out by the glider pilot. What impelled a man, Ed wondered, to soar over Mount Everest in a homemade glider?

Two months, during which Ed had come to dislike Doctor Schenk intensely. Tall, saturnine,[9] smelling strongly of formaldehyde, Schenk classified everything into terms of vertebrate, invertebrate.[10]

So now, standing on this wind-scoured ridge with the shadows falling into the abysses on either side, Ed peered through ice-encrusted goggles, watching Schenk arguing with the guides. He motioned to the ledge above, and obediently the Sherpas moved toward it. Obviously that would be the final camping spot. The two months were over by several days; Schenk was within his rights to call it quits. It was only Ed's assurances that the plateau they were seeking lay just ahead that had kept Schenk from bowing out exactly on the appointed time, that and the burning desire to secure his niche in zoology forever with a new specimen: biped, erect-walking — what?

But the plateau just ahead, and the one after that, and all the rest beyond

---

9. **saturnine** (SAT•uhr•NYN): quiet and gloomy.
10. **vertebrate, invertebrate**: animals with backbones, animals without backbones.

had proved just as empty as those behind. A bust. Whatever the unknown creatures were the glider pilot had photographed, they would remain just that — unknown.

And yet, as Ed slogged slowly up toward where the porters were setting up the bright blue and yellow nylon tents, he was nagged by a feeling that the odd-shaped pinnacle ahead looked awfully much like the one in the blurred photograph. With his unfailing memory for pictures, Ed remembered the tall, jagged cone that had cast a black shadow across a snowy plateau, pointing directly toward the little group that was in the center of the picture.

But Schenk wasn't having any more plateaus. He shook his head vehemently, white-daubed lips a grim line on his sun-blistered face. "Last camp, Ed," he said firmly. "We agreed this would be the final plateau. I'm already a week behind schedule. If the monsoons hit us, we could be in serious trouble below. We have to get started back. I know exactly how you feel, but I'm afraid this is it."

Later that night, while the wind moved ceaselessly, sucking at the tent, they burrowed in sleeping bags, talking.

"There must be some basis of fact in those stories," Ed said to Doctor Schenk. "I've given them a lot of thought. Has it occurred to you that every one of the sightings, the few face-to-face meetings of the natives and these — these unknowns — has generally been just around dawn and usually when the native was alone?"

Schenk smiled dubiously. "Whatever this creature may be — and I'm convinced that it's either a species of large bear, or one of the great anthropoids[11] — it certainly must keep off the well-traveled routes. There are very few passes through these peaks, of course, and it would be quite simple for them to avoid these locales."

"But we're not on any known trail," Ed said thoughtfully. "I believe our methods have been all wrong, stringing out a bunch of men, looking for trails in the snow. All we've done is announce our presence to anything with ears for miles around. That glider pilot made no sound. He came on them without warning."

Ed looked intently at Schenk. "I'd like to try that peak up ahead, and the plateau beyond." When Schenk uttered a protesting cry, Ed said, "Wait. This time I'll go alone, with just one Sherpa guide. We could leave several hours before daybreak. No equipment, other than oxygen, food for one meal, and my cameras, of course. Maintain a strict silence. We could be back before noon. Will you wait long enough for this one last try?" Schenk hesitated. "Only a few hours more," Ed urged.

Schenk stared at him, then he nodded slowly. "Agreed. But aren't you forgetting the most important item of all?" When Ed looked blank, Schenk smiled. "The gas gun. If you should run across one, we'll need more proof than just your word for it."

There was very little wind, no moon, but cold, the cold approaching that of outer space, as Ed and one Sherpa porter started away from the sleeping camp, up the shattered floor of an ice river that swept down from the jagged peak ahead.

The sun came up, and with it the wind began keening[12] again, bitterly sharp, bringing with it a scent of coming snow. In the east, beyond the jagged peak just ahead, the immense escarpment[13] of the Himalayas was lost in approaching cloud. Ed hurried as best he could; it would snow, and soon. He'd have to make better time.

But above, the sky was blue, infinitely blue, and behind, the sun was well up, although the camp was still lost in night below. The peak thrust up ahead, near, with what appeared to be a natural pass skirting its flank. Ed made for it. As he circled an upthrust ridge of reddish, rotten rock, he glanced ahead. The plateau spread out before him, gently sloping, a natural amphitheater full of deep, smooth snow, with peaks surrounding it, and the central peak thrusting a long black shadow directly across the center. He paused, glancing back. The Sherpa had stopped, well below him, his face a dark blur, looking up, gesticulating frantically, pointing to the clouds. Ed motioned, then moved

---

11. **anthropoids:** apes that resemble man, such as gorillas and chimpanzees.

12. **keening:** wailing.
13. **escarpment:** a long, steep ridge.

around, leaning against the rock, peering ahead.

That great shadow against the snow was certainly similar to the one in the photo; only, of course, the shadow pointed west now, when later it would point northwest, as the sun swung to the south. And when it did, most certainly it was the precise. . . . He sucked in a sharp, lung-piercing breath.

He stared, squinting against the rising wind that seemed to blow from earth's outermost reaches. Three figures stirred slightly and suddenly leaped into focus, almost perfectly camouflaged against the snow and wind-blasted rock. Three figures, not more than a hundred feet below him. Two small, one larger.

He leaned forward, his heart thudding terribly at this twenty-thousand-foot height. A tremor of excitement shook him. It was true. They existed. He was looking at what was undeniably a female and two smaller — what? Apes?

They were covered with downy hair, nearly white, resembling nothing so much as tight-fitting leotards. The female was exactly like any woman on earth, except for the hair. No larger than most women, with arms slightly longer, more muscular. Thighs heavier, legs shorter, out of proportion to the trunk. Not apes.

Hardly breathing, Ed squinted, staring, motionless. Not apes. Not standing so erectly. Not with those broad, high brows. Not with the undeniable intelli-

gence of the two young capering about their mother. Not — and seeing this, Ed trembled against the freezing rock — not with the sudden affectionate sweep of the female as she lifted the smaller and pressed it to her breast, smoothing back hair from its face with a motion common to every human mother on earth. A wonderfully tender gesture.

What were they? Less than human? Perhaps. He couldn't be certain, but he thought he heard a faint gurgle of laughter from the female, fondling the small one, and the sound stirred him strangely. Doctor Schenk had assured

394

him that only humans were capable of genuine laughter.

But they laughed, those three, and hearing them, watching the mother tickling the younger one, watching its delighted squirming, Ed knew that in that marvelous little grouping below, perfectly lighted, perfectly staged, he was privileged to observe one of earth's most guarded secrets.

He should get started, shooting his pictures. Afterward he should stun the group into unconsciousness with the gas gun and then send the Sherpa back down for Doctor Schenk and the

others. Clouds were massing, immensities of blue black. Already the first few flakes of snow, huge and wet, drifted against his face.

But for a long moment more he remained motionless, oddly unwilling to do anything to destroy the harmony, the aching purity of the scene below, so vividly etched in brilliant light and shadow. The female, child slung casually on one hip, stood erect, hand shading her eyes, and Ed grinned. Artless, but perfectly posed. She was looking carefully about and above, scanning the great outcroppings of rock, obviously searching for something. Then she paused. She was staring directly at him. Ed froze, even though he knew he was perfectly concealed by the deep shadows of the high cliff behind him. She was still looking directly at him, and then slowly her hand came up. She waved.

He shivered uncontrollably in the biting wind, trying to remain motionless. The two young ones suddenly began to jump up and down, and show every evidence of joy. Suddenly Ed knew.

He turned slowly, very slowly, and with the sensation of a freezing knife plunging deeply into his chest, he saw the male less than five yards away.

It was huge, easily twice the size of the female below. And, crazily, Ed thought of Schenk's little lecture, given what seemed like eons ago, in the incredible tropical grove far below, and six weeks before, where rhododendrons grew in wild profusion and

enormous butterflies flitted about. "In primitive man," Schenk had said, "as in the great apes today, the male was far larger than the female."

The gas gun was hopelessly out of reach, securely strapped to his shoulder pack. Ed stared, knowing there was absolutely nothing he could do to protect himself before this creature, fully eight feet tall, with arms as big as Ed's own thighs, and blue eyes boring into his. There was a light of savage intelligence there, and something else.

The creature made no move against him, and Ed stared at it, breathing rapidly, shallowly and with difficulty, noting with his photographer's eyes the immense chest span, the easy rise and fall of his breathing, the large, square, white teeth, the somber cast of his face. There was long, sandy fur on the shoulders, chest and back, shortening

to off-white over the rest of the magnificent torso. Ears rather small and close to the head. Short, thick neck, rising up from the broad shoulders to the back of the head in a straight line. Toes long and definitely prehensile.[14]

They looked intently at each other, across the abyss of time and mystery. Man and — what? How long, Ed wondered, had it stood there, observing him? Why hadn't it attacked? Had it been waiting for Ed to make a single threatening gesture, such as pointing a gun or camera? Seeing the calm awareness in those long, slanting, blue eyes, Ed sped a silent prayer of thanks upward; most certainly if he had made a move for camera or gun, that move would have been his last.

They looked at each other through

---

14. **prehensile:** able to grasp or hold things.

the falling snow, and suddenly there was a perfect instantaneous understanding between them. Ed made an awkward, half-frozen little bow, moving backward. The great creature stood motionless, merely watching, and then Ed did a strange thing. He held out his hands, palms up, gave a wry grin, and ducked quickly around the outcropping of rock and began a plunging, sliding return, down the way he had come. In spite of the harsh, snow-laden wind, bitterly cold, he was perspiring.

Ed glanced back once. Nothing. Only the thickening veil of swift-blowing snow, blanking out the pinnacle, erasing every trace, every proof that anyone, anything, had stood there moments before. Only the snow, only the rocks, only the unending wind-filled silence of the top of the world. Nothing else.

The Sherpa was struggling up to him from below, terribly anxious to get started back; the storm was rising. Without a word they hooked up and began the groping, stumbling descent back to the last camp. They found the camp already broken, Sherpas already moving out. Schenk paused only long enough to give Ed a questioning look.

What could Ed say? Schenk was a scientist, demanding material proof, if not a corpse, at the very least a photograph. The only photographs Ed had were etched in his mind, not on film. And even if he could persuade Schenk to wait, when the storm cleared, the giant, forewarned, would be gone.

Some farther peak, some remoter plateau would echo to the laughter of his young.

Feeling not a bit bad about it, Ed gave Schenk a barely perceptible[15] negative nod. Instantly Schenk shrugged, turned and went plunging down, into the thickening snow, back into the world of littler men. Ed trailed behind.

On the arduous trek back, through that first great storm, through the snow line, through the rain forest, hot and humid, Ed thought of the giant, back up there where the air was thin and pure.

Who, what was he, and his race? Castaways on this planet, forever marooned, yearning for a distant, never-to-be-reached home? Or did they date in unbroken descent from Pleistocene times,[16] creatures forced to retreat higher and higher, to more and more remote areas, until finally there was only one corner of earth left to them, the high Himalayas? Or were he and his kind earth's last reserves, waiting for the opening of still another chapter in earth's unending mystery story?

Whatever the giant was, his secret was safe with him, Ed thought. For who would believe it, even if he chose to tell?

---

15. **perceptible:** recognizable; visible.
16. **Pleistocene** (PLY·stuh·SEEN) **times:** the geologic epoch lasting from about 1,000,000–10,000 B.C. Sometimes called the Glacial epoch or the Great Ice Age, this period was characterized by widespread glacial ice and major changes in the development of plants, animals, and humans.

Understanding the Story

1. Why did Ed McKale's boss send him to the Himalayas?

2. Ed tells Schenk he wants to make one last try before they leave. What does he plan to do differently this time?

3. What was human about the snow creatures?

4. Why did Ed decide to tell no one about what he saw?

5. Suppose that the expedition had been able to capture the snow creatures. What do you think would have happened to them in today's world? Would you have captured them or left them alone?

6. What kinds of creatures do you think the snow creatures are? Write a brief description of them in your own words and explain how and why they live in the high Himalayas.

Understanding Literature

The short story "Creature of the Snows" begins with Ed McKale staring, cameras ready, across the snow-covered rock of the Himalayas. The setting is the Himalayas of Tibet, and we are told that Ed has been there for two months. Look back at page 389 and notice that the location remains in the Himalayas for only two paragraphs. In the third paragraph, the author shifts the setting back two months to New York. This shift is called a *flashback,* a technique writers use to present scenes or events that occurred before the opening scene of a story.

When earlier events might help the reader better understand the characters or the plot, the writer interrupts the action of the story and uses a flashback to present background information. In this story, the action changes from the present to the past (two months before) on the first page of the story and then back to the present on page 391. What important information do we receive in this flashback?

Writing About the Story

Consult an encyclopedia, recent magazines, or other reference materials to gather information about the Abominable Snowman (the yeti) and Bigfoot (the sasquatch). Take notes on what you read. Then pretend you are broadcasting a news report on a sighting of one of these creatures and write the news copy. Explain who saw the creature, what it looked like, and where and when the sighting occurred.

The Presence

A poem by Maxine Kumin

Something went crabwise[1]
across the snow this morning.
Something went hard and slow
over our hayfield.
It could have been a raccoon
lugging a knapsack,
it could have been a porcupine
carrying a tennis racket,
it could have been something
supple[2] as a red fox
dragging the squawk and spatter
of a crippled woodcock.
Ten knuckles underground
those bones are seeds now
pure as baby teeth
lined up in the burrow.
I cross on snowshoes
cunningly woven from
the skin and sinews of
something else that went before.

---

1. **went crabwise:** moved like a crab, sideways.
2. **supple:** limber.

Illustration by Pat Traub

Galante Garden: II

A poem by Juan Ramón Jiménez

Translated from the Spanish by H. R. Hays

There was no one. The water — no one?
How can the water be no one? There is
No one. There's the flower — is no one there?
But is the flower no one?

There is no one. There was the wind — no one?
Is the wind no one? There is
No one. Illusion — is no one there?
And is the illusion no one?

400

Illustration by Julie Downing

BOOKSHELF

Green Mansions by William E. Hudson. Dodd, Mead, 1949. Lush vegetation, exotic insects, and birds of a tropical rain forest are vividly described in this fanciful tale of a young man's search for the elusive Rima the Bird Girl.

Emma Tupper's Diary by Peter Dickinson. Little, Brown, 1971. On a trip to the Scottish Highlands, Emma keeps a journal which becomes the revelation of a dangerous hoax that threatens the future of the loch itself.

Spill by Chester Aaron. Atheneum, 1978. A family attempts to save a lagoon and a nearby bird sanctuary after an oil spill occurs.

Lost in the Barrens by Farley Mowat. Little, Brown, 1956. Jamie, new to northern Canada, and Awasin Meewasin, a Cree Indian, become friends and explore the far north where survival depends on all their skill and courage.

The Starship and the Canoe by Kenneth Brower. Holt, Rinehart & Winston, 1978. Two remarkable men, a father and son, search for meaning in the stars above and the sea below.

The Outermost House: A Year of Life on the Great Beach of Cape Cod by Henry Beston. Viking Press, 1962. The migrations of birds, the rhythms of the wind, the pageant of stars in the changing seasons — all are captured with wonder and mystery.

Song of the Wild by Allan W. Eckert. Little, Brown, 1980. Caleb Erikson has the ability to transfer his consciousness to any living organism and share what it experiences. He can soar with the blackbird or tremble with a mighty tree during a storm.

Pilgrim at Tinker Creek by Annie Dillard. Harper's Magazine Press, 1974. The author's vision of nature is one of both beauty and terror. This personal narrative chronicles one year's exploration of her woodland surroundings.

6 Another Where, Another When

The Quest of the Unicorn

From the novel *The Last Unicorn* by Peter S. Beagle

Illustrated by Kinuko Craft

The proud, graceful unicorn is perhaps the most fascinating of all mythical creatures. The Roman naturalist Pliny the Elder (A.D. 23–79) named the unicorn the cruelest of the beasts, with a horse's body, a stag's head, elephant's feet, boar's tail, and a black horn. However, by the Middle Ages the unicorn had become a symbol of strength, tenderness, and chastity. It was said that St. Denis Cathedral in France kept a unicorn, its healing magic so potent that even the water it waded in could cure the sick. The unicorn is also found in Chinese mythology as the ch'i-lin, *whose rare appearance marked the birth or death of a great sage or ruler.*

There is always an aura of sadness surrounding tales about the unicorn, as if the creatures were too noble and pure to exist. Yet the unicorn is also a symbol of faith in the impossible. Whenever people think of this fabulous beast prancing proudly on the earth, they can hope for a world beautiful enough to contain unicorns.

THE UNICORN LIVED in a lilac wood, and she lived all alone. She was very old, though she did not know it, and she was no longer the careless color of sea foam, but rather the color of snow falling on a moonlit night. But her eyes were still clear and unwearied, and she still moved like a shadow on the sea.

She did not look anything like a horned horse, as unicorns are often pictured, being smaller and cloven-hoofed,[1] and possessing that oldest, wildest grace that horses have never had, that deer have only in a shy, thin imitation and goats in dancing mockery. Her neck was long and slender, making her head seem smaller than it was, and the mane that fell almost to the middle of her back was as soft as dandelion fluff and as fine as cirrus.[2] She had pointed ears and thin legs, with feathers of white hair at the ankles; and the long horn above her eyes shone and shivered with its own sea-shell light even in the deepest midnight. She had killed dragons

---

1. **cloven-hoofed:** having split hoofs, like cattle.

2. **cirrus** (SIR•uhs): thin, white clouds.

with it, and healed a king whose poisoned wound would not close, and knocked down ripe chestnuts for bear cubs.

Unicorns are immortal. It is their nature to live alone in one place: usually a forest where there is a pool clear enough for them to see themselves — for they are a little vain, knowing themselves to be the most beautiful creatures in all the world, and magic besides. They mate very rarely, and no place is more enchanted than one where a unicorn has been born. The last time she had seen another unicorn the young ones who still came seeking her now and then had called to her in a different tongue;[3] but then, she had no idea of months and years and centuries, or even of seasons. It was always spring in her forest, because she lived there, and she wandered all day among the great beech trees, keeping watch over the animals that lived in the ground and under bushes, in nests and caves, earths and treetops. Generation after generation, wolves and rabbits alike, they hunted and loved and had children and died, and as the unicorn did none of these things, she never grew tired of watching them.

One day it happened that two men with long bows rode through her forest, hunting for deer. The unicorn followed them, moving so

warily that not even the horses knew she was near. The sight of men filled her with an old, slow, strange mixture of tenderness and terror. She never let one see her if she could help it, but she liked to watch them ride by and hear them talking.

"I mislike the feel of this forest," the elder of the two hunters grumbled. "Creatures that live in a unicorn's wood learn a little magic of their own in time, mainly concerned with disappearing. We'll find no game here."

"Unicorns are long gone," the second man said. "If, indeed, they ever were. This is a forest like any other."

"Then why do the leaves never fall here, or the snow? I tell you, there is one unicorn left in the world — good luck to the lonely old thing, I say — and as long as it lives in this forest, there won't be a hunter who takes so much as a titmouse home at his saddle. Ride on, ride on, you'll see. I know their ways, unicorns."

"From books," answered the other. "Only from books and tales and songs. Not in the reign of three kings has there been even a whisper of a unicorn seen in this country or any other. You know no more about unicorns than I do, for I've read the same books and heard the same stories, and I've never seen one either."

The first hunter was silent for a time, and the second whistled sourly

---

3. tongue: a language.

to himself. Then the first said, "My great-grandmother saw a unicorn once. She used to tell me about it when I was little."

"Oh, indeed? And did she capture it with a golden bridle?"

"No. She didn't have one. You don't have to have a golden bridle to catch a unicorn; that part's the fairy tale. You need only to be pure of heart."

"Yes, yes." The younger man chuckled. "Did she ride her unicorn, then? Bareback, under the trees, like a nymph in the early days of the world?"

"My great-grandmother was afraid of large animals," said the first hunter. "She didn't ride it, but she sat very still, and the unicorn put its head in her lap and fell asleep. My great-grandmother never moved till it woke."

"What did it look like? Pliny describes the unicorn as being very ferocious, similar in the rest of its body to a horse, with the head of a deer, the feet of an elephant, the tail of a boar; a deep bellowing voice, and a single black horn, two cubits[4] in length. And the Chinese——"

"My great-grandmother said only that the unicorn had a good smell. She never could abide the smell of

4. **two cubits** (KYOO·bits): about 36 inches.

any beast, even a cat or a cow, let alone a wild thing. But she loved the smell of the unicorn. She began to cry once, telling me about it. Of course, she was a very old woman then, and cried at anything that reminded her of her youth."

"Let's turn around and hunt somewhere else," the second hunter said abruptly. The unicorn stepped softly into a thicket as they turned their horses, and took up the trail only when they were well ahead of her once more. The men rode in silence until they were nearing the edge of the forest, when the second hunter asked quietly, "Why did they go away, do you think? If there ever were such things."

"Who knows? Times change. Would you call this age a good one for unicorns?"

"No, but I wonder if any man before us ever thought his time a good time for unicorns. And it seems to me now that I have heard stories — but I was sleepy, or I was thinking of something else. Well, no matter. There's light enough yet to hunt, if we hurry. Come!"

They broke out of the woods, kicked their horses to a gallop, and dashed away. But before they were out of sight, the first hunter looked back over his shoulder and called, just as though he could see the unicorn standing in shadow, "Stay where you are, poor beast. This is no world for you. Stay in your forest, and keep your trees green and your friends long-lived. And good luck to you."

The unicorn stood still at the edge of the forest and said aloud, "I am the only unicorn there is." They were the first words she had spoken, even to herself, in more than a hundred years.

That can't be, she thought. She had never minded being alone, never seeing another unicorn, because she had always known that there were others like her in the world, and a unicorn needs no more than that for company. "But I would know if all the others were gone. I'd be gone too. Nothing can happen to them that does not happen to me."

Her own voice frightened her and made her want to be running. She moved along the dark paths of her forest, swift and shining, passing through sudden clearings unbearably brilliant with grass or soft with shadow, aware of everything around her, from the weeds that brushed her ankles to insect-quick flickers of blue and silver as the wind lifted the leaves. "Oh, I could never leave this, I never could, not if I really were the only unicorn in the world. I know how to live here, I know how everything smells, and tastes, and is. What could I ever search for in the world, except this again?"

But when she stopped running at last and stood still, listening to crows and a quarrel of squirrels over her head, she wondered, But suppose they are riding together, somewhere far away? What if they are hiding and waiting for me?

From that first moment of doubt, there was no peace for her; from the time she first imagined leaving her forest, she could not stand in one place without wanting to be somewhere else. She trotted up and down beside her pool, restless and unhappy. Unicorns are not meant to make choices. She said no, and yes, and no again, day and night, and for the first time she began to feel the minutes crawling over her like worms. "I will not go. Because men have seen no unicorns for a while does not mean they have all vanished. Even if it were true, I would not go. I live here."

But at last she woke up in the middle of one warm night and said, "Yes, but now." She hurried through her forest, trying to look at nothing and smell nothing, trying not to feel her earth under her cloven hoofs. The animals who move in the dark, the owls and the foxes and the deer, raised their heads as she passed by, but she would not look at them. I must go quickly, she thought, and come back as soon as I can. Maybe I won't have to go very far. But whether I find the others or not, I will come back very soon, as soon as I can.

Under the moon, the road that ran from the edge of her forest gleamed like water, but when she stepped out onto it, away from the trees, she felt how hard it was, and how long. She almost turned back then; but instead she took a deep breath of the woods air that still drifted to her, and held it in her mouth like a flower, as long as she could.

—◦◦✺◦◦—

The long road hurried to nowhere and had no end. It ran through villages and small towns, flat country

and mountains, stony barrens[5] and meadows springing out of stones, but it belonged to none of these, and it never rested anywhere. It rushed the unicorn along, tugging at her feet like the tide, fretting at her, never letting her be quiet and listen to the air, as she used to do. Her eyes were always full of dust, and her mane was stiff and heavy with dirt.

Time had always passed her by in her forest, but now it was she who passed through time as she traveled. The colors of the trees changed, and the animals along the way grew heavy coats and lost them again; the clouds crept or hurried before the changing winds, and were pink and gold in the sun or livid[6] with storm. Wherever she went, she searched for her people, but she found no trace of them, and in all the tongues she heard spoken along the road there was not even a word for them any more.

Early one morning, about to turn off the road to sleep, she saw a man hoeing in his garden. Knowing that she should hide, she stood still instead and watched him work, until he straightened and saw her. He was fat, and his cheeks jumped with every step he took. "Oh," he said. "Oh, you're beautiful."

When he tugged off his belt, made a loop in it, and moved clumsily toward her, the unicorn was more pleased than frightened. The man knew what she was, and what he himself was for: to hoe turnips and pursue something that shone and could run faster than he could. She sidestepped his first lunge as lightly as though the wind of it had blown her out of his reach. "I have been hunted with bells and banners in my time," she told him. "Men knew that the only way to hunt me was to make the chase so wondrous that I would come near to see it. And even so I was never once captured."

"My foot must have slipped," said the man. "Steady now, you pretty thing."

"I've never really understood," the unicorn mused as the man picked himself up, "what you dream of doing with me, once you've caught me." The man leaped again, and she slipped away from him like rain. "I don't think you know yourselves," she said.

"Ah, steady, steady, easy now." The man's sweating face was striped with dirt, and he could hardly get his breath. "Pretty," he gasped. "You pretty little mare."

"*Mare?*" The unicorn trumpeted the word so shrilly that the man stopped pursuing her and clapped his hands to his ears. "Mare?" she demanded, "I, a horse? Is that what you take me for? Is that what you see?"

"Good horse," the fat man panted. He leaned on the fence and

---

5. **barrens**: wastelands.
6. **livid** (LIV·id): here, dark; grayish blue.

wiped his face. "Curry[7] you up, clean you off, you'll be the prettiest old mare anywhere." He reached out with the belt again. "Take you to the fair," he said. "Come on, horse."

"A horse," the unicorn said. "That's what you were trying to capture. A white mare with her mane full of burrs." As the man approached her, she hooked her horn through the belt, jerked it out of his grasp, and hurled it across the road into a patch of daisies. "A horse, am I?" she snorted. "A horse, indeed!"

For a moment the man was very close to her, and her great eyes stared into his own, which were

small and tired and amazed. Then she turned and fled up the road running so swiftly that those who saw her exclaimed, "Now *there's* a horse! There's a real horse!" One old man said quietly to his wife, "That's an Arab horse. I was on a ship with an Arab horse once."

From that time the unicorn avoided towns, even at night, unless there was no way at all to go around them. Even so, there were a few men who gave chase, but always to a wandering white mare; never in the gay and reverent manner proper to the pursuit of a unicorn. They came with ropes and nets and baits of sugar lumps, and they whistled and called her Bess and Nellie. Sometimes

---

7. curry: to comb a horse.

she would slow down enough to let their horses catch her scent, and then watch as the beasts reared and wheeled and ran away with their terrified riders. The horses always knew her.

"How can it be?" she wondered. "I suppose I could understand it if people had simply forgotten unicorns or if they had changed so that they hated all unicorns now and tried to kill them when they saw them. But not to see them at all, to look at them and see something else — what do they look like to one another, then? What do trees look like to them, or houses, or real horses, or their own children?"

Sometimes she thought, "If people no longer know what they are looking at, there may well be unicorns in the world yet, unknown and glad of it." But she knew beyond both hope and vanity that people had changed, and the world with them, because the unicorns were gone. Yet she went on along the hard road, although each day she wished a little more that she had never left her forest.

About PETER S. BEAGLE

Peter S. Beagle describes himself as a "born hider" who has been fascinated all his life by "disguise, camouflage, shape changers." It is no wonder then that he should write fantasy — works of the imagination that bring to life all the *maybe*s and *what if*s lingering on the borders of the everyday.

Peter Beagle feels that animals are the single most important influence on his work, and they inhabit all his worlds. When he was a child, he pretended to be a wolf. He read every book he could find on wolves, bears, and wild horses. Even in high school he preferred animals to people, and he had a black-maned lion as an imaginary friend. Now he finds "there's no book or story of mine that isn't stiff with animal imagery — animal feeling — whether the protagonists are unicorns, werewolves and ravens, or only noblemen and motor scooters." Peter Beagle says he is not really sure just what he thinks of his writing. He explains that people cannot always believe what he says, though, because he makes things up.

■ Understanding the Story

1. How was the unicorn's forest different from all other forests?

2. Why did the unicorn leave her forest?

3. When the unicorn allows people to see her, she makes an amazing and sad discovery. What is it?

4. The events in the story are not true, but the ideas in it may be true. What do you think the author is saying about modern life? Explain.

5. If you had come upon the unicorn as she traveled throughout the modern world, would you have seen a unicorn or a horse? Explain.

■ Understanding Literature

Because many fantasies are written about worlds that exist only in the imagination, they offer a wealth of creative ways to use language. In "The Quest of the Unicorn," author Peter S. Beagle uses *figurative language* to help you discover the unicorn's world and the meaning of her quest.

As you know, figurative language is an unusual way of using words to create new sounds, images, and comparisons. By using figurative language, an author can lend another dimension to the details and meanings in his or her stories. For example, with the following *simile,* a type of figurative language that compares two things by using *like* or *as,* Beagle illustrates the unicorn's love for her forest: "She took a deep breath of the woods air . . . and held it in her mouth like a flower." The word *flower* suggests the way she cherishes the sweetness of the forest air.

Figurative language can also be used to develop character and to create mood. Beagle does both of these by using a kind of figurative language called *metaphor*. A metaphor implies a comparison but does not use *like* or *as*. Notice how, in the following passage, Beagle is able to describe the unicorn while creating a soft, quiet mood: "She was no longer the careless color of sea foam, but rather the color of snow falling on a moonlit night." Beagle is making comparisons about the unicorn's color. He is also suggesting that, after having been the color of something wild and resounding, she has quieted with age.

Find another example of figurative language that describes the fantasy world Beagle has created.

■ Writing About the Story

In "The Quest of the Unicorn," we see and understand the world through the eyes of the unicorn, an imaginary creature. Pretend that you are a different imaginary creature, a real animal, or an object like a comb or pencil. Write about the world from your "new" point of view.

A Fox and a Rose

From *The Little Prince* written and illustrated
by Antoine de Saint-Exupéry
Translated from the French by Katherine Woods

*The little prince lived alone on a tiny planet no larger than a
house. Every day he cleaned his three tiny volcanoes (so that instead of erupting they would burn evenly and cook his breakfast)
and pulled up the shoots of the baobab[1] trees that otherwise would
grow and split the little planet to pieces.*

*One day the winds blew in a seed, which grew to be a beautiful
rose. The prince loved and cared for this flower, but the rose
wanted more. She said she was the only rose in the universe. She
demanded a fence to protect her from tigers and a glass to stop the
breezes. She claimed that where* she *came from, it was much
warmer. . . .*

*As she talked, the little prince began to suspect that his rose
was lying. She had arrived as a seed and couldn't know about the
rest of the universe. The prince thought that perhaps she wasn't
the only rose after all. Sad and curious, the little prince set out to
explore other planets in search of some answers. Finally his journey brings him to Earth, where he is about to learn a lot about his
world back home.*

---

1. baobab (BAY•oh•BAB): a large tree with a very thick trunk; these trees are native to
tropical Africa.

Border illustration by Kinuko Craft

AFTER WALKING for a long time through sand, and rocks, and snow, the little prince at last came upon a road. And all roads lead to the abodes of men.

"Good morning," he said.

He was standing before a garden, all abloom with roses.

"Good morning," said the roses.

The little prince gazed at them. They all looked like his flower.

"Who are you?" he demanded, thunderstruck.

"We are roses," the roses said.

And he was overcome with sadness. His flower had told him that she was the only one of her kind in all the universe. And here were five thousand of them, all alike, in one single garden!

"She would be very much annoyed," he said to

himself, "if she should see that . . . She would cough most dreadfully, and she would pretend that she was dying, to avoid being laughed at. And I should be obliged to pretend that I was nursing her back to life — for if I did not do that, to humble myself also, she would really allow herself to die . . ."

Then he went on with his reflections: "I thought that I was rich, with a flower that was unique in all the world; and all I had was a common rose. A common rose, and three volcanoes that come up to my knees — and one of them perhaps extinct forever . . . That doesn't make me a very great prince . . ."

And he lay down in the grass and cried.

It was then that the fox appeared.

"Good morning," said the fox.

"Good morning," the little prince responded politely, although when he turned around he saw nothing.

"I am right here," the voice said, "under the apple tree."

"Who are you?" asked the little prince, and added, "You are very pretty to look at."

"I am a fox," the fox said.

"Come and play with me," proposed the little prince. "I am so unhappy."

"I cannot play with you," the fox said. "I am not tamed."

"Ah! Please excuse me," said the little prince.

But, after some thought, he added:

"What does that mean — 'tame'?"

"You do not live here," said the fox. "What is it that you are looking for?"

"I am looking for men," said the little prince. "What does that mean — 'tame'?"

"Men," said the fox. "They have guns, and they hunt. It is very disturbing. They also raise chickens. These are their only interests. Are you looking for chickens?"

"No," said the little prince. "I am looking for friends. What does that mean — 'tame'?"

"It is an act too often neglected," said the fox. "It means to establish ties."

" 'To establish ties' ?"

"Just that," said the fox. "To me, you are still nothing more than a little boy who is just like a hundred thousand other little boys. And I have no need of you. And you, on your part, have no need of me. To you, I am nothing more than a fox like a hundred thousand other foxes. But if you tame me, then we shall need each other. To me, you will be unique in all the world. To you, I shall be unique in all the world . . ."

"I am beginning to understand," said the little prince. "There is a flower . . . I think that she has tamed me . . ."

"It is possible," said the fox. "On the Earth one sees all sorts of things."

"Oh, but this is not on the Earth!" said the little prince.

The fox seemed perplexed, and very curious.

"On another planet?"

"Yes."

"Are there hunters on that planet?"

"No."

"Ah, that is interesting! Are there chickens?"

"No."

"Nothing is perfect," sighed the fox.

But he came back to his idea.

"My life is very monotonous," he said. "I hunt chickens; men hunt me. All the chickens are just alike, and all the men are just alike. And, in consequence, I am a little bored. But if you tame me, it will be as if the sun came to shine on my life. I shall know the sound of a step that will be different from all the others. Other steps send me hurrying back underneath the ground. Yours will call me, like music, out of my burrow. And then look: you see the grain fields down yonder? I do not eat bread. Wheat is of no use to me. The wheat fields have nothing to say to me. And that is sad. But you have hair that is the color of gold. Think how wonderful that will be when you have tamed me! The grain, which is also golden, will bring me back the thought of you. And I shall love to listen to the wind in the wheat . . ."

The fox gazed at the little prince, for a long time.

"Please — tame me!" he said.

"I want to, very much," the little prince replied. "But I have not much time. I have friends to discover, and a great many things to understand."

"One only understands the things that one tames," said the fox. "Men have no more time to understand anything. They buy things all ready made at the shops. But there is no shop anywhere where one can buy friendship, and so men have no friends any more. If you want a friend, tame me . . ."

"What must I do, to tame you?" asked the little prince.

"You must be very patient," replied the fox. "First you will sit down at a little distance from me — like that — in the grass. I shall look at you out of the corner of my eye, and you will say nothing. Words are the source of misunderstandings. But you will sit a little closer to me, every day . . ."

The next day the little prince came back.

"It would have been better to come back at the same hour," said the fox. "If, for example, you come at four o'clock in the afternoon, then at three o'clock I shall begin to be happy. I shall feel happier and happier as the hour advances. At four o'clock, I shall already be worrying and jumping about. I shall show you how happy I am! But if you come at just any time, I shall never know at what hour my heart is to be ready to greet you . . . One must observe the proper rites . . ."

"What is a rite?" asked the little prince.

"Those also are actions too often neglected," said the fox. "They are what make one day different from other days, one hour from other hours. There is a rite, for example, among my hunters. Every Thursday they dance with the village girls. So Thursday is a wonderful day for me! I can take a walk as far as the vineyards. But if the hunters danced at just any time, every day would be like every other day, and I should never have any vacation at all."

So the little prince tamed the fox. And when the hour of his departure drew near ——

"Ah," said the fox, "I shall cry."

"It is your own fault," said the little prince. "I never wished you any sort of harm; but you wanted me to tame you . . ."

"Yes, that is so," said the fox.

"But now you are going to cry!" said the little prince.

"Yes, that is so," said the fox.

"Then it has done you no good at all!"

"It has done me good," said the fox, "because of the color of the wheat fields." And then he added:

"Go and look again at the roses. You will understand now that yours is unique in all the world. Then come back to say goodbye to me, and I will make you a present of a secret."

The little prince went away, to look again at the roses.

"You are not at all like my rose," he said. "As yet you

are nothing. No one has tamed you, and you have tamed no one. You are like my fox when I first knew him. He was only a fox like a hundred thousand other foxes. But I have made him my friend, and now he is unique in all the world."

And the roses were very much embarrassed.

"You are beautiful, but you are empty," he went on. "One could not die for you. To be sure, an ordinary passerby would think that my rose looked just like you — the rose that belongs to me. But in herself alone she is more important than all the hundreds of you other roses: because it is she that I have watered; because it is she that I have put under the glass globe;[2] because it is she that I have sheltered behind the screen; because it is for her that I have killed the caterpillars (except the two or three that we saved to become butterflies); because it is she that I have listened to, when she grumbled, or boasted, or even sometimes when she said nothing. Because she is *my* rose."

And he went back to meet the fox.

"Goodbye," he said.

"Goodbye," said the fox. "And now here is my secret, a very simple secret: It is only with the heart that one can see rightly; what is essential is invisible to the eye."

"What is essential is invisible to the eye," the little prince repeated, so that he would be sure to remember.

"It is the time you have wasted for your rose that makes your rose so important."

"It is the time I have wasted for my rose —" said the little prince, so that he would be sure to remember.

"Men have forgotten this truth," said the fox. "But you must not forget it. You become responsible, forever, for what you have tamed. You are responsible for your rose . . ."

"I am responsible for my rose," the little prince repeated, so that he would be sure to remember.

---

2. **glass globe:** a glass ball used to keep plants warm.

■ Understanding the Story

1. The fox has a poor opinion of people because they hunt him. Find one other reason why the fox seems to dislike people. What interest does the fox share with humans?

2. An *aphorism* is a saying that sums up an idea in just a few words. For example, the sentence "Words are the source of misunderstandings" is an aphorism. What other aphorism can you find in the story?

3. Choose one of the following statements and explain what the fox means by it: (a) "It has done me good . . . because of the color of the wheat fields"; (b) "What is essential is invisible to the eye."

4. The fox says that "tame means to establish ties." Do you think the fox's definition of *tame* is different from the ordinary definition? Explain.

5. At his last meeting with the little prince, the fox tells the prince a secret. In your own words, tell what the secret is.

■ Understanding Literature

On the surface, "A Fox and a Rose" is a fantasy tale about a little boy who tames a fox. As soon as the roses say, "Good morning," you know that the story is not about "real" roses—and, of course, no fox in the real world can talk. Yet not everything in a fantasy is false. A fantasy story can contain ideas that are as true as they are important.

Antoine de Saint-Exupéry was a French writer and aviator during the Second World War. *Le Petit Prince (The Little Prince),* from which "A Fox and a Rose" was taken, was written during that war to teach moral and spiritual values. Saint-Exupéry wrote his story as a symbolic story. A *symbol* is an object, character, or incident that stands for something else. The characters in *The Little Prince* stand for types of people, and their actions and dialogue teach ideas that the author feels are important.

Saint-Exupéry uses symbols to express his dissatisfaction with modern life, which he considered too materialistic—that is, too concerned with the accumulation of wealth. For example, in the aphorism "It is only with the heart that one can see rightly," the heart is a symbol for feelings, especially feelings of love. Saint-Exupéry is saying that feelings are the best guide for action. Do you agree with this idea? Explain.

■ Writing About the Story

Choose an aphorism from the story, find another, or make up one of your own. Design a poster on which you carefully write your aphorism. Choose any background you wish that seems appropriate for the idea that is expressed by the aphorism.

From

The Lady of Shalott

A poem by Alfred, Lord Tennyson

The bright white towers of King Arthur's Camelot buzz with the activity of the court. But up the river at Shalott,[1] the gloomy gray castle is quiet. The Lady of Shalott sits alone in her room, weaving day and night. From time to time she breaks the silence with a song, and the workers in the fields gaze up at her window and wonder why she never appears.

On either side the river lie
Long fields of barley and of rye,
That clothe the wold [2] and meet the sky;
And thro' the field the road runs by
    To many-tower'd Camelot;
And up and down the people go,
Gazing where the lilies blow
Round an island there below,
    The island of Shalott.

Willows whiten, aspens quiver,
Little breezes dusk and shiver
Thro' the wave that runs for ever
By the island in the river
    Flowing down to Camelot.
Four gray walls, and four gray towers,
Overlook a space of flowers,
And the silent isle imbowers
    The Lady of Shalott.

By the margin,[3] willow-veil'd,
Slide the heavy barges trail'd
By slow horses; and unhail'd
The shallop flitteth[4] silken-sail'd
    Skimming down to Camelot:
But who hath seen her wave her hand?
Or at the casement seen her stand?
Or is she known in all the land,
    The Lady of Shalott?

Only reapers, reaping early
In among the bearded barley,
Hear a song that echoes cheerly
From the river winding clearly,
    Down to tower'd Camelot:
And by the moon the reaper weary,
Piling sheaves in uplands airy,
Listening, whispers, " 'Tis the fairy
    Lady of Shalott."

---

1. **Shalott** (shuh·LOT).
2. **clothe the wold:** cover the hills.
3. **margin:** shoreline.
4. **The shallop flitteth:** The sailboat skims along.

Illustration by Jaclyne Scardova

Eleanor of Aquitaine

Adapted from the novel *A Proud Taste for Scarlet and Miniver*
by E. L. Konigsburg
Illustrated by Friso Henstra

*Eleanor of Aquitaine[1] (1122–1204), who married two kings and
mothered two more, was the most powerful woman of her era. At
age fifteen, Eleanor inherited the duchy of Aquitaine (then larger
than the kingdom of France) from her father, William X. Soon
thereafter she married King Louis VII of France. She and Louis
ruled together until 1152, when he became jealous of her power
and independence and had their marriage annulled. Two months
later Eleanor married Henry Plantagenet,[2] who became Henry II
of England, and King and Queen both worked to expand and ad-
minister the realm. After Henry's death Eleanor enjoyed greater
influence than ever, managing the kingdom while her son King
Richard the Lion Heart fought in Palestine. Later — when she
was eighty — Eleanor led the troops that successfully defended
England's holdings in France for her son King John.*

*"Eleanor of Aquitaine" is a historical fantasy set in present-day
Heaven. While waiting for Henry II to finish his penance in Hell
so he can come up and join her, Eleanor visits with William, one of
her court officials, and with Henry's mother. Each person in turn
tells a tale about Eleanor's extraordinary life, a life that profoundly
affected the history of twelfth-century England and France.*

---

1. **Aquitaine** (AK·wi·tayn): a region in western France, once a separate kingdom.
2. **Plantagenet** (plan·TAJ·uh·nit): the ruling family of England from 1154 to 1485.

DURING HER LIFETIME Eleanor of Aquitaine had not been a patient woman. While she had lived, she had learned to bide her time,[3] but biding one's time is a very different thing from patience. After she had died, and before she had arrived in Heaven, it had been necessary for Eleanor to learn some patience. Heaven wouldn't allow her Up until she had. But there were times, like today, when she wasn't sure whether she had really learned any patience at all or whether she had simply become too tired to be quarrelsome.

Today she was restless. She paced back and forth so rapidly that the swish of her robes ruffled the tree-tops below. For today was the day when her husband, King Henry II of England, was to be judged. Today she would at last know whether or not — after centuries of waiting — he would join her in Heaven.

Henry had died even before she had. He had died in the year 1189, in July of that year, and Eleanor had spent fifteen years on Earth beyond that. But Eleanor's life had not been perfect; she had done some things on Earth for which there had been some Hell to pay, so she had not arrived in Heaven immediately. Finally, the world's poets had pleaded and won her case; with their pull, Eleanor had moved Up. Even so,

she had not arrived in Heaven until two centuries after she had died and long after her first husband and some of her best friends had made it. Now it was late in the twentieth century, and Henry still had not moved Up.

Eleanor began drumming her fingers on a nearby cloud.

"You keep that up, and you'll have the Angels to answer to for it," said a voice, one cloud removed.

"Oh, Mother Matilda, I swear you could nag a person to a second death."

A man sitting beside Mother Matilda pleaded, "Your mother-in-law is only reminding you that we have all been requested to stop drumming our fingers and to stop racing back and forth. The Angels don't appreciate having to answer hundreds of requests for better television reception."

"I know, William, I know," Eleanor answered.

"After all," Henry's mother Matilda-Empress added, "we are every bit as anxious as you are to know the outcome of today's Judgment."

"You ought to be patient, my lady," William said.

"Yes," Eleanor answered. "I know. I know what I ought to be. I have always known what I ought to be."

But the truth was that Eleanor actually enjoyed not being patient. When she felt impatient, she felt

---

3. **bide her time:** to wait for the right moment to do something.

something close to being alive again. Even after more than five hundred years in Heaven, Eleanor of Aquitaine still missed quarreling and dressing up. Eleanor missed strong, sweet smells. Eleanor missed feeling hot and being cold. Eleanor missed Henry. She missed life.

She sighed. She wanted to be there the minute Henry arrived — if he would; there was a great deal to tell him. It had taken Eleanor almost five hundred years to catch up on the two hundred she had missed.

She often thought that the worst thing about time spent in Hell is that a person has no way of knowing what is happening on Earth. In Heaven at least, one could watch, even if one could not participate.

Eleanor turned around looking toward the night side of Earth. Perhaps she could spot an outdoor movie screen. Watching that would help her pass some minutes.

"Eleanor," Matilda-Empress interrupted, "are you sure you still want Henry with you in Heaven?"

"After all," reminded William, the true and loyal knight, "it was a long time that Henry held you prisoner."

"It certainly was," Eleanor agreed. "Henry kept me locked up for fifteen years."

"And you still want him with you in Heaven?" repeated Matilda.

"Oh, goodness! yes. I think Heaven is much what he deserves. I want him to be every bit as bored as I am . . ." She laughed, looking quickly over at her two friends.

"We all miss living," she said. "Come now. Let us remember. Let us remember life, my life. Come, Mother Matilda, William, come. Let us remember together."

Matilda-Empress's Tale: The Early Years

Eleanor and I had no great love for each other. But Eleanor and I had respect for each other. Where love is not possible, respect will do. I admired Eleanor's efficiency and her willingness to learn. No longer was she the ambitious, spoiled young Queen of the Franks.[4] She was the wife of my handsome young son Henry; she was Queen of England. Now she was energetic, and her energies were well directed.

Discomfort, bad weather, even pregnancy did not stop her. Eleanor bore eight children within the fifteen years I knew her. And of those, only that first, little William, died while I still lived. Even as she embarked on that rough Channel crossing that would take her to England to become their queen, she was pregnant with their second child and second son; they named him Henry. Their next child they named for me: Matilda. Then followed Richard, whom everyone knows as Richard the Lion Heart. Geoffrey[5] came a year later, followed by Eleanor, Joanna and finally John. John was the last of their children and the last of an era.

An era. It was almost that. Eleanor and Henry squeezed a great deal of living into a single week, even into a single day. Since taxes were as often paid in merchandise as they were in money, Eleanor and Henry and the whole royal household often moved from one castle to another to use up their share of a manor's[6] profits. Barley, potatoes and cattle could not be mailed.

And take the question of loyalty. Henry believed that people need to see who they are working for, fighting for. He must not merely be a name. He must be a face. (Doesn't every corporation display pictures of its president, and doesn't every government office in the United States

---

4. **Franks:** the French.

5. Geoffrey (JEF·ree).
6. **manor:** in the Middle Ages, land worked by peasants but owned by a king or lord.

have a picture of the President?) In those days there were no pictures, so the king and queen came in person. They held court, and at these courts they collected homage and taxes, but they also allowed people to tell their grievances.

The matter of justice kept the king and queen most busy, kept them most on the road, and often kept them in separate parts of the kingdom. Everyone was at war with everyone else. Robbers haunted the forests of Sherwood, and the legend of Robin Hood[7] began. The law on one side of a road was different from the law on the other. The island was in chaos. It was my son's job to pull it all together and to be clever about it. Henry did, and Henry was.

There was an old law in England that allowed people to appeal to the king if they felt that justice had been denied them in the court of their lord. During the days of my worthless nephew, no one had dared appeal to the king, for Stephen was stupid and mean and would decide cases only as they suited him.

Henry knew that he could not force people to appeal their cases to the king's court. They had to want to, so he made his courts very attractive. A man would find fairer treatment in the king's court than at any

7. **Robin Hood**: a legendary twelfth-century English outlaw who robbed from the rich to give to the poor.

other. For one thing, Henry used a jury of witnesses. Trial by jury was better than trial by combat or trial by ordeal. What kind of a chance did a man have in a trial by ordeal? Throwing a bound man into a pond of water and claiming him guilty if he floated seemed to me more a matter of a man's habits of eating than his habits with the law.

Everyone began to appeal to the king's court, and Henry had clerks record what happened. When people came with a complaint similar to an earlier one, Henry would check the records and see how the matter had been settled before. In that way everyone received the same treatment under the law, a law common to everyone, the English Common Law.

Back in Heaven

"We seem to have strayed from the subject of Queen Eleanor," said William the Marshal.[8]

Eleanor laughed. "Leave it to a noble knight not to forget his purpose."

"Well, I'm glad you're here to bring us back to Eleanor," Matilda-Empress said.

William the Marshal replied, "I would be most happy to continue the story of Queen Eleanor. That is, if she does not mind."

Eleanor waved her arm and said, "Tell anything you want to."

"I want, my lady, to tell only the truth."

"Ah, yes! The true and noble knight will tell only the true and noble truth. Come, sit, William. Sit and spin your tale."

"You might say, my lady, that I shall weave my tale but not embroider it."[9]

"William!" Eleanor exclaimed, "to find wit in you is to make me believe that in Heaven all things are truly possible."

William the Marshal's Tale: The Middle Years

During these years, more than laws and courts concerned Henry and Eleanor. After years of marriage, they had begun to have their differences, serious differences. Thus, the queen went to France.

Queen Eleanor went South for two reasons. One reason was that King Henry wanted her to. He had recently quieted some rebellions in the Aquitaine, but the peace there was touchy. He hoped that by sending his wife there, the people would stay quiet. The people of the South, he thought, would respond better to one of their own kind. That was the king's reason.

The other reason for Queen Eleanor's going South was that she

---

8. **Marshal:** a high officer in a royal household or court.

9. **embroider it:** add anything untrue to it.

wanted to, and for the first time in fifteen years her reason was not the same as her husband's. Queen Eleanor's reason for leaving England was Rosamond, Rosamond Clifford.

Rosamond Clifford was the girl King Henry had met and fallen in love with while he was fighting in Wales. The queen did not choose to stay in a country where she was number two. She knew what she would do. She would return to France, to her native Aquitaine, and there she would set up court, and there she would rear her sons to manhood. And to rebellion.

I had just been made a knight when I was sent by King Henry to accompany Queen Eleanor to Poitiers.[10] The lords of the Aquitaine were waiting for a chance for revenge. Just outside of Poitiers, they ambushed us. It was my first chance to prove myself as a knight. My horse was killed from under me, but I put my back against a hedge and warded off all who came until I knew that my queen was safely inside the castle.

I was wounded, and I was captured, but my bravery did not go unnoticed. Queen Eleanor herself paid my ransom. I went to the castle to thank her for her generosity, and she rewarded me further. She gave

me a horse, arms and clothing. She also gave me my first job; I was made knight-at-arms[11] to the royal children.

Queen Eleanor was a generous ruler and hostess. Her court at Poitiers was open to everyone, and everyone came. Poets and troubadours[12] came; cousins came, dozens of cousins from the Aquitaine who were happy to have a headquarters again. Second sons[13] of famous dukes and barons came; they had no money and no skills. Besides these cousins and second sons, there were the queen's own children, seven in all, plus the girls her sons were to marry. The castle at Poitiers was nursery, home, school and seat of government. Children and adolescents were aswarming. All of these young people had two things in common: too much time and not enough responsibility.

Some of these young people, especially Eleanor's son Young Henry, resented this lack of responsibility; they felt they had better things to do than play. Eleanor's sons desperately wanted their own lands and their own power. Hard feelings arose between Young Henry and his brother John, who was King Henry's favorite.

---

10. **Poitiers** (pwah·TYAY): a city in Aquitaine.

11. **knight-at-arms**: a guardian.
12. **troubadours** (TROO·buh·DOHRZ): singer-poets.
13. **second sons**: Eldest sons inherited their fathers' title, lands, and wealth. Other sons had to live off of their oldest brothers or become soldiers or clergymen.

Young Henry and Richard were jealous of each other. Moreover, all of King Henry's princes resented their father's power.

By the time the Plantagenets held Christmas court in 1172, Queen Eleanor had had six years to train her sons in chivalry and rebellion. After all the official holiday ceremonies were over, the family found itself together, and King Henry produced a map and pointed out a place here, another there, and a stretch of land as well. He said, "I have promised these castles as well as a few estates to a very rich count who happens to have something I want."

"A few estates!" Young Henry shouted. "Those lands are mine. Why must you always clip my feathers?"

"Ah, my boy, what are a few pinfeathers to a bird of such fine plumage?"

"Yes, Father," Richard interrupted, "we all have fine plumage. Bright plumage, but it is purely ornamental. When will you let us fly?"

"Never," Queen Eleanor answered. "Your father expects you to stay in the nest forever, my sons." Then she looked at her husband and said, "Those are not your castles or your estates to give, my husband. Young Henry has been crowned and recognized by the people of England as their king, and Richard, Geoffrey and Henry have paid homage for their territories in France."

King Henry turned on her. "I built the nest. Those castles and estates are mine. I have fought to keep this land together." Henry came over to Eleanor and spoke directly to her. "Don't you see, Eleanor? We can extend our lands all the way to Italy. What has Young Henry done to keep these lands? He does nothing but play at tournaments and at elaborate games of love in your court at Poitiers."

Young Henry was furious. "When have you ever let me do anything that would show you that I can rule? Mother has let Richard rule the Aquitaine with her. They truly share the work. He mashes rebellion with a hammer, and she follows in his wake and passes out bandages. Mother has convinced the people of the Aquitaine that her father, their beloved Duke William, has come to life again in the person of your son, Richard. The Aquitaine is better off without you, Father. Are you afraid that the people of Normandy, Anjou and England will find me a better overlord than you? Is that why you won't let me do anything more than show my face once here and once there and then only to collect your taxes? Is that why you have to chop up my inheritance?"

Queen Eleanor spoke again. She was calm, controlled. "That is only part of the reason, children. Your father will not let you rule because he considers himself the grandest puppeteer in Europe. He believes that

for a great performance, he needs only a few puppets and one very large stage — say from Scotland to the Pyrenees[14] and a little bit east-ward — say to Italy. That will do for the present. What your father does not realize, children, is that some-one, not him, but someone, has put some guts into his puppets. Guts bleed, my husband. Look well. You have just drawn the first blood."

Then Queen Eleanor left the room. Her sons followed. The queen had at last what she had wanted: two sons unwilling to give up the taste of power they had and another one fighting mad to get it.

War followed. Father against son. Father won. King Henry finished his battles with his sons and headed for Poitiers. He knew now that his queen had cost him a war and his son's loyalty. He was hell-bent for a show down. Queen Eleanor was not in Poitiers when he arrived. His fury grew. "Eleanor! Eleanor!" he shouted in the empty halls. Where was that woman?

---

14. **Pyrenees** (PIR•uh•NEEZ): a mountain range be-tween France and Spain.

The truth was that Queen Eleanor was dressed as a knight and was riding toward the borders of France. Some of the king's men were on a routine mission when they chanced upon a small band of knights close to the borders of the land of King Louis.[15] They asked the knights the nature of their business. "Our business is none of yours," answered one of the knights.

"Whatever happens within these borders is our business. We are the

men of King Henry, and this land is his."

"You are wrong. This land belongs to his wife," answered the same knight.

One of the guards said to another, "Only a very young knight or an old lady could have so brazen a tongue and so high a voice." Saying that, he pulled the cap from the head of the saucy knight and found that the head with the quick tongue belonged to a lady. More than a lady. It belonged to a queen. Eleanor.

_____
15. **King Louis:** Louis VII, Eleanor's first husband.

She was taken to the king. The king looked at his wife and asked, "Was it you, Eleanor? Was it you who inspired the rebellion of my sons?"

"Yes, Henry, it was."

The king nodded his head. "I thought as much. Were you going to Louis in France when you were captured?"

"Yes, Henry, I was."

"You are without shame."

"I am not. A woman without shame has no pride, and I have plenty of that. Pride drove me out of England. Louis is still my overlord. I always say, Henry, that politics makes nicer bedfellows than marriage. Speaking of marriage, Henry, why don't you divorce me? You have excellent grounds. There are no better grounds than treason."

"No, madam," King Henry answered. "I shall not divorce you and set you free to marry someone else and then sue me for the return of the Aquitaine. There are other remedies for treason, my queen."

"Prison! Are you going to put me in jail, Henry?"

"Call it *house arrest,* madam," King Henry looked at his wife and saw her smile. "Why do you smile, madam? Don't you fear being my prisoner?"

"Fear is not something I am familiar with, Henry. *Loathing*[16] is. I know that I shall loathe prison more than I shall fear it."

"Why then, do you smile?"

"Because, Henry, I know that I shall love that loathing, and that spark of love will keep me well."

❦

The queen was taken to England. Henry wanted her far away from him and his sons while he negotiated peace with them. The Channel was high, and the wind was strong when they set sail. Just twenty years before they had made a similar stormy crossing, but that crossing had marked a union and a beginning. This crossing marked a separation and an end. King Henry again stood up in the boat, and again thrust his fist at the storm. "Hear me, Lord?" he shouted, "see us safely through to the other side of the Channel. Let my will be done upon this woman before Thy will be done."

"Amen," the queen said.

King Henry looked at his wife and roared, "Why are you smiling now, madam?"

"You and my father are the only men I have ever known who grab God by the throat instead of whispering into His good ear," she answered.

"One must get His attention, first, madam," Henry said, smiling.

And there, for that moment, the sound of their shared laughter broke through the noise of the storm and the sea.

---

16. loathing (LOH·thing): strong dislike and disgust.

Queen Eleanor was taken to Salisbury. She was allowed to ride in the country, but she was always under guard. She sometimes moved from one castle to another after she had received permission to do so. That, too, was done under guard. She was deprived of the company of her children, and she was deprived of being at the center of affairs. She was deprived of learning of events firsthand and of being the cause of those events.

Not far from Salisbury was the circle of giant stones, called *Stonehenge*.[17] Queen Eleanor loved to ride there and watch the light peek through the openings of the arches made by the stones. The tallest stones were set in an odd pattern of arches, the space between them was too narrow for a horse and rider to pass through.

One day shortly after I had been promoted to marshal, I came to deliver a message. Upon arriving at Salisbury Tower, I was told that the queen had gone to Stonehenge. I rode there to meet her, and I found her sitting astride her horse beside one of the large stones outside the circle.

"My queen seems lost in thought," I said.

"Lost in time," she answered.

"Now that the present is denied me, I wonder about the past. I wonder how these stones got here. I ride here often and wonder. Surely these giants are not native to this flat pancake of land."

"It is said, my lady, that Merlin brought these stones from Ireland."

"Merlin who? And who says?"

"Merlin the magician, the teacher of King Arthur. And Geoffrey Monmouth says. Geoffrey of Monmouth wrote a book called the *Histories of the Kings of Britain;* it tells the story of Merlin and King Arthur."

---

17. *Stonehenge:* probably an ancient place of worship; there are many theories as to how these tremendous prehistoric stones were raised.

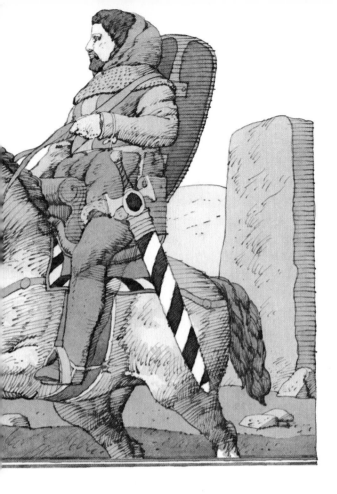

"I want a copy of that book," the queen said.

I promised the queen that she would have a copy of the book before my next visit, and I kept my promise true.

Queen Eleanor did with those histories as she did with everything — she transformed them. She found them interesting, but plain. She thought they could be improved. Especially the history of King Arthur. She called for her poets and her troubadours; she asked each of them to read the stories and to rewrite them. She asked her writers to dress them up. She suggested that King Arthur's knights be more noble, that the ladies of the court be more fair, that the manners of the whole court be more courtly, like Poitiers.

The work of her poets became popular; people from France to Constantinople[18] began to read and to write of Merlin and of the knights of Arthur's court. Galahad, Lancelot, and the traitorous Mordred were lifted from the plain pages of a history book and wrapped around with magic and adventure and romance. And that is how people read of them today. All elegantly clothed in honor and seated at a Round Table[19] in Camelot.

Had I not brought Queen Eleanor that book, King Arthur would have stayed dust bound between Geoffrey of Monmouth's pages, and the people of England would never have had the proud sense of history they have today.

Back in Heaven

Eleanor smiled at William the Marshal and at Matilda-Empress. "I was sixty-seven when I was let out of prison. I believe that my real life began then. I had used that time. I

---

18. Constantinople: a city, now Istanbul, Turkey.
19. Round Table in Camelot: meeting place for Arthur's knights, in his legendary castle in Camelot.

had lost two husbands and two sons before I was released. Yet for all those losses, I felt that I had gained something while I was there."

"What could you have gained in prison?"

"Understanding," Eleanor answered. "Understanding freedom for one thing. It looks even brighter when viewed from its dark side. As a matter of fact, when I arrived Up, and I was asked what age I wanted to be, I answered *sixty-seven* without a moment's hesitation. And I answered, knowing that I would be sixty-seven for all Eternity. I could have chosen twenty-five when I was fresh and comely,[20] and I could have chosen thirty when I was madly in love with Henry, but I chose sixty-seven. For I wanted all those years, even the years in prison, with me in Heaven."

Matilda-Empress said, "One thing you never learned in prison was to slow down your tongue."

Eleanor laughed. "Being in prison is like looking at life inside out. You learn to know its fabric and its seams. After I was released from prison, I learned what it means to be a queen."

"I never knew you to have any doubts about that," Matilda-Empress said.

"Then say that I learned not *to know* but *to understand*."

---

20. **comely** (KUM·lee): pretty.

1. What is the setting of this story?

2. At the beginning of the story, Eleanor is impatiently waiting for something important to happen. What event is about to take place?

3. King Henry and Queen Eleanor wanted everyone to receive the same treatment under the law. How did they improve the trial system?

4. What clue is there in the story that Eleanor and Henry would eventually forgive one another?

5. William the Marshal and Matilda-Empress tell Eleanor's story. If you could choose two people to tell *your* story, which two people would you choose? Why?

■ **Understanding Literature**

"Eleanor of Aquitaine" is an unusual combination of historical fiction, biography, and fantasy. The story accurately portrays the major events in Eleanor's life and also presents a picture of the power and influence the queen wielded.

Queen Eleanor was responsible for a type of literature that had an effect on how men and women saw themselves. At the court in Poitiers, Eleanor and her daughter Marie called together their poets and asked them to rewrite old legends about heroes and battles and to write new songs and poems praising women and emphasizing love. Then they organized an elaborate game called "The Courts of Love." Out of this game grew rules and practices, some of which are still in evidence today.

Such practices, especially the knight's quest for some ideal or treasure to prove himself worthy of a lady's love, were incorporated into a type of literature called *romance.* The word *romance* originally meant anything written in any language other than Latin, which was the language of scholarly and religious works. As wealthy people began to have more leisure time, they wanted to read and hear stories they could enjoy. Thus stories were made up in the commonly spoken language. The quest and courtly love were recurrent themes in these romances. Eleanor's "discovery" of the King Arthur stories, as explained by William the Marshal in "Eleanor of Aquitaine," provided another popular subject for the romances.

■ **Writing About the Story**

Suppose that you could look up at the sky and see a historical figure sitting on a cloud. What historical figure would you choose to see? Write a brief dialogue between the historical figure and yourself. In the dialogue, ask at least two questions that you would like to have this person answer. Make up the answers, too.

The Book of Songs: VIII

A poem translated from the Chinese by Helen Waddell

This Chinese poem, written in 675 B.C., points out the danger of a rigid government and society where everyone is kept in his or her place and new ideas are ignored. Written in a time so long ago that it seems like another world, this poem still speaks to the men and women of today.

I would have gone to my lord in his need,
    Have galloped there all the way,
But this is a matter concerns the State,
    And I, being a woman, must stay.

I watched them leaving the palace yard,
    In carriage and robe of state.
I would have gone by the hills and the fords;
    I know they will come too late.

I may walk in the garden and gather
    Lilies of mother-of-pearl.
I had a plan would have saved the State.
    — But mine are the thoughts of a girl.

The Elder Statesmen sit on the mats,
    And wrangle through half the day;
A hundred plans they have drafted and dropped,
    And mine was the only way.

Illustration by Christa Kieffer

THE LOOSING OF THE SHADOW

From the novel *A Wizard of Earthsea* by Ursula K. LeGuin
Illustrated by Allen Atkinson

The island of Gont, in the stormy Northeast Sea, is a land famous for its mages, wizards who work their magic from isle to isle throughout Earthsea. Some say the greatest mage ever born there was the man called Sparrowhawk, whose true name was Ged.

Ged was mageborn — he had the power to work magic before he had the knowledge to use that power properly. As a teenager, Ged was a brilliant, eager student at the school of magic on Roke Island. "Especially the tricks of illusion came to him so easily that it seemed he had been born knowing them and needed only to be reminded." Ged's only shortcomings were his temper and his pride, which led him into a fierce rivalry with an older apprentice, Jasper. His teachers realized that Ged's abilities outstripped his wisdom, and one Master warned him not to change anything, even a pebble or a grain of sand, until he knew for certain what good and evil would result from the act. "The world is in balance, in Equilibrium. A wizard's power of Changing and of Summoning can shake the balance of the world. It is dangerous, that power. It is most perilous. It must follow knowledge, and serve need. To light a candle is to cast a shadow. . . ."

WHEN THE LONG DANCE was over most people slept the day away, and gathered again at evening to eat and drink. There was a group of young fellows, prentices[1] and sorcerers who had brought their supper out from the refectory to hold private feast in a courtyard of the Great House: Vetch, Jasper, and Ged were there, and six or seven others, and some young lads released briefly from the Isolate Tower. They were all eating and laughing and playing such tricks out of pure frolic as might be the marvel of a king's court. One boy had lighted the court with a hundred stars of werelight,[2] colored like jewels, that swung in a slow netted procession between them and the real stars; and a pair of boys were playing bowls with balls of green flame and bowling-pins that leaped and hopped away as the ball came near; and all the while Vetch sat cross-legged, eating roast chicken, up in midair. One of the younger boys tried to pull him down to earth, but Vetch merely drifted up a little higher, out of reach, and sat calmly smiling on the air. Now and then he tossed away a chicken bone, which turned to an owl and flew hooting among the netted star-lights. Ged shot breadcrumb arrows after the owls and brought them down, and

when they touched the ground there they lay, bone and crumb, all illusion gone. Ged also tried to join Vetch up in the middle of the air, but lacking the key of the spell he had to flap his arms to keep aloft, and they were all laughing at his flights and flaps and bumps. He kept up his foolishness for the laughter's sake, laughing with them, for after those two long nights of dance and moonlight and music and magery[3] he was in a fey[4] and wild mood, ready for whatever might come.

He came lightly down on his feet just beside Jasper at last, and Jasper, who never laughed aloud, moved away saying, "The Sparrowhawk that can't fly . . ."

"Is jasper[5] a precious stone?" Ged returned, grinning. "O Jewel among sorcerers, O Gem of Havnor, sparkle for us!"

The lad that had set the lights dancing sent one down to dance and glitter about Jasper's head. Not quite as cool as usual, frowning, Jasper brushed the light away and snuffed it out with one gesture. "I am sick of boys and noise and foolishness," he said.

"You're getting middle-aged, lad," Vetch remarked from above.

"If silence and gloom is what you want," put in one of the younger

---

1. prentices: apprentice magicians.
2. werelight (WAYR•lyt): artificial light (literally, *man-light*).

3. magery (MAYJ•uh•ree): magic.
4. fey (FAY): enchanted; giddy.
5. jasper: a variety of quartz.

boys, "you could always try the Tower."

Ged said to him, "What is it you want, then, Jasper?"

"I want the company of my equals," Jasper said. "Come on, Vetch. Leave the prentices to their toys."

Ged turned to face Jasper. "What do sorcerers have that prentices lack?" he inquired. His voice was quiet but all the other boys suddenly fell still, for in his tone as in Jasper's the spite between them now sounded plain and clear as steel coming out of a sheath.

"Power," Jasper said.

"I'll match your power act for act."

"You challenge me?"

"I challenge you."

Vetch had dropped down to the ground, and now he came between them, grim of face. "Duels in sorcery are forbidden to us, and well you know it. Let this cease!"

Both Ged and Jasper stood silent, for it was true they knew the law of Roke, and they also knew that Vetch was moved by love, and themselves by hate. Yet their anger was balked, not cooled. Presently, moving a little aside as if to be heard by Vetch alone, Jasper spoke, with his cool smile: "I think you'd better remind your goatherd friend again of the law that protects him. He looks sulky. I wonder, did he really think I'd accept a challenge from him? a fellow who smells of goats, a prentice who doesn't know the First Change?"[6]

"Jasper," said Ged, "What do you know of what I know?"

For an instant, with no word spoken that any heard, Ged vanished from their sight, and where he had stood a great falcon hovered, opening its hooked beak to scream: for one instant, and then Ged stood again in the flickering torchlight, his dark gaze on Jasper.

Jasper had taken a step backward, in astonishment; but now he shrugged and said one word: "Illusion."

The others muttered. Vetch said, "That was not illusion. It was true change. And enough. Jasper, listen —"

"Enough to prove that he sneaked a look in the Book of Shaping behind the Master's back: what then?

Go on, Goatherd. I like this trap you're building for yourself. The more you try to prove yourself my equal, the more you show yourself for what you are."

At that, Vetch turned from Jasper, and said very softly to Ged, "Sparrowhawk, will you be a man and drop this now — come with me —"

Ged looked at his friend and smiled, but all he said was, "Keep Hoeg for me a little while, will you?" He put into Vetch's hands the little otak, which as usual had been riding on his shoulder. It had never let any but Ged touch it, but it came to Vetch now, and climbing up his arm cowered on his shoulder, its great bright eyes always on its master.

"Now," Ged said to Jasper, quietly as before, "what are you going to do to prove yourself my superior, Jasper?"

"I don't have to do anything, Goatherd. Yet I will. I will give you a chance — an opportunity. Envy eats you like a worm in an apple. Let's let out the worm. Once by Roke Knoll you boasted that Gontish wizards don't play games. Come to Roke Knoll now and show us what it is they do instead. And afterward, maybe I will show you a little sorcery."

"Yes, I should like to see that," Ged answered. The younger boys, used to seeing his black temper break out at the least hint of slight or insult, watched him in wonder at his

---

6. the First Change: a spell for changing one thing into another.

446

coolness now. Vetch watched him not in wonder, but with growing fear. He tried to intervene again, but Jasper said, "Come, keep out of this, Vetch. What will you do with the chance I give you, Goatherd? Will you show us an illusion, a fireball, a charm to cure goats with the mange?"

"What would you like me to do, Jasper?"

The older lad shrugged, "Summon up a spirit from the dead for all I care!"

"I will."

"You will not." Jasper looked straight at him, rage suddenly flaming out over his disdain. "You will not. You cannot. You brag and brag —"

"By my name, I will do it!"

They all stood utterly motionless for a moment.

Breaking away from Vetch who would have held him back by main force, Ged strode out of the courtyard, not looking back. The dancing werelights overhead died out, sinking down. Jasper hesitated a second, then followed after Ged. And the rest came straggling behind, in silence, curious and afraid.

The slopes of Roke Knoll went up dark into the darkness of summer night before moonrise. The presence of that hill where many wonders had been worked was heavy, like a weight in the air about them. As they came onto the hillside they thought of how the roots of it were deep, deeper than the sea, reaching down even to the old, blind, secret fires at the world's core. They stopped on the east slope. Stars hung over the black grass above them on the hill's crest. No wind blew.

Ged went a few paces up the slope away from the others and turning said in a clear voice, "Jasper! Whose spirit shall I call?"

"Call whom you like. None will listen to you." Jasper's voice shook a little, with anger perhaps. Ged answered him softly, mockingly, "Are you afraid?"

He did not even listen for Jasper's reply, if he made one. He no longer cared about Jasper. Now that they stood on Roke Knoll, hate and rage were gone, replaced by utter certainty. He need envy no one. He knew that his power, this night, on this dark enchanted ground, was greater than it had ever been, filling him till he trembled with the sense of strength barely kept in check. He knew now that Jasper was far beneath him, had been sent perhaps only to bring him here tonight, no rival but a mere servant of Ged's destiny. Under his feet he felt the hillroots going down and down into the dark, and over his head he saw the dry, far fires of the stars. Between, all things were his to order, to command. He stood at the center of the world.

"Don't be afraid," he said, smiling.

"I'll call a woman's spirit. You need not fear a woman. Elfarran I will call, the fair lady of the *Deed of Enlad*."

"She died a thousand years ago, her bones lie afar under the Sea of Ea, and maybe there never was such a woman."

"Do years and distances matter to the dead? Do the Songs lie?" Ged said with the same gentle mockery, and then saying, "Watch the air between my hands," he turned away from the others and stood still.

In a great slow gesture he stretched out his arms, the gesture of welcome that opens an invocation.[7] He began to speak.

He had read the runes[8] of this Spell of Summoning in Ogion's book, two years and more ago, and never since had seen them. In darkness he had read them then. Now in this darkness it was as if he read them again on the page open before him in the night. But now he understood what he read, speaking it aloud word after word, and he saw the markings of how the spell must be woven with the sound of the voice and the motion of body and hand.

The other boys stood watching, not speaking, not moving unless they shivered a little: for the great spell was beginning to work. Ged's voice was soft still, but changed, with a deep singing in it, and the words he spoke were not known to them. He fell silent. Suddenly the wind rose roaring in the grass. Ged dropped to his knees and called out aloud. Then he fell forward as if to embrace earth with his outstretched arms, and when he rose he held something dark in his straining hands and arms, something so heavy that he shook with effort getting to his feet. The hot wind whined in the black tossing grasses on the hill. If the stars shone now none saw them.

The words of the enchantment hissed and mumbled on Ged's lips, and then he cried out aloud and clearly, "Elfarran!"

Again he cried the name, "Elfarran!"

The shapeless mass of darkness he had lifted split apart. It sundered,[9] and a pale spindle of light gleamed between his opened arms, a faint oval reaching from the ground up to the height of his raised hands. In the oval of light for a moment there moved a form, a human shape: a tall woman looking back over her shoulder. Her face was beautiful, and sorrowful, and full of fear.

Only for a moment did the spirit glimmer there. Then the sallow oval between Ged's arms grew bright. It widened and spread, a

---

7. **invocation:** here, the act of calling upon a spirit or deity for help or inspiration; a summoning of a demon or evil spirit.
8. **runes:** ancient letters used for secret writing or magical spells.

---

9. **sundered:** divided.

rent in the darkness of the earth and night, a ripping open of the fabric of the world. Through it blazed a terrible brightness. And through that bright misshapen breach clambered something like a clot of black shadow, quick and hideous, and it leaped straight out at Ged's face.

Staggering back under the weight of the thing, Ged gave a short, hoarse scream. The little otak watching from Vetch's shoulder, the animal that had no voice, screamed aloud also and leaped as if to attack.

Ged fell, struggling and writhing, while the bright rip in the world's darkness above him widened and stretched. The boys that watched fled, and Jasper bent down to the ground hiding his eyes from the terrible light. Vetch alone ran forward to his friend. So only he saw the lump of shadow that clung to Ged, tearing at his flesh. It was like a black

449

beast, the size of a young child, though it seemed to swell and shrink: and it had no head or face, only the four taloned paws with which it gripped and tore. Vetch sobbed with horror, yet he put out his hands to try to pull the thing away from Ged. Before he touched it, he was bound still, unable to move.

The intolerable brightness faded, and slowly the torn edges of the world closed together. Nearby a voice was speaking as softly as a tree whispers or a fountain plays.

Starlight began to shine again, and the grasses of the hillside were whitened with the light of the moon just rising. The night was healed. Restored and steady lay the balance of light and dark. The shadow-beast was gone. Ged lay sprawled on his back, his arms flung out as if they yet kept the wide gesture of welcome and invocation. His face was blackened with blood and there were great black stains on his shirt. The little otak cowered by his shoulder, quivering. And above him stood an old man whose cloak glimmered pale in the moonrise: the Archmage[10] Nemmerle.

The end of Nemmerle's staff hovered silvery above Ged's breast. Once gently it touched him over the heart, once on the lips, while Nemmerle whispered. Ged stirred, and his lips parted gasping for breath.

---

10. **Archmage:** the chief magician.

Then the old Archmage lifted the staff, and set it to earth, and leaned heavily on it with bowed head, as if he had scarcely strength to stand.

Vetch found himself free to move. Looking around, he saw that already others were there, the Masters Summoner and Changer. An act of great wizardry is not worked without arousing such men, and they had ways of coming very swiftly when need called, though none had been so swift as the Archmage. They now sent for help, and some who came

went with the Archmage, while others, Vetch among them, carried Ged to the chambers of the Master Herbal.

All night long the Summoner stayed on Roke Knoll, keeping watch. Nothing stirred there on the hillside where the stuff of the world had been torn open. No shadow came crawling through moonlight seeking the rent through which it might clamber back into its own domain. It had fled from Nemmerle, and from the mighty spell-walls that surround and protect Roke Island, but it was in the world now. In the world, somewhere, it hid. If Ged had died that night it might have tried to find the doorway he had opened, and follow him into death's realm, or slip back into whatever place it had come from; for this the Summoner waited on Roke Knoll. But Ged lived.

They had laid him abed in the healing-chamber, and the Master Herbal tended the wounds he had on his face and throat and shoulder. They were deep, ragged, and evil wounds. The black blood in them would not stanch, welling out even under the charms and the cobweb-wrapped perriot leaves laid upon them. Ged lay blind and dumb in fever like a stick in a slow fire, and there was no spell to cool what burned him.

Not far away, in the unroofed court where the fountain played, the Archmage lay also unmoving, but cold, very cold: only his eyes lived, watching the fall of moonlit water and the stir of moonlit leaves. Those with him said no spells and worked no healing. Quietly they spoke among themselves from time to time, and then turned again to watch their Lord. He lay still, hawk nose and high forehead and white hair bleached by moonlight all to the color of bone. To check the ungoverned spell and drive off the shadow from Ged, Nemmerle had

451

spent all his power, and with it his bodily strength was gone. He lay dying. But the death of a great mage, who has many times in his life walked on the dry steep hillsides of death's kingdom, is a strange matter: for the dying man goes not blindly, but surely, knowing the way. When Nemmerle looked up through the leaves of the tree, those with him did not know if he watched the stars of summer fading in daybreak, or those other stars, which never set above the hills that see no dawn.

The raven of Osskil that had been his pet for thirty years was gone. No one had seen where it went. "It flies before him," the Master Patterner said, as they kept vigil.

The day came warm and clear. The Great House and the streets of Thwil were hushed. No voice was raised, until along towards noon iron bells spoke out aloud in the Chanter's Tower, harshly tolling.

On the next day the Nine Masters of Roke gathered in a place somewhere under the dark trees of the Immanent Grove. Even there they set nine walls of silence about them, that no person or power might speak to them or hear them as they chose from amongst the mages of all Earthsea him who would be the new Archmage. Gensher of Way was chosen. A ship was sent forth at once across the Inmost Sea to Way Island to bring the Archmage back to Roke. The Master Windkey stood in the stern and raised up the mage-wind into the sail, and quickly the ship departed, and was gone.

Of these events Ged knew nothing. For four weeks of that hot summer he lay blind, and deaf, and mute, though at times he moaned and cried out like an animal. At last, as the patient crafts of the Master Herbal worked their healing, his wounds began to close and the fever left him. Little by little he seemed to hear again, though he never spoke. On a clear day of autumn the Master Herbal opened the shutters of the room where Ged lay. Since the darkness of that night on Roke Knoll he had known only darkness. Now he saw daylight, and the sun shining. He hid his scarred face in his hands and wept.

Still when winter came he could speak only with a stammering tongue, and the Master Herbal kept him there in the healing-chambers, trying to lead his body and mind gradually back to strength. It was early spring when at last the Master released him, sending him first to offer his fealty[11] to the Archmage Gensher. For he had not been able to join all the others of the School in this duty when Gensher came to Roke.

None of his companions had been allowed to visit him in the months of his sickness, and now as he passed

---

11. **fealty:** loyalty; allegiance; devoted service.

some of them asked one another, "Who is that?" He had been light and lithe and strong. Now, lamed by pain, he went hesitantly, and did not raise his face, the left side of which was white with scars. He avoided those who knew him and those who did not, and made his way straight to the court of the Fountain. There where once he had awaited Nemmerle, Gensher awaited him.

Like the old Archmage the new one was cloaked in white; but like most men of Way and the East Reach Gensher was black-skinned, and his look was black, under thick brows.

Ged knelt and offered him fealty and obedience. Gensher was silent a while.

"I know what you did," he said at last, "but not what you are. I cannot accept your fealty."

Ged stood up, and set his hand on the trunk of the young tree beside the fountain to steady himself. He was still very slow to find words. "Am I to leave Roke, my lord?"

"Do you want to leave Roke?"

"No."

"What do you want?"

"To stay. To learn. To undo . . . the evil. . . ."

"Nemmerle himself could not do that. — No, I would not let you go from Roke. Nothing protects you but the power of the Masters here and the defenses laid upon this island that keep the creatures of evil away. If you left now, the thing you loosed

453

would find you at once, and enter into you, and possess you. You would be no man but a *gebbeth*, a puppet doing the will of that evil shadow which you raised up into the sunlight. You must stay here, until you gain strength and wisdom enough to defend yourself from it — if ever you do. Even now it waits for you. Assuredly it waits for you. Have you seen it since that night?"

"In dreams, lord." After a while Ged went on, speaking with pain and shame, "Lord Gensher, I do not know what it was — the thing that came out of the spell and cleaved[12] to me — "

———

12. **cleaved:** held on.

"Nor do I know. It has no name. You have great power inborn in you, and you used that power wrongly, to work a spell over which you had no control, not knowing how that spell affects the balance of light and dark, life and death, good and evil. And you were moved to do this by pride and by hate. Is it any wonder the result was ruin? You summoned a spirit from the dead, but with it came one of the Powers of unlife. Uncalled it came from a place where there are no names. Evil, it wills to work evil through you. The power you had to call it gives it power over you: you are connected. It is the shadow of your arrogance, the shadow of your ignorance, the shadow you cast. Has a shadow a name?"

Ged stood sick and haggard. He said at last, "Better I had died."

"Who are you to judge that, you for whom Nemmerle gave his life? — You are safe here. You will live here, and go on with your training. They tell me you were clever. Go on and do your work. Do it well. It is all you can do."

So Gensher ended, and was suddenly gone, as is the way of mages. The fountain leaped in the sunlight, and Ged watched it a while and listened to its voice, thinking of Nemmerle. Once in that court he had felt himself to be a word spoken by the sunlight. Now the darkness also had spoken: a word that could not be unsaid.

He left the court, going to his old room in the South Tower, which they had kept empty for him. He stayed there alone. When the gong called to supper he went, but he would hardly speak to the other lads at the Long Table, or raise his face to them, even those who greeted him most gently. So after a day or two they all left him alone. To be alone was his desire, for he feared the evil he might do or say unwittingly.

Neither Vetch nor Jasper was there, and he did not ask about them. The boys he had led and lorded over were all ahead of him now, because of the months he had lost, and that spring and summer he studied with lads younger than himself. Nor did he shine among them, for the words of any spell, even the simplest illusion-charm, came halting from his tongue, and his hands faltered at their craft.

In autumn he was to go once again to the Isolate Tower to study with the Master Namer. This task which he had once dreaded now pleased him, for silence was what he sought, and long learning where no spells were wrought, and where that power which he knew was still in him would never be called upon to act.

The night before he left for the Tower a visitor came to his room, one wearing a brown travelling-cloak and carrying a staff of oak shod with iron. Ged stood up, at sight of the wizard's staff.

"Sparrowhawk — "

At the sound of the voice, Ged raised his eyes: it was Vetch standing there, solid and foursquare[13] as ever, his black blunt face older but his smile unchanged. On his shoulder crouched a little beast, brindle-furred and bright-eyed.

"He stayed with me while you were sick, and now I'm sorry to part with him. And sorrier to part with you, Sparrowhawk. But I'm going home. Here, hoeg! go to your true master!" Vetch patted the otak and set it down on the floor. It went and

---

13. **foursquare**: steady; firm.

sat on Ged's pallet, and began to wash its fur with a dry brown tongue like a little leaf. Vetch laughed, but Ged could not smile. He bent down to hide his face, stroking the otak.

"I thought you wouldn't come to me, Vetch," he said.

He did not mean any reproach, but Vetch answered, "I couldn't come to you. The Master Herbal forbade me; and since winter I've been with the Master in the Grove, locked up myself. I was not free, until I earned my staff. Listen: when you too are free, come to the East Reach. I will be waiting for you. There's good cheer in the little towns there, and wizards are well received."

"Free . . ." Ged muttered, and shrugged a little, trying to smile.

Vetch looked at him, not quite as he had used to look, with no less love but more wizardry, perhaps. He said gently, "You won't stay bound on Roke forever."

"Well . . . I have thought, perhaps I may come to work with the Master in the Tower, to be one of those who seek among the books and the stars for lost names, and so . . . so do no more harm, if not much good. . . ."

"Maybe," said Vetch. "I am no

456

seer, but I see before you, not rooms and books, but far seas, and the fire of dragons, and the towers of cities, and all such things a hawk sees when he flies far and high."

"And behind me — what do you see behind me?" Ged asked, and stood up as he spoke, so that the werelight that burned overhead between them sent his shadow back against the wall and floor. Then he turned his face aside and said, stammering, "But tell me where you will go, what you will do."

"I will go home, to see my brothers and the sister you have heard me speak of. I left her a little child and soon she'll be having her Naming — it's strange to think of! And so I'll find me a job of wizardry somewhere among the little isles. Oh, I would stay and talk with you, but I can't, my ship goes out tonight and the tide is turned already. Sparrowhawk, if ever your way lies East, come to me. And if ever you need me, send for me, call on me by my name: Estarriol."

At that Ged lifted his scarred face, meeting his friend's eyes.

"Estarriol," he said, "my name is Ged."

Then quietly they bade each other farewell, and Vetch turned and went down the stone hallway, and left Roke.

Ged stood still a while, like one who has received great news, and must enlarge his spirit to receive it.

It was a great gift that Vetch had given him, the knowledge of his true name.

No one knows a man's true name but himself and his namer. He may choose at length to tell it to his brother, or his wife, or his friend, yet even those few will never use it where any third person may hear it. In front of other people they will, like other people, call him by his use-name, his nickname — such a name as Sparrowhawk, and Vetch, and Ogion which means "fir-cone." If plain men hide their true name from all but a few they love and trust utterly, so much more must wizardly men, being more dangerous, and more endangered. Who knows a man's name, holds that man's life in his keeping. Thus to Ged who had lost faith in himself, Vetch had given that gift only a friend can give, the proof of unshaken, unshakable trust.

Ged sat down on his pallet and let the globe of werelight die, giving off as it faded a faint whiff of marsh-gas. He petted the otak, which stretched comfortably and went to sleep on his knee as if it had never slept anywhere else. The Great House was silent. It came to Ged's mind that this was the eve of his own Passage, the day on which Ogion had given him his name. Four years were gone since then. He remembered the coldness of the mountain spring through which he had walked naked and unnamed. He

457

fell to thinking of other bright pools in the River Ar, where he had used to swim; and of Ten Alders, his village, under the great slanting forests of the mountain; of the shadows of morning across the dusty village street, the fire leaping under bellows-blast in the smith's smelting-pit on a winter afternoon, the witch's dark fragrant hut where the air was heavy with smoke and wreathing spells. He had not thought of these things for a long time. Now they came back to him, on this night he was seventeen years old. All the years and places of his brief broken life came within mind's reach and made a whole again. He knew once more, at last, after this long, bitter, wasted time, who he was and where he was.

But where he must go in the years to come, that he could not see; and he feared to see it.

About URSULA K. LE GUIN

Ursula K. Le Guin has been writing for as long as she can remember. "I started writing poetry and stories about as soon as I learned how to write," she says, "and I always intended and expected to go on writing, and did so."

Although Ursula Le Guin has become known for her science fiction, her first published works were poems and, after that, some short stories. Then she turned her efforts to book-length science fiction. "I started out as a science fiction writer," she explains, "because editors and publishers need a label for writers who don't have a name yet, and science fiction was about the only thing I could do that they could label. Since then I have written science fiction, fantasy, a realistic novel, a historical novel, a mixed realistic and fantasy novel, a picture book, more poems, and worked on a movie, and haven't the faintest idea what might happen next."

What did happen next was a television show. Ursula Le Guin dramatized some of her work for television, and it was a tremendous success. The show touched on the theme that interests her most: the future possibilities of the human spirit. She believes that the past and the present are not nearly as exciting as the future, for that is where we are headed.

■ Understanding the Story

1. Even though Ged has supernatural powers, he is a realistic character because he has both bad and good qualities. What bad qualities in Ged drive him to call up a spirit from the dead?

2. At the end of the selection, how does Vetch show his trust and love for Ged?

3. At the climax of this story, the night world is compared to a dark piece of cloth. What happens to the "fabric of the world" after the spirit of Elfarran appears?

4. What causes the death of the Archmage Nemmerle?

5. What do you think the shadow-beast in this story stands for? What do you think might happen in the chapters that follow this one in the novel?

■ Understanding Literature

Fantasy allows you to escape the real world while it gives you insights into universal truths that are important in the real world.

In "The Loosing of the Shadow," you strongly identify with Ged, the major character. In spite of his magical powers, Ged is a lifelike character who grows and changes in the story. At the beginning of the story he is impatient and hot-tempered, eager to show off his power. Then the shadow-beast at-tacks, and Ged is struck down in both body and mind. No longer strong, he is sick and scarred. He realizes that he is responsible for a terrible evil that has been let loose on the world. He fears the evil power, the shadow, that is in him.

Like many other stories, "The Loosing of the Shadow" contains the universal theme that each person has a potentially evil side to his or her character, which must be recognized and dealt with before he or she can really grow up. To face your shadow is to take responsibility for your actions. Like any young person in the real world, Le Guin's main character, Ged, must face the same ordeal.

■ Writing About the Story

Ged calls for Elfarran, the fair lady of the *Deed of Enlad*, part of the folklore of Earthsea. Who do you think Elfarran was? Why was she famous? Make up a legend or story about Elfarran that explains her important position. Write your story, but be prepared to tell it aloud, as it would have been told or sung in Earthsea.

Rescue at the Dragon Stones

From the novel *Dragonsong* by Anne McCaffrey

Illustrated by David Wiesner

Between Threadfalls, life on the planet Pern was pleasant, if a bit narrow and dull. The men worked at their crafts while the women kept house in cave towns called holds. The Harpers and the music they made provided the only form of entertainment and celebration. Every two hundred years, though, deadly silver strands of plant spore called Thread rained down on Pern, consuming every living thing in its path. Then the people had to wait in fear while Pern's fire-breathing dragons and their dragonriders fought off the Thread.

It wasn't growing up in a time of Threadfall that made Menolly miserable so much as it was living without music. The girl had loved to sing and play more than anything and had shown great talent. Encouraged by the old Harper, Petiron, "her friend, her ally and mentor," Menolly had even written her own songs. When Petiron died, however, Menolly was left terribly alone. Her father Yanus thought it improper for a girl to seek a career in music, a craft reserved for male Harpers. He grudgingly allowed Menolly to teach music to the other children until a new Harper arrived, but made her promise not to sing her own tunes. She did her best to obey, but absentmindedly started "tuning" during lessons one day just as her father walked by. Yanus dismissed the class, gave Menolly a beating, and forced her to give up music altogether in favor of household chores.

Sent by her mother to pick greens near the rocks called the Dragon Stones, Menolly happened upon a group of fire lizards, tiny relations to the huge dragons of Pern. Menolly felt so joyous and free around the little creatures that she made up a song about them.

It was the last tune she would compose for a long time. Upon her return home, Menolly was put to work cleaning fish. Her knife slipped, and she cut her hand horribly. Her mother told her she would never again be able to play music. It was not until Menolly had the good fortune to come upon the fire lizards once again that she found anything to hope for.

MENOLLY HEARD THE FIRE LIZARDS before she saw them. Their excited chirpings and squeals indicated something was upsetting them. She dropped to a crouch and crept to the edge of the bluff, overlooking the little beach. Only there wasn't much beach left, and the fire lizards were hovering over a spot on the small margin of sand, almost directly below her.

She inched up to the edge, peering down. She could see the queen darting at the incoming waves as if she could stop them with her violently beating wings. Then she'd streak back, out of Menolly's line of sight, while the rest of the creatures kept milling and swooping, rather like frightened herdbeasts running about aimlessly when wild wherries[1] circled their herd. The queen was shrieking at the top of her shrill little voice, obviously trying to get them to do something. Unable to imagine what the emergency could be, Menolly leaned just a little further over the edge. The whole lip of the cliff gave way.

Clutching wildly at sea grasses, Menolly tried to prevent her fall. But the sea grass slipped cuttingly through her hand and she slid over the edge and down. She hit the beach with a force that sent a shock through her body. But the wet sand absorbed a good deal of the impact. She lay where she'd fallen for a few minutes, trying to get her breath into her lungs and out

again. Then she scrambled to her feet and crawled away from an incoming wave.

She looked up the side of the bluff, rather daunted by the fact that she'd fallen a dragon length or more. And how was she going to climb back up? But, as she examined the cliff face, she could see that it was not so unscalable as she'd first thought. Almost straight up, yes, but pocked by ledges and holds, some fairly large. If she could find enough foot and hand holds, she'd be able to make it. She dusted the sand from her hands and started to walk towards one end of the little cove, to begin a systematic search for the easiest way up.

She'd gone only a few paces when something dove at her, screeching in fury. Her hands went up to protect her face as the little queen came diving down at her. Now Menolly recalled the curious behavior of the fire lizards. The little queen acted as if she were protecting something from Menolly as well as the encroaching sea, and she looked about her. She was within handspans of stepping into a fire lizard clutch.[2]

"Oh, I'm sorry. I'm sorry. I wasn't looking! Don't be mad at me," Menolly cried as the little fire lizard came at her again. "Please! Stop! I won't hurt them!"

To prove her sincerity, Menolly backtracked to the far end of the beach. There she had to duck under

---

1. **wherries:** large, wild birds of Pern.

2. **clutch:** a group of eggs.

a small overhang. When she looked around, there wasn't a sign of the little queen. Menolly's relief was short-lived, for how was she to find a way up the cliff if the little fire lizard kept attacking her every time she approached the eggs. Menolly hunched down, trying to get comfortable in her cramped refuge.

Maybe if she kept away from the eggs? Menolly peered up the cliff directly above her. There were some likely looking holds. She eased herself out the far side, keeping one eye on the clutch, basking in the hot sun, and reached for the first ledge.

Immediately the fire lizard came at her.

"Oh, leave me alone! Ow! Go away. I'm trying to."

The fire lizard's talons had raked her cheek.

"Please! I won't hurt your eggs!"

The little queen's next pass just missed Menolly, who ducked back under the ledge.

Blood oozed from the long scratch, and Menolly dabbed at it with the edge of her tunic.

"Haven't you got any sense?" Menolly demanded of her now invisible attacker. "What would I want with your silly eggs? Keep 'em. I just want to get home. Can't you understand? I just want to go home."

Maybe if I sit very still, she'll forget about me, Menolly thought and pulled her knees up under the chin, but her toes and elbows protruded from under the overhang.

Suddenly a bronze fire lizard materialized above the clutch squeaking worriedly. Menolly saw the queen swooping to join him, so the queen must have been on the top of the ledge, waiting, just waiting for Menolly to break cover.

And to think I made up a pretty tune about you, Menolly thought as she watched the two lizards hovering over the eggs. The last tune I ever made up. You're ungrateful, that's what you are!

Despite her discomfort, Menolly had to laugh. What an impossible situation! Held under a cramped ledge by a creature no bigger than her forearm.

At the sound of her laughter, the two fire lizards disappeared.

Frightened, were they? Of laughter?

"A smile wins more than a frown," her mother, Mavi, was fond of saying.

Maybe if I keep laughing, they'll know I'm friendly? Or get scared away long enough for me to climb up? Saved by a laugh?

Menolly began to chuckle in earnest, for she had also seen that the tide was coming in rather quickly. She eased out of her shelter, flung the carry-sack over her shoulder, and started to climb. But it proved impossible to chuckle and climb. She needed breath for both.

Abruptly both the little queen and the bronze were back to harry her, flying at her head and face. The fragile looking wings were dangerous when used as a weapon.

No longer laughing, Menolly ducked back under her ledge, wondering what to do next.

If laughter had startled them, what about a song? Maybe if she gave that pair a chorus of her tune, they'd let her go. It was the first time she'd sung since before she'd cut her hand, so her voice sounded rough and uncertain. Well, the lizards would *know* what she meant, she hoped, so she sang the saucy little song. To no one.

"Well, so much for that notion," Menolly muttered under her breath. "Which makes the lack of interest in your singing absolutely unanimous."

No audience? Not a fire lizard's whisker in sight?

As fast as she could, Menolly slipped from her shelter and came face to face, for a split second, with two fire lizard faces. She ducked down, and they evidently disappeared because when she cautiously peered again, the ledge where they'd been perched was empty.

She had the distinct impression that their expressions had registered curiosity and interest.

"Look, if wherever you are, you can hear me . . . will you stay there and let me go? Once I'm on the top of the cliff, I'll serenade you til the sun goes down. Just let me get up there!"

She started to sing, a dutiful dragon

song as she once again emerged from her refuge. She was about five steps upward when the queen fire lizard emerged, with help. With squeaks and squeals she was driven back down. She could even hear claws scraping on the rock above her. She must have quite an audience by now. When she didn't need one!

Cautiously she looked up, met the fascinated whirling of ten pairs of eyes.

"Look, a bargain! One long song and then let me up the cliff? Is that agreed?"

Fire lizard eyes whirled.

Menolly took it that the bargain was made and sang. Her voice started a flutter of surprised and excited chirpings, and she wondered if by any possible freak they actually understood that she was singing about grateful holds[3] honoring dragonriders. By the last verse she eased out into the open, awed by the sight of a queen fire lizard and nine bronzes entranced by her performance.

"Can I go now?" she asked and put one hand on the ledge.

The queen dived for her hand, and Menolly snatched it back.

"I thought we'd struck a bargain."

The queen chirped piteously, and Menolly realized that there had been no menace in the queen's action. She simply wasn't allowed to climb.

"You don't want me to go?" Menolly asked.

---

3. **holds:** towns built in caves by the colonists on Pern. Menolly lives in Half-Circle Sea Hold.

The queen's eyes seemed to glow more brightly.

"But I have to go. If I stay, the water will come up and drown me." And Menolly accompanied her words with explanatory gestures.

Suddenly the queen let out a shrill cry, seemed to hold herself midair for a moment and then, her bronzes in close pursuit, she glided down the sandy beach to her clutch. She hovered over the eggs, making the most urgent and excited sounds.

If the tide was coming in fast enough to endanger Menolly, it was also frighteningly close to swamping the nest. The little bronzes began to take up the queen's plaint and several, greatly daring, flew about Menolly's head and then circled back to the clutch.

"I can come there now? You won't attack me?" Menolly took a few steps forward.

The tone of the cries changed, and Menolly quickened her step. As she reached the nest, the little queen secured one egg from the clutch. With a great laboring of her wings, she bore it upward. That the effort was great was obvious. The bronzes hovered anxiously, squeaking their concern but, being much smaller, they were unable to assist the queen.

Now Menolly saw that the base of the cliff at this point was littered with broken shells and the pitiful bodies of tiny fire lizards, their wings half-extended and glistening with egg-fluid.

The little queen now had raised the egg to a ledge, which Menolly had not previously noticed, about a half-dragon length up the cliff-face. Menolly could see the little queen deposit the egg on the ledge and roll it with her forelegs towards what must be a hole in the cliff. It was a long moment before the queen reappeared again. Then she dove towards the sea, hovering over the foamy crest of a wave that rolled in precariously close to the endangered clutch. With a blurred movement, the queen was hovering in front of Menolly and scolding.

Although Menolly couldn't help grinning at the thought, she was filled with a sense of pity and admiration for the courage of the little queen, single-handedly trying to rescue her clutch. If the dead fire lizards were that fully formed, the clutch was near to hatching. No wonder the queen could barely move the eggs.

"You want me to help you move the eggs, right? Well, we'll see what I can do!"

Ready to jump back if she had mistaken the little queen's imperious command, Menolly very carefully picked up an egg. It was warm to the touch and hard. Dragon eggs, she knew, were soft when first laid but hardened slowly on the hot sands of the Hatching Grounds in the Weyrs.[4] These definitely must be close to hatching.

Closing the fingers of her damaged hand carefully around the egg, Menolly searched for and found foot and hand holds, and reached the queen's ledge. She carefully deposited the egg. The little queen appeared, one front talon resting proprietarily on the egg, and then she leaned forward, towards Menolly's face, so close that the fantastic motion of the many-faceted eyes was clearly visible. The queen gave a sort of sweet chirp and then, in a very business-like manner, began to scold Menolly as she rolled her egg to safety.

Menolly managed three eggs in her hand the next time. But it was obvious that between the onrushing tide and the startling number of eggs in the clutch, there'd be quite a race.

"If the hole were bigger," she told the little queen as she deposited three eggs, "some of the bronzes could help you roll."

The queen paid her no attention, busy pushing the three eggs, one at a time, to safety.

Menolly peered into the opening, but the fire lizard's body obscured any view. If the hole was bigger and the ledge consequently broader, Menolly could bring the rest of the eggs up in her carry-sack.

Hoping that she wouldn't pull down the cliffside and bury the queen, clutch and all, Menolly prodded cautiously at the mouth of the opening. Loose sand came showering down.

The queen took to scolding frantically as Menolly brushed the rubble

---

4. **Hatching Grounds in the Weyrs** (WEERZ): where dragons' eggs are kept. A weyr is a dragon hold.

from the ledge. Then she felt around the opening. There seemed to be solid stone just beyond. Menolly yanked away at the looser rock, until she had a nice tunnel exposed with a slightly wider opening.

Ignoring the little queen's furious complaints, Menolly climbed down, unslinging her sack when she reached the ground. When the little queen saw Menolly putting the eggs in the sack, she began to have hysterics, beating at Menolly's head and hands.

"Now, look here," Menolly said sternly, "I am not stealing your eggs. I am trying to get them all to safety in jig time. I can do it with the sack but not by the handful."

Menolly waited a moment, glaring at the little queen who hovered at eye level.

"Did you understand me?" Menolly pointed to the waves, more vigorously dashing up the small beach. "The tide is coming in. Dragons couldn't stop it now." Menolly put another egg carefully in the sack. As it was she'd have to make two, maybe three trips or risk breaking eggs. "I take this," and she gestured up to the ledge, "up there. Do you understand, you silly beast?"

Evidently, the little creature did because, crooning anxiously, she took her position on the ledge, her wings half-extended and twitching as she watched Menolly's progress up to her.

Menolly could climb faster with two hands. And she could, carefully, roll the eggs from the mouth of the sack well down the tunnelway.

"You'd better get the bronzes to help you now, or we'll have the ledge stacked too high."

It took Menolly three trips in all, and as she made the last climb, the water was a foot's width from the clutch. The little queen had organized her bronzes to help, and Menolly could hear her scolding tones echoing in what must be a fair-sized cave beyond the tunnel. Not surprising since these bluffs were supposed to be riddled with caverns and passages.

Menolly gave a last look at the beach, water at least ankle deep on both ends of the little cove. She glanced upward, past the ledge. She was a good halfway up the cliff now, and she thought she could see enough hand and foot holds ahead.

"Good-bye!" She was answered by a trill of chirps, and she chuckled as she imagined the scene: the queen marshalling her bronzes to position her eggs just right.

Menolly did not make the cliff top without a few anxious moments. She was exhausted when she finally flopped on the sea grasses at the summit, and her left hand ached from unaccustomed gripping and effort. She lay there for some time, until her heart stopped thudding in her ribs and her breath came more easily. An inshore

breeze dried her face, cooling her; but that reminded her of the emptiness of her stomach. Her exertions had reduced the rolls in her pouch to crumby fragments, which she gobbled as fast as she could find them.

All at once the enormity of her adventure struck her, and she was torn between laughter and awe. To prove to herself that she'd actually done what she remembered, she crept cautiously to the bluff edge. The beach was completely underwater.

Menolly felt her cheek. The fire lizard's scratch was crusted with dried blood and sand.

"So it did happen!"

However did the little queen know I could help her? No one had ever suggested that fire lizards were stupid. Certainly they'd been smart enough for endless Turns[5] to evade every trap and snare laid to catch them. The creatures were so clever, indeed, that there was a good deal of doubt about their existence, except as figures of overactive imaginations. However, enough trustworthy men had actually seen the creatures, at a distance, like her brother Alemi when he'd spotted some about the Dragon Stones, that most people did accept their existence as fact.

Menolly could have sworn that the little queen had understood her. How else could Menolly have helped her?

That proved how smart the little beast was. Smart enough certainly to avoid the boys who tried to capture them . . . Menolly was appalled. Capture a fire lizard? Pen it up? Not, Menolly supposed with relief, that the creature would stay caught long. It only had to pop *between*.[6]

Now why hadn't the little queen just gone *between* with her eggs, instead of arduously transporting them one by one? Oh, yes, *between* was the coldest place known. And cold would do the eggs harm. At least it did dragon eggs harm. Would the clutch be all right now in the cold cavern? Hmmm. Menolly peered below. Well, if the queen had as much sense as she'd already shown, she'd get all her followers to come lie on the eggs and keep them warm until they did hatch.

Menolly turned her pouch inside out, hoping for some crumbs. She was still hungry. She'd find enough early fruits and some succulent reeds to eat, but she was curiously loath[7] to leave the bluff. Though, it was unlikely that the queen, now her need was past, would reappear.

Menolly rose finally and found herself stiff from the unaccustomed exercise. Her hand ached in a dull way, and the long scar was red and slightly swollen. But, as Menolly flexed her fingers,

---

5. **Turns:** similar to our years. Menolly is fourteen Turns old.

6. ***between:*** Dragons are capable of *teleportation,* transporting themselves through time and space. During teleportation they pass through a black, cold nothingness known as *between.*

7. **loath** (LOHTH): unwilling; reluctant.

it seemed that the hand opened more easily. Yes, it did. She could almost extend the fingers completely. It hurt, but it was a stretchy-hurt. Could she open her hand enough to play again? She folded her fingers as if to chord. That hurt, but again, it was a stretchy-hurt. Maybe if she worked her hand a lot more . . . She had been favoring it until today when she hadn't given it a thought. She'd used it to climb and carry and everything.

"Well, you did me a favor, too, little queen," Menolly called, speaking into the breeze and waving her hands high. "See? My hand is better."

There was no answering chirp or sound, but the soft whistle of the sea-born breeze and the lapping of the waves against the bluff. Yet Menolly liked to think that her words had been heard. She turned inland, feeling considerably relieved and rather pleased with the morning's work.

She'd have to scoot now and gather what she could of greens and early berries. No point in trying for spider-claws[8] with the tide so high.

--- · ---

No one, as usual, noticed Menolly when she got back to the Hold. Dutifully she saw the harbormaster and told him about the tides.

"Don't you go so far, girl," he told her kindly. "Thread's due any day now, you know. How's the hand?"

She mumbled something, which he didn't hear anyway, as a shipmaster shouted for his attention.

The evening meal was hurried since all the masters[9] were going off to the Dock Cavern to check tide, masts and ships. In the bustle Menolly could keep to herself.

And she did — seeking the cubicle and the safety of her bed as soon as possible. There she hugged to herself the incredible experience of the morning. She was certain that the queen had understood her. Just like the dragons, fire lizards knew what was in the mind and heart of a person. That's why they disappeared so easily when boys tried to trap them. They'd liked her singing, too.

Menolly gave herself a squeeze, ignoring the spasm of pain in her now stiff hand. Then she tensed, remembering that the bronzes had been waiting to see what the queen would do. She was the clever one, the audacious one. What was it her friend Petiron, the Harper, was always quoting? "Necessity breeds solution."

Did fire lizards really understand people, even when they kept away from them, then, Menolly puzzled again. Of course, dragons understood what their riders were thinking, but dragons Impressed at Hatching to their riders.[10] The link was never broken, and

---

8. **spiderclaws**: plump shellfish.

9. **masters**: master craftspeople.
10. **dragons Impressed at Hatching to their riders**: As each dragon emerges from its shell, it chooses a rider with whom it forms a telepathic bond that binds the two together for life.

the dragon would only hear that one person, or so Petiron had said. So *how* had the little queen understood her?

"Necessity?"

Poor queen! She must have been frantic when she realized that the tide was going to cover her eggs! Probably she'd been depositing her clutches in that cove for who knows how long? How long did fire lizards live? Dragons lasted the life of their rider. Sometimes that wasn't so long, now that Thread was dropping. Quite a few riders had been so badly scored they'd died and so had their dragons. Would the little fire lizards have a longer life, being smaller and not in so much danger? Questions darted through Menolly's mind, like fire lizard's flashing, she thought, as she cuddled into the warmth of her sleeping fur. She'd try to go back tomorrow, maybe, with food. She rather thought fire lizards would like spiderclaws, too, and maybe then she'd get the queen's trust. Or maybe it would be better if she didn't go back tomorrow? She should stay away for a few days. Then, too, with Thread falling so often, it was dangerous to go so far from the safety of the Hold.

What would happen when the fire lizard eggs hatched? What a sight that would be! Ha! All the lads in the Sea Hold talking about catching fire lizards and she, Menolly, had not only seen but talked to them and handled their eggs! And if she were lucky, she might even see them hatching, too. Why, that would be as marvelous as going to a

dragon Hatching at one of the Weyrs! And no one, not even her father, Yanus, had been to a Hatching!

Considering her exciting thoughts, it was a wonder that Menolly was able to sleep.

The next morning her hand ached and throbbed, and she was stiff from the fall and the climbing. Her half-formed notion of going back to the Dragon Stones' cove was thwarted by the weather, of all things. A storm had blown in from the sea that night, lashing the harbor with pounding waves. Even the Dock Cavern waters were turbulent, and a wind whipped with such whimsical force that walking from Hold to Cavern was dangerous.

That evening Menolly couldn't escape the Great Hall. Since everyone had been in all day, everyone needed entertainment and was going. The new Harper would surely play. Menolly shuddered. Well, there was no help for it. She had to hear music sometime. She couldn't avoid it forever. And at least she could sing along with the others. But she soon found she couldn't even have that pleasure. Mavi gestured to her when the Harper began to tune his gitar. And when the Harper beckoned for everyone to join in the choruses, Mavi pinched Menolly so hard that she gasped.

"Don't roar. You may sing softly as befits a girl your age," Mavi said. "Or don't sing at all."

Across the Hall, Menolly's sister, Sella, was singing, not at all accurately and loud enough to be heard in Benden Hold;[11] but when Menolly opened her mouth to protest, she got another pinch.

So she didn't sing at all but sat there by her mother's side, numb and hurt, not even able to enjoy the music and very conscious that her mother was being monstrously unfair.

Wasn't it bad enough she couldn't play anymore — yet — but not to be allowed to sing? Why, everyone had encouraged her to sing when the old Harper, Petiron, had been alive. And been glad to hear her. Asked her to sing, time and again.

Then Menolly saw her father watching her, his face stern, one hand tapping not so much to the time of the music but to some inner agitation. It was her father who didn't want her to sing! It wasn't fair! It just wasn't fair! They didn't want her here.

She wrenched herself free from her mother's grip and, ignoring Mavi's hiss to come back and behave herself, she crept from the Hall. Those who saw her leave thought sadly that it was such a pity she'd hurt her hand and didn't even want to sing anymore.

Wanted or not, creeping out like that would send Mavi looking for her when there was a pause in the evening's singing. So Menolly took her sleeping furs and a glow and went to one of the unused inner rooms where no one would find her. She brought her clothes, too. If the storm cleared, she'd be away in the morning to the fire lizards. *They* liked her singing. They liked *her!*

Before anyone else was up, she had risen. She gulped down a cold klah[12] and ate some bread, stuffed more in her pouch and was almost away. Her heart beat fast while she struggled with the big metal doors of the Hold entrance. She'd never opened them before and hadn't appreciated how very solid they were. She couldn't, of course, bar

---

12. **klah**: a nutritious breakfast drink, usually served hot.

---

11. **Benden Hold**: a fort built for two hundred dragons and their riders in an extinct volcano.

them again, but there was scarcely any need.

Sea mist was curling up from the quiet harbor waters, the entrances to the dock Cavern visible as darker masses in the gray. But the sun was beginning to burn through the fog, and Menolly's weather-sense told her that it would soon be clear.

She struck somewhat inland, towards the first of the marshes. One cup of klah and a hunk of bread was not enough food, and she remembered some unstripped marshberry bushes.

She was over the first humpy hill and suddenly the mist had left the land, the brightness of the spring sun almost an ache to the eyes.

She found her patch of marshberry and picked one handful for her face, then one for the pouch.

Now that she could see where she was going, she jogged down the coast and finally dropped into a cove. The tide was just right to catch spiderclaws. These should be a pleasant offering to the fire lizard queen she thought as she filled her bag. Or could fire lizards hunt in fog?

When Menolly had carried her loaded sack through several long valleys and over humpy hills, she was beginning to wish she'd waited a while to do her netting. She was hot and tired. Now that the excitement of her unorthodox behavior had waned, she was also depressed. Of course, it was quite likely that no one had noticed she'd left.

No, no one was likely to notice that she was gone until there was some unpleasant or tedious job for a one-handed girl to do. So they wouldn't assume that *she'd* opened the Hold door. And since Menolly was apt to disappear during the day, no one would think anything about her until evening. Then someone might just wonder where Menolly was.

That was when she realized that she didn't plan to return to the Hold. And the sheer audacity of that thought was enough to make her halt in her tracks.

Not return to the Hold? Not go back to the endless round of tedious tasks? Of gutting, smoking, salting, pickling fish? Mending nets, sails, clothes? Cleaning dishes, clothes, rooms? Gathering greens, berries, grasses, spiderclaws? Not return to tend old uncles and aunts, fires, pots, looms, glowbaskets? To be able to sing or shout or roar or play if she so chose? To sleep . . . ah, now where would she sleep? And where would she go when there was Thread in the skies?

Menolly trudged on more slowly up the sand dunes; her mind churning with these revolutionary ideas. Why, everyone had to return to the Hold at night! The Hold, any hold or cot[13] or weyr. Seven Turns had Thread been dropping from the skies, and no one travelled far from shelter.

Some stillness in the air, some vague unease caused Menolly to glance about her apprehensively. There was certainly no one else about at this early hour. She scanned the skies. The mist banking the coast was rapidly dispersing. She could see it retreating across the water to the north and west. Towards the east the sky was brilliant with sunrise, except for what were probably some traces of early morning fog in the northeast. Yet something disturbed Menolly. She felt she should know what it was.

She was nearly to the Dragon Stones now, in the last marsh before

the contour of the land swept gently up towards the seaside bluff. It was as she traversed the marsh that she identified the odd quality: it was the stillness. Not of wind, for that was steady seaward, blowing away the fog, but a stillness of marsh life. All the little insects and flies and small wrigglers, the occasional flights of wild wherries who nested in the heavier bushes were silent. Their myriad activities and small noises began as soon as the sun was up and didn't cease until just before dawn, because the nocturnal insects were as noisy as the daytime ones.

It was this quiet, as if every living thing was holding its breath, that was disturbing Menolly. Unconsciously she began to walk faster and she had a strong urge to glance over her right shoulder, towards the northeast — where a smudge of gray clouded the horizon . . .

A smudge of gray? Or silver?

Menolly began to tremble with rising fear, with the dawning knowledge that she was too far from the safety of the Hold to reach it before Thread reached her. The heavy metal doors, which she had so negligently left ajar, would soon be closed and barred against her, and Thread. And, even if she were missed, no one would come for her.

She began to run, and some instinct directed her towards the cliff edge before she consciously remembered the queen's ledge. It wasn't big enough, really. Or she could go into the sea? Thread drowned in the sea. So would

---

13. **cot:** a cottagelike dormitory.

she, for she couldn't keep under the water for the time it would take Thread to pass. How long would it take the leading edge of a Fall[14] to pass over? She'd no idea.

She was at the edge now, looking down at the beach. She could see her ledge off to the right. There was the lip of the cliff that had broken off under her weight. That was the quick way down, to be sure, but she couldn't risk it again, and didn't want to.

She glanced over her shoulder. The grayness was spreading across the horizon. Now she could see flashes against that gray. Flashes? Dragons! She was seeing dragons fighting Thread, their fiery breath charring the dreaded stuff midair. They were so far away that the winking lights were more like lost stars than dragons fighting for the life of Pern.

Maybe the leading edge wouldn't reach this far? Maybe she was safe. "Maybes seldom are" as her mother would say.

In the stillness of the air, a new sound made itself heard: a soft rhythmic thrumming, something like the tuneless humming of small children. Only different. The noise seemed to come from the ground.

She dropped, pressing one ear to a

_____

14. **leading edge of a Fall**: the farthest inland penetration of a Threadfall.

475

patch of bare stone. The sound was coming from within.

Of course! The bluff was hollow . . . that's why the queen lizard . . .

On hands and knees, Menolly scooted to the cliff edge, looking for that halfway ledge of the queen's.

Menolly had enlarged the entry once. There was every chance she could make it big enough to squirm through. The little queen would certainly be hospitable to someone who had saved her clutch!

And Menolly didn't come empty-handed as a guest! She swung the heavy sack of spiderclaws around to her back. Grabbing handfuls of the grasses on the lip of the cliff, she began to let herself slowly down. Her feet fumbled for support; she found one toehold and dug half that foot in, the other foot prodding for another place.

She slithered badly once, but a rock protrusion caught her before she'd slipped far. She laid her face against the cliff, gulping to get back her breath and courage. She could feel the thrumming through the stone, and oddly, that gave her heart. There was something intensely exciting and stimulating about that sound.

Sheer luck guided her foot to the queen's ledge. She'd risked only a few glances beneath her — the aspect was almost enough to make her lose her balance completely. She was trembling so much with her exertions that she had to rest then. Definitely the

humming came from the queen's cavern.

She could get her head into the original opening. No more. She began to tear at the sides with her bare hands until she thought of her belt knife. The blade loosened a whole section all at once, showering her with sand and bits of rock. She had to clean her eyes and mouth of grit before she could continue. Then she realized that she'd gotten to sheer rock.

She could get herself into the shelter only up to her shoulders. No matter how she turned and twisted, there was an outcropping that she could not pass. Once again she wished she were as small as a girl ought to be. Sella would have had no trouble crawling through that hole. Resolutely, Menolly began to chip at the rock with her knife, the blows jarring her hand to the shoulder, and making no impression at all on the rock.

She wondered frantically how long it had taken her to get down the cliff. How long did she have before Thread would be raining down on her unprotected body?

Body? She might not get past the bobble in the wall with her shoulders . . . but . . . She reversed her position, and feet, legs, hips, all right up to the shoulders passed into the safety of solid rock. Her head was covered, but only just, by the cliff overhang.

Did Thread *see* where it was going when it fell? Would it notice her, crowded into this hole as it flashed by?

Then she saw the thong of the carry-sack where she'd looped it over the ledge to keep it handy but out of her way. If Thread got into the spider-claws. . . .

She pulled herself far enough out of the hole to cast an eye above. No silver yet! No sound but the steadily increasing thrumming. That wouldn't have anything to do with Thread, would it?

The carry-sack thong had bitten into the ledge and she had a job freeing it, having to yank rather hard. The next thing she knew the sack came free, the force of her pull threw her backwards, cracking her head on the roof of her tunnel, and then the surface beneath her started to slide, out and down. Menolly clawed her way into the tunnel, as the ledge slowly detached itself from the face of the cliff and tumbled down onto the beach.

Menolly scrambled back quickly, afraid more of the entrance would go, and suddenly she was in a cave, wide, high, deep, clutching the carry-sack and staring at the greatly widened mouth.

The thrumming was behind her and, startled at what she could only consider to be an additional threat, she whirled.

Fire lizards were perched around the walls, clinging to rock spur and ledge. Every eye glinted at the mound of eggs in the sandy center of the cave. The thrumming came from the throats of all the little fire lizards, and they were far too intent on what was happening to

the eggs to give any heed to her abrupt appearance.

Just as Menolly realized that she was witnessing a Hatching, the first egg began to rock and cracks appeared in its shell.

It rocked itself off the mound of the clutch and, in hitting the ground, split. From the two parts emerged a tiny creature, not much bigger than Menolly's hand, glistening brown and creeling with hunger, swaying its head back and forth and tottering forward a few awkward steps. The transparent brown wings unfolded, flapping weakly to dry, and the creature's balance improved. The creel turned to a hiss of displeasure, and the little brown peered about defensively.

The other fire lizards crooned, encouraging it to some action. With a tiny shriek of anger, the little brown launched itself towards the cave opening, passing so close to Menolly she could have touched it.

The brown fire lizard lurched off the eroded lip of the cave, pumping its wings frantically to achieve flight. Menolly gasped as the creature dropped, and then sighed with relief as it came into sight briefly, airborne, and flew off, across the sea.

More creeling brought her attention back to the clutch. Other fire lizards

had begun to hatch in that brief period, each one shaking its wings and then, encouraged by the weyrmates,[15] flopping and weaving towards the cave mouth, defiantly independent and hungry.

Several greens and blues, a little bronze and two more browns hatched and passed Menolly. And then, as she watched a little blue launch itself, Menolly screamed. No sooner had the blue emerged from the safety of the cliff than she saw the thin, writhing silver of Thread descending. In a moment, the blue was covered with the deadly filaments. It uttered one hideous shriek and disappeared. Dead? Or *between?* Certainly badly scored.

Two more little fire lizards passed Menolly, and she reacted now.

"No! No! You can't! You'll be killed." She flung herself across their path.

The angry fire lizards pecked at her unprotected face and while she covered herself, made their escape. She cried aloud when she heard their screams.

"Don't let them go!" She pleaded with the watching fire lizards. "You're older. You know about Thread. Tell them to stop!" She half-crawled, half-ran to the rock where the golden queen was perched.

"Tell them not to go! There's Thread out there! They're being killed!"

The queen looked at her, the many-

faceted eyes whirling violently. The queen chuckled and chirped at her, and then crooned as yet another fledgling spread its wings and began to totter towards sure death.

"Please, little queen! Do something! Stop them!"

The thrill of being the witness to a Hatching of fire lizards gave way to horror. Dragons had to be protected because they protected Pern. In Menolly's fear and confusion, the little lizards were linked to their giant counterparts.

She turned to the other lizards now, begging them to do something. At least until the Threadfall was over. Desperately she plunged back to the cave mouth and tried to turn the little fire lizards back with her hands, blocking their progress with her body. She was overwhelmed with pangs of hunger, belly-knotting, gut-twisting hunger. It took her only a moment to realize that the driving force in these fire lizards was that sort of hunger: that was what was sending them senselessly forth. They had to eat. She remembered that dragons had to eat, too, when they first Hatched, fed by the boys they Impressed.

Menolly wildly grabbed for her carry-sack. With one hand she snatched a fire lizard back from the entrance, and with the other, a spiderclaw from the sack. The little bronze screeched once and then bit the spiderclaw behind the eye, neatly killing it. Wings beating, the bronze lifted itself free of Menolly's

---

15. **weyrmates:** other newborn lizards in the nest.

grasp and with more strength than Menolly would have thought the new-born creature could possess flew its prey to a corner and began tearing it apart.

Menolly reached out randomly now and, with some surprise, found herself holding the one queen in the clutch. She snagged two spiderclaws from the sack in her other hand, and deposited them and the queen in another corner. Finally realizing she couldn't handfeed the whole clutch, she upended the sack, spilling the shellfish out.

Newly hatched fire lizards swarmed over and after the spiderclaws. Menolly caught two more lizards before they could reach the cave mouth and put them squarely in the center of their first meal. She was busy trying to make sure that each new fire lizard had a shellfish when she felt something prick-ing her shoulder. Surprised, she looked up to find the little bronze clinging to her tunic. His round eyes were whirling and he was still hungry. She gave him an unclaimed spiderclaw and put him back in his corner. She tossed the little queen another and snared several other spiderclaws for her "specials."

Not many more of the newly-hatched got out, not with a source of food so nearby. She'd had a fair haul in the sack, but it didn't take long for the hungry fire lizards to devour every last morsel. The poor things were still sounding starved as they creeled about, tipping over claws and body shells, trying to find any scraps over-looked. But they stayed in the cave and now the older fire lizards joined them, nuzzling or stroking, making affection-ate noises.

Utterly exhausted, Menolly leaned back against the wall, watching their antics. At least they'd not all died. She glanced apprehensively at the entrance and saw no more writhing lengths of Thread falling past. She peered further. There wasn't even a trace of the men-acing gray fog on the horizon. Thread-fall must be over.

And not a moment too soon. Now

she was experiencing hunger thoughts from all the fire lizards. Rather overpoweringly, in fact. Because she realized how hungry she herself was.

The little queen, the old queen, began to hover in the cave, squeaking an imperious command to her followers. Then she darted out and the old clutch began to follow her. The fledglings, moving awkwardly, made their virgin flight, and within moments, the cave was empty of all but Menolly, her torn sack, and a pile of empty spiderclaw and fire lizard shells.

With their exit, some of Menolly's hunger eased and she remembered the bread she'd tucked in her pocket. Feeling a bit guilty at this belated discovery, she gratefully ate every crumb.

Then she made herself a hollow in the sand, pulled the torn carry-sack over her shoulders, and went to sleep.

About ANNE MCCAFFREY

Dragonhold, Ireland, is a long way from Cambridge, Massachusetts, where Anne McCaffrey was born, but it seems a proper setting for the author of *Dragonflight, Dragonquest,* and *Dragonsong.* McCaffrey lives at Dragonhold with two of her children; her cat, Mr. Magoofey; and her horse, Mr. Ed. She relaxes from writing by riding Mr. Ed, by cooking, and by doing needlework. She says of herself, "My hair is silver, my eyes are green and I freckle: the rest is subject to change without notice."

Anne McCaffrey's books are set in the imaginary land of Pern, which is inhabited by dragons, fire lizards, and a tribe of humans. McCaffrey has an eye for detail, for she has mapped and described Pern so thoroughly that it seems like a real place. Her writing has been highly praised, and she has won both the Hugo and Nebula awards for outstanding science fiction.

Her first book was neither fantasy nor science fiction but a novel she wrote during high school Latin class. It was far from outstanding, so she tried a western. That was not very good either, so she gave up writing and studied acting. Eventually she came back to writing and finally tried science fiction. In that world she has found her place as a writer, for indeed Pern seems to be a second home, which she graciously shares with her readers.

Understanding the Story

1. Why did Menolly decide to leave the Hold?

2. How did Menolly save some of the newly hatched fire lizards from Thread?

3. Explain the meaning of these three aphorisms: (a) Necessity is the mother of invention; (b) A smile wins more than a frown; (c) Maybes seldom are.

4. The harbormaster warns Menolly not to go far: "Thread's due any day now, you know." Find one other clue that foreshadows Threadfall.

5. Does the world of Pern sound to you like an interesting place to visit? Tell why you would or would not like to go there.

Understanding Literature

An author who creates an imaginary world like the planet Pern wants you to believe in the fantasy while you read the story. To give you the feeling that you are indeed in a different world, author Anne McCaffrey invents new words and gives some English words meanings that you will not be able to find in any dictionary.

You can get the meaning of some Pernese words because they combine two English words you already know. *Spiderclaws* and *marshberry* are examples of such combination words. *Glow* and *glowbasket* are easy because you

know that they must have something to do with light.

You can figure out the meaning of most Pernese words the same way you get the meaning of unfamiliar English words: by using *context clues*. Context is the part of a sentence or paragraph that comes just before and after a word.

When you read "Quite a few riders had been so badly *scored*, they'd died," you realize that *scored* means injured by Threadfall. Having read the story, how would you define the *italicized* words in the following two sentences?

> a. "She gulped down a cold *klah* and ate some bread."
> b. ". . . the occasional flights of wild *wherries* who nested in the heavier bushes were silent."

Perhaps you will try inventing some words for a make-believe world. Make up five new words or a new meaning for each of five English words. For each word write a sentence that will help someone else understand its meaning.

Writing About the Story

Design a travel poster for Pern. On your poster, feature an aspect of the planet that tourists from Earth might find beautiful or exciting. Your poster should contain few words, but every word will be important in making Pern sound as attractive as possible.

The Man with the Blue Guitar

From

A poem by Wallace Stevens

I

The man bent over his guitar,
A shearsman of sorts. The day was green.

They said, "You have a blue guitar,
You do not play things as they are."

The man replied, "Things as they are
Are changed upon the blue guitar."

And they said then, "But play, you must,
A tune beyond us, yet ourselves,

A tune upon the blue guitar
Of things exactly as they are."

VI

A tune beyond us as we are,
Yet nothing changed by the blue guitar;

Ourselves in the tune as if in space,
Yet nothing changed, except the place

Of things as they are and only the place
As you play them, on the blue guitar.

Illustration by Richard Brown

483

Fasten your seatbelt. Your imagination is about to take flight when you encounter words like these:

"The unicorn lived in a lilac wood. . . ."
"'Good morning,' said the roses."
". . .Vetch sat cross-legged, eating roast chicken up in mid-air."

Fantasy transports you to a magical world where impossible events often happen—sometimes without a proper explanation, but almost always for a reason. Fantastic stories are not true, but they often contain ideas that are true. You certainly don't believe foxes can talk, yet you listen with wonder to what the fox in "A Fox and a Rose" has to say about love. Not many people believe that unicorns have ever existed. Yet while you are reading "The Quest of the Unicorn," you believe in the unicorn, and you want her to find that innocence and purity still exist today. In the world of fantasy, you find ideas about such things as love, faith, good, and evil that are important to you in the real world.

A writer of fantasy makes you believe in an imaginary world by carefully blending the real and the fantastic.

Fantasy writers include familiar sights, even in the strangest scenes. Supernatural events occur along with ordinary happenings. Monsters, wizards, and sorcerers do the impossible, but they also show strengths and weaknesses that make them seem surprisingly human.

Many fantasy tales have characters who seem much like ourselves and people we know. Ursula Le Guin has said that the idea for her three novels about Earthsea, the setting for "The Loosing of the Shadow," began with the character of Ged. Although Ged can work magic, he is in all other ways a believable human being with good and bad qualities.

The events in "The Loosing of the Shadow" are fantastic when measured against reality. Nevertheless, they seem quite believable as they occur in the story. Le Guin has given Earthsea its own natural laws, and everything in this fantasy world abides by them. For instance, not everyone in Earthsea can do magic, and those who learn magic make foolish mistakes now and then, showing themselves to be only too human. Ged studies magic for many years at a school for wizards, only to bring an evil shadow into the world when he uses his power wrongly.

The fantasy world of Ursula Le Guin suggests that there are mysteries people are not meant to understand

and forces in the world that we cannot know or control. Anne McCaffrey, who created for her science fantasy books the world of Pern (the setting for "The Rescue at the Dragon Stones"), takes a different approach.

McCaffrey makes the laws of Pern seem as rational as possible. She uses earthly scientific principles to explain the *how*s and *why*s of life on Pern. Supernatural forces are not seen or felt; no one on Pern can work magic. Even the flying, fire-breathing dragons are logically explained in McCaffrey's introductions to the books about Pern.

While you read about Earthsea and Pern, vivid sights and sounds are brought to your attention. The odd landscapes of these worlds are painted for you. Bits of history and culture emerge. Earthsea has its own poetry; Ged summons the dead Elfarran, "the fair lady of the *Deed of Enlad*," which is an important epic poem. Pern's literature consists mostly of folk songs, especially ballads that recount "the legends of past braveries"; each chapter in McCaffrey's book *Dragonsong* begins with a verse from a Pernese ballad. Ursula Le Guin and Anne McCaffrey both use these elements to give depth to fantasy worlds, making them seem more real.

PERN

● HOLDS
★ WEYRS

HIGH REACHES · RUATHA · TELGAR · BIFKA · LEMOS · BENDEN WEYR · TILLEK · FORT · IGEN · KEROON · BOLL · HOLDS · WEYRS · NERAT · HALF-CIRCLE SEA HOLD

Fantasy worlds are often carefully mapped. A map not only gives you a feeling that the mapped region exists, but it also helps you follow the action of the story. Look at the map of Pern; notice that it has two continents. What might you guess about life on Pern just from studying the map?

Notice that some place names on the map of Pern seem to give descriptive information. For example, an area labeled "Snowy Wastes" on a map might indicate an area similar to polar regions on Earth. Find the following place names on the map of Pern: *High Reaches* and *Half-Circle Sea Hold.* Think about why each place might have been given its name.

Often names in a fantasy world suggest what something is like without actually describing it. Ursula Le Guin has written that most of the names and words she invents do not "mean" anything, although the *sound* of each word is "more or less meaningful." For example, *Gont,* Ged's home island in Earthsea, is a "single mountain that lifts its peak a mile above the storm-racked Northeast Sea." Le Guin chose the name *Kurremkarmerruk* for the Master namer, who lives in the Isolate Tower, because she meant the word "to look formidable"—huge, awesome, and rather frightening.

Action is important in a fantasy story: it makes you want to know what happens next. But to make the reader *care* about what happens, the author must make the fantasy world seem amazing, and yet somehow believable. Most authors do this by filling the story with clearly drawn details — maps, customs, tools, special words, names, and bits of history—all of which fit with one another.

There must also be a measure of wisdom in any good fantasy. Though fantasies deal with imaginary beings and strange worlds, they hold our interest because they teach us so much about ourselves and how we behave here in the world we know.

The strange creatures that inhabit fantasy worlds often resemble real animals found on Earth. For example, the fire lizards of Pern seem to be similar to lizards that are alive today as well as to prehistoric lizardlike creatures. Make up two creatures that inhabit a fantasy world of your invention. Model each of your creatures after something that lives on the earth today. Write a paragraph about each creature, giving details about such things as appearance, behavior, and diet.

488

BOOKSHELF

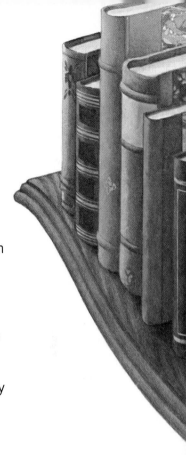

The Perilous Gard by Elizabeth Marie Pope. Houghton Mifflin, 1974. In 1558, while imprisoned in a remote castle, a young girl discovers an underground labyrinth peopled by the last practitioners of Druidic magic.

Wraiths of Time by Andre Norton. Atheneum, 1977. Hurtled through space and time into the ancient Nubian kingdom of Meroe, a museum expert in African archaeology finds she must play a key role in preserving their civilization from evil power seekers.

Weirdstone of Brisingamen: A Tale of Alderley by Alan Garner. Henry Z. Walck, 1963. Susan and Colin discover that the area around Alderley is haunted, and that Susan's pendant is really a magic weirdstone.

Beauty: A Retelling of the Story of Beauty and the Beast by Robin McKinley. Harper & Row, 1978. This charming retelling has all the enchantment of the original fairy tale.

Beyond Silence by Eleanor Cameron. E. P. Dutton, 1980. Andrew Cames's visionary encounters with a young woman confuse him until he sees a connection — his his guilt over his failure to prevent his older brother's death.

Z for Zachariah by Robert C. O'Brien. Atheneum, 1975. After a nuclear war, Ann Burden believes she is the last person on Earth. When she sees the distant smoke of a campfire, she wonders if friend or foe has found her.

The String in the Harp by Nancy Bond. Atheneum, 1976. Peter is unhappy living in Wales until he finds a strange key that can transport him back to the sixth century.

Watership Down by Richard Adams. Macmillan, 1972. Fiver's frightening premonition begins an adventure of courage and survival in this remarkable fantasy about a society of rabbits.

LITERARY TERMS

ALLUSION   *A reference in one literary work to another literary work.* If you were to call someone a "Romeo," for example, you would be making an allusion to William Shakespeare's play *Romeo and Juliet*. In "The Great Bagthorpe Daisy Chain," by Helen Cresswell, Tess makes an allusion to the classical Greek myth of Hercules when she talks about "a task of Herculean proportions" and "the Augean stables."

ANECDOTE   *A short narrative usually told to illustrate or clarify an idea.* In "I Hate Mornings," Richard Cohen uses an anecdote to illustrate how he could sleep through anything that threatened to wake him up in the morning.

> Once, for instance, I dreamed that my father had been locked out of the house and was calling me. I dreamed that because my father had been locked out of the house and was calling me.

BALLAD   *A song or a poem that tells a story.* The classic ballad form is a series of four-line stanzas (verses) that tell the story, with a four-line refrain (chorus) repeated after each verse. The rhyming pattern is always AABB for the story and ABCB for the chorus. The content of the story is often an adventure ending in the hero's death. "The Ballad of the Harp-Weaver," by Edna St. Vincent Millay, is not a true ballad, but rather a poem that is similar in both structure and content to traditional ballads.

CHARACTERS   *The people (or animals) in a story, poem, play, or film.* Sometimes authors are mainly concerned with bringing their story characters to life. How the characters think, feel, act, and change is more important than the story's main action or plot. For example, in "Aggie," author Irene Hunt develops the character of Julie more than she develops the plot. It is important for us to learn what Julie thinks and feels, for the story is about Julie and how she changes. Other stories are built around the plot, and little attention is given to the personalities of the characters. These characters are flat, like paper dolls on which the events of the story are hung. In "Lazy Peter and His Three-Cornered Hat," as in many folk tales, the characters are much less important than their playfully mischievous deeds or the lessons they learn.

A story can contain both a strong plot *and* interesting characters, and within a story some characters may be fully developed while others may not. But the most memorable characters in literature are those whose personalities are fully developed. Such characters seem to live on in our minds long after we finish the story.

CHARACTERIZATION   *The methods a writer uses to reveal a character's personality traits and thus make the character seem real.* The following are several ways writers develop characters:

1. *By giving a physical description of the character:* "She stood in the doorway as though she had been stacked there like bricks and a dress drawn hastily down over the stack and a face sketched on beneath a fuzz of hair."

2. *By showing the character's actions and speech:* " 'I'm not crying.' Ollie stamped her foot, but the tears kept coming and before she could stop herself she was howling, right there in the middle of the street and not even caring who saw her."

3. *By revealing the character's thoughts and feelings:* ''I had a terrible sinking feeling in my stomach. Something was wrong. I looked down at the pages in my notebook.''

4. *By revealing what others think of the character:* '' 'It's my crazy brother,' he replied. 'He's not quite thirteen, and he wants to fight.' ''

5. *By commenting directly on the characters:* ''Grandma was a schemer of the first order. If she had a project in hand, she executed it with the ruthless efficiency of a military genius.''

DIALECT   *A variety of language that differs from the standard.* A dialect is passed down orally and reflects the vocabulary, usage, and pronunciation of a particular region of a country, an ethnic origin, or an occupation. Occupational dialects are sometimes known as **jargon**.

Authors may use dialect to give ''local color'' and authenticity to a story, as in MacKinlay Kantor's story ''The Purple Moccasin.''

> ''Arkansas!'' cried out Uncle Andrew, and I had to hang my head. ''Why this boy ain't no more than fourteen mile from home this minute. He was born right here in Barbary County, and we all live on Rosy Ridge, and we'd admire to have you come a-visiting us.''

DIALOGUE   *Conversation between or among characters.* Dialogue is used in almost all forms of literature to move the plot forward and to tell the reader something about the characters. Dialogue is especially important in drama, where speech is the main way of moving the action of a play forward. When you read a play, you see that the script is almost all dialogue, except for stage directions. In forms other than drama, dialogue is set apart with quotation marks.

In Robert Sheckley's story ''The King's Wishes,'' Bob and Janice are trying to find out what country the ferra is from by asking him questions.

> ''What country are you from?'' Bob asked, wiping perspiration from his forehead.
>
> ''Sorry,'' the ferra said. ''But if you knew that, you might find the right spell to use against me. And I'm in enough trouble as it is.''
>
> ''Now look,'' Janice said. ''If the king is so rich, why can't he pay?''
>
> ''The king never pays for anything he can get free,'' the ferra said. ''That's why he's so rich.''
>
> Bob and Janice glared at him, their marriage fading off into the future.
>
> ''See you tomorrow night,'' the ferra said.
>
> He waved a friendly hand, and vanished.

In this passage, a few lines of dialogue help to move the plot along and keep us wondering if the characters will ever find out what they want to know.

FICTION   *A story invented by the writer.* A work of fiction may be based on real events, but it always includes made-up (fictional) characters and/or experiences. A work of fiction may be brief, like a fable, folk tale, or short story. A longer fictional story, with many characters and incidents, is called a **novel**.

''The Battle of the Rosebud'' is an example of **historical fiction** — fiction based on fact. Author Nathaniel Benchley researched the history of certain Native American tribes and the circumstances that led to the Battle of the Rosebud, but he used his imagination to fill in the missing details and to develop the characters for his story.

Two other types of fiction are **fantasy** and **science fiction**. A fantasy may take place in the "real" world and may have ordinary people and animals doing impossible things. Often, however, fantasies take place in an imaginary world, as in "The Loosing of the Shadow," by Ursula Le Guin. Fantasy offers us the chance to wonder *"What if . . . ?" What if* you could be three inches tall or travel through time? By presenting a world where fantastic events are possible, writers of fantasy sometimes make the "real" world and its problems more clear to us. (See page 484 for more about fantasy.)

Most science fiction deals with scientific possibilities and the changes these "advancements" may bring about. Some writers suggest that the difference between science fiction and fantasy is one of purpose. Unlike fantasy, science fiction suggests real theories about the future. (See page 230 for more about science fiction.)

FIGURATIVE LANGUAGE *Words used in unusual, rather than exact or literal, ways.* Whenever you say you feel as "free as a bird" or think that a task is "a piece of cake," you are using figurative language.

The most common forms of figurative language in literature are **simile** and **metaphor**. A simile uses the words *like* or *as* to compare two very different things. We often use similes such as "wound up like a clock" and "stubborn as a mule." A metaphor *suggests* a comparison by saying one thing *is* another, without using *like* or *as*. Everyday **metaphors** include "this car is a lemon" or "she is a tower of strength."

In "The Quest of the Unicorn," Peter S. Beagle uses similes to describe the Unicorn.

> . . . the mane that fell almost to the middle of her back was as soft as dandelion fluff and as fine as cirrus. . . . and she still moved like a shadow on the sea.

In another description, from "maggie and milly and molly and may," poet e.e. cummings uses metaphor to compare a starfish to a hand:

> milly befriended a stranded star whose rays five languid fingers were.

Writers sometimes use metaphor to create imagery by replacing a common verb with one that suggests a comparison. Instead of saying "the basketball player ran across the court," we might say he or she "darted across the court," which suggests a comparison between the player and a swift dart. Anne McCaffrey uses the word *dart* in this way in her story "Rescue at the Dragon Stones" when she says, "Questions darted through Menolly's mind. . . ." In "The Ballad of the Harp-Weaver," poet Edna St. Vincent Millay writes that "a wind with a wolf's head/Howled about our door." By using the verb *howled*, she suggests that the wind and cold resembled a powerful and menacing wolf. (See also **Imagery**.)

Another type of figurative language, called **personification**, occurs when a writer gives human characteristics to an animal or object. In Geoffrey Godbey's poem "The Television," we meet a television set that "crept" to the window and "sat/looking out/at the night."

FLASHBACK *A technique writers use to present scenes or events that occurred* *before the opening scene of a story.* When earlier events might help the reader understand the characters or plot, the writer interrupts the action of the story and uses a flashback to present background information. "Eleanor of Aquitaine," by E.L. Konigsburg, is made up almost entirely of flashbacks, as each of the characters recalls events in Eleanor's life.

FOLKLORE *The customs, traditions, beliefs, stories, and sayings preserved among a people and passed down orally from generation to generation.* Folklore that was eventually written down developed into several types of literature, including **folk tales, myths, epics,** and **legends.**

All cultures have folk tales, which mirror the lives of their people. Many similar characters, plots, and themes appear in folk tales that come from very different parts of the world. "Lazy Peter and His Three-Cornered Hat," adapted from a Puerto Rican folk tale by Ricardo E. Alegría, has a common theme: even a lazy rascal can trick powerful people blinded by greed. *Fairy tales* are a type of folk tale.

Myth, epic, and legend are other kinds of folk literature. Myths dramatize a particular civilization's view of how the world began, the origins of the earth's creatures, and the workings of nature. Most myths involve gods or other supernatural beings. An epic is a long, formal narrative poem about the adventures of a hero. A legend is a story of a hero (often a real person) whose strength and deeds become exaggerated over the years. In the United States, legends based on humorous exaggeration are known as *tall tales.*

FORESHADOWING *Clues or hints that suggest what will happen later.* In Jane Yolen's "Johanna," Mrs. Chevril warns her daughter:

"Never, never go to the woods at night. . . . Your father went though he was told not to. He never returned."

When Johanna sets out into the woods at night later in the story, the reader is prepared for something unusual or fantastic to happen. Foreshadowing adds to suspense by giving us just enough clues to keep us guessing about what will happen next.

IMAGERY *The use of images in a literary work.* Images are pictures that the writer paints with words. They communicate an experience of the senses (sight, sound, touch, taste, and smell) or of the emotions. In the poem "Those Winter Sundays," Robert Hayden lets us *hear* a freezing house warm up: "I'd wake and hear the cold splintering, breaking." In "The Door," poet Miroslav Holub presents a series of visual images of what might be outside the door. Then, suddenly, he switches to a sound image — "the darkness ticking." In "Johanna," writer Jane Yolen uses a variety of images to portray how Johanna's senses intensify as she changes into a deer.

IRONY *A contrast between what is said and what is really meant, or between what is expected to happen and what actually does happen.* The following are three kinds of irony:

1. **Verbal irony,** in which a writer or a speaker says one thing and means something entirely different. **Sarcasm** is a type of verbal irony, usually a critical comment on others' behavior. In "The Dummy," by Kin Platt, when Mr. Alvarado "congratulates" Neil Comstock for making fun of Alan, the boy who is called the Dummy, he is being sarcastic.

2. **Dramatic irony,** in which a reader or an audience knows something a character in

the story or play does not know. In Graham Greene's "The News in English," Mary Bishop knows that her husand has been heroic, as does the reader, but David Bishop's mother does not know and cannot be told. She says, " 'He ought never to have been born. I never wanted him. The coward!' "

3. **Irony of situation,** in which the development of the plot prepares the reader for one conclusion — yet the opposite takes place. In "Creature of the Snows," author William Sambrot prepares the reader for a dramatic scene in which the snow creatures are captured. However, when Ed McKale finally encounters them in the snow, he finds it impossible even to reach for his camera.

METAMORPHOSIS *A change in form.* Scientists use the term to describe a marked change in an animal's appearance during its life cycle, such as the metamorphosis of a caterpillar into a butterfly. In literature, metamorphosis refers to a magical change, especially of humans into animals (or animals into humans). This theme, common to many cultures, seems to express the idea that humans, animals, and nature are closely related. "Johanna," by Jane Yolen, is a story about metamorphosis.

MOOD *The overall emotional atmosphere or feeling in a story, poem, or play.* An author's choice of setting, language, and writing style help create the mood. In "The Loosing of the Shadow," author Ursula Le Guin wants her readers to feel the same enchantment that her characters are feeling as a spell is being recited.

> Suddenly the wind rose roaring in the grass. Ged dropped to his knees and called out aloud. Then he fell forward as if to embrace earth with his outstretched arms, and when he rose he held something dark in his straining hands and arms, something so heavy that he shook with effort getting to his feet. The hot wind whined in the black tossing grasses on the hill. If the stars showed now none saw them.

Through descriptive details of the setting along with the repetition of words that contain *oh* and *ah* sounds, Le Guin creates a mood that tells us something magical is happening.

NARRATOR *The person who tells a story.* All writing — be it a story, poem, or play — has a narrator. The angle from which the narrator tells the story is called the **point of view.** In poetry the narrator is usually referred to as the **speaker.**

NONFICTION *A true (factual) account; any writing that describes things as they actually happened, or that presents information or opinions about something.* One type of nonfiction is the written history of a person's life. When a person writes his or her own life story, that story is called an **autobiography.** "Lincoln School" is a selection from Ernesto Galarza's autobiography. When someone else writes a person's life story, the story is called a **biography.** "A Wagon Load of Bricks" is a chapter of Ann Petry's biography of Harriet Tubman. Other common forms of nonfiction include news reports, travel stories, personal journals and diaries, articles on science and history, and essays. The humorous essay "I Hate Mornings," by Richard Cohen, is nonfiction, as are the interviews collected by Studs Terkel for his book *Working.*

PARODY *A humorous imitation of a literary work, a type of literature, or an author's style of writing.* The writer of a parody imitates a well-known serious form, but the content of the parody is ridiculous or exaggerated. In "The Affair at 7, Rue de M ——,"

John Steinbeck carefully imitates the style of Edgar Allan Poe's detective tales. In contrast to Poe's stories, however, the "terrifying" villain of Steinbeck's parody is not a mad murderer, but a piece of bubble gum that has come to life.

(For more about Steinbeck's parody, see the Introduction and the Understanding Literature for "The Affair at 7, Rue de M — ," which begins on page 188.)

PLOT   *The action in a story.* When you tell what happens in a story, you are talking about the plot. For example, in "Big Chris," by William Saroyan, the plot is simple: a little boy gets caught in an animal trap and is rescued by a big man who breaks that trap.

The plot is also the writer's overall plan of the action — how, when, and why things happen. The writer uses this plan to arrange the action in an interesting and logical order. Each incident becomes a link in a chain of events that makes sense and holds the reader's attention.

The most important ingredient in plot is **conflict,** the characters' struggle with opposing forces. Sometimes the conflict is external (from an outside source): the character struggles against nature, as in Scott O'Dell's "The Secret of Blue Beach," or with another character, as in Ursula Le Guin's "The Loosing of the Shadow." At other times the conflict is internal (within the character's own mind), as in "The Dummy," by Kin Platt, where Neil Comstock struggles to overcome his own cruelty. Some stories include all three types of conflict.

Usually a plot progresses through four stages. Most stories or plays begin with **exposition,** which reveals information about the setting, the characters, and the conflict. The events that come after the exposition are often called **rising action.** As this action progresses, you become more and more involved until the story reaches the **climax,** or turning point. At this point you learn how the story will turn out. The events following the climax are called the **resolution** or the **falling action.** Here you find answers to your questions about the outcome of the story or play.

POINT OF VIEW   *The angle from which a narrator tells a story.* Most authors use one of the following points of view:

1. **First-person,** or personal, point of view, where the writer chooses one character to be the narrator and to tell the story from his or her own point of view. We see and hear only what this character sees and hears. Yoshiko Uchida's "The Bracelet" is told from Ruri's point of view.

2. **Third-person objective** point of view, where the narrator of the story is an outsider. All of the characters are spoken of in the third person: *he, she, it,* or *they.* The narrator reports only what is happening and does not give any opinions about or reveal the thoughts of the characters in the story. The poem "The Television" by Geoffrey Godbey is written from this point of view.

3. **Third-person omniscient** (om·NISH·ənt) point of view, where the narrator of the story is also an outsider, but can give us insight into what the characters are thinking or feeling. In "Lucas and Jake," by Paul Darcy Boles, we learn what Lucas thinks and how he feels about "his charge," the great aging lion named Jake. **Third-person limited** is a type of omniscient point of view because the narrator can give us some insight into the characters' thoughts and feelings, but this is limited to one character or only a few characters.

PUN   *A "play on words"— that is, a joke based on the different uses of a word or on* words that sound alike but have different meanings. The first type is seen in E.L. Konigsburg's "Eleanor of Aquitaine," when Eleanor asks William to sit and *spin* his tale. William replies, "You might say, my lady, that I shall *weave* my tale but not *embroider* it." William's puns are based on the literal and figurative meanings of the three needlework terms. (See Figurative Language.) To spin or weave a tale means simply to tell a story; to embroider it means — just as in needlework — to add something extra. Abbott and Costello's "Who's on First?" is loaded with puns — in fact, the entire skit is based on Sebastian's mixing up the meanings of words.

Other puns are made with homophones — words that sound the same — such as "He's called the *weather* man because he tells us *whether* or not it will rain." In "The Great Bagthorpe Daisy Chain," author Helen Cresswell makes a pun when she has young Daisy refer to the "Beginner's Book of Records." Of course, Daisy is really trying to say the *Guinness Book of Records.*

REPETITION *The repeated use of a sound, word, phrase, or chorus.* Repetition is used in all forms of literature, most commonly in poetry. In "I Hear America Singing" the repetition of the words *I hear* and *singing* in the phrases about the working people of America make it seem as if the poet, Walt Whitman, is singing at his work — the work of writing poems. In her graduation speech from the teleplay "I Know Why the Caged Bird Sings," Maya Angelou repeats the word *hero* many times. When she finally says, "And I got another hero. Me. . . ." she emphasizes her pride in who she is.

The repetition of an initial sound in a phrase or line of poetry is called **alliteration.** In "The Loosing of the Shadow," Ur-

sula Le Guin creates a commotion of sound so that we can almost hear the glow of the spirit in Ged's arms.

> Through it *blazed* a terrible *brightness.* And through that *bright* misshapen *breach* clambered something like a clot of *black* shadow.

This passage illustrates how alliteration can be an effective device for adding emphasis and rhythm to writing.

RHYME *The repetition of syllable sounds, especially at the ends of lines of poetry.* The rhyming of sounds at the ends of lines is called **end rhyme.** Maxine Kumin's poem "The Microscope" consists of lines that rhyme:

> Impossible! Most Dutchmen *said.*
> This Anton's crazy in the *head.*
> We ought to ship him off to *Spain.*
> He says he's seen a housefly's *brain.*

The pattern made by the rhymes at the ends of lines is called the **rhyme scheme.** We label the rhyming sounds with letters so we can describe the rhyme scheme. "The Microscope" has an AABB rhyme scheme because the words at the end of every two lines rhyme. These pairs of lines are also called **rhyming couplets.** Poets frequently play with rhyme schemes to write different kinds of poems. A different kind of rhyme scheme is used by Edna St. Vincent Millay in "The Ballad of the Harp-Weaver." This is an ABCB rhyme scheme because the second and fourth lines rhyme while the first and third do not.

> "Son," said my mother, (A)
>   When I was knee-*high,* (B)
> "You've need of clothes to cover you, (C)
>   And not a rag have *I.*" (B)

The rhyming of two words on the same

line, such as *day* and *away* in the following lines from the song "I'm Only Sleeping" by John Lennon and Paul McCartney, is known as **internal rhyme:**

> Please don't spoil my *day,* I'm miles *away,*
> And after all, I'm only sleeping.
> Keeping an *eye* on the world going *by* my window.

RHYTHM *The pattern of stressed and unstressed syllables, especially in poetry; also known as the* beat *of a poem.* A poem may have a regular rhythm throughout, or the rhythm may vary within the poem. People of many ancient cultures recited long verses from memory. Rhythm, along with rhyme, helped poets and singers remember these verses, and modern poets often continue this tradition. Notice how, in the following lines from e.e. cummings's "maggie and milly and molly and may," the rhyme and the regular rhythm pattern help the words to stay in the mind:

> may came home with a smooth round stone
> as small as a world and as large as alone.

> For whatever we lose (like a you or a me)
> it's always ourselves we find in the sea.

SATIRE *A literary work that criticizes persons, behaviors, ideas, or social institutions by holding them up to ridicule.* Satirists often attack the follies, vices, and social ills of their times. Robert Sheckley, in "The King's Wishes," uses satire to poke fun at people who tackle life's problems as if they were still in the army or at college.

SETTING *When and where a story takes place.* If you say, "Today at school, Susan won a race," you've given the setting (when and where) before describing the action. Authors can choose any time or any place as a setting for a story.

On the first page of "The Bracelet," author Yoshiko Uchida describes a family leaving an empty house, then tells us precisely when and where this takes place.

> It was almost time to leave our home, but we weren't moving to a nicer house or to a new town. It was April 21, 1942. The United States and Japan were at war, and every Japanese person on the West Coast was being evacuated by the government to an internment camp. My Mama, my sister Keiko, and I were being sent from our home, and out of Berkeley, and eventually, out of California.

A writer doesn't always give us the setting so directly — sometimes we must figure it out as the story goes along. A story may begin in the morning in a person's room, for instance. As the story unfolds, we may find that the room is in an apartment, that the building is in New York City, and that the story takes place during a particular time, for example, the 1960s.

When the setting is essential to understanding the characters and their conflicts, it is called an **integral setting.** Sometimes the setting is even the *source* of the conflict. In nature adventures such as "Creature of the Snows," by William Sambrot, characters struggle against their environment. Science fiction and fantasy stories are often set in other worlds to give a different perspective on our own world. Sometimes such stories are based on the many difficulties a character faces when living in a new setting. Zenna Henderson's story "Something Bright" deals with the Klevitys' experience in another world (our own) and their efforts to get back home.

When the setting is relatively unimportant, it is called a **backdrop setting**, because it is like the scenery in a stage play. The characters or their conflicts are more important, so the story could take place just about anywhere at any time. "Lazy Peter and His Three-Cornered Hat" takes place in a Puerto Rican market town, but the setting is merely a backdrop — this story could take place wherever rascals and greedy misers get together.

STANZA   *A group of lines forming a unit in a poem, comparable to a paragraph in a story.* Some poems, such as the Mbundu poem "Preoccupation," have only one stanza, but most poems have several. "The Ballad of the Harp-Weaver," by Edna St. Vincent Millay, has many stanzas that repeat the same pattern of rhyme and rhythm. Maxine Kumin's poem "The Microscope" does not repeat the same pattern of rhyme or rhythm in every stanza, yet each group of lines is still called a stanza.

SUSPENSE   *Tension and uncertainty about what will happen next.* When suspense enters our daily lives, it is often unpleasant, like waiting for the results of a test or of a job interview. In literature, however, suspense can be exciting — it is often what keeps us interested in a story. Suspense is also present whenever we worry about the fate of a character, as when Menolly flees from the deadly Thread in "Rescue at the Dragon Stones," by Anne McCaffrey.

SYMBOL   *An object, character, or incident that stands for something else.* Our everyday lives are filled with different kinds of symbols. They tell us when we need to take an action, the way the colors of traffic lights do, or they signify something, as a red heart signifies affection on Valentine's Day.

In literature, writers often use everyday objects or ideas to represent something of greater significance. Author Antoine de Saint-Exupéry uses the rose in "A Fox and a Rose" to symbolize love and friendship. Because of the characters' statements, we know that what the Little Prince values is love and friendship and not just a rose. The unicorn, a character in Peter S. Beagle's "The Quest of the Unicorn," has often been used to symbolize ideas about beauty, hope, and religion. Both the rose and the unicorn are meaningful symbols because they have symbolized so many important things throughout history.

THEME   *The meaning of a story — that is, the main idea, or the point the writer is trying to make.*

Plot answers the question "What happens in the story?" *Theme* answers the question "What does it all mean?" A story has a theme when the author uses the events and characters to make a comment about life, society, or individuals. For instance, the main theme of Yoshiko Uchida's "The Bracelet" is that friendship is a greater gift than any material object.

Authors sometimes write stories purely to entertain their readers and may not have any specific theme in mind. When they do want to convey an important message, however, they will often use **key passages.** Key passages point out the theme of a story in a brief and simple way. In "The Dummy," by Kin Platt, Mr. Alvarado sums up the main theme of the story when he tells the class, "A certain amount of courage is needed to resist mass opinion." In "A Fox and a Rose," the fox's speech to the Little Prince — "It is the time you have wasted for your rose that makes your rose so important" — is a key passage that author Antoine de Saint-Exupéry uses to state his theme, a comment on the nature of love.

GLOSSARY

This glossary gives the meanings of unfamiliar words used in the text of this book. The meanings given here define words only the way they are used in the book. You can find other meanings for these words in a dictionary.

The correct pronunciation of each glossary word is given in the special spelling after that word. The sounds used in these spellings are explained in the following Pronunciation Key. Each symbol, or letter, stands for a sound, a sound you can recognize in the words following it. In addition to these sounds, each glossary pronunciation includes marks to show the kind of force, or stress, with which certain syllables are pronounced. A heavy mark, ′, shows that the syllable it follows is given the strongest, or primary, stress, as in **sis·ter (sis′·ter)**. A lighter mark, ′, shows that the syllable it follows is given a secondary, or lighter, stress, as in **tax·i·cab (tak′·sē·kab′)**.

Several abbreviations are used in the glossary: *v.,* verb; *adv.,* adverb; *n.,* noun; *adj.,* adjective; *pl.,* plural.

Pronunciation Key

a	add, map	m	move, seem	u	up, done
ā	ace, rate	n	nice, tin	û(r)	urn, term
â(r)	care, air	ng	ring, song	yōō	use, few
ä	palm, father	o	odd, hot	v	vain, eve
b	bat, rub	ō	open, so	w	win, away
ch	check, catch	ô	order, jaw	y	yet, yearn
d	dog, rod	oi	oil, boy	z	zest, muse
e	end, pet	ou	out, now	zh	vision, pleasure
ē	even, tree	ōō	pool, food	ə	the schwa,
f	fit, half	o͝o	took, full		an unstressed
g	go, log	p	pit, stop		vowel representing
h	hope, hate	r	run, poor		the sound spelled
i	it, give	s	see, pass		a in above
ī	ice, write	sh	sure, rush		e in sicken
j	joy, ledge	t	talk, sit		i in possible
k	cool, take	th	thin, both		o in melon
l	look, rule	t͡h	this, bathe		u in circus

ab·er·ra·tion (ab′·ə·rā′·shən) *n.* A defect; an abnormality.

ab·ra·sive (ə·brā′·siv) *adj.* Having a rough, scraping surface, as of sandpaper.

a·byss·es (ə·bis′·iz) *n., pl.* Deep, seemingly bottomless pits or canyons.

ac·claim (ə·klām′) *n.* An act of praise or approval.

ac·cli·ma·tized (ə·klī′·mə·tīzd′) *adj.* Used to a different climate or environment.

ac·quit (ə·kwit′) *v.* To behave; to do well.

ag·i·tat·ed (aj′·ə·tā′·tid) *adj.* Upset; disturbed. — **ag·i·ta·tion,** *n.*

am·phi·the·a·ter (am′·fə·thē′·ə·tər) *n.* A theater consisting of a level area in the center surrounded by upward-sloping rows of seats.

ap·palled (ə·pôld′) *adj.* Horrified. — **ap·pall·ing**, *adj.*

ap·pa·ri·tion (ap′·ə·rish′·ən) *n.* A ghostly figure.

ap·pre·hen·sion (ap′·ri·hen′·shən) *n.* An anxious feeling that something bad may happen soon; fear.

ap·pro·pri·at·ing (ə·prō′·prē·āt′·ing) *v.* Taking possession for oneself.

ar·du·ous (är′·jo͞o·wəs) *adj.* Very difficult; demanding great care. — **ar·du·ous·ly**, *adv.*

ar·ro·gance (ar′·ə·gəns) *n.* Extreme pride; acting superior to others.

as·sert·ed (ə·sərt′·id) *v.* To state positively; to affirm.

as·sur·ed·ly (ə·sho͞or′·id·lē) *adv.* Certainly.

a·tro·cious (ə·trō′·shəs) *adj.* Extremely bad; horrible.

at·tain·ments (ə·tān′·məntz) *n.* Accomplishments; achievements; skills one has learned.

at·tire (ə·tīr′) *n.* Clothing.

au·da·cious (ô·dā′·shəs) *adj.* Bold; daring. — **au·dac·i·ty** (ô·da·si·tē), *n.*

av·a·rice (av′·ə·rəs) *n.* Greed.

bar·ren (bar′·ən) *adj.* Without leaves or fruit; bare.

be·fits (bi·fits′) *v.* Is suitable or appropriate for.

be·lat·ed·ly (bi·lāt′·əd·lē) *adv.* Delayed beyond the usual or proper time.

bunt (bənt) *v.* To tap a baseball lightly without swinging the bat.

butte (byo͞ot) *n.* An isolated steep hill.

cap·i·tal·ist (kap′·ə·təl·ist) *n.* A person who invests money in business. *adj.* Favoring private rather than state ownership of business and industry.

car·niv·o·rous (kär·niv′·ə·rəs) *adj.* Meat-eating.

cast (kast) *n.* Shape; structure.

cha·os (kā′·äs) *n.* Total confusion or disorder.

chiv·al·ry (shiv′·əl·rē) *n.* The qualities associated with knighthood, such as bravery and courtesy.

cir·cu·lat·ed (sər′·kyə·lā′·tid) *v.* Moved from one place to another.

cir·cum·vent (sər′·kəm·vent′) *v.* To avoid.

claim·ants (klā′·mənts) *n.* People who claim something, such as those who claim to be the rightful rulers of a country.

clam·bered (klam′·bərd) *v.* Climbed awkwardly.

col·lo·qui·al (kə·lō′·kwē·əl) *adj.* Used in conversation but not in formal writing.

com·mod·i·ty (kə·mäd′·ə·tē) *n.* A thing; an item.

com·pas·sion (kəm·pash′·ən) *n.* An awareness of others' suffering, along with the desire to help.

con·sci·en·tious (kän′·chē·en′·shəs) *adj.* Thorough; careful in fulfilling one's duties.

con·sort (kän′·sôrt) *n.* The wife of a king or the husband of a queen.

con·strict·ed (kən·strikt′·id) *v.* Squeezed tightly together.

con·tempt (kən·tempt′) *n.* Lack of respect; dislike.

con·vic·tion (kən·vik′·shən) *n.* The state of being convinced that what one is saying is true.

coun·te·nance (koun′·tə·nəns) *n.* Look, expression.

coun·ter·parts (koun′·tər·pärts) *n., pl.* Things that correspond to other things; equivalents.

cow·ered (kou′·ərd) *v.* Cringed out of fear.

crev·ice (krev′·əs) *n.* A narrow crack or opening.

croon·ing (kro͞on′·ing) *v.* Singing or humming; murmuring.

cu·bi·cle (kyo͞o′·bi·kəl) *n.* A small sleeping compartment.

cyn·ic (sin′·ik) *n.* Someone who has a low opinion of people or things.

de·barred (di·bärd′) *v.* Excluded; ruled out.

de·bris (də·brē′) *n.* Scattered remains of something broken; rubble.

de·ci·sive (di·sī′·siv) *adj.* Having the power to settle a question once and for all; conclusive.

de·mean·or (di·mē′·nər) *n.* The way a person behaves; manner.

de·mot·ed (di·mō′·tid) *v.* Lowered in rank.

de·ri·sion (di·rizh′·ən) *n.* Ridicule; scorn.

des·o·late (des′·ə·lət) *adj.* Miserable; unhappy.

de·spoiled (di·spoild′) *v.* Caused widespread injury and desolation; destroyed.

de·te·ri·o·rates (di·tir′·ē·ə·rātz′) *v.* Falls apart or wears away.

dig·i·tal (dij′·ət·əl) *adj.* Of or relating to fingers.

dis·cred·it·a·ble (dis·kred′·it·ə·bəl) *adj.* Deserving a loss of reputation; disgraceful.

dis·en·gage (dis′·ən·gāj′) *v.* To release something entangled or held tightly.

dis·patch (dis·pach′) *n.* Promptness and efficiency.

dis·pers·ing (dis·pərs′·ing) *v.* Scattering or breaking up; causing to evaporate.

dis·tor·tions (dis·tôr′·shənz) *n., pl.* Things that are twisted, exaggerated, or changed in meaning.

doc·ile (däs′·əl) *adj.* Easy to manage; obedient.

du·bi·ous·ly (do͞o′·bē·əs·lē) *adv.* Doubtfully; with hesitation.

ec·sta·cy (ek′·stə·sē) *n.* Extreme joy; intense pleasure. — **ec·stat·ic**, *adj.*

ef·fi·cient·ly (ə·fish′·ənt·lē) *adv.* Producing the desired results without waste.

e·lab·o·rate (i·lab′·ə·rit) *adj.* Made with attention to detail; fancy. — **e·lab·o·rate·ly,** *adv.*

e·lab·o·rat·ed (i·lab′·ə·rāt′·id) *v.* Gave more details.

e·lude (ē·lood′) *v.* To avoid or escape from.

em·ber (em′·bər) *n.* A small piece of glowing coal or wood in a dying fire.

e·merg·ing (i·mərj′·ing) *v.* Coming out of.

e·mit·ted (ē·mi′·tid) *v.* Released; sent out.

en·camp·ment (in·kamp′·mənt) *n.* A camp.

en·ig·mat·ic (en′·ig·mat′·ik) *adj.* Puzzling; mysterious.

e·nor·mi·ty (i·nôr′·mə·tē) *n.* The quality or state of being huge or outrageous.

en·ter·prise (en′·tər·prīz′) *n.* An undertaking; a difficult task.

en·throned (in·thrōnd′) *adj.* Seated in a place associated with a position of importance, as on a throne.

e·ons (ē′·ənz) *n.* Generations or ages; extremely long periods of time.

e·rod·ed (i·rōd′·əd) *v.* Gradually worn away.

e·vac·u·at·ed (i·vak′·yoo·āt′·id) *v.* Moved people from one region to another during a war or disaster.

e·vade (i·vād′) *v.* To escape having to do something; avoid.

e·voked (i·vōkt′) *v.* Produced or inspired some emotion or state of mind.

ex·ceed·ing·ly (ik·sēd′·ing·lē) *adv.* Extremely.

ex·hil·a·rat·ed (ig·zil′·ə·rāt′·id) *adj.* Invigorated; thrilled; stimulated.

ex·tract (ik′·strakt) *v.* To pull out; to remove.

fast·ness·es (fast′·nəs·ez) *n.* Remote or secret places.

fe·ro·cious (fə·rō′·shəs) *adj.* Fierce; savage.

fes·tooned (fes·toond′) *adj.* Decorated with hanging flowers or ornaments.

fledg·ling (flej′·ling) *n.* A young bird that is just learning to fly; a beginner.

for·ays (for′·āz) *n.* Raids aimed especially at plundering.

for·mal·de·hyde (fôr·mal′·də·hīd′) *n.* A chemical used as a disinfectant and preservative.

fur·rowed (fər′·ōd) *adj.* Deeply wrinkled.

gal·li·vant·ing (gal′·ə·vant′·ing) *v.* Moving about in search of excitement.

gar·bled (gär′·bəld) *v.* Spoke in a distorted way that is difficult to understand.

gaunt (gônt) *adj.* Overly thin, often as a result of suffering.

ges·tic·u·lat·ing (jes·tik′·yə·lāt′·ing) *v.* Making vigorous motions or gestures in order to communicate something.

gran·deur (gran′·jər) *n.* Greatness; splendor.

hag·gard (hag′·ərd) *adj.* Worn out; exhausted.

halt·ing (hôl′·ting) *adj.* Hesitant; wavering.

har·ried (har′·ēd) *v.* Harassed; annoyed by constant attacks.

haugh·ti·ly (hôt′·il·ē) *adv.* Acting as if one were superior to someone else.

heath (hēth) *n.* Area of land covered with shrubs or similar plants.

heaves (hēvz) *v.* Rises up or swells.

her·e·sy (her′·ə·sē) *n.* A statement or action that goes against commonly held beliefs.

hid·e·ous (hid′·ē·əs) *adj.* Horrible; repulsive.

hom·age (häm′·ij) *n.* Public expression of respect or admiration.

hy·poc·ri·sy (hi·päk′·rə·sē) *n.* Insincerity; saying what one does not believe.

id·i·o·cies (id′·ē·ə·sēz) *n., pl.* Notable stupidities.

im·bed·ded (im·bed′·id) *adj.* Stuck; snugly enclosed. Also spelled **em·bed·ded.**

im·mac·u·late (im·ak′·yə·lət) *adj.* Perfectly clean; spotless.

im·men·si·ty (i·men′·sə·tē) *n.* The quality or state of being large.

im·mor·tal·i·ty (im′·ôr·tal′·ə·tē) *n.* 1. An endless life. 2. A long-lasting fame.

im·pec·ca·ble (im·pek′·ə·bəl) *adj.* Faultless; without a flaw.

im·pelled (im·peld′) *v.* Driven or forced to an action.

im·pend·ing (im·pen′·ding) *adj.* Due to happen soon; approaching.

im·pe·ri·ous (im·pir′·ē·əs) *adj.* Domineering, as of a person used to ordering people around.

im·per·ti·nence (im·pər′·tən·əns) *n.* Rudeness.

im·po·tence (im′·pə·təns) *n.* Powerlessness.

in·ac·ces·si·ble (in′·ak·ses′·ə·bəl) *adj.* Impossible to reach.

in·com·pe·tence (in·käm′·pə·təns) *n.* The state of not being capable of doing something.

in·cur·sions (in·kər′·zhənz) *n.* Raids; invasions.

in·dict·ment (in·dīt′·mənt) *n.* A detailed account of someone's faults or crimes.

in·dif·fer·ent (in·dif′·ə·rənt) *adj.* Marked by lack of interest; not caring. — **in·dif·fer·ent·ly,** *adv.*

in·dig·nant·ly (in·dig′·nənt·lē) *adv.* With anger, aroused by some untruthfulness or injustice. — **in·dig·na·tion,** *n.*

in·es·cap·a·ble (in·ə·skā′·pə·bəl) *adj.* Certain; unavoidable.

in·ex·o·ra·bly (in·eks′·ə·rə·blē) *adv.* Without letting up; unyieldingly.

in·fer·nal (in·fər′·nəl) *adj.* Evil; fiendish.

in·ten·si·ty (in·ten′·sə·tē) *n.* An extreme degree of force; power.

in·tent (in·tent′) *adj.* Having one's attention fixed on one thing.

in·tern·ment (in·tərn′·mənt) *adj.* Confinement, especially during wartime. — **in·terned,** *v.*

in·tol·er·a·ble (in·tä′l·ər·ə·bəl) *adj.* Impossible to put up with; unbearable.

ir·rel·e·vant (i·rel′·ə·vənt) *adj.* Off the subject.

ir·res·o·lute·ly (i·rez′·ə·l ōōt′·lē) *adv.* Not firmly doing something or making up one's mind; indecisively.

ir·rev·o·ca·bly (i·rev′·ə·kə·blē) *adv.* Without being able to be undone.

ju·bi·la·tion (jōō′·bə·lā′·shən) *n.* Great joy.

le·git·i·mate (lə·jit′·ə·mit) *adj.* Lawful.

lithe (līth) *adj.* Limber.

mar·shal·ing (mär′·shə·ling) *v.* Arranging in proper order.

mar·tyr (mär′·tər) *n.* One who suffers for a belief.

ma·son (mā′·sən) *n.* A bricklayer or stoneworker. — **ma·son·ry,** *n.*

mel·an·chol·y (mel′·ən·kôl′·ē) *adj.* Sad; depressed.

mor·bid (môr′·bid) *adj.* Characterized by gloomy or unwholesome feelings; unhealthy.

myr·i·ad (mir′·ē·əd) *adj.* Innumerable; a very large number of.

mys·ti·cal (mis′·ti·kəl) *adj.* Supernatural; mysterious.

ne·go·ti·at·ed (ni·gō′·shē·āt′·id) *v.* Bargained in order to reach an agreement.

niche (nich) *n.* A safe place; a position suited to one's abilities.

non·com·mit·tal·ly (nän′·kə·mit′·əl·ē) *adv.* Without expressing any opinion.

non·plused (nän·pləst′) *adj.* Baffled; at a loss for words. Also spelled **non·plussed.**

nymph (nimf) *n.* A nature goddess who lives in trees, rivers, etc.

ob·scure (äb·skyōōr′) *adj.* Vague; unclear.

ob·ses·sive·ly (äb·ses′·iv·lē) *adv.* Abnormally involved in something to the exclusion of anything else.

of·fense (ə·fens′) *n.* A violation of a rule or law.

om·i·nous (äm′·ə·nəs) *adj.* Threatening; menacing; evil.

op·ti·mis·tic (äp·tə·mis′·tik) *adj.* Expecting the best possible result; hopeful.

pac·i·fy·ing·ly (pas′·ə·fī′·ing·lē) *adv.* Soothingly; in such a way as to calm someone down.

par·a·dox (par′·ə·däks′) *n.* A statement that seems to be impossible.

Pa·tri·ot (pā′·trē·ət) *n.* A person loyal to the anti-British, pro-independence cause during the American Revolution.

per·fec·tion·ist (pər·fek′·shə·nist′) *n.* A person who insists that everything be done just right.

per·plexed (pər·plekst′) *adj.* Puzzled.

per·sist·ent (pər·sis′·tənt) *adj.* Repeated; continuous. — **per·sist·ent·ly,** *adv.*

per·verse (pər·vərs′) *adj.* Against what is accepted; backward.

pe·ti·tion (pə·tish′·ən) *n.* A request.

pin·na·cle (pin′·i·kəl) *n.* The top of a hill; a mountain peak.

pi·ous·ly (pī′·əs·lē) *adv.* In a religious or falsely religious manner; self-righteous, as if offended at being suspected of wrongdoing.

pip·ing (pīp′·ing) *adj.* High-pitched.

plac·id (plas′·id) *adj.* Calm; quiet.

plum·age (plōō′·mij) *n.* The feathers of a bird.

pon·der·ing·ly (pän′·dər·ing·lē) *adv.* In a carefully considering manner.

pon·der·ous·ly (pon′·dər·əs·lē) *adv.* Slowly, as when one is weighed down by a heavy burden or is sick or injured.

prat·tling (prat′·ling) *v.* Meaningless talking or babbling.

pre·car·i·ous·ly (pri·kar′·ē·əs·lē) *adv.* Dangerously.

pre·dic·a·ment (pri·dik′·ə·mənt) *n.* A difficult situation.

pre·lim·i·nar·y (pri·lim′·ə·ner′·ē) *adj.* Before; in preparation for.

pro·fuse·ly (prə·fyōōs′·lē) *adv.* Exceedingly; abundantly. — **pro·fu·sion,** *n.*

pro·pri·e·tar·i·ly (prə·prī′·e·ter′·i·lē) *adv.* In a way showing that something is one's property.

pro·trude (prō·trōōd′) *v.* To stick out. — **pro·tru·sion,** *n.*

pru·dent·ly (prōōd′·ənt·lē) *adv.* Cautiously; avoiding any risk.

pul·sat·ed (pul′·sāt′·id) *v.* Expanded and contracted rhythmically.

pup·pet·eer (pup′·ə·tir′) *n.* 1. One who operates puppets. 2. One who controls people as if they were puppets.

pu·ri·ty (pyōōr′·ə·tē) *n.* Innocence; cleanness.

ra·di·ant (rā′·dē·ənt) *adj.* Bright; beaming.

raft·ers (raf′·tərz) *n., pl.* Large beams of wood supporting a roof.

rav·aged (rav′·ijd) *adj.* Overrun by some destructive force; devastated.

re·as·sert·ed (rē′·ə·sərt′·id) *v.* Demanded to be recognized.

re·buked (ri·byōōkd′) *v.* Sharply criticized.

502

re·cede (ri·sēd′) v. To withdraw; to fade away.

re·cep·tive (ri·sep′·tiv) adj. Open; ready to receive something.

re·coil (rē·kôil′) n. Bounce back.

reg·is·tered (rej′·əs·tərd) v. Shown or expressed.

re·it·er·at·ed (rē·it′·ə·rāt′·id) v. Said or done over again; repeated.

re·lent·less·ly (ri·lent′·ləs·lē) adv. Without letting up; steadily; persistently.

rem·i·nis·cent (rem′·ə·nis′·ənt) adj. Suggestive of the past; nostalgic.

ren·der·ing (ren′·də·ring) v. Making or causing to become.

ren·dez·vous (rän′·dā·voo′) n. An arranged meeting or a place where one has arranged a meeting.

re·proach (ri·prōch′) n. A cause for blame or discredit.

res·o·lute·ly (rez′·ə·loot′·lē) adv. Firmly doing something or making up one's mind; decisively.

re·solved (ri·zälvd′) v. Decided.

res·o·nant (rez′·ə·nənt) adj. Deep, full sound.

res·to·ra·tion (res′·tə·rā′·shən) n. The act of repairing something so that it is in as good a condition as when it was first made.

re·sur·gence (ri·sər′·jəns) n. A rising again of activity.

re·tal·i·a·tion (ri·tal′·ē·ā′·shən) n. The act of getting back at someone.

ric·o·chet·ing (rik′·ə·shā′·ing) v. Bouncing; rebounding.

rid·dled (rid′·əld) adj. Pierced with many holes or openings.

ro·man·ti·cized (rō·man′·tə·sīzd) v. Imagined as something more exciting or heroic than it really is.

sab·o·tage (sab′·ə·täzh′) n. An act of deliberate, underhanded destruction.

sar·casm (sär′·kaz′·əm) n. The act of making a cutting, ironic remark.

sa·vored (sā′·vərd) v. Tasted or smelled with pleasure.

scourged (skurjd) v. Made to endure suffering; punished.

se·er (sē′·ər) n. One able to perceive things outside the normal range of human senses; a prophet.

sen·try (sen′·trē) n. A lookout guard.

se·ren·i·ty (sə·ren′·ə·tē) n. Calmness; tranquility. — **se·rene**, adj.

sin·cer·i·ty (sin·ser′·ə·tē) n. The quality of saying what one believes; honesty.

sin·gu·lar (sing′·gyə·lər) adj. Set apart as being remarkable; unusual.

skep·ti·cism (skep′·tə·siz′·əm) n. An attitude of doubting things unless they are proved to be true.

skir·mish·es (skûr′·mish·iz) n., pl. Brief fights between small numbers of soldiers.

slip·shod (slip′·shäd′) adj. Poorly or carelessly done; shabby.

sloughed (sluft) v. Shed, as of the dead outer skin of an animal.

som·ber (säm′·bər) adj. Dark; sad.

sparse (spärs) adj. Not plentiful; scarce.

spec·u·lat·ed (spek′·yə·lāt′·id) v. Thought about something; tried to figure something out.

squall·ing (skwäl′·ing) v. Screaming or crying loudly.

squeam·ish (skwē′·mish) adj. Easily shocked or offended.

stead·fast·ly (sted′·fast′·lē) adv. With a fixed or unchanging manner.

stealth·i·ly (stel′·thə·lē) adv. In a secretive manner; slyly.

stench (stench) n. A strong and unpleasant odor.

stren·u·ous (stren′·yoo·wəs) adj. Requiring great effort; energetic.

sub·sides (səb·sīdz′) v. Sinks or settles down; decreases.

sub·stan·tial (səb·stan′·shəl) adj. Solid; strong.

suc·cu·lent (suk′·yə·lənt) adj. Juicy.

suc·cumbed (sə·kumd′) v. Yielded to an overpowering force.

sym·bol·ic (sim·bäl′·ik) adj. Meaningful; representative of something.

taunt (tônt) n. An insult; a scornful remark. — **taunt**, v.

ten·ta·cle (tent′·i·kəl) n. A long, flexible arm, such as that of an octopus.

thwart·ed (thwôrt′·id) v. Prevented from happening; blocked.

tinc·ture (tingk′·chər) n. A trace of something.

tol·er·ate (täl′·ə·rāt′) v. To put up with.

To·ry (tôr′·ē) n. A person loyal to the British cause during the American Revolution.

trav·ersed (trə·vərsd′) v. Traveled through or across.

trem·or (trem′·ər) n. A shiver.

trill·ing (tril′·ing) adj. Having a fluttering sound like the warbling of some birds.

tu·mor·ous (too′·mər·əs) adj. Resembling an abnormal, swollen growth in the body.

tu·mult (too′·mult) n. A commotion or disturbance.

tur·bu·lent (tur′·byə·lənt) *adj.* Violently agitated or disturbed.

ty·ran·ni·cal (tə·ran′·i·kəl) *adj.* Severe, strict, or oppressive, as of the laws of a tyrant or all-powerful ruler.

u·nan·i·mous (yōō·nan′·ə·məs) *adj.* Agreed on by everyone.

un·com·pre·hend·ing (un·käm′·pri·hen′·ding) *adj.* Lacking understanding.

un·de·ni·a·ble (un′·di·nī′·ə·bəl) *adj.* Certain; impossible to be denied. — **un·de·ni·a·bly,** *adv.*

un·du·late (un′·jə·lāt′) *v.* To move in a smooth, wavelike motion.

un·e·mo·tion·al (un′·i·mō′·shən·əl) *adj.* Not showing any strong feelings.

un·nerv·ing (un·nərv′·ing) *adj.* Taking away courage or strength; upsetting.

un·ob·struct·ed (un′·əb·strukt′·id) *adj.* Unblocked; clear.

un·or·tho·dox (un·or′·thə·däks′) *adj.* Opposed to what is traditional or customary.

un·re·sist·ing (un·ri·zist′·ing) *adv.* Not working against; not opposing.

un·sa·vor·y (un·sāv′·ə·rē) *adj.* Disagreeable; unpleasant; offensive.

un·scal·a·ble (un·skāl′·ə·bəl) *adj.* Impossible to climb to the top of.

un·scru·pu·lous (un·skrōō′·pyə·ləs) *adj.* Dishonest.

up·surge (əp′·sərj) *n.* A powerful rising up, as of a wave or emotion.

vain (vān) *adj.* Showing excessive pride in oneself; conceited.

ve·he·ment·ly (vē′·ə·mənt′·lē) *adv.* Vigorously.

vein·ous (vān′·əs) *adj.* Having veins that stick out.

ven·ture (ven′·chər) *n.* A daring undertaking. — **ven·ture,** *v.*

ver·ba·tim (vər·bāt′·əm) *adv.* Word for word.

vir·tu·al (vurch′·ə·wəl) *adj.* Near; almost the same as something.

vy·ing (vī′·ing) *v.* Competing with someone; trying to win a contest.

war·y (war′·ē) *adj.* Cautious; on the lookout.

way·far·er (wā′·fer′·ər) *n.* One who travels, especially on foot.

whim·si·cal (hwim′·zi·kəl) *adj.* Playful; unpredictable; subject to sudden changes.

wield·ed (wēld′·id) *v.* Handled effectively.

winced (winsd) *v.* Flinched; made a sudden involuntary movement out of fear.

writh·ing (rīth′·ing) *v.* Twisting or squirming.

wrought (rôt) *adj.* Formed; shaped; put together.

zest (zest) *n.* Lively interest.

INDEX

AUTHORS AND TITLES

The page numbers in *italics* indicate where a brief biography of the author is located.